MU01939543

"The books of 1 and 2 Thessalonians have a crucial message for the world today, but they can be hard to understand. What does the Bible teach about the return of Christ? What should we think about the 'rapture'? Who is the man of lawlessness? With theological precision and the care of a seasoned pastor, Richard Phillips reveals the sure biblical path through the underbrush of end-times confusion, and explains the relevance of Paul's letters for today. Readers will be instructed and encouraged to follow Christ anew, trusting in the God who sovereignly directs history. Highly recommended."

> —**Brandon D. Crowe**, Associate Professor of New Testament, Westminster Theological Seminary; Book Review Editor, *Westminster Theological Journal*

"The author of this worthy volume is conversant with the extensive literature on 1 and 2 Thessalonians and has given us a commentary informed by his long commitment to Christ-centered reformational theology. But this is not a trudging tome; it was preached *viva voce* by a busy, caring pastor-scholar to his own flock week by week and is lively, engaging, and wholly relevant. *1 & 2 Thessalonians* is sure to be a grace to the church and her shepherds."

> —**R. Kent Hughes**, Senior Pastor Emeritus, College Church, Wheaton, Illinois; Visiting Professor of Pastoral Theology, Westminster Theological Seminary

"As Christians, Bible teachers, or gospel ministers, we take our first step in the study of the Bible by going directly to our copy of God's Word. Then, seeking to plumb the depths of the text and avoid handling it wrongly, we secure accurate and thoughtful commentaries from trusted commentators. That is precisely what we have in Rick Phillips's insightful, faithful, and instructive commentary on 1 and 2 Thessalonians, which navigates Paul's Holy Spirit–inspired treatment of wide-ranging, yet ever-relevant gospel issues for life and eternity."

> —**Harry L. Reeder**, Pastor/Teacher, Briarwood Presbyterian Church, Birmingham, Alabama

"Paul wrote 1 and 2 Thessalonians to a young church endeavoring to live for Christ in the midst of a hostile culture. These two little letters have a lot to say to the contemporary church. We may be grateful, then, that Richard D. Phillips has provided us with this fine expositional commentary, a sure and insightful guide to understanding and applying these epistles. Whether you want to be a better reader of God's Word or are called to preach or teach the Bible in the church, pick up this book and let it help you to prize afresh the riches of these two epistles."

—**Guy Prentiss Waters**, James M. Baird Jr. Professor of New Testament, Reformed Theological Seminary, Jackson, Mississippi

1 & 2 Thessalonians

Reformed Expository Commentary

A Series

Series Editors

Richard D. Phillips
Philip Graham Ryken

Testament Editors

Iain M. Duguid, Old Testament
Daniel M. Doriani, New Testament

1 & 2 Thessalonians

RICHARD D. PHILLIPS

P&R PUBLISHING

P.O. BOX 817 • PHILLIPSBURG • NEW JERSEY 08865-0817

ISBN: 978-1-59638-977-9 (cloth)
ISBN: 978-1-59638-978-6 (ePub)
ISBN: 978-1-59638-979-3 (Mobi)

Printed in the United States of America

Library of Congress Cataloging-in-Publication Data

Phillips, Richard D. (Richard Davis), 1960-
 1 & 2 Thessalonians / Richard D. Phillips.
     pages cm. -- (Reformed expository commentary)
 Includes bibliographical references and index.
 ISBN 978-1-59638-977-9 (cloth : alk. paper) -- ISBN 978-1-59638-978-6 (epub) --
ISBN 978-1-59638-979-3 (mobi)
 1. Bible. Thessalonians--Commentaries. I. Title.
 BS2725.53.P484 2015
 227'.8107--dc23
                            2015017406

To L. Edgar Barnhill III,
with thanks for his stalwart friendship in Christ,
and to Him who is coming
when the final trumpet sounds (1 Thess. 4:16).

CONTENTS

Contents

Series Introduction

In every generation there is a fresh need for the faithful exposition of God's Word in the church. At the same time, the church must constantly do the work of theology: reflecting on the teaching of Scripture, confessing its doctrines of the Christian faith, and applying them to contemporary culture. We believe that these two tasks—the expositional and the theological—are interdependent. Our doctrine must derive from the biblical text, and our understanding of any particular passage of Scripture must arise from the doctrine taught in Scripture as a whole.

We further believe that these interdependent tasks of biblical exposition and theological reflection are best undertaken in the church, and most specifically in the pulpits of the church. This is all the more true since the study of Scripture properly results in doxology and praxis—that is, in praise to God and practical application in the lives of believers. In pursuit of these ends, we are pleased to present the Reformed Expository Commentary as a fresh exposition of Scripture for our generation in the church. We hope and pray that pastors, teachers, Bible study leaders, and many others will find this series to be a faithful, inspiring, and useful resource for the study of God's infallible, inerrant Word.

The Reformed Expository Commentary has four fundamental commitments. First, these commentaries aim to be *biblical*, presenting a comprehensive exposition characterized by careful attention to the details of the text. They are not exegetical commentaries—commenting word by word or even verse by verse—but integrated expositions of whole passages of Scripture. Each commentary will thus present a sequential, systematic treatment of an entire book of the Bible, passage by passage. Second, these commentaries are unashamedly *doctrinal*. We are committed to the Westminster Confession of Faith and Catechisms as containing the system of doctrine taught in the Scriptures of the Old and New Testaments. Each volume will teach, promote, and defend the doctrines of the Reformed faith as they are found in the Bible. Third, these commentaries are *redemptive-historical* in their orientation. We believe in the unity of the Bible and its central message of salvation in Christ. We are thus committed to a Christ-centered view of the Old Testament, in which its characters, events, regulations, and institutions are properly understood as pointing us to Christ and his gospel, as well as giving us examples to follow in living by faith. Fourth, these commentaries are *practical*, applying the text of Scripture to contemporary challenges of life—both public and private—with appropriate illustrations.

The contributors to the Reformed Expository Commentary are all pastor-scholars. As pastor, each author will first present his expositions in the pulpit ministry of his church. This means that these commentaries are rooted in the teaching of Scripture to real people in the church. While aiming to be scholarly, these expositions are not academic. Our intent is to be faithful, clear, and helpful to Christians who possess various levels of biblical and theological training—as should be true in any effective pulpit ministry. Inevitably this means that some issues of academic interest will not be covered. Nevertheless, we aim to achieve a responsible level of scholarship, seeking to promote and model this for pastors and other teachers in the church. Significant exegetical and theological difficulties, along with such historical and cultural background as is relevant to the text, will be treated with care.

We strive for a high standard of enduring excellence. This begins with the selection of the authors, all of whom have proved to be outstanding communicators of God's Word. But this pursuit of excellence is also reflected in a disciplined editorial process. Each volume is edited by both a series editor and a testament editor. The testament editors, Iain Duguid for the Old Testament and Daniel Doriani for the New Testament, are accomplished pastors and respected scholars who have taught at the seminary level. Their job is to ensure that each volume is sufficiently conversant with up-to-date scholarship and is faithful and accurate in its exposition of the text. As series editors, we oversee each volume to ensure its overall quality—including excellence of writing, soundness of teaching, and usefulness in application. Working together as an editorial team, along with the publisher, we are devoted to ensuring that these are the best commentaries that our gifted authors can provide, so that the church will be served with trustworthy and exemplary expositions of God's Word.

It is our goal and prayer that the Reformed Expository Commentary will serve the church by renewing confidence in the clarity and power of Scripture and by upholding the great doctrinal heritage of the Reformed faith. We hope that pastors who read these commentaries will be encouraged in their own expository preaching ministry, which we believe to be the best and most biblical pattern for teaching God's Word in the church. We hope that lay teachers will find these commentaries among the most useful resources they rely on for understanding and presenting the text of the Bible. And we hope that the devotional quality of these studies of Scripture will instruct and inspire each Christian who reads them in joyful, obedient discipleship to Jesus Christ.

May the Lord bless all who read the Reformed Expository Commentary. We commit these volumes to the Lord Jesus Christ, praying that the Holy Spirit will use them for the instruction and edification of the church, with thanksgiving to God the Father for his unceasing faithfulness in building his church through the ministry of his Word.

Richard D. Phillips
Philip Graham Ryken
Series Editors

PREFACE

Paul's letters to the church in Thessalonica provide an enlightening snapshot of the life and concerns of the earliest Christian churches. Written from Corinth within weeks of Paul's sudden need to depart from his beloved Thessalonian converts, the letters express the apostle's joy that these believers excel in the most important of graces: faith and love. From this perspective, 1 and 2 Thessalonians set forth vital teaching on what makes for a good church. Paul's converts did not have political power, financial resources, or perhaps even great numbers. But having received the gospel "not as the word of men but as . . . the word of God" (1 Thess. 2:13), they possessed true spiritual riches and power. In this way these two letters, among the earliest of the New Testament, provide an excellent primer on what constitutes a healthy and thriving church, even amid adversity and with a need for continued spiritual growth. As such, these letters are a vital study for pastors and especially those called into church-planting, and also for every Christian who longs for a healthy and growing Christian life.

The letters to the Thessalonians are particularly known, however, for their concentrated doctrinal teaching regarding the second coming of Jesus Christ. Indeed, Paul's eschatology in these letters is of primary importance for those seeking a firm understanding of end-times teaching. It is my conviction that Paul's teaching here reproduces in a doctrinally clear fashion the teaching of Jesus' Olivet Discourse in Matthew 24–25 and Luke 21. Thessalonians also provides an essential doctrinal grid for approaching the book of Revelation. As such, the apostle's clear and orderly teaching in these letters is a vital resource not only for properly understanding Christ's return but also for inciting a joyful anticipation that agrees with the earliest Christians' fervent desire. In my view, one of the great tragedies today is that so many Christians have been led to face the thought of Jesus' return with fear and dread. But for Paul and his Thessalonian readers, Christ's coming is nothing less than "our blessed hope, the appearing of the glory of our great God and Savior Jesus Christ" (Titus 2:13). This joyful expectation of Christ's return is clearly communicated in 1 and 2 Thessalonians, so that a careful study of this material will lead to a life-and-death transformation of our hope for the future in the Lord.

The expositions in this commentary were preached to the congregation of Second Presbyterian Church, Greenville, South Carolina. I thank this beloved congregation, with special thanks for the encouragement I have received from the session for my commitment to study and writing. I am always grateful for the ministry partnership of my wife, Sharon, together with the blessing of our five children. This volume is dedicated to L. Edgar Barnhill III, who for many years has been a devoted friend and who is a stalwart servant of Christ and his church. Most of all, I thank and praise the Lord and Savior Jesus Christ, who will soon return "with a cry of command, with the voice of an archangel, and with the sound of the trumpet of God" (1 Thess. 4:16). To him be glory forever.

Richard D. Phillips
Greenville, South Carolina
June 2015

1 Thessalonians

STANDING FAST IN THE LORD

1

To the Thessalonians

1 Thessalonians 1:1

*Paul, Silvanus, and Timothy, To the church of the Thessalonians
in God the Father and the Lord Jesus Christ: Grace to you and
peace.* (1 Thess. 1:1)

Everyone can use a little encouragement. When the famous painter Benjamin West was a boy, he decided to paint a picture of his sister while his mother was out. Gathering some bottles of ink and paper, he soon made an awful mess in the house. When his mother returned, she saw the mess but also her son's attempt at making art. Instead of scolding him, she picked up the portrait and declared, "What a beautiful picture of your sister!" and kissed her son. West later recalled, "With that kiss I became a painter."[1]

PAUL'S ENCOURAGEMENT OVER THE THESSALONIANS

Encouragement is so valuable that even the apostle Paul needed it. Having recently arrived in the decadent port city of Corinth, the apostle could only

1. Quoted in Michael P. Green, *1500 Illustrations for Biblical Preaching* (Grand Rapids: Baker, 1982), 119.

have been discouraged by his recent experience as an evangelist. Landing in Greece at the city of Philippi, he had gained noteworthy converts such as Lydia and the Philippian jailer. But after a false arrest and savage beating, Paul and his colleagues were asked to leave the city (Acts 16:11–40). Moving along the Aegean coast, he next came to Thessalonica. After preaching in the synagogue there, some Jews and "a great many" devout Greeks came to faith in Christ (17:4). This success roused the anger of the Jewish leaders, who raised a disturbance against the Christians, so that once again Paul left town after only a short stay. On the apostle went to Berea and then Athens, where he preached a famous sermon on Mars Hill but once again had to leave only a small band of converts behind.

From Athens, Paul sent his young assistant Timothy back to Thessalonica to minister to the believers whom they had left there (1 Thess. 3:1–2). Shortly after Paul arrived in Corinth, Timothy returned with news that lifted the apostle's spirits: "Now that Timothy has come to us from you, and has brought us the good news of your faith and love . . . we have been comforted about you through your faith" (vv. 6–7). "For now we live," Paul exclaimed, "if you are standing fast in the Lord" (v. 8).

Paul wrote 1 Thessalonians to express his joy in the believers' faith. Based on information from the book of Acts, scholars date this letter during the year A.D. 50 or 51, making it one of the oldest New Testament documents, with only Galatians and James likely to have been written earlier. First Thessalonians is one of Paul's most encouraging writings, expressing his relief and joy. Leon Morris comments:

> [Paul] wrote in exultation of spirit, having just heard the good news of the way in which they were standing fast. He wrote to let them know how thankful he was. He wrote to let them know of his tender concern for them. He wrote to encourage them in the face of the opposition, even persecution, that still confronted them. He wrote to give them fuller information about matters in which their zeal had outdistanced their knowledge. He wrote to put them further along the Christian way that meant so much to him and to them.[2]

These are matters in which we, too, need to be encouraged and instructed, for which purpose the Holy Spirit inspired 1 Thessalonians and preserved it for many generations of Christians.

---

2. Leon Morris, *The First and Second Epistles to the Thessalonians*, New International Commentary on the New Testament (Grand Rapids: Eerdmans, 1959), 23.

Paul and Friends

Our letters today normally begin by addressing the recipient: "Dear So and So." First Thessalonians follows the ancient practice of first identifying the author(s): "Paul, Silvanus, and Timothy" (1 Thess. 1:1). These opening words remind us that this book is not an abstract theological treatise, but a letter. The teaching given here is not intended for highly trained specialists but for ordinary Christians of all kinds. The letter served to bridge the gap of space between apostle and church for the sake of ministry. The same letter bridges the gap of time between Christians today and the apostles who were charged to provide the foundational teaching of doctrine and practice for the followers of Christ.

It is noteworthy that Paul's salutation includes the names of his two assistants, both of whom had helped to plant the Thessalonian church. *Silvanus* is a Greek rendering of *Silas*; one bearing that name preached the gospel alongside Paul. Silas is first seen at the Jerusalem Council, where he is described as one of the "leading men" of the Jerusalem church (Acts 15:22). After the Jerusalem Council affirmed the acceptance of the Gentile churches, Silas was sent with Paul and Barnabas to Antioch with this news. He is identified as a prophet (v. 32), which means that while he was not formally invested with apostolic authority, he was inspired by the Holy Spirit to provide revelation from God. After Paul and Barnabas disputed and parted ways, Paul chose Silas, whose character and gifts made him a valuable partner in evangelism and church-planting (v. 40).

Early in Paul and Silas's first missionary journey together (Paul's third journey), they encountered Timothy at the church of Lystra. Timothy was a young man of good reputation whose mother was a Jewish believer and whose father was Greek. He joined Paul and Silas as an assistant (Acts 16:1–3) and would go on to serve as Paul's ministerial son and most valued deputy, ultimately serving as pastor of the strategically important church in Ephesus (1 Tim. 1:3).

Paul's pattern of ministering as a team fits the overall New Testament approach of joint rule by a plurality of spiritually gifted and qualified men. Not only did Paul usually minister with partners, but he also gave instructions that a plurality of elders would be placed in charge of local churches after he had departed (see Titus 1:5). This practice reflects a general principle

3

that is rooted in Christ's own instruction. Midway in his own ministry, when Jesus commissioned seventy-two evangelists, he sent them throughout Galilee "two by two" (Luke 10:1).

The benefits of this team approach to ministry include emotional, physical, and spiritual support, a balancing of complementary gifts, and a combination of fellowship and accountability that reduces the likelihood of a leader's falling into sin. Moreover, the modeling of camaraderie among a ministry team encourages similar fellowship in the church and encourages all believers to participate in the work of spreading the gospel and building the body of Christ. Although Paul is plainly the principal author of this letter, we can imagine him consulting with his partners and praying with them as they communicated their joint concern together for this fledgling church.

The leading author of 1 Thessalonians was the apostle Paul. Formerly known as *Saul of Tarsus*, this titanic figure of the New Testament is first encountered in the Bible as one of the chief persecutors of the followers of Christ. Saul was so zealous to oppose the gospel that he journeyed from Jerusalem to Damascus to root out the church there. Along the way, he was confronted by a vision of the exalted Lord Jesus, who called him to both faith and apostleship (Acts 9:15–16). With his conversion, Saul's name was changed to *Paul*, meaning "little," perhaps to convey the humility to which the proud Pharisee was called in service to Christ.

As the leading apostle to the Gentiles, Paul wrote thirteen biblical books, making up just under a quarter of the New Testament. In most of his letters, Paul identifies himself as "an apostle" of Jesus Christ. The fact that he did not use this designation in 1 Thessalonians probably reflects how recently he had ministered there, so that his apostolic credentials were well known and accepted.

An apostle is "one who is sent" or "commissioned," and Christ's apostles were commissioned to preach the gospel and form the initial churches. Most importantly, the resurrected Lord Jesus granted them authority to teach and rule on his behalf, empowering them with the inspiration of the Holy Spirit (John 16:13; Acts 1:8). Peter O'Brien states, "As an apostle [Paul] has the authority to proclaim the gospel in both oral and written form, as well as to establish and build up churches."[3]

---

3. Peter T. O'Brien, *The Letter to the Ephesians*, Pillar New Testament Commentary (Grand Rapids: Eerdmans, 1999), 84.

Christ's apostles consisted of the original twelve disciples of Jesus, with Matthias added to replace the betrayer Judas Iscariot (Acts 1:16–26). Acts 1:22 establishes the qualifications that an apostle must have been personally discipled by Jesus and an eyewitness of the resurrection. These qualifications show that there can be no apostles today. Moreover, the work of the apostles in founding the church and establishing its doctrine was completed during the initial era of the church. Paul fulfilled the criteria for the apostolic office by means of his conversion and commissioning on the Damascus road. What Jesus said to the Twelve just before his ascension into heaven applies equally to Paul: "You will receive power . . . , and you will be my witnesses" (v. 8). Paul's writing, like that of the other apostles, is the exalted Christ's own Word as the Holy Spirit inspired these official messengers from Christ to his church.

The Church in God and in Christ

After identifying the senders, ancient letters typically stated the recipients. Paul addressed this letter: "To the church of the Thessalonians in God the Father and the Lord Jesus Christ" (1 Thess. 1:1).

The Greek word for *church* is *ekklesia*, which has the general meaning of "assembly." In the Greek society of Paul's audience, this word evoked images of the great democratic assemblies in which free citizens met for shared rule. Speaking generally, an *ekklesia* was any body joined together for political, social, or other purposes. The Christian church is a unique kind of assembly that has turned to God through faith in Jesus Christ. Paul's later writings will convey the distinctiveness of the church by referring to his readers as "saints," that is, holy ones who have been separated by God for faith, godliness, ministry, and worship in Christ's name. John Lillie comments: "Called out . . . from the surrounding mass, whether of unbelieving Jews or of heathen idolaters, and quickened individually with a new life, they were, as a church, incorporate one with another, set apart and furnished for holy service, and consecrated to a glorious destiny."[4]

Most important to the meaning of *church* is the Old Testament background of Israel as the assembly of the Lord. The Greek translation of the

4. John Lillie, *Lectures on Paul's Epistles to the Thessalonians*, Tentmaker Classic Commentaries (1860; repr., Stoke-on-Trent, UK: Tentmaker Publications, 2007), 22.

Old Testament commonly used in Paul's day (the Septuagint) used *ekklesia* to render the Hebrew word *qahal,* which designated the gathering of Israel as the congregation of God's people. Thus, Paul sees the Christians to whom he is writing as an extension of the ancient people of God who were redeemed in the exodus and called out as a pilgrim nation to serve and worship the Lord. G. K. Beale observes: "In this light, the Thessalonian church was part of the true Israelite congregation of God's people who had been established by Messiah Jesus' latter-day redemptive work."[5]

Seeing the church as the great assembly of God's people throughout history highlights its importance to the Christian faith and life. To be a Christian is to be part of the church, both locally and universally. The church provides the communal context for Christian evangelism, discipleship, worship, and ministry. When Christians are saved out of the world, they are saved into Christ's church, which serves "to establish group boundaries between saved and unsaved humanity."[6]

Paul wrote his letter to an assembly of Christians at a particular place and time. His original audience was "the church of the Thessalonians" (1 Thess. 1:1). Christian life and ministry will always have a local feel and flavor. There is a tendency today, however, to exaggerate these differences when it comes to the witness of the gospel. When we think of Paul's various places of ministry, we should note that his strategy varied little, and his doctrine not at all, despite the wide variety of cultural and social contexts in which he served. Paul explained to the Corinthians that he had come to preach "Jesus Christ and him crucified" (1 Cor. 2:2). In a city with a large Jewish population, such as Thessalonica, Paul would begin preaching in the synagogue, proving from the Old Testament that Jesus was the promised Messiah. In a city without many Jews, such as Athens, Paul still preached in order to declare Jesus as Savior and Lord. After his preaching had caused conversions, Paul then discipled and organized a local church to continue preaching the message of Christ.

As the chief city of the northern Greek region of Macedonia, Thessalonica was a strategic location, with probably a quarter-million residents. Since its main street was the primary east-west highway of the Roman Empire, a

5. G. K. Beale, *1–2 Thessalonians,* IVP New Testament Commentary Series (Downers Grove, IL: InterVarsity Press, 2003), 42.

6. Charles A. Wanamaker, *Epistles to the Thessalonians,* New International Greek Text Commentary (Grand Rapids: Eerdmans, 1990), 71.

strong church in Thessalonica would be well situated to spread the gospel to others. This strategic potential did not cause Paul to change his ministry approach, but it could account in part for the interest and attention he showed to this important church.

Paul's audience may have been located in Thessalonica, but their identity came from God. Paul thus refers to them as "the church of the Thessalonians in God the Father and the Lord Jesus Christ" (1 Thess. 1:1). The worldly city of Thessalonica had proved to be inhospitable to the Christians, causing Paul and his friends to leave and exposing the church to persecution (see Acts 17:1–9). So how encouraging it was for them to know that their life was rooted in God himself, who through Jesus Christ had become their loving Father. Thessalonica might reject them, but God had received them as children. Thessalonica might vilify and persecute them, but God the Father would provide for and save them. Paul's language of being "in God the Father" emphasizes that the church dwells in God, "as not merely the ground of her existence, but as her fortress and high tower, and her eternal home."[7] Although these Thessalonians are "newborn Christians, freshly converted from either Judaism or paganism," though their beliefs and "moral standards have been recently adopted," and though "they are being sorely tested by persecution," Paul is still confident of their perseverance "because he knows it is God's church, and because he has confidence in God."[8]

In addition to its grounding in God the Father, the church is also in "the Lord Jesus Christ" (1 Thess. 1:1). By placing Jesus alongside God the Father, Paul emphasizes the full deity of Christ. This expression, penned a mere twenty years after Christ's death and resurrection, identifies the deity of Christ as an essential article of faith for believers. Paul further notes the deity of Jesus by referring to him as *Lord*. The title *kurios*, or *Lord*, was used in the Greek translation of the Old Testament for *Yahweh*, the personal and covenant name that God had revealed to his people (Ex. 3:14–15). This divine name is now given to Jesus. As Lord, Jesus is sovereign over his people. As *Christ*, which means "Messiah," or "Anointed One," Jesus is the Savior who has atoned for our sins and reconciled us to God. With Jesus as Lord and Savior, the church is to respond obediently to Christ's Word through his

7. Lillie, *Thessalonians*, 23.
8. John R. W. Stott, *The Message of 1 & 2 Thessalonians*, The Bible Speaks Today (Downers Grove, IL: InterVarsity Press, 1994), 26–27.

apostles, relying on his saving work as the ground of our blessings from God and drawing near to him as the source of our vitality and joy. Since the church is rooted, saved, and enlivened "in God the Father and the Lord Jesus Christ," then the way for a church to most powerfully experience the life and blessings of Christian salvation is to be a God-centered and Christ-captivated church. This includes making the Great Commission that Jesus gave us to proclaim the gospel to the world our overarching concern.

PEACE TO YOU

Having identified himself and his partners, and then having biblically defined his audience, Paul concludes his salutation with an expression of divine blessing. Writing out of the encouragement that they had given to him, Paul encourages the Thessalonians with God's rich blessing: "Grace to you and peace" (1 Thess. 1:1). Paul interjects theology into all his greetings, and here he notes the two great themes of salvation: grace and peace.

When we think of the peace of Christ's salvation, we should first think of receiving peace *with* God. The Bible shows that mankind's greatest need is to be restored to a relationship of peace with the God whom we have alienated and offended by our sin. The great problem of humanity is not caused by illiteracy, disease, or bad government. Our true problem is that, having rejected God's rule, we are at war with the sovereign Creator. Paul writes that "the sinful mind is hostile to God. It does not submit to God's law, nor can it do so" (Rom. 8:7 NIV). As a result of our guilt for breaking God's law, all men and women are justly condemned under God's wrath (Eph. 2:1–2). "All have sinned and fall short of the glory of God," Paul laments, with this dreadful result: "the wages of sin is death" (Rom. 6:23).

Given the great problems of alienation and condemnation, our great need is the peace with God that Jesus came to provide. The angels proclaimed at his birth: "Glory to God in the highest, and on earth peace among those with whom he is pleased!" (Luke 2:14). Jesus reconciled sinners to God by dying to pay the penalty for our sins, so that through faith we may be justified before God. Paul concludes, "Therefore, since we have been justified by faith, we have peace with God through our Lord Jesus Christ" (Rom. 5:1).

Along with peace *with* God, Christ ministers the peace *of* God in our hearts. The world thinks of peace as the cessation of hostilities: we sign peace treaties and the fighting temporarily stops. The hatred is still there, however, the causes of strife are unrelieved, and no unity or true love arises. But Jesus gives a true and abiding inward peace, producing unity and harmony among men and women. Jesus told his disciples, "Peace I leave with you; my peace I give to you. Not as the world gives do I give to you" (John 14:27).

The biblical idea of peace is designated by the Hebrew word *shalom*, the deep and abiding peace that results when people are right with God. Leon Morris has defined this peace as "a flourishing state of soul."[9] This is the peace that David celebrated in Psalm 23: "The LORD is my shepherd," he sang. "I shall not want. He makes me lie down in green pastures. He leads me beside still waters. He restores my soul. . . . Even though I walk through the valley of the shadow of death, I will fear no evil . . . . Surely goodness and mercy shall follow me all the days of my life, and I shall dwell in the house of the LORD forever."

Inner peace comes only through the resurrection power sent by the exalted, reigning Jesus Christ, who restores us to God and gives us his own peace. Indeed, "he himself is our peace" (Eph. 2:14). Do you know peace with God? Are you conscious of his favor and love? Do you love him in return, longing to do his will and know him better? Peace with God comes by confessing your sin to God, trusting Christ's life, death, and resurrection for your salvation, and surrendering your life to "the God of peace," who will "sanctify you completely" through the blood of his Son, Jesus Christ (1 Thess. 5:23). Having received God's peace in Christ, we then are to pursue peace in our relationships and in the world. In his Sermon on the Mount, Jesus challenged each believer to make a practical commitment to peace: "Blessed are the peacemakers, for they shall be called sons of God" (Matt. 5:9).

GRACE TO YOU

It is wonderful to know that we can have peace with God and especially encouraging to know that this peace comes as a gift of God's grace in Jesus Christ. This may be why Paul blesses the Thessalonians with the greeting, "Grace to you and peace." It is by grace that we receive the peace of God through Jesus Christ.

9. Quoted in J. Philip Arthur, *Patience of Hope: 1 and 2 Thessalonians Simply Explained*, Wellwyn Commentary Series (Ross-shire, UK: Evangelical Press, 1996), 22.

One way for us to think about grace is as a description of what God is like. *Grace* is often defined as "God's unmerited favor." This is true, but it does not go far enough. Grace is God's favor to us when we have merited his condemnation. We have earned God's hatred and wrath, yet he causes us to be forgiven and makes us his precious children. God gives that which is most precious to himself, his only Son, that he might remove our guilt on the cross, reconciling us to his love. The measure of God's grace is the costliness of his gift, and in the giving of Jesus to die for our sins, God has shown himself to abound in grace for sinners.

God's grace finds expression in an unstoppable plan of grace for our salvation. Paul refers to this plan in 1 Thessalonians 1:4–5: "For we know, brothers loved by God, that he has chosen you, because our gospel came to you not only in word, but also in power and in the Holy Spirit and with full conviction." This states that God graciously chose his people in advance (see Eph. 1:4), sent Jesus into the world to achieve their salvation, and then, when the apostles came to preach that good news, granted them his grace so that they would believe and be saved. The entirety of salvation is the work of God's grace! How encouraging it is for beleaguered Christians today, like the Thessalonians of old, to know that our salvation is the free gift of God, according to his sovereign and eternal plan of grace. We may therefore rely utterly on God's grace, giving God all the glory for our blessings in Christ. Though we have all sinned, believers "are justified by [God's] grace as a gift, through the redemption that is in Christ Jesus" (Rom. 3:24).

Grace describes God's unmerited favor and his method of saving sinners. Finally, grace is God's power working in us for newness of life. Later in this letter, Paul will exhort the Thessalonian believers to live in a holy manner that pleases the Lord. "For this is the will of God, your sanctification," he will announce, "that you abstain from sexual immorality" and "that no one transgress and wrong his brother" (1 Thess. 4:3–6). The Thessalonians were no longer to live in the sinful and harmful manner in which they had previously lived as unbelievers, and that their society, like ours, had come to think was inevitable and unavoidable. How can morally depraved sinners change so as to live in a holy and loving way? Paul says at the end of 1 Thessalonians that the God of peace will "sanctify you completely" (5:23). What an encouragement it is to know, Paul exults, the power of God's grace to empower us to live in a way that pleases the Lord and brings blessing to us.

In the Face of Christ

This chapter began with an incident from the life of Benjamin West, who was encouraged to be a painter by his mother's kiss. Something similar occurred to Mercedes Ruehl when she attended her first Broadway play as a little girl. The star actress on the stage noticed young Mercedes gazing at her with adoring eyes, and looked back directly at the girl, holding her gaze for several moments. Mercedes considered that gaze an invitation to fulfill her dream to be an actress, and with that simple encouragement she went on to be one of the few stage performers to win both an Academy Award and a Tony Award in the same year.

If you will look in faith to the Lord Jesus Christ as he is revealed in the Bible, you will gain from him the greatest encouragement of all as God's grace invites you into his heavenly peace. For when you look to Jesus, the "star" of all history looks back to you with grace, revealing himself as the Savior who died for your sins. Jesus invites you to believe in him, to enter the church over which he is Lord, and, encouraged by his grace, to extend his offer of peace to a sinful, broken world.

2

A PRAYER OF THANKS

1 Thessalonians 1:2–3

We give thanks to God always for all of you, constantly mentioning you in our prayers, remembering before our God and Father your work of faith and labor of love and steadfastness of hope in the Lord Jesus Christ. (1 Thess. 1:2–3)

*I*n most of the apostle Paul's letters, the greeting is followed by an expression of thanks to God. Since 1 Thessalonians is an entire letter of thanks for the readers' faith, Paul expresses his gratitude throughout the first three chapters. This thanksgiving begins with a long sentence that runs from 1 Thessalonians 1:2–5, in which Paul rejoices over the proofs of their salvation: "For we know, brothers loved by God, that he has chosen you" (v. 4). Paul had been concerned about the reality of the Thessalonians' faith when he was forced to hastily leave them in the midst of trials, and he thanks God for proof of his grace in their lives.

Assurance of salvation is based on biblically sanctioned evidences, and in 1 Thessalonians 1:2–3 Paul identifies the proofs that mark the Thessalonians as God's elect: "your work of faith and labor of love and steadfastness of hope in our Lord Jesus Christ" (v. 3). In doing this, Paul identifies the qualities of a healthy church and a thriving Christian life, while also noting the graces for which believers should pray to God.

PAUL'S CONTINUAL PRAYERS

Before commending the proofs of their salvation, Paul assures his readers of his fervent prayers on their behalf: "We give thanks to God always for all of you, constantly mentioning you in our prayers" (1 Thess. 1:2). This statement is one of many references in his letters that present Paul's commitment to prayer. It says much that the first thing said about Paul after his conversion is, as the King James Version eloquently puts it, "Behold, he prayeth" (Acts 9:11). This is not a bad beginning to anyone's spiritual biography. "It is as though," says Arthur Pink, "that struck the keynote of his subsequent life, that he would, to a special degree, be marked as a man of prayer."[1]

One of the keys to Paul's prayer is the word "constantly" (1 Thess. 1:2). Paul seems to have maintained an incessant prayer vigil for his persecuted friends in Thessalonica. In his former days as a Pharisee, Paul would have kept the practice of formal prayers at least three times a day: in the morning, at midday, and in the evening. It is hard to imagine that as an apostle he would have prayed less frequently than this. We, too, would benefit from regular periods of prayer in our daily schedules. Like Paul, we should pray for a wide range of family, friends, and servants of Christ. Some faithful Christians keep a list of those whom they will pray for on each day of the week. Others pray through the church directory one letter at a time so as to be constantly praying for fellow believers. We can easily imagine Paul, Silas, and Timothy meeting regularly—perhaps at every meal—to pray together for new converts and persecuted churches. G. K. Beale writes: "Paul is a spiritual parent to the Thessalonians (2:7–8, 11), and just as little children are never far from the thoughts of their parents, so Paul is continually mindful of his children, the Thessalonians."[2]

The English Standard Version continues Paul's description by saying that his prayer consisted of "remembering before our God and Father" (1 Thess. 1:3). It is likely that the reference to God the Father belongs later in verse 3,

1. Arthur W. Pink, *The Ability of God* (Chicago: Moody Press, 2000), 13.
2. G. K. Beale, *1–2 Thessalonians*, IVP New Testament Commentary Series (Downers Grove, IL: InterVarsity Press, 2003), 45.

asserting that the Christian virtues for which Paul prays are lived out in the sight of God. It certainly is true that the fervor of Paul's prayer life arose from his awareness of God the Father's presence. We have a tendency to think most about what we or others are doing in our families, our businesses, and our churches. This is why so little attention is often given to prayer and so much attention is paid to influencing men and women. Paul, however, realized that the blessings he sought in the Thessalonian church come only from God. This is why he sought the favor not of men but of God, and therefore why he prayed constantly. To the extent that we realize that the spiritual blessings we desire cannot be procured by man but are freely given by the God of grace, we like Paul will devote ourselves more constantly and earnestly to prayer.

Moreover, our prayers, like Paul's, should be richly adorned with thanks, realizing that, as James put it, "every good and every perfect gift is from above, coming down from the Father" (James 1:17). Thanksgiving is a distinctive mark of Christian prayer. Geoffrey Wilson points out that pagan writers such as Homer included a great many prayers in their works, yet virtually no prayers of thanksgiving. The reason for this pagan thanklessness, just like its current form in our thankless, cynical secular society, is an ignorance of God's grace. Wilson notes, in contrast, that "a constant spirit of thankfulness marks out those who have been made sensible of God's multiplied mercies. Hence Paul, Silas, and Timothy are daily filled with fervent thanksgiving to God as they think of what his grace has wrought in the lives of these Thessalonians."[3] We, too, through our faith in Christ, have ample reasons to pray continually with thanksgiving because of the saving grace that has flowed to us from the cross of Christ and from the throne in heaven where he reigns for us. As Paul writes toward the end of this letter: "pray without ceasing, give thanks in all circumstances; for this is the will of God in Christ Jesus for you" (1 Thess. 5:17–18).

EVIDENCES OF SALVATION

Paul's opening prayer identifies the marks of grace that bear testimony to the believers' salvation. He writes to express his joy over the report that

3. Geoffrey B. Wilson, *New Testament Commentaries*, 2 vols. (Edinburgh: Banner of Truth, 2005), 2:134.

Timothy brought back from Thessalonica, noting their "work of faith and labor of love and steadfastness of hope" (1 Thess. 1:3). Readers familiar with Paul will recognize the threefold virtues about which he often spoke: faith, love, and hope (see Rom. 5:2–5; 1 Cor. 13:13; Gal. 5:5f.; Col. 1:4f.). In writing to the Corinthians, Paul changed the order, saying: "So now faith, hope, and love abide, these three; but the greatest of these is love" (1 Cor. 13:13). To the divided Corinthians, Paul stressed love, whereas here, writing to believers harassed by persecution, Paul places the stress on hope. In every case, Paul notes faith as the initial grace, from which spring both love and hope in the believer's heart. John Lillie explains that "wherever true faith is, there also you are sure to find the other two. If faith is the indispensable root, the unfailing fruit is love and hope."[4]

The first evidence of salvation is faith as it is observed through good works: "your work of faith" (1 Thess. 1:3). Some Christians become alarmed whenever the concepts of works and faith appear together in the Bible. Paul makes clear in his writings that sinners are justified by faith alone, apart from any good works: "We know that a person is not justified by works of the law but through faith in Jesus Christ" (Gal. 2:16). As sinners, we could never cover our guilt before God with any number of good works, since works cannot erase the record of our sin. Being imperfect, they cannot merit salvation. Instead, God justifies us through the finished work of his Son, Jesus Christ, who paid the penalty of our sin on the cross and achieved righteousness for us by his perfect life of obedience. Having been justified through faith, however, a Christian is called to the "work of faith." Paul makes this connection explicit in Ephesians 2:8–10: "For by grace you have been saved through faith. And this is not your own doing; it is the gift of God, not a result of works, so that no one may boast. For we are his workmanship, created in Christ Jesus for good works, which God prepared beforehand, that we should walk in them." While we are most certainly not saved *by* works, Paul specifies that we are certainly saved *to* good works.

What exactly does Paul have in mind in speaking of the "work of faith"? We might think of a wide range of godly results of trusting in Christ. One result is turning from sin in practical areas of life. Paul will emphasize this later in the letter: "For this is the will of God, your sanctification" (1 Thess.

4. John Lillie, *Lectures on Paul's Epistles to the Thessalonians*, Tentmaker Classic Commentaries (1860; repr., Stoke-on-Trent, UK: Tentmaker Publications, 2007), 38–39.

4:3). Paul could be referring to faithful work in the home or in a vocational calling, both of which are important to Christian living. The work of faith might also include evangelism and other vital ministries in the church, another topic that Paul writes about extensively in this epistle.

Benjamin Morgan Palmer points out, however, that Paul speaks of *work* in the singular rather than *works* in the plural. This suggests that faith produces work as "an undivided whole, a continuous career of activity."[5] The apostle has in view a life of increasing fruitfulness in obedience to God's instruction and commands in the Bible. Leon Morris notes that sincere faith in Christ "cannot but transform the whole of life, and issue in 'work' of many kinds."[6] The writer of Hebrews celebrated such a life when he remembered Bible heroes "who through faith conquered kingdoms, enforced justice, obtained promises, stopped the mouths of lions, quenched the power of fire, escaped the edge of the sword, were made strong out of weakness, became mighty in war, put foreign armies to flight" (Heb. 11:33–34).

Second, Paul rejoices in the Thessalonians' "labor of love." The Greek word *kopou* emphasizes sacrificial exertions that go beyond ordinary works. Whereas *work* focuses on the deeds, *labor* considers the arduous effort required. Paul rejoices that the Thessalonians were willing to serve in costly ways because of the love that had arisen from their faith in Christ. Paul envisions love in labor among fellow Christians (1 Thess. 3:12), in esteem for spiritual leaders (5:13), in concern for Christians in other places (4:9), and "for all" (3:12), which includes non-Christians.

A "labor of love" was discovered by a visitor to a Bulgarian peasant's house. During the long stay, the peasant's daughter busily stitched at a dress the whole time. The visitor asked her, "Don't you ever get tired of that eternal sewing?" "Oh no!" she said; "you see this is my wedding dress."[7] It was for her a labor of love, and the weariness and difficulty seemed as nothing to her heart. So is the labor of love that Christians offer to one another and to the world.

The most common New Testament word for *love* is *agape*, a word seldom used in earlier Greek writings. The more common word among the Greeks

5. Benjamin Morgan Palmer, *Sermons*, 2 vols. (1875; repr., Harrisonburg, VA: Sprinkle, 2002), 1:585.
6. Leon Morris, *The First and Second Epistles to the Thessalonians*, New International Commentary on the New Testament (Grand Rapids: Eerdmans, 1959), 51.
7. William Barclay, *The Letters to the Philippians, Colossians, and Thessalonians* (Louisville: Westminster, 1975), 186.

was *eros*, which not only meant romantic love but also spoke more generally of love for something desirable. A young man has romantic love toward a woman who catches his eye. Leon Morris warns us, however, of the contrast between the love of desire and the love that God gives: "The Hollywood brand of love will never do if we wish to understand the New Testament."[8] In contrast to the *eros* love common to humanity, God's love moves his people to costly labor apart from any desire for gain. Morris explains:

> God loves us, not because we are worthy, nor even, as some think, because He sees in us possibilities as yet unrealized. God loves us although He knows full well our complete unworthiness. . . . He loves, moreover, without thought of advantage, for there is nothing that we can bring to Him who made all things. He loves because it is His nature to love. He loves because He *is* love. Continually He gives Himself in a love which is for the blessing of others, not for the enrichment of Himself.[9]

God's love became known to believers most fully through the sacrifice of God's Son, Jesus Christ, to atone for our sins. John wrote, "In this is love, not that we have loved God but that he loved us and sent his Son to be the propitiation for our sins" (1 John 4:10). That gracious love of God works in the hearts of those who receive it, so that we begin to see others as God sees them and to love them without thought of gain or cost to ourselves. Hearing of the "labor of love" among the Thessalonians, Paul rejoices at this evidence of God's saving power at work within them.

Third, Paul notes their "steadfastness of hope" (1 Thess. 1:3). The hope to which he refers is not mere wishful thinking, as when we say, "I hope it snows on Christmas morning!" Rather, biblical hope is the certainty of receiving what God has promised, including forgiveness of sin and an inheritance in eternal glory. Like love, hope springs from a living faith in Christ and his Word. Paul wrote to Titus: "He saved us, . . . so that being justified by his grace we might become heirs according to the hope of eternal life" (Titus 3:5-7). The result of this hope is the ability to remain steadfast in the face of present trials, knowing that by persevering in faith we will be saved.

The steadfastness of Christian hope is not a grim, stoic resignation to hardship but a believing fortitude that faces trials in the certain expectation of

8. Morris, *First and Second Thessalonians*, 52.
9. Ibid.

victory through Jesus Christ. Alexander the Great showed this attitude when he divided all his property before setting off to war. A friend exclaimed, "But you are keeping nothing for yourself." "O yes, I am," Alexander answered. "I have kept my hopes." William Barclay comments: "A man can endure anything so long as he has hope, for then he is walking not into the night but to the dawn."[10] Christians have a far greater hope than even the fondest desires of a conqueror such as Alexander: we have, Paul wrote, "Christ in you, the hope of glory" (Col. 1:27).

GROUNDED IN GRACE

Credible evidences are important to Christian assurance, which is why those who do not live out their faith in practical godliness and love will often be tormented with doubts about their salvation. Yet the evidences are not the source or cause of salvation. Instead, Paul explains, these are signs of God's saving work and even of a believer's eternal election (1 Thess. 1:4). With this in mind, Paul concludes verse 3 by directing his readers to look to Jesus Christ and to God the Father for the security of their salvation.

Notice that the Thessalonians' faith, love, and hope are located "in our Lord Jesus Christ" (1 Thess. 1:3). This reference to Christ is especially linked to the concluding matter of hope. Since Paul is writing to new believers who are struggling with persecution and other hardships, his particular concern is that they will press on in hope. This letter goes on to emphasize that believers' hope is grounded in the promised return of Jesus Christ to complete the salvation of his people: "For the Lord himself will descend from heaven with a cry of command, with the voice of an archangel, and with the sound of the trumpet of God . . . , and so we will always be with the Lord" (4:16–17). Anticipating Christ's return, they are to "encourage one another" amid the brief struggles of this life (5:11).

Of course, the whole of a Christian's salvation is in Christ. We look back in faith to Christ's saving work, in the present we love Christ and share that love in the labor of ministry, and we look forward to his future return and the final victory of his people. To hope in the Lord, then, is "to wait for [God's] Son from heaven, . . . who delivers us from the wrath to come" (1 Thess. 1:10).

10. Barclay, *The Letters to the Philippians, Colossians, and Thessalonians*, 186–87.

In the Greek text, the final words of verse 3 refer to God the Father: "before our God and Father." Some English translations insert this statement earlier, with Paul describing his prayers as "remembering before our God and Father" (1 Thess. 1:3 ESV), since the idea of being in God's presence fits the topic of prayer. The problem with such translations is that by putting these words at the end of the sentence, it is more likely that Paul relates the presence of God with the practice of Christian virtues. Probably the King James Version is right to translate verse 3 this way: "Remembering without ceasing your work of faith, and labour of love, and patience of hope in our Lord Jesus Christ, in the sight of God and our Father." In this case, Paul is wrapping up his expression of thanksgiving by first relating the believers' hope to Jesus Christ and then reminding them that God sees and is glorified by their evidences of his saving grace.

In this respect, Paul emphasizes the fatherhood of God for believers, who are his children in Jesus Christ. As children, we are reminded of our responsibilities by the presence of our father. But even more so, we are encouraged by the love, support, and provision of our Father. Just as children want their earthly father to be present for baseball or soccer games, drawing strength and encouragement from his supportive presence, so Christians are emboldened in the work of faith, labor of love, and steadfastness of hope by their awareness of God's love, acceptance, and provision. The Father's presence motivates us to glorify him through lives transformed by the grace he gives.

The Christian's Potential and Calling

In applying Paul's prayer of thanks, we should be reminded not only of the high calling but also of the high potential that every believer possesses through faith in Christ. Paul told the Corinthians that "if anyone is in Christ, he is a new creation. The old has passed away; behold, the new has come" (2 Cor. 5:17). As sinners, we are saved by grace alone, apart from anything of our own to commend us to God. But while God receives sinners, he does not leave us in our sin. We can and must be transformed by the mighty grace of God!

Christians who do not realize their potential as born-again children of God may live in defeated resignation toward their sin. Sometimes it is taught that since we are such sinners, we simply have to accept the bondage of our corruption. This teaching is completely contrary to the New Testament. Paul exhorted the Ephesians to remember Christ's resurrection and "the immeasurable greatness of his power toward us who believe" (Eph. 1:19), which enables us "to put off your old self, which belongs to your former manner of life and is corrupt through deceitful desires, and to be renewed in the spirit of your minds, and to put on the new self, created after the likeness of God in true righteousness and holiness" (4:22–24). Some false teachers will describe an emphasis on good works and a changed life as a legalistic denial of Paul's principle of salvation by grace. But Paul himself rejoiced in the "work of faith" (1 Thess. 1:3). He explained to Titus that "the grace of God has appeared, . . . training us to renounce ungodliness and worldly passions, and to live self-controlled, upright, and godly lives in the present age" (Titus 2:11–12).

The record of the Thessalonians, who had only recently become believers, shows that everyone who is born again in Christ has God's power for radical change. Trusting Christ therefore calls us to strive in God's Word and in prayer to realize this potential and grow in God's grace. In raising Christian children, we likewise should aspire to far more than keeping them from getting into trouble or abandoning the faith. Instead, we should minister God's Word in confident expectation of divine blessing, setting an inspiring example through our own transformed lives and praying fervently that God will empower our children in the "work of faith and labor of love and steadfastness of hope" in Jesus Christ.

Moreover, Paul provides us with an apostolic definition of a good church. Notice how little attention Paul pays to the size of the Thessalonian congregation, much less to the impressiveness of their building, their church budget, or the personality traits of their leaders. What really matters in a church is faith, love, and hope: faith arising from the ministry and practice of God's Word, love flowing from Christ through the fellowship of the church members, and hope that brings joy and zeal for witness to a hostile world. This is the kind of church that we should desire to be, and that we can become as we consciously live before God the Father through faith in Jesus Christ.

Furthermore, Paul's example in prayer should inform our own intercessions. We should think frequently of other Christians and also of the well-being and ministry of the church, constantly bearing their needs in prayer before God. We should pray in keeping with the priorities of Christ's kingdom, in which the things that really matter are faith, love, and hope. And we should often thank God for the evidences that his saving power is at work among us.

A LIFE WORTH REMEMBERING

Everything that we have noted about a good church is also true of a fruitful Christian life. A successful Christian is not one who has attained to a high position in society but one who has advanced in evidences of God's grace. A rich Christian is not one who boasts of a great deal of money but one who abounds in faith, love, and hope through Jesus Christ. As Paul remembers the evidences of salvation among the Thessalonians, we realize that a life worth remembering is one sketched out on the canvas of Paul's prayer of thanks.

We see such a portrait in the life of Joseph A. Maybin, an elder at First Presbyterian Church of New Orleans, who died on May 14, 1876. Maybin was a man blessed with a great intellect, a high position in society, and an eminently successful career. Yet after his conversion to faith in Christ as an adult, he increasingly devoted his attention to ministry to fellow Christians and service to Christ's church. At his memorial service, Maybin's pastor, Benjamin Morgan Palmer, preached from 1 Thessalonians 1:3. He stated: "Should it occur to this church to set a monumental slab upon the wall of this sanctuary, as a fitting memorial of one whose ministerial service dates back almost to her origin—beneath the honored name and the dates of his official career, I would have traced simply these words: 'Remembering without ceasing your work of faith, and labor of love, and patience of hope in our Lord Jesus Christ, in the sight of God and our Father.'"[11]

Maybin's example, with the eulogy given to his life, invites us to ask what words would sum up our own lives as believers in Christ. Many good verses might adorn a memorial to our names. But if those who knew us best should choose to note our "work of faith and labor of love and steadfastness of hope" (1 Thess. 1:3), then surely Christ will also bless us, saying, "Well done, good and faithful servant" (Matt. 25:21, 23), and the people of God will remember our lives with both thanks to God and assurance of his saving work in us.

11. Palmer, *Sermons*, 1:584.

3

ELECTION AND ITS EFFECTS

1 Thessalonians 1:4–5

For we know, brothers loved by God, that he has chosen you,
because our gospel came to you not only in word, but also
in power and in the Holy Spirit and with full conviction.
(1 Thess. 1:4–5)

According to author James R. White, the Trinity is the forgotten doctrine of Christianity:

> Most Christian people have forgotten the central place the doctrine is to hold in the Christian life. It is rarely the topic of sermons and Bible studies, rarely the object of adoration and worship . . . . The doctrine is misunderstood as well as ignored. . . . It does not hold the place it should in the proclamation of the Gospel message, nor in the life of the individual believer in prayer, worship, and service.[1]

This could not be said about the apostle Paul, who structured his whole teaching of salvation around the Trinity. Paul's opening section of

1. James R. White, *The Forgotten Trinity* (Minneapolis: Bethany House, 1998), 16.

thanksgiving in 1 Thessalonians makes mention of each person of the Trinity and that person's respective contributions to our salvation.

The Doctrine of the Trinity

The Trinity is Christianity's highest and greatest mystery. The Bible presents the one God in three persons: Father, Son, and Holy Spirit. As the Westminster Larger Catechism explains, they are "the same in substance, equal in power and glory; although distinguished by their personal properties" (WLC 9). This statement emphasizes that each member of the Trinity is equally God in every respect, yet in his personhood he is distinct and individual. To be a Christian is to relate to all three persons of the Trinity; according to Jesus, the full Christian name for God is "Father, Son, and Holy Spirit" (Matt. 28:19).

In his teaching of salvation, Paul emphasizes the role that each of the three persons plays and the distinctive work that each provides. God the Father chiefly *administers* our salvation. This means that God ordains, plans, and supervises his will for our redemption. Speaking of the Father, Paul writes in Ephesians 1:11 that we have been "predestined according to the purpose of him who works all things according to the counsel of his will." The ultimate cause of our salvation is the sovereign plan and will of the Father.

Meanwhile, God the Son *accomplishes* the work of our salvation. Paul says in Ephesians 1:7, "In [Christ] we have redemption through his blood, the forgiveness of our trespasses." Christ's saving achievement includes his perfect life as our representative, his sin-atoning death and glorious resurrection, his present reign on the throne of heaven, and his soon return to bring his people to glory. These are all things that Christ does for us, accomplishing a definite work for our salvation. How can sin condemn us when Christ has paid its penalty? How will the flesh, the world, or the devil destroy us while Christ now reigns in power, interceding for us in heaven?

But there is still need for the work of God the Spirit, who plays the role of *applying* salvation to individual believers. How can I be included in God's salvation? How can I know that these things are not merely true in the abstract but true for *me*? The answer is in the work of God the Spirit, who gives us faith and unites us to Christ.

23

Seeing how all three members of the Trinity collaborate to provide a sure and certain salvation, we understand why James White began his book by writing, "I love the Trinity."[2] Paul loved the Trinity, too, which is why his exclamation of thanksgiving for the Thessalonians points to Father, Son, and Holy Spirit working together for and in us. The God displayed in the Trinity is a God of unfathomable glory, who meets our every need. Our salvation rests on the sovereign authority of God the Father, who *administers* salvation, on the finished work of God the Son, who *accomplishes* salvation, and on the mighty intervention performed by God the Holy Spirit, who *applies* salvation to believers.

THE DOCTRINE OF ELECTION

At the beginning of Paul's thanks for the Thessalonians, he prays to "our God and Father" because of their faith in "our Lord Jesus Christ" (1 Thess. 1:3). Paul then thanks the Father because faith in Christ indicates that the believers were chosen by God for salvation: "For we know, brothers loved by God, that he has chosen you" (v. 4). Here, Paul makes clear reference, as he so often does in his letters, to the doctrine of election.

The doctrine of election gets its name from the Greek word *eklektos*, which means "chosen." When America holds an election, its citizens choose their leaders. The Bible's doctrine of election declares that God chooses his people for salvation. All the blessings that we enjoy as Christians are grounded in God's sovereign election and predestination, which took place in eternity past. Paul asserts in Ephesians 1:4 that God "chose us in [Christ] before the foundation of the world." God's eternal purpose provides the strongest, firmest ground for salvation, and it is on this foundation that Paul rests our hope for salvation. John Calvin explains:

> God having chosen us before the world had its course, we must attribute the cause of our salvation to His free goodness; we must confess that He did not take us to be His children, for any deserts of our own; for we had nothing to recommend ourselves into His favor. Therefore, we must put the cause and fountain of our salvation in Him only, and ground ourselves upon it.[3]

2. Ibid., 13.
3. John Calvin, *The Mystery of Godliness* (1830; repr., Morgan, PA: Soli Deo Gloria, 1999), 11.

If we ask the question, "Why is someone a Christian?" we might answer, "Because he believed the gospel." This is true. But we go on to ask, "Why did he believe while others did not?" The issue is this: "Was it because of something in the Christian that is better in some way, enabling him to believe while others hear the same message and do not?" The Bible says, No! Salvation is not caused by anything in the Christian, but because of God's sovereign election of individuals to be saved through faith in Christ. This is good news to all who believe, for election assures us that our salvation does not ultimately rest on anything in ourselves—we who are so weak and changing, so mixed in our affections, so inconstant in our faith—but on God's sovereign choice from eternity past. Paul's firmest and ultimate cause for the Thessalonians' salvation is "that he has chosen you" (1 Thess. 1:4).

Notice that Paul joins election to both the love of God and the brotherhood of believers: it is "brothers loved by God" who are chosen by God. The Bible consistently sees God's love as the operative principle in election. The Lord told Israel, "It was not because you were more in number than any other people that the Lord set his love on you and chose you, for you were the fewest of all peoples, but it is because the Lord loves you and is keeping the oath that he swore to your fathers" (Deut. 7:7–8). Paul wrote in Ephesians 1:4–5, "In love he predestined us for adoption as sons through Jesus Christ." Being bound together in sovereign grace, believers are joined into the brotherhood of God's family. To help the Thessalonians think of themselves together as "members of one family and the objects of God's special love,"[4] Paul mentions their brotherhood nineteen times in this letter.

Objections to Election Answered

Despite the overwhelming biblical evidence for election, many Christians raise objections to the doctrine. Some argue that believing in election leads to pride, since if we believe that we have been chosen by God, we will think that we are somehow special and superior. On the contrary, the biblical doctrine of election promotes humility and not pride.

Election promotes humility by ascribing salvation not to any merit in the Christian but only to the sovereign grace of God. Election goes together with the doctrine of total depravity, which declares that sinners are not able to

4. Andrew W. Young, *Let's Study 1 & 2 Thessalonians* (Edinburgh: Banner of Truth, 2001), 12.

contribute anything positive to their own salvation, which therefore must be wholly of God. Where is the ground for human boasting when we realize that our salvation is in spite of our utter unworthiness and thorough corruption, and only because of God's sovereign and amazing grace? Paul states the humbling truth in Titus 3:3–5: "For we ourselves were once foolish, disobedient, led astray, slaves to various passions and pleasures, passing our days in malice and envy, hated by others and hating one another. But when the goodness and loving kindness of God our Savior appeared, he saved us, not because of works done by us in righteousness, but according to his own mercy."

A second objection to election complains that it leads to laziness and loose living. After all, it is argued, if my salvation is caused not by my effort but by God's mercy, then what motive do I have to press on with the difficult work of sanctification? The Bible answers by emphasizing that election promotes holiness and not license.

The objection that election promotes license fails to realize that holiness is the goal for which we are saved. It is God's purpose in our salvation that we should be holy. Paul wrote that God "chose us . . . , that we should be holy and blameless before him" (Eph. 1:4). Martyn Lloyd-Jones writes that according to Paul, "we are not chosen with the possibility of holiness, but to the realization of holiness. . . . Being 'chosen' and being 'holy' are inseparable. . . . God will make you holy because He has chosen you unto holiness."[5]

This teaching warrants the categorical statement that if you are not bearing evidence of holiness and if you do not even desire to be holy, then you have no reason to think you are elect. God elected sinners to holiness, and this is the particular mark of the elect. Paul wrote to the Thessalonians, "This is the will of God, your sanctification" (1 Thess. 4:3). Once we realize that holiness is our destiny in Jesus Christ, we no longer look upon sanctification as an unrealizable ideal, but pursue it with vigor and anticipation. In this way, election promotes and greatly stimulates the pursuit of holiness, as we rely on God's grace and not on our works.

ELECTION'S GOSPEL EFFECTS

A further objection to election argues that believing the doctrine discourages zeal in evangelism. Critics say, "If God predestines people to salvation,

5. D. Martyn Lloyd-Jones, *God's Ultimate Purpose: An Exposition of Ephesians 1* (Grand Rapids: Baker, 1978), 103–4.

then why bother to preach the gospel?" The answer is that God ordains not merely the ends but also the means. God predestines some to be saved and commands us to preach the gospel to that end. If we do not witness the gospel, then none will be saved. But God has ordained that they will be; so he has also ordained that we would preach the gospel so that his chosen people will come to faith. John Stott thus argues that "the doctrine of election, far from making evangelism unnecessary, makes it indispensable. For it is only through the preaching and receiving of the gospel that God's secret purpose comes to be revealed and known."[6] James Montgomery Boice adds:

> Besides it is only election that gives us any hope of success as we evangelize. If God cannot call people to faith effectively, how can we? We cannot persuade them. But if God is working, then he can work in us even if we are inept witnesses. We do not know who God's elect are, but we can find out who some of them are by telling them about Jesus. . . . We can speak to them boldly because we know that God has promised to bless his Word.[7]

The relationship between God's sovereign election and the preaching of the gospel is seen in Paul's continuing thanks for the Thessalonians. In verse 3, Paul saw the evidence of their faith, love, and hope as proof of their election. Now, Paul expresses confidence in their election because of the way the gospel came to them: "For we know, brothers loved by God, that he has chosen you, because our gospel came to you not only in word, but also in power and in the Holy Spirit and with full conviction" (1 Thess. 1:4–5). F. F. Bruce comments: "While the act of election took place in God's eternal counsel, its effects are seen in the lives of the elect, as they were seen now in the lives of the Thessalonian Christians."[8]

Paul sees God's sovereign grace at work in three ways in which the gospel came to the Thessalonians. First, Paul says that the gospel came to them "not only in word" (1 Thess. 1:5). This tells us that the witness of the gospel must first come "in word," that is, in the form of clear, biblical teaching. When we consider Paul's ministry in the book of Acts to widely different people, it was always the case that he ministered "in word." Typically, he

---

6. John R. W. Stott, *The Message of 1 & 2 Thessalonians*, The Bible Speaks Today (Downers Grove, IL: InterVarsity Press, 1994), 31–32.

7. James Montgomery Boice, *Amazing Grace* (Wheaton, IL: Tyndale House, 1993), 56.

8. F. F. Bruce, *1 & 2 Thessalonians*, Word Biblical Commentary 45 (Waco, TX: Word, 1982), 13.

went to the synagogue, where the Jews met for worship, and "reasoned with them from the Scriptures" (Acts 17:2). This means that he expounded the text, "explaining and proving . . . , 'This Jesus, whom I proclaim to you, is the Christ'" (v. 3). On the occasions when he ministered to Gentiles who did not know the Scriptures, Paul still reasoned with them so as to explain the biblical message about Jesus (see vv. 30–31). As he put it to the Romans, "How then will they call on him in whom they have not believed? And how are they to believe in him of whom they have never heard? And how are they to hear without someone preaching? . . . So faith comes from hearing, and hearing through the word of Christ" (Rom. 10:14, 17). Gospel ministry is always a ministry "in word."

Theologians refer to preaching as the *general call* of the gospel. When the pastor opens the Bible in the pulpit and proclaims Jesus Christ, or when a Christian witnesses the gospel to a neighbor, this is the general call that invites everyone to come to Jesus in faith for salvation. Without the general call, no one can be saved. Yet by the general call alone, no one still can be saved, because of the blinding effects of sin. So complete is the sinner's corruption that he "does not accept the things of the Spirit of God . . . , and he is not able to understand them because they are spiritually discerned" (1 Cor. 2:14). Because of man's total depravity in sin, no one is able to respond to a gospel ministry that is "only in word" (1 Thess. 1:5).

Paul thanks God and sees evidence of his readers' election because the gospel did not come to them "only in word, but also in power and in the Holy Spirit" (1 Thess. 1:5). We remember that the gospel is "the power of God for salvation to everyone who believes" (Rom. 1:16) as the Holy Spirit attends to the ministry of the Word to bring faith to life. When Paul speaks of *power*, he is not referring to the miracles that the apostles sometimes performed, for which the New Testament employs a plural form of the word for *power*.[9] Instead, he refers here to the regenerating power of the Holy Spirit with and through the Word of God to bring the spiritually dead sinner to life. This is the *effectual call* of the gospel. The general call offered by the preacher through the Word is made effectual by the Spirit's power in opening the hearer's heart so as to believe.

---

9. See Robert L. Thomas, "1, 2 Thessalonians," in *The Expositor's Bible Commentary*, ed. Frank E. Gaebelein, 12 vols. (Grand Rapids: Zondervan, 1978), 11:244. The singular *dynamei* means "power," whereas the plural *dynamis* means "miracles."

One classic example of the Spirit's bringing power to the gospel Word is the conversion of the apostle Matthew, then known as Levi the tax collector. Living in Jesus' headquarters town of Capernaum, he would have seen Jesus, known about Christ's miracles, and heard the gospel message on a number of occasions. None of this availed for his salvation. But Matthew 9:9 tells us that on one occasion Jesus came directly to him: "He said to him, 'Follow me,'" and the tax collector "rose and followed him." If you are a Christian, it is only because Christ likewise came to you through the ministry of the Spirit and gave power to the gospel Word in order to bring you to spiritual life and salvation. If you are not a Christian but are being drawn by God's Word, realize that it could be the Holy Spirit who is bringing you near to Christ in order to believe. When we engage in evangelism, even with the most difficult and hardened objectors, Christians may have confidence in knowing that the Holy Spirit has power to save anyone who is called by God.

Paul's teaching that election is seen not merely in word but also in the Spirit's power reminds us of the necessity of a transformed life in Christian salvation. We do not transform our lives in order to be saved; but having been saved, we are changed by the power of God, starting with the reborn hearts that believe the gospel. Those whose Christianity consists only in talk, in word only, unadorned with a growing holiness and spiritual fruit, are warned by Paul's teaching that "the kingdom of God does not consist in talk but in power" (1 Cor. 4:20). Only when the Word is confirmed in the power of the Spirit may we be assured regarding our election. The Welsh evangelist Rowland Hill once met a drunken man in the street. "Mr. Hill, I am one of your converts," the man stammered. "Yes, I dare say you are one of mine," Hill answered; "but if you were one of God's you would not be in the state in which you are now."[10] Why was Hill right to answer this way? Because, Paul wrote to Timothy, "God gave us a spirit not of fear but of power and love and self-control" (2 Tim. 1:7).

Those involved in Christian ministry are hereby reminded of our total reliance on the Spirit and his power for salvation. Paul was strongly persuaded of this in his own gospel outreach. Therefore, he did not preach in a way that relied on his rhetorical skills or a dynamic personality, but rather he preached "in demonstration of the Spirit and of power, that your

10. Charles Haddon Spurgeon, *Metropolitan Tabernacle Pulpit* (Pasadena, TX: Pilgrim, 1978), 51:54.

faith might not rest in the wisdom of men but in the power of God" (1 Cor. 2:4–5). Second Corinthians 4:2 explains his simple approach to preaching, that "by the open statement of the truth we would commend ourselves to everyone's conscience in the sight of God." Our encouragement in preaching is to know that the Spirit attends the true proclamation of God's Word with power even by his deeply flawed servants. As a result, all of God's chosen and beloved people have known what it means to have the power of God's Word impressed on their hearts.

Paul concludes his statement in 1 Thessalonians 1:5 by asserting that the faith given to Christians by the Holy Spirit is not bare faith but one that is fully persuaded regarding Jesus Christ. Paul thus completes his thought: "our gospel came to you not only in word, but also in power and in the Holy Spirit and with full conviction." Paul is not saying that true faith requires believers always to have complete assurance of their salvation. A true believer may often doubt his or her election, and will have ups and downs in his or her spiritual life. Paul is referring, instead, to the full persuasion of Christ and his gospel that endures under trials and temptations to turn away.

In his important parable of the soils, Jesus said that the kingdom of God is like a farmer going about sowing seeds, with the seeds representing the Word of God (Luke 8:11). In one case, the seed fell on rocky soil, where the seed would not grow strong roots. Jesus explained that this person "hears the word and immediately receives it with joy, yet he has no root in himself, but endures for a while, and when tribulation or persecution arises on account of the word, immediately he falls away" (Matt. 13:20–21). Paul rejoices that this example does not describe the Thessalonians. They had given testimony to their election by enduring under hardships and persecution, so that they not only received the Word with an initial experience of the Spirit's power but also continued persuaded in their faith and showed their salvation by refusing to give way under trials.

With Power and Persuasion

In thanking God for the tangible signs of his readers' election, Paul provides us with a helpful framework for evaluating the spiritual authenticity and health of our churches and our lives. Is the Word of God going forth plainly from our pulpits and being received earnestly by God's people? Are our evangelism and our spiritual growth based on God's Word, instead of worldly methods and techniques? Paul presupposes that ministry must be centered on the Word. But then are there evidence of and experience of the Spirit's power working in our lives through the Word? Are we finding that long-cherished errors are yielding place to scriptural truth, however unpalatable these errors are to the spirit of our age? Is the Spirit of God bringing Bible verses to our minds so as to restrain our sin or motivate our service? Are we embracing Christian duties in the home, church, and society more freely and with a more fervent commitment? True Christians revel in the excitement of hearing and reading God's Word, knowing the power with which the Holy Spirit attends the Word, a power that testifies to our eternal election and reveals itself through a persevering, conquering persuasion of faith.

4

RECEIVING GOD'S WORD

1 Thessalonians 1:5–7

You became imitators of us and of the Lord, for you received the
word in much affliction, with the joy of the Holy Spirit,
so that you became an example to all the believers in
Macedonia and in Achaia. (1 Thess. 1:6–7)

ohn Wesley experienced a powerful example of true and living Christianity during his voyage from England to Georgia
to be a missionary. His ship contained a number of Moravians, members of a movement that in the late eighteenth century was alive
in the gospel. Wesley was astonished by their conduct, describing these
often-persecuted people as "always employed, always cheerful themselves,
and in good humour with one another; . . . they adorned the gospel of our
Lord in all things."[1] This was the kind of Christianity that Paul wanted to
see flourishing in Thessalonica. What is it, then, that gives this description
to a church? According to Paul, it is by receiving God's Word in true faith
that we become the Christians that God wants us to be.

In 1 Thessalonians 1:5–10, Paul sketches three movements of the gospel

---

1. Quoted in Iain H. Murray, *Wesley and Men Who Followed* (Edinburgh: Banner of Truth, 2003), 19.

as it progressed in northern Greece. In verse 5, he says that "our gospel came to you." Then, in verse 6, "you received the word." Finally, Paul states in verse 8 that "the word of the Lord sounded forth from you." This is the gospel progression that has continued throughout the church age, as the gospel has come to people who received it by faith and became in turn heralds who bore God's Word to others. This is the progression that God intends for the gospel to follow in our lives as well.

Verses 5–7 center on the Thessalonians' receiving God's Word in saving faith. This stage is the key to our salvation, for when we believe the gospel in faith, we enter into Christ's salvation and become his servants for the spread of the gospel in the world. Paul notes four characteristics of these early believers' receiving of God's Word: (1) they received it through human agents; (2) they received it from God; (3) they received it in great affliction; and (4) having received God's Word, they became a model for other believers to follow.

A WORD RECEIVED THROUGH MEN

Paul refers to the message about Jesus Christ as "our gospel" (1 Thess. 1:5). This does not mean that the apostle claimed to be the originator of the doctrines he taught. Nor did he think that the gospel's success depended on his own strength or ability. He will refer to it in this letter as "the gospel of God" (2:2, 8–9) and "the gospel of Christ" (3:2). Paul's gospel was not about himself but about God and his Son, Jesus, and the salvation they offer by grace and through faith. It was Paul's gospel, however, in the sense that Paul had embraced it for his own salvation. He was relying on this gospel for his own soul's destiny. It was also a message that had been entrusted to him. When Christ converted Paul on the Damascus road, Jesus identified him as "a chosen instrument of mine to carry my name before the Gentiles and kings and the children of Israel" (Acts 9:15).

Christians today have not received the apostolic office, but we have all been inducted as participants in Jesus' Great Commission: "Go therefore and make disciples of all nations, baptizing them in the name of the Father and of the Son and of the Holy Spirit, teaching them to observe all that I have commanded you" (Matt. 28:19–20). The gospel has thus been committed to us in a way similar to how it was entrusted to the apostles. We will be effective in spreading the gospel to the extent that we embrace this calling and rely on the good news of Jesus for our own salvation blessing.

Paul makes it clear that the gospel message requires an authentic messenger to the world. He writes: "You know what kind of men we proved to be among you for your sake" (1 Thess. 1:5). It is obvious that Paul became personally involved in the lives of the Thessalonians, since he can state that they have personal knowledge of his character and spirit. He had ministered "among" them, so that they could assess in his life the credibility of his message.

Today, increasing percentages of Christians attend churches that are so large that few attendees have personal contact with their preachers. Many other Christians depend on media personalities whom they may never meet in the flesh. When such preachers are faithfully proclaiming God's Word, some real good will be done. But the biblical model involves heralds of the gospel whose lives are personally known by those to whom they preach. Such men are never going to be perfect, of course, but there should be a strong correspondence between their message and the pattern of their lives.

Moreover, it should be obvious that true ministers of the gospel are motivated not by personal gain but, as Paul writes, "for your sake" (1 Thess. 1:5). Some people are reluctant to receive God's Word from a minister's lips until experience demonstrates his love and sincerity in ministry, after which people will receive even hard teachings from his trusted lips. Peter's injunction to elders sets the model for preachers and evangelists who would earn the trust of their hearers: "Shepherd the flock of God that is among you, exercising oversight, not under compulsion, but willingly, as God would have you; not for shameful gain, but eagerly; not domineering over those in your charge, but being examples to the flock" (1 Peter 5:2–3).

Paul's emphasis on the credibility of the human witnesses applies not only to pastors and elders but also to every other Christian. The evidence of the gospel in our lives provides an important commendation of our witness to the gospel. John MacArthur writes:

> Most people do not come to Christ as an immediate response to a sermon they hear in a crowded setting. They come to Christ because of the influence of an individual. . . . In the overwhelming majority of [new believers' testimonies], they tell us they came to Christ primarily because of the testimony of a coworker, a neighbor, a relative, or a friend. . . . There's no question that the

most effective means for bringing people to Christ is one at a time, on an individual basis.[2]

This principle shows how important is the individual sincerity, godliness, and love of every Christian to the spread of the gospel and the salvation of the lost. Tim Shenton writes: "There is no point in preaching the truth if we are living a lie."[3] Hypocrisy is perhaps the single greatest deterrent to a Christian's effectiveness as a witness, while the evidence of the gospel's power provides a compelling testimony to the gospel's truth.

A WORD RECEIVED FROM GOD

Together with Silas and Timothy, Paul was a vital agent in bringing the gospel to the Thessalonians. It was not his word, however, but God's Word that they received in faith. In his many letters, Paul insists that a divine message was committed to him directly by the resurrected Lord Jesus Christ. To the Galatians he wrote that he was "an apostle—not from men nor through man, but through Jesus Christ and God the Father" (Gal. 1:1). Later, he amplified: "I would have you know, brothers, that the gospel that was preached by me is not man's gospel. For I did not receive it from any man, nor was I taught it, but I received it through a revelation of Jesus Christ" (vv. 11–12). First Thessalonians 2:13 makes a similar claim: "When you received the word of God, which you heard from us, you accepted it not as the word of men but as what it really is, the word of God."

The Bible teaches that the prophets and apostles received God's Word by means of *inspiration*. Inspiration does not speak to the inspiring character of the message or the effect of God's Word in a fervent, believing heart. Instead, inspiration refers to the process by which the Holy Spirit conveyed God's Word to his chosen messengers. Paul's classic statement on inspiration says: "All Scripture is breathed out by God" (2 Tim. 3:16). By this definition, we would do better to refer to the *expiration* of Scripture rather than its *inspiration*, since Paul says that God's Word is "out-breathed." Isaiah paints the same picture: "For as the rain and the snow come down from heaven and do not return there but water the earth, making it bring forth and sprout,

2. John MacArthur, *Twelve Ordinary Men* (Nashville: Thomas Nelson, 2002), 68–69.
3. Tim Shenton, *Opening Up 1 Thessalonians* (Leominster, UK: Day One, 2006), 20.

giving seed to the sower and bread to the eater, so shall my word be that goes out from my mouth" (Isa. 55:10–11). Peter adds that "no prophecy was ever produced by the will of man, but men spoke from God as they were carried along by the Holy Spirit" (2 Peter 1:21). Each of these verses gives emphasis to the divine origin of the message given by the prophets and apostles.

As a result of divine inspiration, the apostles' message is the very Word of God, written to the first Christians and faithfully preserved for us. When Paul says to the Thessalonians, "You received the word" (1 Thess. 1:6), urging them to welcome it gladly in the way that a treasured guest is received into the home, Paul might have said, "You embraced the Word to your heart" by receiving it gladly with faith.

Since Paul's gospel was not a human but a divine message, we truly receive the Scriptures only when we receive them as a word from God. John Calvin wrote: "The Holy Scripture will never be of any service to us, unless we [are] persuaded that God is the author of it. . . . Therefore the Holy Scripture will be lifeless, and without force, until we know it is God [who speaks] in it, and thereby reveal[s] His will to man."[4]

To receive the Bible as God's Word is to bow before its sovereign *authority*, just because it is the Word of God. Some people complain that evangelical Christians worship the book instead of God. This is a false charge once we recognize that God wrote the book in order to aid us in living before him in faith. If a king leaves instructions before he goes away, it is hardly rebellion for his servants to pay careful attention to what he has written, and when the king returns he will surely reward those who have kept his word. Likewise, Christians are to embrace the Bible to our hearts as the divine mandate for our faith and life, simply because it is the Word of God. "Our wisdom," Calvin taught, "ought to be nothing else than to embrace with humble teachableness . . . whatever is taught in Sacred Scripture."[5]

Receiving the Bible as God's Word also means accepting its *inerrancy*, receiving it as without error in all that it teaches and affirms. We believe the Bible's inerrancy not because we can harmonize every apparent discrepancy (although they all have good explanations) but because it is the Word of God and therefore is perfect. God's attributes of omniscience, omnipotence, and sublime wisdom enable him to declare perfect truth at all times, while his

---

4. John Calvin, *The Mystery of Godliness* (1830; repr., Morgan, PA: Soli Deo Gloria, 1999), 131.

5. John Calvin, *Institutes of the Christian Religion*, ed. John T. McNeill, trans. Ford Lewis Battles (Philadelphia: Westminster, 1960), 1.18.4.

attributes of holiness and faithfulness oblige him to speak only the truth. Martyn Lloyd-Jones thus ascribes divine authority to the Bible's teaching:

> The Christian faith is not what I think or what anybody else thinks; it is what is plainly taught in the Scriptures. The Christian church is established on the foundation of the apostles and prophets. . . . The moment people begin to stand in judgment upon it and say, "This is not true, I accept that but I do not accept this," then they have substituted their authority, and what they think, for the teaching of the Bible.[6]

We further rely on the Bible's *power* as God's Word. Paul proclaimed, "I am not ashamed of the gospel, for it is the power of God for salvation to everyone who believes" (Rom. 1:16). Martin Luther exclaimed: "We must make a great difference between God's Word and the word of man. A man's word is a little sound, that flies into the air, and soon vanishes; but the Word of God is greater than heaven and earth, yea, greater than death and hell, for it forms part of the power of God, and endures everlastingly."[7]

Because the Bible is inspired, authoritative, and true, the Christian is not on a quest seeking after truth. Instead, the Christian has found truth by receiving God's Word, which he or she is faithfully to believe and boldly to proclaim.

A great example of someone who received God's Word is Lydia, a business-woman in Philippi. Not long before Paul's ministry to the Thessalonians, he arrived in Philippi on a Sabbath day. He and his friends went down to the river, seeking a place to pray, and found Lydia gathered with other women for prayer. Paul declared the gospel, and we read of Lydia: "The Lord opened her heart to pay attention to what was said by Paul" (Acts 16:14). Here we have both the divine and human sides of receiving God's Word. It is the Lord alone who can open the heart, so faith in God's Word is a sovereign act of saving grace. The effect is that we not only affirm God's Word but also "pay attention" to it with the greatest diligence. This is the way for us also to welcome God's Word: by giving it our full attention, believing all that Scripture teaches, and putting into action all that we are taught by God in his Word.

6. D. Martyn Lloyd-Jones, *Love So Amazing: Expositions of Colossians 1* (Grand Rapids: Baker, 1995), 9–10.
7. Quoted in James Montgomery Boice, *Foundations of the Christian Faith* (Downers Grove, IL: InterVarsity Press, 1986), 69.

A WORD RECEIVED IN AFFLICTION

Paul notes that in receiving God's Word, the Thessalonians "became imitators of us and of the Lord" (1 Thess. 1:6). Discipleship is learned by imitating the example of those who have gone before us. Paul does not hesitate to tell new believers, "Be imitators of me." He can urge this humbly because he goes on to say "as I am of Christ" (1 Cor. 11:1). If as mature Christians we can sincerely tell new believers, "Watch what I do and how I live," then we will be greatly used by God in helping fellow believers to walk in faith. G. K. Beale writes: "As we become more conformed to the image of Christ, we are to live in such a way that others would be influenced by our lives and so become conformed also to Christ's image."[8] Likewise, those who have believed in Jesus are then called to replace sinful and worldly patterns in their lives by imitating biblical patterns that they see being lived out in the church around them.

In urging his readers to follow him, Paul is not claiming spiritual perfection. His example, rather, is in receiving God's Word, as he has urged them to do as well. Those who teach the Bible should be the most eager students of the Bible. We should be able to urge others to believe all that is taught in Scripture by receiving ourselves the whole counsel of God in obedient faith. We should lead a life that is growing in the truth and delights in God's Word so that others will do the same. This calling is just as important for parents as it is for pastors. It should be evident to those who are following our example that we believe the Bible to be the holy, inerrant, and life-giving Word of God as we revere it, study it, and obey it in sincere faith.

Paul emphasizes that his readers followed his example not only in receiving the Word but also in believing in the context of "much affliction" (1 Thess. 1:6). The Thessalonians had suffered violent persecution with the possibility of imprisonment and death. Being "jealous" over Paul's success in that city, the Jewish leaders organized a mob to raise an uproar. The throng came to one of the new Christian leaders, Jason, in whose house the church seems to have been meeting. They dragged Jason before the civil authorities on the false charge that the Christians were "acting against the decrees of Caesar"

---

8. G. K. Beale, *1–2 Thessalonians*, IVP New Testament Commentary Series (Downers Grove, IL: InterVarsity Press, 2003), 58.

and setting up Jesus as a rebel king against the government (Acts 17:7). Later in this letter, Paul will commend his readers for suffering "the same things from your own countrymen" as the Christians in Jerusalem suffered from the Jews, "who killed both the Lord Jesus and the prophets, and drove us out, and displease God and oppose all mankind" (1 Thess. 2:14–15). In this way, Paul points out that believing God's Word will generally lead to opposition from the world and in many cases overt persecution.

Paul himself had suffered very great afflictions through his service to Christ (see 2 Cor. 11:23–30), and when he first arrived in Thessalonica he was probably still bruised from the beating he had just taken in Philippi (see Acts 16:23). Now by imitating him, the Christians were suffering similar trials. Ultimately, our example in suffering is Jesus himself. Peter wrote, "To this you have been called, because Christ also suffered for you, leaving you an example, so that you might follow in his steps" (1 Peter 2:21). We are especially to follow Christ's manner of suffering: "He committed no sin, neither was deceit found in his mouth. When he was reviled, he did not revile in return; when he suffered, he did not threaten, but continued entrusting himself to him who judges justly" (vv. 22–23).

The word that Paul uses for *affliction* (*thlipsis*) refers to severe pressure being applied to an object. Therefore, Paul is speaking of great trouble that results in serious and harmful difficulty. Christians in the West today are most likely to suffer social rejection, the loss of valued relationships, or the limiting of career prospects because of our discipleship to Jesus. Christians in other parts of the world know that a wider range of suffering could result from our salvation. Geoffrey Wilson comments: "It was never Paul's practice to portray an easy road to heaven, for he knew that all who became imitators of the Lord are called to share in the rejection which He met from an unbelieving world."[9] In teaching this truth, Paul is again following the example of Christ, who said, "If anyone would come after me, let him deny himself and take up his cross daily and follow me. For whoever would save his life will lose it, but whoever loses his life for my sake will save it" (Luke 9:23–24).

What particularly distinguished the early Christians, as well as the apostles whose example they followed, was the joy they experienced in the midst

9. Geoffrey B. Wilson, *New Testament Commentaries*, 2 vols. (Edinburgh: Banner of Truth, 2005), 2:138.

of tribulation. The Thessalonians may well have heard of Paul and Silas's experience in the Philippian jail, not long before their arrival in Thessalonica. The two preachers had been unjustly arrested and severely beaten by the civil authorities. They were then placed in a cell with their feet fastened to stocks. Most people would feel discouragement or even despair in such a situation, but Paul and Silas rejoiced. Acts 16:25–26 tells us: "About midnight Paul and Silas were praying and singing hymns to God, and the prisoners were listening to them, and suddenly there was a great earthquake, so that the foundations of the prison were shaken. And immediately all the doors were opened, and everyone's bonds were unfastened." Christians who rejoice in Christ amid afflictions unleash a similar power today, as those who witness the power of the gospel in our joy are often made eager to embrace Christ for themselves.

The Holy Spirit is the key to knowing joy in the midst of trials, which is why Paul observes that his readers exhibited the "joy of the Holy Spirit" (1 Thess. 1:6). This is not to say that Christians never grieve or walk in spiritual shadows. Instead, even with tears on our cheeks we can access a joy that comes from above. This happens when we take our griefs to the Lord and receive the peace and joy that only his Spirit can give. The question is: As you suffer afflictions, are your eyes on the world and all that you have lost, or are they on the beauty and glory of Christ and all that you have gained in him? The answer will make all the difference in how you respond to difficulty.

It is God's design that our afflictions would bring out a spiritual joy from our lives as we draw close to Christ, who suffered for us and who sends the Spirit to his suffering people. Often, it is precisely in our afflictions that Christians experience the most precious joy. John Lillie describes this joy as one "that springs only from His presence and operation in the soul, and which, perhaps, is never in this world so pure, and deep, and full, as when a man is enabled to suffer faithfully for Christ's sake and the gospel's."[10] Rejoicing in Christ amid afflictions is so important that it was the very last subject that Jesus addressed with his disciples before leaving the upper room for the garden of Gethsemane: "In the world you will have tribulation. But take heart; I have overcome the world" (John 16:33).

10. John Lillie, *Lectures on Paul's Epistles to the Thessalonians*, Tentmaker Classic Commentaries (1860; repr., Stoke-on-Trent, UK: Tentmaker Publications, 2007), 52.

A Word Passed on by Example

The complaints made against Christians by the world will often be our highest compliment. So it was for Paul and his companions. When the Thessalonian mob came to Jason's house, looking for the apostle, the Christians' accusers described them as "these men who have turned the world upside down" (Acts 17:6). How did Paul and his friends have such a mighty impact despite their earthly weakness? By preaching the gospel in God's power so that it was received in faith by those who heard. They further influenced the world through the joy of the Holy Spirit that shone through their afflictions. We now have the privilege of following their example in having this effect on our world.

Paul's formula for the gospel's spread is that Christ's people are to receive God's Word in imitation of those who brought it and then to become bearers of the same gospel message so that others may follow their example. Paul reported this as happening in and through the Thessalonians, rejoicing "that you became an example to all the believers in Macedonia and in Achaia" (1 Thess. 1:7).

The word that Paul uses for *example* is the Greek word *tupos*, denoting a model or representation of an object. Receiving God's Word in faith, imitating those from whom we heard it, and rejoicing in Christ amid worldly persecution enable us to serve as examples for our children and others who come to faith through the gospel. This calling to be an example to others is not given to only a few highly educated and gifted Christians but to all believers; it is the thrilling calling that will enable each of us to make an eternal difference, one believer and one church at a time, as we follow Christ and offer ourselves as an example to others.

I mentioned the powerful example of Christianity that John Wesley encountered in the Moravians of the eighteenth century. Their lives were made vibrant by receiving God's Word in faith. Believers who live out God's Word not only bring blessing to themselves, but also have a mighty gospel influence on others. Wesley experienced this influence during his year in the American Colonies, where he had regular contact with these Thessalonian-minded believers. On his way home to England, he told of the effect that their example had had on him, having learned "what I least suspected, that I, who went to America to convert others, was never myself converted to God."[11] Shortly afterward, Wesley attended a Moravian meeting where the gospel was clearly presented, and he believed. Recording the event in his journal, Wesley recalled: "I felt my heart strangely warmed. I felt I did trust in Christ, Christ alone for salvation; and an assurance was given me, that He had taken away *my* sins, even *mine*, and saved *me* from the law of sin and death."[12]

Wesley's experience confirms Paul's idea of how the gospel spreads. First the Word is brought through faithful, credible witnesses. Then God's Word is received into hearts opened by the Holy Spirit. Rejoicing in the midst of afflictions, these believers display a living faith before the world so that others see, hear the gospel, and by God's grace are brought to saving faith.

Where are you in this progression? Are you just now hearing God's Word as it is preached to you? Then God calls you to welcome his gospel into your heart through faith, believing that Jesus died for your sins and offers you eternal life. Or have you long since received the gospel in faith? Then draw near to God for the joy in the midst of afflictions that will enable you to be an example to others. Jesus said, "As the Father has sent me, even so I am sending you" (John 20:21).

11. Quoted in Murray, *Wesley and Men Who Followed*, 20.
12. Ibid., 8–9.

5

A Model Reputation

1 Thessalonians 1:8–10

For not only has the word of the Lord sounded forth from
you in Macedonia and Achaia, but your faith in God
has gone forth everywhere. (1 Thess. 1:8)

ew accolades are more meaningful than to be told "well done" by a trusted and admired leader. Such praise was given by the apostle Paul to the fledgling church in the northern Greek city of Thessalonica. Having terminated his second missionary journey in the southern city of Corinth, Paul was delighted to learn that his labor among the Thessalonians had borne such strong fruit. As he put it later in this letter, "Now we live, if you are standing fast in the Lord" (1 Thess. 3:8). Among his reasons for writing to them was his desire to share his joy and praise their faith.

Paul's praise for the Thessalonians is also heartening to readers of this letter today. Many Christians in America and in the West in general sense that the church has lost touch with the spirit that animated the early believers. The New Testament enables us to access their experience—an example that can still instruct and inspire us. Paul's praise for the Thessalonians is especially important, since he sees this church as a model for all others. So fully did Paul approve of their reputation that he could respond, "We need not say anything" (1 Thess. 1:8), since their actions said enough. In the last three verses of this opening section of Paul's letter, he notes three characteristics that made their reputation so commendable: theirs was a *gospel-spreading*, a *God-serving*, and a *Christ-awaiting* reputation. If we will follow this model, we may gain not only the praise of the Lord's servants but also a strong assurance of Christ's saving presence in our midst.

A GOSPEL-SPREADING REPUTATION

Paul had heard, first, about the Thessalonians' *gospel-spreading* reputation: "The word of the Lord sounded forth from you in Macedonia and Achaia" (1 Thess. 1:8). Apparently, even before Timothy had returned with his report from Thessalonica, news had come to Paul down the great Egnetian Way, the main east-west corridor of the Roman Empire that ran straight through that city. Paul had met traveling Christians (such as Priscilla and Aquila in Corinth) who brought reports of the wider world. Since Paul says that the Thessalonians' "faith in God has gone forth everywhere" (v. 8), many such travelers would have passed on the gospel-spreading reputation of this church.

Paul says that "the word of the Lord sounded forth" from the Thessalonians. This means that their witness to the person and work of Christ was being heralded throughout the ancient world. The apostle compares their gospel proclamation to a trumpet blast that summons people to attention. F. F. Bruce comments: "Having received the gospel, the Thessalonian Christians had no thought of keeping it to themselves; by word and life they made it known to others."[1]

Paul's praise for this witness completes his threefold description of how the gospel spread in northern Greece: it came to them through the apostle's preaching (1 Thess. 1:5), the Thessalonians "received the word" (v. 6), and now "the word of the Lord sounded forth from you" to others (v. 8). God intends for the gospel to spread in this manner through every church and every Christian life. John Stott compares a gospel-spreading church to a "telecommunications satellite which first receives and then transmits messages." This is "God's simplest plan for world evangelization," he observes, and every church is to play its part.[2]

---

1. F. F. Bruce, *1 & 2 Thessalonians*, Word Biblical Commentary 45 (Waco, TX: Word, 1982), 16–17.
2. John R. W. Stott, *The Message of 1 & 2 Thessalonians*, The Bible Speaks Today (Downers Grove, IL: InterVarsity Press, 1994), 43.

We should note that it was not just any witness that the Thessalonians gave. It was the "word of the Lord" that they received and spread. It was their belief that the gospel is the very Word of God that empowered their witness. We, too, must be completely persuaded about the divine character of the Bible if we are to have a similar impact. This is why attacks on the divine authority and inerrancy of Scripture always weaken the church and its witness. Leon Morris writes: "If men think of the gospel only as another philosophy, as the result of the reflection of certain, admittedly profound, first-century thinkers on religious topics, they will never have the burning zeal which sent the first Christian preachers through the world to proclaim what God had done for man."[3] Only if we, like them, are persuaded that we have received by grace an authoritative, true Word of salvation from God will we readily suffer scorn and spread without apology or permission a bold witness of gospel light into the darkness of our world. Moreover, when Paul speaks of the word "of the Lord," he is referring specifically to Jesus, so that a truly apostolic witness not only will be biblical in a general sense but will center on the biblical testimony to Jesus as God's Son and the Savior of the world through the blood of his cross.

As word spread though Greece and beyond about the Thessalonian Christians, the news told not only of their God-revealed message but also of their faith in it. When Paul says that the gospel sounded forth from them, he adds, "Your faith in God has gone forth everywhere, so that we need not say anything" (1 Thess. 1:8). This reputation for faith in God likely began at home. Husbands were astonished at the new conduct of their wives who had converted to Christ. Friends and neighbors commented on the new priorities seen among those who embraced the gospel. So profound was the change among so many people that news of a significant event in Thessalonica began spreading. Especially when the Christians would not give up their faith in the midst of persecution, but responded to trials with a steadfast hope (v. 3) and the "joy of the Holy Spirit" (v. 6), more and more people took notice of these believers in Jesus. Only with the same testimony of faith that the Thessalonians gave, showing the power of the gospel they preached, can any Christians sound forth the Word of the Lord with real credibility and persuasiveness.

3. Leon Morris, *The First and Second Epistles to the Thessalonians*, New International Commentary on the New Testament (Grand Rapids: Eerdmans, 1959), 61.

This first item characterizing the Thessalonians' reputation prompts us to ask whether something similar could be said of us. Would people be struck by our conviction as a church that the Bible is God's very Word that declares salvation through his Son, Jesus? What do we desire to be known for: our social standing, our cultural refinement, our trendy sophistication, or our biblical fervor and faithfulness? Here is a reputation for preachers to seek: not a reputation for humor, oratorical refinement, or good storytelling, but a reputation for a bold and faithful heralding of the divine truth revealed in Scripture about Jesus Christ. What kind of reputation do we desire as individual Christians? If we would be regarded as spreaders of the gospel, then we will prayerfully seek to be Christians who enlighten, encourage, and challenge others by our living testimony to the Word of the Lord.

A GOD-SERVING REPUTATION

Second, the Thessalonians had gained a reputation as a *God-serving* church: "For they themselves report concerning us the kind of reception we had among you, and how you turned to God from idols to serve the living and true God" (1 Thess. 1:9). John Stott aptly describes this verse as presenting "the fullest account of [Christian conversion] in the New Testament."[4]

The conversion of the Thessalonians began with the manner in which they received Paul and his associates. How people receive a sincere ministry of God's Word largely determines their spiritual state. Today there are churches that claim the name of Jesus but resist clear and faithful Bible teaching. Such Christians are not likely to advance far in godliness or make much real spiritual impact, however much outward success they might enjoy. Instead, humble Christians who rejoice to have God's Word opened and who respect faithful Christian leaders are most likely to make a lasting gospel impact.

As Paul preached the Scriptures in Thessalonica, many who heard his message were converted to faith in Christ. Verse 9 sets forth in clear language what this conversion entailed: "You turned to God from idols to serve the living and true God." Notice how the early Christians understood that becoming a Christian requires a definite and radical break with one's former life. Paul's statement indicates that many Thessalonian believers had been converted out of pagan idolatry, rather than from Judaism. They realized

4. Stott, *The Message of 1 & 2 Thessalonians*, 38.

that they could not place Christ alongside the idols of their former lives. The Thessalonians recognized that embracing Christ required a revolution in their worship and service; the early Christians saw a basic antithesis that required them to turn to God from the idolatrous culture around them and embrace a distinctive and biblical Christian approach to life, worship, and ministry.

Starting in the apostolic age, the history of Christian missions has witnessed the rejection of false and enslaving gods for the worship of "the living and true God" (1 Thess. 1:9). With this phrase, Paul was pointing out that idols are false deities who neither possess life nor pass it on to others. Idols are themselves dead, whereas the true God is the author and giver of life. Still, idols can possess a powerful hold on the mind and heart, through superstitious habit or the bondage of fear and desire.

In the Roman world, idol-worship was associated with the local economy and ruling structure. Acts 19 shows the prevailing attitude when Paul challenged the idol-making industry in Ephesus. Complaining that Paul had "persuaded and turned away a great many people, saying that gods made with hands are not gods" (Acts 19:26), the local tradesmen formed a mass riot that threw the whole city into uproar. A great crowd gathered to oppose the apostle, crying out, "Great is Artemis of the Ephesians!" (v. 28). The idols were symbols of civic identity and sources of communal identity for those who saw in them a source of protection and prosperity. To demand that converts to Christ should turn from the idols was virtually to disenfranchise them from the polis and the trade guilds.

In the many centuries since Paul called the Thessalonians from idolatry, Christian missionaries have contended with false gods and their enslaving worship. John Stott records a letter written by a Burmese evangelist who explained what converting to Christ required among tribesmen who had formerly been dominated by animist spirits:

> We explained to them the pure simple gospel and Christ's lordship over the devil and all evil forces, after which they were counseled to confess and forsake their evil deeds and to receive Christ Jesus as their Saviour and Lord. With brokenness and tears and guilt they responded. Then we burned up the charms and amulets, took a wood-cutting knife, and broke down a spirit's house made of bamboo and wood, claiming the lordship of Jesus Christ, and singing Christ's victory songs, and putting all of ourselves under the

47

blood of the Lamb of God and the rule of the Holy Spirit, and claiming God's protection.[5]

Paul's statement regarding the Thessalonians' rejection of idols is particularly poignant when we recognize that the peak of Mount Olympus—the supposed home of the Greek pantheon of gods—was visible from their location a bare fifty miles away. It is less easy, perhaps, for us to see the gods that faith in Christ requires us to renounce today. In his book *Counterfeit Gods*, Tim Keller points out that while Americans will probably never encounter a shrine to Athena, Aphrodite, Ares, or Artemis—some of the more prominent Greek gods—nonetheless our culture is deeply involved in the worship of the very things that these idols represented:

> Each culture is dominated by its own set of idols. Each one has its shrines—whether office towers, spas and gyms, studios or stadiums—where sacrifices must be made in order to procure the blessings of the good life and ward off disaster. What are the gods of beauty, power, money, and achievement but these same things that have assumed mythic proportions in our individual lives and in our society? We may not physically kneel before the statue of Aphrodite, but many young women today are driven into depression and eating disorders by an obsessive concern over their body image. We may not actually burn incense to Artemis, but when money and career are raised to cosmic proportions, we perform a kind of child sacrifice, neglecting family and community to achieve a higher place in business and gain more wealth and prestige.[6]

An idol is anything that we trust and serve in the place of God. There is nothing wrong with desiring to be successful, but when success provides our identity, significance, and security, we have made it an idol. Likewise, there is nothing wrong with fitness and beauty, but when the focus of our lives is given to glorifying our physique and form, then we are worshiping an idol in the place of God. One of the most common forms of idolatry today is the worship of money and all that it can buy. Keller recounts a series of suicides in New York City—men who took their lives during the financial crises of 2008. Their spirits had been broken, and they could see no reason

5. Ibid., 40.
6. Timothy Keller, *Counterfeit Gods: The Empty Promises of Money, Sex and Power, and the Only Hope That Matters* (New York: Dutton, 2009), xi–xii.

to continue living without their wealth. These people despaired over their loss of money—as others despair over lost relationships, an inability to lose weight, or failure to achieve coveted career success—because they had made good things into ultimate things.[7] "An idol is something we cannot live without. We must have it, and therefore it drives us to break rules we once honored, to harm others and even ourselves in order to get it. Idols are spiritual addictions that lead to terrible evil."[8]

For this reason, Paul saw the rejection of idols not only as a necessity in Christian conversion but also as part of the deliverance that Christ achieves in our salvation. Believing the gospel and embracing Jesus involves a change of the will from trusting, worshiping, and serving false gods to a new faith in which God is trusted, worshiped, and served through a saving relationship with Jesus Christ. Just like the converted animists of Burma who "turned to God from idols" (1 Thess. 1:9), we must claim the lordship of Christ, put ourselves under his blood, trust in the Holy Spirit's power, and claim God's fatherly protection for our salvation.

Along with the negative movement of turning from idols, conversion to Christ involves the positive step of submitting ourselves to a life of serving God. Christ is not only our Savior but also our Lord and Master. He has called us to service, urging: "Take my yoke upon you, and learn from me, for I am gentle and lowly in heart, and you will find rest for your souls" (Matt. 11:29). Jesus also said, "If anyone would come after me, let him deny himself and take up his cross daily and follow me" (Luke 9:23). The living God both gives and commands life; the true God calls his people into the service of truth. Having rejected idols, we now are to trust, worship, and serve God above all others. John Calvin wrote: "No one, therefore, is properly converted to God, but the man who has learned to place himself wholly under subjection to him."[9]

Here again, we have a diagnostic question that we can use to assess ourselves. Do we have a reputation for being radically converted to God and his ways, forsaking the idols of our generation? As individuals, do we exhibit to those who know us a clear rejection of worldly values and a deliberate commitment to the liberating service of God? If we have such a reputation, it will be evident in how we spend our time, use our money,

7. Ibid., ix–x.
8. Ibid., xv.
9. John Calvin, *Commentaries*, 22 vols. (1854; repr., Grand Rapids: Baker, 2009), 21:245.

and offer our talents and energies in pursuing a decidedly biblical lifestyle as servants of the Lord.

A CHRIST-AWAITING REPUTATION

The third component of the Thessalonians' exemplary reputation was that they were a *Christ-awaiting* church. Paul concludes this opening section of his letter by writing that they turned to God in order "to wait for his Son from heaven, whom he raised from the dead, Jesus who delivers us from the wrath to come" (1 Thess. 1:10).

The word that Paul uses for *wait* (*anameno*) appears only here in the New Testament. It conveys the idea of patient expectation and trust. The Thessalonian Christians were gospel-spreading and God-serving believers who were persuaded that Christ would return soon to bring the fullness of the salvation for which they longed.

This waiting has a passive component, in that the early Christians did not expect to achieve salvation through their own witness and ministry. They were counting on Jesus—the same Savior who had died for their sins—to return in glory to deliver them from evil. Paul writes later in this letter to assure them that they had not missed the return of Christ (1 Thess. 4:1ff.). Although they were right to expect Christ to come soon, they should have also realized that God's timing is not known to man (5:2). With this in mind, the Thessalonians were to live with an eye on the horizon, waiting for Jesus to return and give them victory over the world.

At the same time, the waiting that Paul describes has an important active component. While they were anticipating Jesus' return, the Thessalonian readers should ready themselves to greet him. William Hendriksen writes: "When you await a visitor, you have prepared everything for his coming. You have arranged the guest-room, the program of activities, your time and your other duties, and all this in such a manner that the visitor will feel perfectly at home. So also, awaiting the very Son of God who is coming out of the heavens implies the sanctified heart and life."[10] As this description suggests, Christians are waiting not merely for the coming of heaven on earth but for Christ himself, who is coming for us. Jesus spoke this way

10. William Hendriksen, *1 and 2 Thessalonians*, New Testament Commentary (Grand Rapids: Baker, 1974), 57.

to the disciples before departing for the cross: "If I go and prepare a place for you, I will come again and will take you to myself, that where I am you may be also" (John 14:3). The heaven for which we wait is bound up in the person of Jesus, and our expectation is fixed on the One who comes to take us not merely to heaven but to himself in glory (see Matt. 24:45–25:13).

Paul goes on to cite a good reason for Christians to believe in Christ's return. He speaks of God's Son from heaven, "whom he raised from the dead" (1 Thess. 1:10). The Christian hope of Christ's return would be preposterous were it not joined to the doctrine of his resurrection. If the Father promised to raise his Son and then fulfilled this most unlikely pledge, however, then God's promise to send Jesus back is equally worthy of being believed and trusted. Moreover, if we believe that Jesus is God the Son, in possession of full deity, then in his sovereign omnipotence he is able to return from heaven to bring salvation to his people forever.

To go with this reason to *believe*, Paul adds a reason for us to *hope* in Christ's return with great joy and expectation, saying that we wait for "Jesus who delivers us from the wrath to come" (1 Thess. 1:10). Jesus' first coming had the aim of redeeming us from our sins by his blood. His second coming completes this salvation by actually delivering us from the sphere and power of everything cursed by sin. Hebrews 9:28 promises: "Christ, having been offered once to bear the sins of many, will appear a second time, not to deal with sin but to save those who are eagerly waiting for him."

Jesus died on the cross to remove the guilt and curse of sin from his people. God's wrath is not a capricious, sinful outburst of anger but rather his right, just, holy, and burning resolve to punish all evil. Apart from his wrath, God would be unworthy of our worship, since he would then be a deity who tolerated evil and rebellion against his sovereign rights. As sinners, we tend to dread even the thought of divine wrath against sin. Trusting in Jesus, however, we face our Judge without fear, since he has paid the penalty of our sins by bearing them on the cross and is coming soon to fully deliver us "from the wrath to come" (1 Thess. 1:10).

With nothing to fear from God's judgment and literally everything to gain, believers in Christ look forward to his return with a conquering hope. Paul therefore calls the return of Christ "our blessed hope, the appearing of the glory of our great God and Savior Jesus Christ" (Titus 2:13). Jesus comes to enter us into his glory, which we anticipate now with a great longing, gaining courage and strength to face this dark world. Whatever sorrows we have here, in the age to come we will know only the peace and joy of Christ. Then, as John's vision declared, "He will dwell with them, and they will be his people, and God himself will be with them as their God. He will wipe away every tear from their eyes, and death shall be no more, neither shall there be mourning, nor crying, nor pain anymore, for the former things have passed away" (Rev. 21:3–4).

This raises a final question to diagnose ourselves as a church and as individual believers. Is it evident to others that we are depending on a power that is not of this earth but comes from heaven through our faith in Christ? Are we seeking rewards and storing treasures in heaven, where our riches never fail or fade? Or are we, as C. S. Lewis put it, like children who are happy "making mud pies in a slum" because we have never imagined "a holiday at the sea,"[11] settling for mere earthly glories because we know so little of the heavenly splendor of God? Jesus declared, "Where your treasure is, there your heart will be also" (Matt. 6:21). Does our lifestyle give us the reputation of people whose treasure is most truly in the world to come, so that our thoughts, passions, and longings are directed to Christ, who dwells there now?

AN ETERNAL REPUTATION

The key to the faith of the Thessalonians, who gained accolades for their gospel-spreading, God-serving, and Christ-awaiting reputation, is found in 1 Thessalonians 1:6: "You received the word." If we have believed the good news of Jesus as the message of salvation for the world, then we must spread it. If our heavenly Father is the living and true God, then we must turn from the dead and false gods in order to serve the Lord. And if Jesus is returning soon to bring salvation, then surely we should await his coming and prepare ourselves for the greatest moment in our entire future to come: our meeting in the flesh with the Son of God, when he returns to take us to himself.

It would be a fine thing to have a reputation among the churches like that of the Thessalonians. It would be an especially high honor to receive the kind of praise that this church received from no less than the apostle Paul. Yet

---

11. C. S. Lewis, *The Weight of Glory and Other Addresses* (New York: Macmillan, 1980), 4.

we await the coming of One who is infinitely higher than the choicest of his human servants, who will call us to give an account of our service to him.

Jesus foretold such a future interview in his parable of the talents. The Lord had given each of his servants a certain number of gifts and opportunities, and he wanted to see how faithfully and fruitfully his followers had served him. Jesus concluded that a professing believer who had done nothing for him while supposedly awaiting his return could only be a false believer who did not truly belong (Matt. 25:24–28). But to those who had vigorously employed the gospel resources that Christ had given them—some greater and some lesser, but all important—and sincerely offered themselves to serve Christ's glory and kingdom, Jesus gave the word of praise that every Christian is seeking to hear when he returns. "Well done, good and faithful servant," Jesus will say to everyone who spread the gospel, served God, and waited for his return. "Enter into the joy of your master" (vv. 21, 23).

Jesus, who died and was raised for our salvation, is coming soon, and then the reputation we have gained by his grace in this world will be the beginning of an eternal legacy. The Bible speaks of an eternal glory for faithful servants of Christ. As the angel proclaimed to Daniel: "Those who are wise shall shine like the brightness of the sky above; and those who turn many to righteousness, like the stars forever and ever" (Dan. 12:3).

6

MINISTRY NOT IN VAIN

1 Thessalonians 2:1–8

Just as we have been approved by God to be entrusted with the
gospel, so we speak, not to please man, but to please
God who tests our hearts. (1 Thess. 2:4)

*I*n John Bunyan's classic allegory of the Christian life, *Pilgrim's Progress*, Christian was led into a room where the Interpreter pointed out a portrait hanging on the wall. The picture depicted a faithful minister in these words:

> The man whose picture this is, is one of a thousand. . . . You see him with his eyes lifted up to heaven, the best of books in his hand, and the law of truth written on his lips. This shows that his work is to know and unfold dark things to sinners. You see him standing as if he was pleading with men. The world behind him, a crown hanging over his head. This shows that by neglecting and despising present things for the love that he has for his Master's service, he is sure to have glory for his reward in the next world.[1]

Christian needed to be able to recognize a true minister because his own journey to the Celestial City required him to discern between true and false spiritual guides.

1. John Bunyan, *Pilgrim's Progress* (Nashville: Thomas Nelson, 1999), 26–27.

When any pastor compares himself to Bunyan's portrait, he is as likely to be discouraged as he is to be inspired. The pastor knows all too well the many ways in which he falls short of this godly ideal. Even the apostle Paul was discouraged about his fitness to preach God's Word. "Who is sufficient for these things?" he cried (2 Cor. 2:16). Anyone who has ministered in a church has learned to his distress that he is simply not able to meet even the many legitimate needs of his congregation. He knows even better that he will never live up to the likely expectations. Philip Ryken recounts a description of the "Perfect Pastor" that is not far from the expectations that some ministers face:

> He condemns sins, but never upsets anyone. He works from 8:00 A.M. until midnight and is also the janitor. He makes $60.00 a week . . . and gives about $50.00 a week to the poor. He is 28 years old and has been preaching for 30 years . . . . The Perfect Pastor smiles all the time with a straight face because he has a sense of humor that keeps him seriously dedicated to his work . . . . He spends all his time evangelizing the unchurched and is always in his office when needed.[2]

Between the high biblical ideal and the frequently unreasonable expectations of church members, it is no wonder that pastors are often criticized for their performance. It seems from what Paul writes in 1 Thessalonians chapter 2 that his ministry was under attack in that city in such a way that might jeopardize the advances made there for the gospel. John MacArthur writes: "False teachers assailed Paul, as they often do other faithful shepherds, by impugning his character and challenging his authority. . . . They hoped to ruin the new church by destroying its confidence in the person God had used to found it."[3]

When it came to his actual faults, Paul appealed to God's grace for his ministry: "not that we are sufficient in ourselves," he wrote, "but our sufficiency is from God" (2 Cor. 3:5). Paul could also defend himself by appealing to the personal experience of church members. In the opening section of 1 Thessalonians chapter 2, he points out that his was a true ministry in terms of his message, his motives, and his manner among them. Therefore,

2. Philip Graham Ryken, *Galatians*, Reformed Expository Commentary (Phillipsburg, NJ: P&R Publishing, 2005), 175.
3. John MacArthur, *1 & 2 Thessalonians* (Chicago: Moody, 2002), 32–33.

he begins, "You yourselves know, brothers, that our coming to you was not in vain" (1 Thess. 2:1).

THE MESSAGE OF MINISTRY

Paul's ministry was effective because of the message that he proclaimed among the Thessalonians. In preaching this message, Paul was undaunted by the context of great affliction. He reminds his readers that "though we had already suffered and been shamefully treated at Philippi, as you know, we had boldness in our God to declare to you the gospel of God in the midst of much conflict" (1 Thess. 2:2). Paul is referring to what had taken place in Philippi shortly before his arrival in Thessalonica. When Paul cast a demon out of a slave girl who had been annoying him, her owners "seized Paul and Silas and dragged them into the marketplace before the rulers" (Acts 16:19). After accusing Paul of disturbing the city, the crowd attacked them and "the magistrates tore the garments off them and gave orders to beat them with rods" (v. 21). Thus Paul's preaching had brought him intense physical suffering and public shame, which made a strong impression on the Thessalonians. Andrew Young comments: "[Paul and his friends] had not strolled into the city as relaxed and overfed tourists. They had entered still sporting the scars of woeful mishandling in Philippi. . . . Treatment like this would have been enough to stop any phoney mission in its tracks."[4]

Paul's boldness in ministry did not come from his own native courage. It was, he said, "boldness in our God," as he preached "the gospel of God" (1 Thess. 2:2). John Lillie wrote that this boldness "sprang from the preacher's assurance of his own personal relations to God as a redeemed sinner, and from his consciousness of a Divine strength strengthening him for the fulfilment of a Divine commission, in the delivery of a Divine message."[5]

We get a clear impression of the charges leveled against Paul in the denials that he makes. He insisted that his message did not "spring from error or impurity or any attempt to deceive" (1 Thess. 2:3). In Paul's day, there were multitudes of traveling religious charlatans who were notorious for the things alleged against Paul. Perhaps the closest analogy today would be televange-

---

4. Andrew W. Young, *Let's Study 1 & 2 Thessalonians* (Edinburgh: Banner of Truth, 2001), 20.
5. John Lillie, *Lectures on Paul's Epistles to the Thessalonians*, Tentmaker Classic Commentaries (1860; repr., Stoke-on-Trent, UK: Tentmaker Publications, 2007), 69.

lists, many of whose scandals taint the reputation of ministers in general. Unlike the vain philosophers of his day, Paul did not teach error. Certainly his Jewish opponents would have charged Paul with falsely interpreting the Old Testament. But Paul could show from the Scriptures that his teaching was true to God's Word. Every preacher today should be able to do the same. It should be evident, for instance, that the sermons we preach are faithful expositions of the Scriptures rather than our own personal musings. This is also why churches with strong and clear doctrinal standards are most likely to be faithful, since their teaching can be evaluated in light of God's Word.

Moreover, Paul did not preach "impurity." This probably refers to sexual impurity. The mainstream culture in which Paul ministered was sexually lax, to say the least, and at least some of the idolatrous cults employed sexual intercourse as a means of achieving an ecstatic union with God. Added to this were dynamic spiritual gurus who often succeeded in luring many women into their service. Since Acts 17:4 notes that Paul's converts in Thessalonica included "not a few of the leading women," the accusation of impropriety would be a convenient slander against his ministry. The apostle, however, insisted on and practiced sexual purity as taught in the Bible, and those who knew him personally could attest to the outrageous falsehood of this charge against Paul. Similarly, the moral purity of ministers today should be evident to all.

Finally, Paul did not teach with "any attempt to deceive" (1 Thess. 2:3). In Paul's world, rhetoricians could be hired to argue with great eloquence for any cause, much as some lawyers today will argue any legal case for a large enough fee. But the apostle did not manipulate the Scriptures or speak with skillful cunning so as to entrap his audiences. Instead, as he insisted in 2 Corinthians 4:2, "we have renounced disgraceful, underhanded ways. We refuse to practice cunning or to tamper with God's word, but by the open statement of the truth we would commend ourselves to everyone's conscience in the sight of God." Paul spoke with an integrity that should be observed by all ministers of God's Word, as Christ's servants rely on the power of God for salvation rather than manipulative techniques designed to allure or bemuse.

Paul preached his message with integrity because of his sense of obligation to God. He explained: "Just as we have been approved by God to be entrusted with the gospel, so we speak, not to please man, but to please

God who tests our hearts" (1 Thess. 2:4). Paul was a steward of the message that had been entrusted to him by Jesus Christ, so he was constrained to preach it faithfully. The apostle had received his message directly from the risen and exalted Jesus, who appeared to him on the Damascus road and entrusted him with the mission of bringing the gospel to the Gentiles (see Acts 26:16–18). Paul preached under the constraining appointment of Christ himself.

Looking down on the desk where I write my sermons, I see a photograph of the man who mentored me in ministry. I placed it there so that if I were ever tempted not to preach the whole truth of God's Word, that picture would shame me into faithfulness. Paul looked up to the risen and reigning Christ as the One to whom he was accountable, as all gospel ministers should do. Moreover, he could rightly say both that he had been "approved by God" and that God would test his integrity (1 Thess. 2:4). On the one hand, knowing this challenged Paul always to minister "the gospel of God" that he had received. On the other hand, this knowledge liberates ministry, since God will approve sincere faithfulness to his Word regardless of how a message may be criticized in the court of worldly opinion.

THE MOTIVE OF MINISTRY

Not only was Paul's message criticized in his absence, but even stronger attacks were launched against his motives. His opponents suggested that he sought the approval of men through flattery, that he was greedy for money, and that he advanced his own glory at the people's expense. Paul answered: "For we never came with words of flattery, as you know, nor with a pretext for greed—God is witness. Nor did we seek glory from people, whether from you or from others" (1 Thess. 2:5–6).

First, Paul was not motivated by a desire for the approval of men, which is why he refused to flatter in his preaching. The apostle knew that it is not possible to preach the gospel faithfully without giving offense to some listeners. Yes, there are those who enthusiastically believe, but there are others for whom the gospel is "a fragrance from death" (2 Cor. 2:16). Jesus offended the Pharisees of his day by showing their sin and condemning their self-righteous works. To preach the gospel faithfully today requires the minister to deliver this very same message. We not only condemn all men in their sin, but also seek to destroy every false message of salvation, so that sinners might be saved through faith in Jesus.

A prime example of Paul's attitude is found in his highly critical letter to the Galatians. There, Paul was also accused of seeking human approval. After severely rebuking their false doctrine, Paul asked, "For am I now seeking the approval of man, or of God? Or am I trying to please man? If I were still trying to please man, I would not be a servant of Christ" (Gal. 1:10). Given the priority of pleasing God, while rejection and scorn may be more painful to the minister, praise is probably more dangerous. Rowland Hill understood this on an occasion when he descended from the pulpit after preaching. A woman rushed up with praise for his sermon, to which Hill replied, "That's just what the devil told me as soon as I had finished!"[6] Following Paul's example, Hill did not want to be tempted to preach for the approval of men. As Charles Spurgeon is reputed to have said, "I cannot afford to love your praise lest I should fear your scorn!"

A second false charge leveled against Paul's motives was that he preached out of a covetous desire for financial gain. Given the widespread reputations of luxury-living televangelists, ministers today are used to being ridiculed on this charge. I once had a non-Christian neighbor who virtually never saw me without asking, "So how are those tithes and offerings coming?" Paul had to deal with similar ridicule, in large part because of the greedy religious charlatans of his day. Paul would be especially susceptible to this charge because of his zealous efforts to raise money to assist the famine-stricken believers in Judea (1 Cor. 16:1–3), just as ministers today often raise money for gospel causes. "We never came," Paul retorted, however, "with a pretext for greed—God is witness" (1 Thess. 2:5). The word for *pretext* means "cloak": Paul did not use his ministry to conceal a true desire to lay hands on the people's money.

The New Testament teaches that those involved in full-time ministry ought to be paid fairly for their work, ideally in such a way that would allow them to focus on spiritual rather than worldly burdens. Paul wrote, "The Lord commanded that those who proclaim the gospel should get their living by the gospel" (1 Cor. 9:14). As Jesus taught, "the laborer deserves his wages" (Luke 10:7). Quoting the Old Testament, Paul added, "You shall not muzzle an ox when it treads out the grain" (1 Cor. 9:9). Paying Christian

6. Quoted in Tim Shenton, *Opening Up 1 Thessalonians* (Leominster, UK: Day One, 2006), 33.

workers according to their worth helps them not to be tempted by greed or preoccupied with money.

As an apostle, Paul had the right to expect worldly support from the congregations he served. Since he was actually founding these churches, however, Paul thought it wise to refrain from this privilege. "We could have made demands as apostles of Christ" (1 Thess. 2:6), he said, but to avoid the charge of greed he did not. Paul was able to do this because of his calling to lifelong singleness, so that he had no direct family of his own to support (see 1 Cor. 7:7, 32–34). Paul frequently worked to provide for himself, except when he received support from other churches while beginning a new church elsewhere. We know from 2 Corinthians 11:8–9, for example, that the Thessalonians provided financial support to Paul during his ministry in Corinth. For the sake of the churches, the apostle made every effort to avoid a charge of greed, and ministers today should also conduct themselves with an obvious concern for the well-being of their people rather than for the acquisition of money. For some pastors, this attitude will mean serving cheerfully despite poor financial compensation. Paul's approach will always mean that ministers should speak about their own compensation only as is truly needed, seeking God's help to live frugally if our ministry calling requires it. Church history is replete with sterling examples of pastors who remained zealous in ministry despite even desperate financial circumstances.

The third charge against Paul's motives was that he was aiming to increase his own glory through his ministry. He answered: "Nor did we seek glory from people, whether from you or from others" (1 Thess. 2:6). The only glory that Paul sought was the eternal glory that only Christ can give. Here, Paul was exactly like the true minister of John Bunyan's portrait: "The world behind him, a crown hanging over his head." Because of his rejection of worldly glory and his zeal to serve Christ and his gospel, Paul was able to write, "There is laid up for me the crown of righteousness, which the Lord, the righteous judge, will award to me on that Day, and not only to me but also to all who have loved his appearing" (2 Tim. 4:8). Motivated by this consuming aspiration, Paul ministered "not to please man, but to please God who tests our hearts" (1 Thess. 2:4). John Lillie urges every pastor, indeed every Christian, to guide our lives according to Paul's motivation:

Oh then, that in speaking God's word to men, we may please God! From
him alone this word of salvation came. By Him alone have we been intrusted
with it. To Him alone, the all-seeing, infallible, impartial Judge, must we
finally render our account. And only in His hand is the beaming crown, our
exceeding great reward.[7]

THE MANNER OF MINISTRY

To preserve his gospel labors, Paul defended his message, his motives, and
finally his manner among the Thessalonians. Not only was he not motivated
for approval, money, or self-glory, but his manner was, first, gentle among the
new believers: "But we were gentle among you, like a nursing mother taking
care of her own children" (1 Thess. 2:7). Gene Green describes gentleness
as "the virtue of being tender and considerate, concerned for the well-being
of the other, instead of being severe, brusque, or hard."[8] We should not be
surprised that Paul used a feminine analogy for his labors as an apostle,
since God's grace had touched his heart in order to expand rather than
contract his range of human emotions and actions. As Paul looked on the
virtues of self-sacrifice and tender love exemplified by nursing mothers, he
saw an example that should inspire gospel ministers in their attentive care
of their congregations.

Just as a mother does not stand on her dignity when meeting the needs
of her baby, neither did Paul lord his authority over the Thessalonians as he
sought to shepherd them into faith and godliness. The New Testament urges
that ministers of the gospel should be treated with respect: Paul wrote, "Let
the elders who rule well be considered worthy of double honor, especially
those who labor in preaching and teaching" (1 Tim. 5:17). Pastors should not
amplify their titles and honors so as to create distance from the congregation, but should lead, as Peter urged, "not domineering over those in your
charge, but being examples to the flock" (1 Peter 5:3).

Not only was Paul gentle in his manner, but he was also affectionate
toward the Thessalonians. He wrote that he was "affectionately desirous of
you . . . , because you had become very dear to us" (1 Thess. 2:8). The apostle
admits that while he did not covet the believers' money, he did desire the

7. Lillie, *Thessalonians*, 74.
8. Gene L. Green, *The Letters to the Thessalonians*, Pillar New Testament Commentary (Grand
Rapids: Eerdmans, 2002), 127.

believers themselves, because of his love for them and his longing for their salvation. Paul realized that his preaching of truth must be combined with love. Elsewhere he said, "If I speak in the tongues of men and of angels, but have not love, I am a noisy gong or a clanging cymbal" (1 Cor. 13:1). Leon Morris writes: "Paul had come to see the Thessalonians as the objects of God's love, and therefore as the objects of the love of God's servants also."[9] All ministers should pray for God to grant in their hearts an increasing portion of the great love that Jesus has for every sheep in his flock.

Finally, because of his affection for the Thessalonians, Paul could point out the obviously sacrificial character of his ministry. Since the apostle and his associates desired the believers for Christ and because they had become so very dear to them, they shared not only the gospel with them "but also our own selves" (1 Thess. 2:8). Here again, Paul's example of the nursing mother is instructive. G. K. Beale explains: "She conforms her life around the life of the newborn in order properly to meet the child's needs. . . . She is 'delighted to give of her life' to her children because she loves them."[10] Love will cause a true minister to pour out his life for the spiritual well-being of the church, just as every Christian is called to make a sacrificial offering of his or her life in service to Christ and his people.

Not in Vain!

Everything that Paul said in defense of his ministry provides valuable guidelines for those called to ministry, and also for believers who, like Christian in Bunyan's *Pilgrim's Progress*, need discernment in selecting their spiritual guides. Moreover, Paul's description of a true ministry ought to inform the prayers of both the pastor for himself and the congregation for him. Although we are not told, it may be that Paul's sense of inadequacy for ministry was at least a part of the thorn in the flesh about which he complained in 2 Corinthians 12. If so, then every servant of Christ may be encouraged, as Paul was, by the sufficiency of Christ for those who trust him. "He said to me, 'My grace is sufficient for you, for my power is made perfect in weakness,'" Paul reported. "Therefore," he exclaimed, "I will boast

9. Leon Morris, *The First and Second Epistles to the Thessalonians*, New International Commentary on the New Testament (Grand Rapids: Eerdmans, 1959), 80.
10. G. K. Beale, *1–2 Thessalonians*, IVP New Testament Commentary Series (Downers Grove, IL: InterVarsity Press, 2003), 73.

all the more gladly of my weaknesses, so that the power of Christ may rest upon me" (2 Cor. 12:9).

Paul defended his ministry in terms of his message, his motives, and his manner. This kind of faithful godliness was not impressive according to the standards of the world (see 1 Cor. 2:1–5). To realize the significance of what Paul did, however, and of what we are called to do today, we may look back to his opening words in this chapter, where Paul stated that "our coming to you was not in vain" (1 Thess. 2:1). A message of integrity according to God's Word, motives formed by sincerity before God, and a manner that is guided by love will not fail. It will achieve, as Paul wrote to the Ephesians, "far more abundantly than all that we ask or think, according to the power at work within us" (Eph. 3:20).

The word that Paul used in 1 Thessalonians 2:1 for *in vain* (Greek *kenos*) can be taken in two ways, both of which are important. First, it means that Paul's ministry was not "empty" as it came to the Thessalonians. Paul had not come to take from them and to fill up himself; rather, he brought a powerful message and ministry of salvation to give to those to whom he spoke. Christians today, especially pastors, must realize that the same will be true of us if we follow Paul's example. There is nothing more valuable that we can ever bring to anyone—whether people in distant places, neighbors and coworkers, or our own spouses and children—than the message of God's Word as it proclaims Jesus as the Savior of sinners. This is especially true when we offer this message from a life that is pleasing to God and sacrificially offered for others. No church, however obscure in worldly terms, and no life, however insignificant it may seem in worldly things, will ever be empty if it is offered to God to deliver the good news of Jesus to others with the integrity of message, sincerity of motives, and loving manner that Paul could claim for his own labors.

The second meaning of the word *vain* is "ineffective." Paul's coming was not ineffective in bringing salvation to those chosen by God's grace. So also Christians will accomplish mighty things in God's power if we will offer ourselves in the manner described by the apostle. Any Christian who serves as a true messenger of the gospel, ministering with sincere motives and a loving heart, will be used greatly by God to accomplish works of eternal significance, especially the salvation of precious souls through our humble, honest, sincere, and loving witness to Jesus Christ.

63

Paul's testimony regarding his ministry speaks a vitally important word to those who hear the gospel today. If the message that is preached comes with integrity from the Word of God, then it is the same "gospel of God" that Paul preached. It is God who appeals to you now with the good news of forgiveness through the blood of his Son, and God who commands you to honor him by believing. John Lillie writes: "God is the Author of it. God is the Sender of it. God is the Avenger of it. And remember, that, however feeble and unworthy the ministration of it under which you sit, it is the same gospel that Paul preached, and the Thessalonians received, and now it comes to you, laden and enforced, not only by the Divine authority and sanction, but by the experience also and testimony, living and dying, of all past generations of the Church."[11]

Ours is a generation in which so many rich, high, and exalted people are crumbling under the gravity of spiritual emptiness and in which the swollen pride of man inevitably fails of its boasting. In our age, like Paul's, how great is the need for the humblest sinner to believe, and then for every Christian to show how full and powerful a life that is offered to Jesus can be for the service of his gospel. With Paul, we may boldly claim: "I am not ashamed of the gospel, for it is the power of God for salvation to everyone who believes" (Rom. 1:16).

11. Lillie, *Thessalonians*, 74–75.

7

WORTHY OF THE CALLING

1 Thessalonians 2:9—12

For you know how, like a father with his children, we exhorted
each one of you and encouraged you and charged you to walk
in a manner worthy of God, who calls you into his own
kingdom and glory. (1 Thess. 2:11–12)

n today's world, it is not typical for sons to follow in the occupations of their fathers. Throughout most of human history, however, virtually all sons followed in the steps of their fathers. If your father was a farmer, you were going to be a farmer. If he was a merchant, you would be a merchant. In that world, fatherhood involved training your sons to enter into your work. Along these lines, Paul writes to the Thessalonians that he ministered to them "like a father with his children" (1 Thess. 2:11). A father obligates himself to prepare his sons for life in the world, and likewise Paul sought to raise his converts to maturity in faith and godliness.

Together with verse 7, in which Paul compared himself to "a nursing mother taking care of her own children," verse 11 provides a balanced parental picture of spiritual leadership. John MacArthur writes: "It is not enough for leaders just to be compassionate, tender, and caring as spiritual mothers. They also need to live . . . lives that, in their motives and actions, set the standard for all to follow. Furthermore, they need to teach the truth faithfully . . . and call their spiritual children to obedience."[1]

As Paul continues to defend his ministry from the accusations of those who opposed the gospel, he not only sets a standard for pastors and other spiritual leaders today, but also tells us how any of us can be used by God to make a decisive difference in the lives of other believers.

THE FAMILY CALLING

Many families have medieval crests, complete with a Latin motto that provides a family exhortation. The crest of the Phillips family reads *Ducit Amor Patriae*, which means "Love of Country Leads." In keeping with that motto, I was raised to place a high value on patriotism and national service. As Paul exhorts his spiritual children in Thessalonica, his motto for the family of believers might be "Worthy of the Calling." This was the theme, at least, to which Paul directed his fatherly leadership: "walk in a manner worthy of God, who calls you into his own kingdom and glory" (1 Thess. 2:12). As other fathers trained their sons to follow in the work of blacksmiths, farmers, or soldiers, Paul was training his spiritual sons and daughters to consecrate their lives in service to God and Christ's kingdom.

According to Paul, these believers should think of themselves as those called by God "into his own kingdom and glory" (1 Thess. 2:12). They were saved not because they had sought God but because God had sought and called them to himself. Salvation results from God's sovereign summons, which, in tandem with the ministry of his Word, brings about the new birth and saving faith. These Christians had been born again to faith in Christ, and now they were to live as those who had been called by God to enter into his kingdom and glory.

God's kingdom is the realm of his saving activity in the world. According to the Bible, God's full and unopposed reign is a future event that will consummate salvation history. Revelation 11:15 shows that when Christ returns, the angelic host will rejoice to sing: "The kingdom of the world has become the kingdom of our Lord and of his Christ, and he shall reign forever and ever." Christians enter into that eternal reign by receiving Christ as Lord and Savior

1. John MacArthur, *1 & 2 Thessalonians* (Chicago: Moody, 2002), 52–53.

66

through faith, thus coming under his saving rule even in this present evil age. While the Christian is a citizen of the earthly realm, he or she is also a citizen of the heavenly kingdom that rules our spirits and will soon manifest its reign over all. While the present world persists in rebellion against the kingship of Christ, the believer has surrendered to his rule and come under the lordship of Christ. "Take my yoke upon you, and learn from me," Jesus calls, "for I am gentle and lowly in heart, and you will find rest for your souls" (Matt. 11:29).

In reminding believers of their calling into God's kingdom, Paul emphasizes the glory of that kingdom. Like God's kingdom, Christ's glory will be fully manifested in the future, when believers enter into their eternal inheritance together with Jesus. There is, Peter writes, "an inheritance that is imperishable, undefiled, and unfading, kept in heaven for you" (1 Peter 1:4). Included in the eternal glory is our own resurrection into a glorified condition, which Paul describes with these words: "What is sown is perishable; what is raised is imperishable. It is sown in dishonor; it is raised in glory. It is sown in weakness; it is raised in power. It is sown a natural body; it is raised a spiritual body" (1 Cor. 15:42–44). Looking forward to this glory, Christians are to live now in a manner that is worthy of our calling. Leon Morris comments: "They have been saved by such a wonderful God. They have been brought into His kingdom. They face a glorious future. Let them so live here and now as to be worthy of such a God!"[2]

Walking Worthily

When Paul speaks of "walking" in a worthy manner, he refers to the lifestyle that believers are to embrace. We may understand this from secular examples. When a soldier is called into an elite special-forces unit, he is expected to display a standard of valor, fitness, and skill that is a cut above that of the average fighter. When a wife embraces the calling into marriage, she understands that there are duties and obligations, along with many blessings, that now pertain to her life. Likewise, when a sinner has been called into salvation through Jesus Christ, entering God's kingdom and becoming an heir of glory, he or she is obligated to leave behind former ways of sin and embrace a new life of practical godliness and service to the Lord.

2. Leon Morris, *The First and Second Epistles to the Thessalonians*, New International Commentary on the New Testament (Grand Rapids: Eerdmans, 1959), 86.

Paul explained the Christian life in part as a rejection of sin: "Do not present your members to sin as instruments for unrighteousness, but present yourselves to God as those who have been brought from death to life, and your members to God as instruments for righteousness" (Rom. 6:13). Paul also spoke of our spiritual renewal: the believer is called "to be renewed in the spirit of your minds, and to put on the new self, created after the likeness of God in true righteousness and holiness" (Eph. 4:23–24). Andrew Young summarizes: "As God's children, believers are to live to please their Father. As those in union with Jesus Christ, they are to live in the power of his Spirit and not in the strength of the sinful nature (Rom. 8:12–13). The new life we have through the gospel demands a new way of living."[3]

Are you pursuing a walk that is worthy of your calling? Or are you living a life of halfhearted obedience to God's Word? Do you sincerely trust in Jesus Christ, yet are portions of your life governed by the world's rules instead of his? While giving your worship to Jesus, are you withholding your time, your money, or some sinful habit from him? According to Paul, this is no way for a Christian to live. Nor should you think that Christ will settle for a lukewarm devotion and halfhearted service (cf. Rev. 3:16). For a Christian to be worldly is to walk in a manner unworthy of his or her calling. Since Paul insists that "he who began a good work in you will bring it to completion at the day of Jesus Christ" (Phil. 1:6), you should expect him to intervene in your life so as to motivate you to embrace the high calling that you have received.

A few observations are important. The first is that Paul does not give this motto to non-Christians. This is not Paul's gospel charge to unbelievers, nor is his exhortation to walk worthily of God the Christian way of gaining salvation. Paul urged the unbelieving world to "believe in the Lord Jesus, and you will be saved" (Acts 16:31). A fuller version of his gospel message would include the call to confess our sins and trust in the atoning blood of Jesus for our justification: "for all have sinned and fall short of the glory of God, and are justified by his grace as a gift, through the redemption that is in Christ Jesus, ... to be received by faith" (Rom. 3:23–25). Sinners are justified not by living up to God's call but by receiving Christ's saving work in faith.

Second, having noted Paul's gospel call to unbelievers, we must realize that the apostle immediately urged believers to press on in practical godli-

---

3. Andrew W. Young, *Let's Study 1 & 2 Thessalonians* (Edinburgh: Banner of Truth, 2001), 31.

ness. In the terms of one recent controversy, Paul makes it clear that one cannot embrace Jesus as Savior without also submitting to him as Lord. Faith in Christ obliges us to obey God's Word and offer our lives in the pursuit of holiness and gospel service. Although we are not saved *by* our works, Christians most definitely are saved *to* good works and a changed life. So essential is the link between saving faith and holy living that the New Testament candidly declares: "Without [holiness] no one will see the Lord" (Heb. 12:14).

Third, given the necessity for Christians to obey God's Word and grow in godliness, it is part of a gospel minister's calling to exhort the people with Bible commands and precepts. Many voices today complain against biblical exhortations as legalism. The apostle Paul was no legalist, yet he exhorted his followers to "walk worthily" of God's calling! Some insist that gospel preaching should present only the indicatives of the Bible—the promises of God and the declarations of what God has done for us in Christ—without emphasizing the imperative commands of the New Testament for practical godliness. Paul's example shows how wrong this idea is. Although he powerfully delivered the gospel indicatives of Christ's saving work, the apostle was also forceful, like a father, in setting forth the imperative obligations that God's children must embrace in practical faithfulness.

THE FATHER'S EXAMPLE

Paul had a clear idea of what he was aiming to see in the new believers' lives. He also knew that in order to serve as a good spiritual father, he must first set a worthy example for his children. He thus reminded the Thessalonians of their personal experience in watching how Paul lived. Not only should they realize that the slanderous accusations against the apostle were false, but they should also notice his example in order to imitate his lifestyle of faith.

First, Paul set an example of hard work: "For you remember, brothers, our labor and toil: we worked night and day, that we might not be a burden to any of you" (1 Thess. 2:9). The apostle was careful not to give the impression that the purpose of his ministry was to enrich himself; rather, his motive was to bring salvation to his hearers. He therefore refused financial support from the new believers. Paul received financial aid from other, more established churches (see 2 Cor. 11:8), but he also engaged in manual labor to support his needs. We find in Acts 18:3 that his trade was tentmaking. It was probably concerning this work that he spoke of his "labor and toil," words that denote strenuous and demanding effort.

While refusing support as an apostle, Paul made it clear that churches should support their full-time pastors to the best of their ability (see 1 Cor. 9:8–14). Therefore, at least in reasonably well-to-do communities, it should be unusual today for pastors to engage in "tentmaking" trades to provide for their families' needs. In more impoverished communities, pastors often need to work to support their financial needs, sometimes to the detriment of the church. At the same time, a church ought to be able to see that its pastors are working hard and are willing to endure pains on behalf of the spiritual needs of the people. Children in the home similarly should be able to respect their fathers for their hard work in providing for the family, as well as in their service to the church. In every way, including in our battle against sin, the Christian life requires hard work and strain if we are to progress in godliness. Elsewhere, Paul compared the Christian life to the training of athletes: "Train yourself for godliness; for while bodily training is of some value, godliness is of value in every way, as it holds promise for the present life and also for the life to come" (1 Tim. 4:7–8). Growth in grace will require believers to go to bed early and rise before the sun so as to spend time in the Bible and in prayer with God. To have a growing faith, we must study, serve, and participate fully in the life of the church, all of which is hard work. Christian leaders, including pastors and fathers, are to set an example for those they lead, so that they will respect our hard work and learn to embrace the same walk for themselves.

Second, Paul set an example in faithfully witnessing the gospel: "while we proclaimed to you the gospel of God" (1 Thess. 2:9). Paul was a herald called to preach the gospel. It was not a message concerning which he had liberty to innovate or modify doctrines on his own, but rather he preached the "gospel of God," a message fixed by God's revelation. Leon Morris notes: "This conviction that the message comes from God is fundamental to effective preaching. . . . What gives Christianity its power is the fact that the gospel is 'of God.' "[4]

As Paul had disputed with Jewish leaders in the synagogue and also chal-

4. Morris, *First and Second Thessalonians*, 82.

70

lenged pagan delusions, the Thessalonians had seen his refusal to compromise his message or alter his teaching so as to avoid controversy. Instead, Paul had steadfastly set forth the gospel truth of Jesus, relying on God's power to win converts. Christian leaders today must likewise refuse to compromise the Word of God and instead show others by their example that God is able to defend his Word and save all who believe despite worldly objections and even persecution.

Moreover, Paul's zeal for evangelism must have motivated the believers to spread the gospel. Already, Paul has spoken of how the gospel "sounded forth from you" (1 Thess. 1:8), which suggests that the Thessalonians had learned from the apostle's example in witnessing about Jesus Christ. We can only imagine how many of them heard the gospel as they labored with Paul in the workplace or conducted business with him in the market. Likewise, Christian leaders today should set an example of personal evangelism that will inspire and instruct those who follow to show a similar zeal for spreading the gospel.

Third, Paul set a clear example of personal holiness before his spiritual children: "You are witnesses, and God also, how holy and righteous and blameless was our conduct toward you believers" (1 Thess. 2:10). By emphasizing "you believers," Paul suggests that while the world might be slandering him, the believers knew the truth about Paul's life. According to this statement, Paul would have agreed with the later Scottish preacher John Murray M'Cheyne, who said that in his ministry, "my people's greatest need is my personal holiness."[5] The same is true of every spiritual leader, whether a pastor, a father, or anyone else who desires his or her example to promote the spiritual well-being of other believers.

It is possible that Paul used these three terms for godly behavior—"holy and righteous and blameless"—without a clear difference in their meaning. Yet scholars suggest that we can see three complementary orientations to his conduct. First, with respect to his relationship to God, Paul was "holy." The most basic meaning of being holy is to be "set apart," and Paul lived in such a way that he was focused on pleasing and serving God. Even though he did secular work so as to provide for his needs, the purpose behind all his toil lay in his commitment to glorify the Lord and spread the gospel. Second, with respect to people, Paul was "righteous." This does not mean that he

5. Quoted in Tony Sargent, *The Sacred Anointing: The Preaching of Dr. Martyn Lloyd-Jones* (Wheaton, IL: Crossway, 1994), 128.

never sinned (see Phil. 3:12), but that there were no obvious sin patterns in his behavior. Third, with respect to the world, Paul was "blameless" (1 Thess. 2:10). Enemies might accuse him, but there was no dirt to stick on Paul, since he conducted himself with careful honesty, integrity, and godliness.

These are all areas in which spiritual leaders of all kinds should apply themselves: holiness toward God, righteousness toward people, and blamelessness before the world. How great is the need today for fathers—spiritual fathers in the church and literal fathers in the home—to live uprightly before God, their children, and the world. And how great an impact such godliness will make as we show that by the power of God's grace, we are able "to renounce ungodliness and worldly passions, and to live self-controlled, upright, and godly lives in the present age" (Titus 2:12).

The Father's Exhortation

In addition to setting a godly example for his spiritual children through his labor, his witness, and his godliness, Paul also faithfully ministered to them: "We exhorted each one of you and encouraged you and charged you to walk in a manner worthy of God, who calls you into his own kingdom and glory" (1 Thess. 2:12). John MacArthur observes: "Fathers are not only examples, but also instructors. So the spiritual father is not to be merely a model but also a personal teacher and motivator."[6]

Paul describes his ministry in three ways, the first of which focuses on exhortation: "We exhorted each one of you" (1 Thess. 2:12). This means that Paul set before his people the clear biblical expectations for a believer. As an adult convert to Jesus, I well remember being exhorted by friends whom the Lord used to train me in the new life of Christianity. There were occasions when I was told very plainly that I should break certain habits and cease certain behaviors, while taking up new habits and godly actions. The purpose was not to tear me down but to build me up, and I was grateful for those who cared enough about me to exhort me in godliness.

Later in this letter, Paul will give some pointed exhortations, commanding the Thessalonians to pursue sexual purity (1 Thess. 4:3–8), brotherly love (vv. 9–10), and a quiet, useful life (vv. 11–12). In 2 Thessalonians, Paul will add exhortations against idleness and gossip: "For we hear that some among

6. MacArthur, *1 & 2 Thessalonians*, 51.

you walk in idleness, not busy at work, but busybodies. Now such persons we command and encourage in the Lord Jesus Christ to do their work quietly and to earn their own living" (2 Thess. 3:11–12). Like any other pastor or father, Paul had many commands to give to his spiritual children, and those under his care did well to pay attention to his instruction and respond humbly to his rebukes. The same is true for us today as we are exhorted in the Bible and as spiritual leaders confront us when there is need for godly change in our lives.

Second, Paul ministered encouragement to the Thessalonians: "We . . . encouraged you" (1 Thess. 2:12). One of the most touching pictures of biblical encouragement is Jonathan's coming to David in a time of bitter distress, when Jonathan's father, King Saul, nearly had David cornered and defeated. First Samuel 23:16 relates that Jonathan "went to David at Horesh, and strengthened his hand in God." If we are to encourage others, we also need to go to them. Paul indicates that he engaged in extensive personal ministry to each of the believers in Thessalonica, saying that he exhorted and encouraged "each one of you" (1 Thess. 2:12). We must also give personal attention to those who are discouraged or weak. Jonathan strengthened David's faith by reminding him of God's promises for his safety and success. We encourage one another by recalling God's promises of salvation for all who trust in Jesus. One encouraging promise was spoken by Jesus in John 10:27–28: "My sheep hear my voice, and I know them, and they follow me. I give them eternal life, and they will never perish, and no one will snatch them out of my hand."

Every Christian—not just those who are spiritual fathers—is called to encourage his or her brothers and sisters. This requires us to come alongside others with words and actions that will strengthen them in Christ. Encouragement may mean bearing a load for them; it may mean prayer, companionship, or sharing our conviction that God is faithful based on our experience of his loving care.

Third, Paul entreated the believers to press on in faith and godliness: "We . . . charged you to walk in a manner worthy of God, who calls you into his own kingdom and glory" (1 Thess. 2:12). The idea here is bearing testimony so as to motivate those who may be growing weary in their lives of faith. Here the caring heart of a father comes alongside a child and reminds him that all his labors will be worthwhile in the end, that the cause is noble and true, and that the power to persevere will be given in answer to the prayer of faith. Paul would provide this ministry to his closest spiritual son, Timothy, in his final letter. Foretelling his own approaching death, Paul wrote: "I have fought the good fight, I have finished the race, I have kept the faith. Henceforth there is laid up for me the crown of righteousness, which the Lord, the righteous judge, will award to me on that Day." Then, to entreat Timothy to keep going in a life worthy of the calling, Paul added: "and not only to me but also to all who have loved his appearing" (2 Tim. 4:7–8). With this hope in mind, Paul urged his spiritual son: "As for you, always be sober-minded, endure suffering, do the work of an evangelist, fulfill your ministry" (v. 5). Just as Paul counseled Timothy, our spiritual encouragement in Christ is intended to keep us going on the path of faith, godliness, and Christian service.

LOOKING TO JESUS

Do you need to be exhorted, encouraged, or entreated in your calling to walk worthily of God and his kingdom of glory? The best way to do all of these is to point to Jesus Christ, as the writer of Hebrews did in his letter of exhortation to the early church. We run the race with endurance, he wrote, "looking to Jesus, the founder and perfecter of our faith, who for the joy that was set before him endured the cross, despising the shame, and is seated at the right hand of the throne of God" (Heb. 12:2).

Do you need to be exhorted to start living more fervently in obedience to God's Word? Then consider Jesus, who died for you, and realize how right it is that you would therefore live for him.

Do you need encouragement as you struggle with sanctification? Consider Jesus, who is the author and completer of your faith, and realize that, enthroned in heaven with power, he is able to give you the strength that you need as you call on him in prayer. Do you need to be entreated so that you will have courage to walk worthily of God in a world of sin? God's Word urges you to look to Jesus, "who for the joy that was set before him endured the cross, despising the shame . . . . Consider him who endured from sinners such hostility against himself, so that you may not grow weary or fainthearted" (Heb. 12:2–3).

8

Not of Men but of God

1 Thessalonians 2:13–17

When you received the word of God, which you heard from
us, you accepted it not as the word of men but as what it
really is, the word of God, which is at work in you believers.
(1 Thess. 2:13)

One of the most dramatic scenes from the Protestant Reformation was the 1521 trial of Martin Luther at the Diet of Worms.
Luther was summoned to account for his writings that attacked
the Roman Catholic doctrines of penance, purgatory, and papal supremacy.
Present at the council were cardinals—princes of the church—along with
high secular princes. Presiding was no one less than Charles V, the Holy
Roman Emperor, who held the power to put Luther to death for his teachings. Not only was the death threat heavy in the air, but the likely method of
execution would be public burning, as had been done to Luther's predecessor
John Hus at the Council of Constance a hundred years before.

Luther could not fail to be intimidated by this scene, and if the record
of his prayer on the night before his final hearing is any indication, he was
frightened. For this reason, Johann von Eck, the papal accuser, had high
expectations for a triumphant humbling of the Reformer and his doctrines.

The preliminaries all complete, time for prayer and reflection having been given to the accused, and with the emperor and the cardinals glowering down on Luther, Eck pressed the final question: "Will you recant?" Luther's bold answer consisted of these famous words: "Unless I am convinced by the testimony of the Scriptures or by clear reason, for I do not trust in the pope or the councils alone, since it is well known that they often err and contradict each other, I am bound to the Scriptures I have quoted and my conscience is captive to the Word of God. . . . I cannot do otherwise. Here I stand. May God help me. Amen."[1]

What was it that enabled an obscure monk to stand unmoved before so dire a threat? What gives a man the conviction to withstand the assault of high worldly authorities? The answer was given by the apostle Paul in his first letter to the Thessalonians—Christians who, like Luther, were also willing to die for their belief in Jesus Christ. Paul wrote that "when you received the word of God, which you heard from us, you accepted it not as the word of men but as what it really is, the word of God" (1 Thess. 2:13). The issue on which courageous faith contends against capitulation to the vaunted spirit of the age is always the same: is the Bible—the Holy Scripture given through the prophets and apostles—the word of man or the Word of God? Our ability to stand firm against persecution with conviction and courage continues to turn on this question today.

GOD'S WORD FROM MEN

First Thessalonians is an enjoyable letter because of the praise and thanksgiving that Paul heaps on these fledgling Christians. The apostle praises them for their "work of faith and labor of love and steadfastness of hope in our Lord Jesus Christ" (1 Thess. 1:3), and marvels at how "the word of the Lord sounded forth" from them (v. 8). The Thessalonian church was a remarkable body of believers making a striking impact on their world for Jesus Christ, despite their weakness and persecution. Seeing this causes us to ask, "What made the Thessalonians such dynamic Christians?" The same answer is repeatedly given by Paul: the Thessalonians "received the word" (v. 6), the gospel's having come to them "not only in word, but also in power

---

1. Quoted in Stephen J. Nichols, *The Reformation: How a Monk and a Mallet Changed the World* (Wheaton, IL: Crossway, 2007), 32.

and in the Holy Spirit and with full conviction" (v. 5). These believers had been brought to life through the mighty working of God's Word! And what was their chief conviction regarding the message they had received? Paul states: "You received the word of God, . . . not as the word of men but as what it really is, the word of God" (2:13). This same question—is the Bible the word of man or of God?—will largely determine the vigor and fidelity of Christians today.

The first part of this question is much disputed today. Is the Bible merely the word of men? In answering this question, we must admit that in a number of important ways, the answer is Yes. This is why Paul refers to the Word "which you heard from us" (1 Thess. 2:13).

The sixty-six books of the Bible were written down by real men, with all their limitations and peculiarities. The Bible did not fall down from heaven completely written, leather-bound, with maps and concordance appended! Instead, the Bible came together through a process that took place over a thousand years. The human writers of Scripture possessed a wide variety of experience, personality, and character. Moreover, the full range of human characteristics is evident in the biblical materials. Moses was one kind of man, David another, and the apostle Peter yet another. Isaiah's soaring brilliance can be seen in his prophecy, Jeremiah's heart is broken in Lamentations, Paul's rigorous mind turns in his letters, and John's passionate spirit burns in his Gospel and epistles. Using 1 Thessalonians as just one example, this letter was written because of the human circumstances described in it, with the personal experiences of Paul and his readers on full display, including joy, thanksgiving, anxiety, and relief. It is a letter written by a man to other men and women, with its humanity integrally woven into every verse.

In saying that God's Word is not the word of men, therefore, Paul does not mean to deny the genuinely human process involved in its composition. Rather, his particular concern has to do with the origin of the Bible and its teaching. Does the Bible present ideas, convictions, doctrines, promises, commands, and precepts that merely reflect what man—the human author—has to say, or is it instead the Word of God, so that ultimately it is God who speaks to us through the very words of Holy Scripture? On this Paul is insistent: the Bible presents to us, through human means, the very Word of God.

God's Word Teaching about Itself

When Christians are challenged to defend the assertion that the Bible is God's Word, there are two main ways to do so. The first is to point out the Bible's self-attestation, that is, what the Bible says about itself. Does the Bible present the ideas of fallible men, so that however well meaning the human authors were, their ideas were limited, historically and culturally, and at least occasionally wrong? According to its own testimony concerning itself, the Bible is God's revealed Word to mankind and not the word of man about God.

Consider the way in which the prophets described the revelation they communicated. Over and over we read: "the word of the LORD came to me" (Jer. 1:4); "the word of the LORD came to Ezekiel the priest" (Ezek. 1:3); and "the word of the LORD that came to Hosea" (Hos. 1:1). On some occasions we are told that a book presents the words of a certain prophet, but we are quickly reminded that the prophet also delivered the Word of God. The opening section of Amos provides an example. It begins, "The words of Amos, who was among the shepherds of Tekoa," and then immediately states, "Thus says the Lord" (Amos 1:1, 3). In no book of the Bible are we told by a prophet, "I have been wrestling with some difficult matters," or "I just want to tell you what is on my heart." Without exception, they all represent themselves as revealing God's Word.

The same doctrine is taught in the New Testament. Peter helpfully states that "no prophecy of Scripture comes from someone's own interpretation. For no prophecy was ever produced by the will of man, but men spoke from God as they were carried along by the Holy Spirit" (2 Peter 1:20–21). Here Peter explicitly denies two things: that the Bible is a collection of human thoughts and ideas, and that it originated in the will or mind of any man. How, then, did human beings give a revelation that is God's Word? Peter answers in terms of what the Bible means by *inspiration*: "men spoke from God as they were carried along by the Holy Spirit." The Holy Spirit made use of real men, moving and employing them in the process of writing the Bible, so that they said exactly what God wanted said and in the way that God wanted it said. James Montgomery Boice summarizes: "What makes the Bible different from other books is that in their speaking (or writing) the biblical authors were moved upon by God. . . . They wrote as people, but as people moved by the Holy Spirit. The result was the revelation of God."[2]

This teaching answers the question as to how erring men could write an inerrant Bible: even their personal characteristics and limitations were employed by God to present the Scriptures in exactly the way that God wanted them to be presented. Benjamin Warfield used the example of a great cathedral with light shining through a number of stained-glass windows. The pigment in the various panes color the light, causing critics to assert that "any word of God which is passed through the mind and soul of a man must come out discolored by the personality through which it is given, and just to that degree ceases to be the pure word of God." What such critics forget, Warfield states, is that the cathedral was designed by a builder who intended for every colored pane of glass to filter the light exactly as it does. "What if the colors of the stained-glass window have been designed by the architect for the express purpose of giving to the light that floods the cathedral precisely the tone and quality it receives from them?"[3] Similarly, it was God who providentially created, guided, and through the Holy Spirit inspired each biblical writer to give exactly the message that God had designed. Therefore, as Hebrews 1:1 teaches, "Long ago, at many times and in many ways, God spoke to our fathers by the prophets."

What, then, are we to believe about the Bible? If we believe the Bible, then we must believe what it teaches about itself. Paul summarizes this teaching as he commends the Thessalonians for receiving his teaching "not as the word of men but as what it really is, the word of God" (1 Thess. 2:13).

The second and even more potent way of demonstrating the divine nature of Scripture is simply to read it and have the Holy Spirit press upon our hearts the awareness that God is speaking to us through his Word. The writers of the Westminster Confession of Faith articulated this in their paragraph explaining how Christians know that Scripture is God's Word. There are many compelling testimonies to the Bible's divine character, including "the testimony of the Church[,] . . . the heavenliness of the matter, the efficacy of the doctrine," and "many other incomparable excellencies." These all present good reasons to receive the Scripture as God's Word. Yet the ultimate

---

2. James Montgomery Boice, *Foundations of the Christian Faith* (Downers Grove, IL: InterVarsity Press, 1986), 38–42.

3. Benjamin B. Warfield, "Inspiration," in *The International Standard Bible Encylopaedia*, ed. James Orr, 4 vols. (Chicago: Howard-Severance Co., 1915), 3:1478.

and most compelling reason on which "our full persuasion and assurance of the infallible truth and divine authority" of the Bible rests "is from the inward work of the Holy Spirit bearing witness by and with the Word in our hearts" (WCF 1.5). Paul wrote of this inward testimony to the Corinthians: "Now we have received not the spirit of the world, but the Spirit who is from God, that we might understand the things freely given us by God" (1 Cor. 2:12). The direct testimony of the Holy Spirit by and with the Word of God remains the surest proof of the Bible as God's Word, so that the best advice we can give to anyone is that which St. Augustine overheard from nearby children on the day of his conversion: *tolle lege, tolle lege*; "take and read, take and read."

GOD'S WORD WORKING

The Thessalonian Christians became strong in the Lord not only because they received Paul's teaching as the Word of God but also because of the mighty working of God's Word in and among them. It is "the word of God, which is at work in you believers" (1 Thess. 2:13). The Thessalonians grew strong in grace not merely because they received God's Word but also because of what God's Word did in them as they believed it.

What work does God's Word do in us through our faith? Isaiah answered in another classic passage on the nature of Scripture:

> For as the rain and the snow come down from heaven
> and do not return there but water the earth,
> making it bring forth and sprout,
> giving seed to the sower and bread to the eater,
> so shall my word be that goes out from my mouth;
> it shall not return to me empty,
> but it shall accomplish that which I purpose,
> and shall succeed in the thing for which I sent it. (Isa. 55:10–11)

According to Isaiah, God's Word conveys life to our souls in the same way that rain from heaven brings life to the ground. Peter makes the same point about the life-giving power of God's Word in applying it to the believer's conversion: "You have been born again, not of perishable seed but of imperishable, through the living and abiding word of God" (1 Peter

1:23). Jesus said that God's Word makes God's people holy: "Sanctify them in the truth," Jesus prayed; "your word is truth" (John 17:17). According to Paul, God's Word transforms our minds so that we are able to make decisions in keeping with God's will: "Do not be conformed to this world, but be transformed by the renewal of your mind, that by testing you may discern what is the will of God, what is good and acceptable and perfect" (Rom. 12:2). David sang of how God's Word brings sweetness and light into our otherwise dark and dreary lives:

> The law of the LORD is perfect,
>   reviving the soul;
> the testimony of the LORD is sure,
>   making wise the simple;
> the precepts of the LORD are right,
>   rejoicing the heart;
> the commandment of the LORD is pure,
>   enlightening the eyes;
> the fear of the LORD is clean,
>   enduring forever;
> the rules of the LORD are true,
>   and righteous altogether.
> More to be desired are they than gold,
>   even much fine gold;
> sweeter also than honey
>   and drippings of the honeycomb. (Ps. 19:7–10)

What else can be described in such glowing terms: *perfect, sure, right, pure, clean, true,* and *righteous*? What else is readily available for our use that promises to revive the soul, make wise the simple, rejoice the heart, enlighten the eyes, and taste sweeter than honey? What an incomparable blessing we have in the Bible! What folly it is, then, for us to neglect the Word of God that is given to us from heaven, which works so wonderfully and with such power for our salvation! Realizing the power of God's Word made John Wesley cry out: "O give me that book! At any price give me the Book of God!"[4]

4. Quoted in Bill T. Arnold, *1 & 2 Samuel*, NIV Application Commentary (Grand Rapids: Zondervan, 2003), 90.

The power of God's Word was experienced by a Chinese man named Xiao-Hu Huang, who was living in Germany with his wife, Kirstin. Xiao was a Buddhist and his wife an unbeliever. Wanting a special birthday gift for her husband, Kirstin sought a book written in Chinese, but the only such book she could find was a Chinese translation of the Bible. Displeased by her options, she nonetheless bought the Bible, hoping that her husband would appreciate the gesture after all. Xiao was not pleased to receive a Bible, but longing for his native tongue he began reading it anyway. As he did so, he began to be struck by the truth revealed in the Bible's pages; before long, he was persuaded and began believing God's Word. This, in turn, displeased his wife, since Kirstin was a Westerner who had rejected Christianity. As they came into conflict over the book, Kirstin began to read it, simply to argue more effectively against her husband. In the process, she was also persuaded and became a believer in Jesus. Before long, they began studying their Chinese Bible together and grew in their faith. Soon they realized that they needed the fellowship and support of other believers, so they attended a faithful church where they heard the preaching of God's Word. There, they were baptized as followers of Christ and continued to grow as his disciples.[5] Marvelous as it is, this example of the Bible's saving power joins countless others like it. It is by the power of God working through his Word that all believers are saved.

Paul rejoices that God's Word works "in you believers" (1 Thess. 2:13), which reminds us that God's Word calls us to a faith that believes and receives. Thankfully, it is God's Word itself that produces the faith by which it works. As Paul wrote, "faith comes from hearing, and hearing through the word of Christ" (Rom. 10:17). Having believed God's Word, we must further open our hearts and minds to the Scriptures, which not only are "breathed out by God," but are also "profitable for teaching, for reproof, for correction, and for training in righteousness, that the man of God may be competent, equipped for every good work" (2 Tim. 3:16–17).

God's Word and Perseverance

One result of God's Word in every true believer's life is the strengthening of faith that enables the Christian to persevere under hardship. Paul emphasizes

5. Ibid., 89–90.

this work in the Thessalonians: "For you, brothers, became imitators of the churches of God in Christ Jesus that are in Judea. For you suffered the same things from your own countrymen as they did from the Jews" (1 Thess. 2:14). Paul knew all about the persecution that the original believers had suffered in Jerusalem, since he himself had been their chief persecutor. After he was brought to faith by the resurrected Jesus, Paul himself shared in the suffering of the church. The unbelieving Jews, he said, "killed both the Lord Jesus and the prophets, and drove us out" (v. 15).

Paul is not the only one who emphasized the importance of persevering in faith under hardship and persecution. Jesus made this same point in his important parable of the soils, in Matthew 13. In the parable, he focused on the coming of God's kingdom by the spreading of God's Word. The problem is that the Word falls on different kinds of soil, which Jesus used to represent different conditions of heart. Sometimes the Word falls on a heart that is like a stony path, so the Word does not penetrate and Satan can remove it just as birds devour seeds on the path. Another is like thorn-infested ground, where worldly cares and desires grow and choke the Word. Still another kind of heart is like rocky ground, "where [the seeds of the Word] did not have much soil, and immediately they sprang up, since they had no depth of soil, but when the sun rose they were scorched . . . [and] withered away" (Matt. 13:5–6). Jesus explained that this type of soil describes "one who hears the word and immediately receives it with joy, yet he has no root in himself, but endures for a while, and when tribulation or persecution arises on account of the word, immediately he falls away" (vv. 20–21). Here is the point that Paul made to the Thessalonians: it is not enough to respond with initial excitement over the gospel. True faith is always tested by hardship and persecution, so that only those who endure under trial, after the Word of God has taken root in their lives, are truly converted and saved.

Are you willing to endure persecution for your faith? Are you willing to remain faithful to Christ and live according to his Word even if it means being shunned, ridiculed, or wickedly injured? The only true faith is that which is willing to suffer with Jesus. He said, "Whoever would save his life will lose it, but whoever loses his life for my sake will save it" (Luke 9:24). Are you willing to miss out on worldly pleasures in order to live boldly for Jesus and offer your life for his gospel? True faith answers Yes, because the Word has worked mightily through faith. This is how Christians today stand boldly next to Martin Luther, holding fast to the Word of God before the world, declaring, "Here I stand. I can do no other!"

Having stood firmly on God's Word, Martin Luther would go on to change the world. So, too, will every other Christian who takes his or her stand with God's Word. Concerning the heart into which the seed of his Word penetrates with life-giving power, Jesus said: "This is the one who hears the word and understands it. He indeed bears fruit and yields, in one case a hundredfold, in another sixty, and in another thirty" (Matt. 13:23).

GOD'S WORD CHALLENGING UNBELIEF

Paul's description of the persecution suffered by the Thessalonians contains a final word of warning that challenges anyone who hears God's Word but does not combine hearing with faith. Paul said that unbelieving Jews "killed both the Lord Jesus and the prophets, and drove us out, and displease God and oppose all mankind by hindering us from speaking to the Gentiles that they might be saved—so as always to fill up the measure of their sins" (1 Thess. 2:15–16).

These verses describe what the unbelieving world has always done: having crucified Jesus under Pontius Pilate, the world continues to crucify him in mocking unbelief, despising the cross on which Jesus died to save sinners. As unbelieving Israel so frequently slew the prophets who spoke God's Word, Israel also refused to tolerate the apostles and the early Christians who preached the gospel of God's grace through faith. Today, secular humanism devotes its energies to removing a witness to Christ from every public sphere and place. Since the gospel is God's good news of salvation through Jesus, God is displeased by the persecution of his Word. Such persecution opposes the true well-being of all mankind "by hindering us from speaking . . . that they might be saved" (1 Thess. 2:16).

Militant unbelief might justify its hostility toward Jesus with claims of tolerance, but in reality its sin continues to fill the measure that one day will be poured out in the judgment of God. Paul did not hesitate to point out that for those who refuse the salvation offered in God's Word and provided at such cost by God's Son, there can be only divine wrath in the final judgment. God's wrath equates to the just and violent punishment that will be inflicted from heaven on all who persist in sin and unbelief. Indeed, according to Paul, those who persecute Christians and the gospel have already begun experiencing judgment through their unbelief. Notice the present tense, as Paul sees their hostility to the gospel as an advance installment on the punishment that is yet to come: "God's wrath has come upon them at last!" (1 Thess. 2:16).

Yet above all other men, Paul knew that God has saving grace even for persecutors who are living out the curse of God's wrath against their sins. The apostle described himself as the chief of sinners "because I persecuted the church of God" (1 Cor. 15:9). Yet Paul had a testimony of saving grace that came to him through hearing the gospel. That grace came to him through the Bible's message, which is not of men but of God. God's Word declares God's holy wrath on sin, especially for those who wickedly oppress Christ and his gospel. But that same Bible offers salvation to anyone who believes the Word of salvation that Paul loved to preach. The apostle wrote:

> In Christ God was reconciling the world to himself, not counting their trespasses against them, and entrusting to us the message of reconciliation. Therefore, we are ambassadors for Christ, God making his appeal through us. We implore you on behalf of Christ, be reconciled to God. (2 Cor. 5:19–20)

If you doubt this witness to God's Word, Christians are happy to give to you the same advice we give to ourselves. Take up for yourself and read the Bible, the Word not from men but of God. Take and read; take and read.

9

MOVED BY AFFLICTIONS

1 Thessalonians 2:17—3:5

*We sent Timothy, our brother and God's coworker in the gospel
of Christ, to establish and exhort you in your faith, that no
one be moved by these afflictions.* (1 Thess. 3:2–3)

*I*n our technologically driven times, we are paradoxically able to communicate with vastly more people while becoming increasingly isolated from one another. Much of our communication takes place in such a way that we never see the face of the person to whom we are speaking, whether it is by e-mail, Internet chat room, or telephone. Convenience has removed the communion from communication! This trend toward efficiency in the place of fellowship has impacted the church. According to Robert Putnam, the percentage of Americans who find meaningful community in their church has dropped from 48 percent in prior generations to 22 percent today.[1]

Unfortunately, at a time when the community aspects of church are most needed, the trend in America has been toward larger and more impersonal churches. The most recent tendency is for megachurches, defined as congregations larger than two thousand attendees, to plant satellite campuses

---

1. Robert Putnam, *Bowling Alone* (New York: Simon & Schuster, 2000).

in other cities and even in other states, where large crowds are drawn to a pastor who is present only via video projection.[2] The implicit assumption of the megachurch model is that a church is defined primarily by the celebrity status of its preacher and the experiential quality of its worship service.

Reading the New Testament gives a different perspective, however— especially Paul's letters to the Thessalonians. It would be hard to find someone more strategically involved in spreading the gospel than Paul, yet we find him deeply and personally involved with congregations and people. G. K. Beale asks, "Why was Paul so concerned, not only to preach the gospel, but to spend time personally with new converts and to disciple them in their new faith?"[3] An answer is found in 1 Thessalonians 2:17–3:5, where Paul writes of his "great desire to see you face to face," because of the love that knit the church together, the danger to the church through afflictions, and the need for the church to be strengthened in faith. Paul was moved by the Thessalonians' afflictions out of a passionate concern that they not be moved from their faith.

A Community Knit Together by Love

It is obvious from Paul's statements that he sees the church as a community knit together by love. We see this, first, in the nature of the *relationships* of love that he describes. "But since we were torn away from you, brothers," he writes (1 Thess. 2:17), using a family model for the bonds between believers, involving deep affection and loyalty. We see an example of this relationship in Paul's description of his protégé: "We sent Timothy, our brother and God's coworker in the gospel of Christ" (3:2). Though Paul functions as Timothy's superior, he still regards him primarily as a brother in Christ, and he is eager to honor Timothy and promote his ministry. Earlier in this letter, Paul used a parental metaphor to describe his relationship to the fledgling church. He loved the Thessalonians with the tender devotion of a mother for a nursing child (2:7), and like a father he took an encouraging interest in their spiritual growth (2:11). Now, in 2:17, Paul uses a word for *torn away* that means "to be orphaned." Being separated from the believers makes him feel like a doting parent who has lost a child. As Paul sees it, the

2. Bob Smietana, "Multi-Site Churches Go Interstate," *Christianity Today* 55, 7 (July 2011): 11–12.
3. G. K. Beale, *1–2 Thessalonians*, IVP New Testament Commentary Series (Downers Grove, IL: InterVarsity Press, 2003), 89.

church is the furthest thing from a corporate business entity; it is a family knit together by Christian love. A famous hymn puts it well: "Blest be the tie that binds our hearts in Christian love: the fellowship of kindred minds is like to that above."[4]

In keeping with these relationships, Paul expresses strong *feelings* of love toward the church under his care. Scholars believe that Paul might be defending himself from charges that he had abandoned the Thessalonians and that once he was out of sight, they were out of his mind. He counters by writing, "But since we were torn away from you, brothers, for a short time, in person not in heart, we endeavored the more eagerly and with great desire to see you face to face, because we wanted to come to you" (1 Thess. 2:17–18). The separation had been only geographical, not spiritual or emotional, since they remained close to Paul's heart. He had a "great desire" to be rejoined to them but had been hindered by Satan. Paul was so anxious for them, being unable to bear a lack of news, that he was willing to be separated from Timothy, sending the younger minister to check on the Thessalonians' progress. Andrew Young comments: "[Paul's] life was bound up in the welfare of those he served (3:8). He loved them, felt for them, and agonized over them. What an example he provides for Christian workers in every age. . . . The Christian church needs pastors, elders, leaders, and members who care deeply for people."[5]

The most significant comment that Paul makes about his attitude toward the Thessalonian believers is found in 1 Thessalonians 2:19–20: "For what is our hope or joy or crown of boasting before our Lord Jesus at his coming? Is it not you? For you are our glory and joy." Paul saw himself as bound up with his converts not only in terms of the service that he offered to Christ, but also in terms of his own salvation. They were fruits of his labor and of Christ's grace in his life, and Paul looked forward to presenting them firm and steadfast in the faith when Christ returned. The term for Christ's *coming* is *parousia*, which was often used of the visits of kings or emperors to cities within their realm, which was a source of great anxiety for those concerned. We know of examples in which cities receiving the emperor were expected to provide a laurel crown of gold for him to wear. This could be the sense in which the apostle speaks of his converts as his "crown of boasting" at

---

4. John Fawcett, "Blest Be the Tie That Binds" (1782).
5. Andrew W. Young, *Let's Study 1 & 2 Thessalonians* (Edinburgh: Banner of Truth, 2001), 42.

Christ's coming (v. 19). In this way, Paul was "anticipating glorying in the successful completion of their faith as a part of the successful outcome of his own at Christ's final coming."[6]

Paul looked forward to the return of Christ at the end of this age with even more fervor than Roman citizens awaited their ruler, and he understood that the fruit of his salvation, the crown that he would lay before Jesus, was none other than these dearly beloved believers, who were therefore Paul's "glory and joy" (1 Thess. 2:20). So it will be for every other believer, each according to our gifts and calling, that the stewardship entrusted to us in marriage, in families, in the church, and in the world constitutes the precious opportunity we have to glorify Jesus Christ and to present him at his coming with the harvest yield he deserves from our lives.

In keeping with his loving feelings, Paul engaged in *actions* of love toward his beloved converts. Being separated at a time when they were afflicted, he writes, "We endeavored the more eagerly and with great desire to see you face to face, because we wanted to come to you—I, Paul, again and again—but Satan hindered us" (1 Thess. 2:17–18). This shows that Paul had made a determined effort to return and minister to the Thessalonians. He had been frustrated by Satan, however, in a manner that is not known to us. We do know that when Paul could not personally come to them, he sent help that could arrive and he performed perhaps the most vital ministry by laboring in prayer on their behalf (1:2).

This passage presents a compelling picture of the church as a community knit together by love: loving relationships, loving feelings, and loving actions. Paul provides the example that every Christian should follow, as he himself followed the example of Christ, who calls believers to loving servanthood. John's Gospel begins its account of Jesus' crucifixion this way: "Having loved his own who were in the world, he loved them to the end" (John 13:1). We are likewise to love one another to the end of our resources, in Christ's behalf.

A COMMUNITY TRIED BY AFFLICTIONS

One reason why God called early believers to love one another is that the world did not love them. They were a community tried by afflictions, not only in the ordinary sense in which everyone faces trials, but also in the

6. Beale, *1–2 Thessalonians*, 92.

special sense that God himself has ordained trials for every believer. Paul had made this clear earlier, and he was taking pains to teach it again: "For you yourselves know that we are destined for this. For when we were with you, we kept telling you beforehand that we were to suffer affliction, just as it has come to pass, and just as you know" (1 Thess. 3:3–4). John Calvin comments: "Paul teaches that there is no reason why believers should feel dismayed on occasion of persecutions, as though it were a thing that was new and unusual, inasmuch as this is our condition, which the Lord has assigned to us. For this manner of expressions—*we are appointed to it*—is as though he had said, that we are Christians on this condition."[7]

The primary reason why Christians are tried by afflictions is that God apportions them to us. Since God has proved his love and faithfulness to his people by sending his Son to die for our sins, we may be certain that these troubles are necessary for our salvation. John Lillie writes:

> It is enough for us to know that such is the will of God; that this fiery trial happens not without His knowledge, and consent, and purpose, and control; that He sits by the mouth of the furnace into which His people are cast; and that both the fervor and the duration of the process are regulated by His infinite, fatherly wisdom and love. Gladly, we may be sure, would He spare us . . . were it not for the necessities of the case, arising from the prevalence of sin and death in the world, and the presence of both in the Church itself.[8]

So powerful is the presence of sin in our lives and so ingrained are the habits of unbelief that the troubles of this life play a vital role in motivating us to be rid of them. Moreover, trials play a vital role in shaping the qualities of Christian character that are needed in the church. Whenever you are helped by a more seasoned believer whose presence has been a vital aid in your need, the gracious character and wisdom of that Christian have likely been forged in the furnace of affliction, without which you would not have been helped.

The story is told of a Christian man who was overthrown by a series of troubles, including career disaster, financial ruin, and the loss of a loved one. He was wandering the streets of his city in depression when he came

---

7. John Calvin, *Commentaries*, 22 vols. (1854; repr., Grand Rapids: Baker, 2009), 21:266.
8. John Lillie, *Lectures on Paul's Epistles to the Thessalonians*, Tentmaker Classic Commentaries (1860; repr., Stoke-on-Trent, UK: Tentmaker Publications, 2007), 135–36.

to the place where a tall cathedral was being erected. As he gazed at the construction, he noticed a workman chiseling at a piece of stonework and asked him what he was doing. The man explained that he was shaping an ornamental stone that had to be a precise shape and size to fit into its space at the very top of the church. Looking at the workman for a while, the man lifted his face upward and began to pray. He said to the Lord, "Now I understand what you are doing in my life. You are shaping me down here so that I will fit up there."

Another reason why the church is a community tried by afflictions is the presence of an active enemy who is maliciously committed to our destruction: Paul feared "that somehow the tempter had tempted you and our labor would be in vain" (1 Thess. 3:5). The tempter here is Satan, the spiritual potentate who is chief among the evil powers in this world. Leon Morris describes Satan as being "always opposed to God and to man's best interests. . . . His activities in the realm of the spirit are seen in the taking away the good seed from the heart of men (Mark 4:15), and 'sowing' evil people in the world (Matt. 13:39). As 'the god of this world' he blinds the minds of the unbelieving (2 Cor. 4:4). He tempted our Lord (Matt. 4, Luke 4) and he tempts His followers (Luke 22:3; 1 Cor. 7:5)."[9] As Paul tells us in 1 Thessalonians 2:18, Satan also hinders the work of Christ's servants. The word that Paul uses for *hindered* means to "break up the road or place obstacles in the path," and Christians who seek to serve the Lord have to deal with such opposition in the work of the gospel. When it comes to persecution, Satan desires to tempt new converts into unbelief. In the case of those who were never truly saved, Satan succeeds in thwarting the work of the gospel, so that it seems—this was Paul's concern—that "our labor would be in vain" (3:5). In the case of the elect, whose salvation Satan cannot stop, he tempts them through trials into a weak and unfruitful faith that complains against the Lord instead of praising him with thanksgiving.

Paul states his concern for the Thessalonians "that no one be moved by these afflictions" (1 Thess. 3:3). This was not a hypothetical but an actual concern. John Lillie says of the devil: "How experienced, how subtle, how assiduous, how relentless, alas, how successful, in seducing, blinding, misleading, destroying the human soul!"[10] Paul thus realized that our afflictions

9. Leon Morris, *The First and Second Epistles to the Thessalonians*, New International Commentary on the New Testament (Grand Rapids: Eerdmans, 1959), 104.
10. Lillie, *Thessalonians*, 138.

must move us in one way or another. His concern was that trials should move believers to live closer to God and be more careful about their lives, rather than move them to discouragement or apostasy. He intended, as John Calvin asserts, "that they may be carefully upon their watch, and may stir themselves up the more vigorously to resistance."[11]

A COMMUNITY STRENGTHENED BY FAITH

When we consider the dire threat to the Thessalonians, we understand why Paul was so determined to find out how they were doing while he was off ministering the gospel elsewhere in Greece. The whole purpose of this letter is to express his rejoicing upon learning that this church was not only tried by afflictions but also strengthened by faith as a community. This news gave Paul such confidence in their ultimate victory that he exulted in 1 Thessalonians 3:8, "For now we live, if you are standing fast in the Lord."

Faith is so essential to enduring the trials of this world that the writer of Hebrews penned a long chapter detailing how faith had enabled the earlier people of God to gain salvation. It was by faith that Noah built the ark and escaped the flood. It was by faith that Abraham obeyed God's call and became an heir of God's promise (Heb. 11:7–9). By faith Moses "left Egypt, not being afraid of the anger of the king, for he endured as seeing him who is invisible . . . [and] by faith the walls of Jericho fell down" (Heb. 11:27, 30). If the Thessalonians were to prevail over persecution and advance to salvation, it would also be by faith.

For this reason, Paul sent Timothy back to Thessalonica "to learn about your faith" (1 Thess. 3:5). This was a significant sacrifice for Paul to make: "when we could bear it no longer, we were willing to be left behind at Athens alone" (v. 1). Paul's urgency on this matter ought to persuade us to inquire about our own faith. Are we careful to guard and nurture our faith, without which we cannot be saved? Do we daily present our minds and hearts before God's Word so that our faith might be protected from the assaults of Satan and the world and so that our faith may be increased? When we face trials, is our first concern for the brightness of our faith? If not, then we fail to see with Paul that on the issue of faith or unbelief our entire well-being depends. He sent Timothy not to inquire about the

11. Calvin, *Commentaries*, 21:266.

financial state of the Thessalonians or their physical stamina, but "to learn about your faith" (v. 5).

We should follow his lead and make regular inquiries not only about our own faith, but also about the faith of those who are close to us, especially Christian friends and family members. Parents go to great expense to ensure that their children gain a first-class education, musical training, and athletic competition. Are we placing as much priority on our children's faith, and is this seen in our ministry of God's Word and prayer in the home, and the priority we place on the life and worship of the church?

Timothy went to Thessalonica not only to inquire about the new converts' faith, but also to minister to it. Paul says that Timothy went "to establish and exhort you in your faith, that no one be moved by these afflictions" (1 Thess. 3:2–3). The word for *to establish* has the idea of "putting in a buttress, a support" for the sake of strengthening. Timothy did this through a ministry of exhortation and encouragement. Just as a building requires the proper support pillars and beams to handle its weight, the Christian life must be erected on the faithful application of the "ordinary means of grace"—God's Word, prayer, and the sacraments. There are occasions, however, when special strains and assaults require personal encouragement and exhortation through God's Word and prayer.

The writer of Hebrews called the entire church into this ministry of encouragement: "Take care, brothers, lest there be in any of you an evil, unbelieving heart, leading you to fall away from the living God. But exhort one another every day, as long as it is called 'today,' that none of you may be hardened by the deceitfulness of sin" (Heb. 3:12–13).

When I served in the army, you could tell a good unit from a poor one by the way it performed its morning fitness training. A unit with good leadership and strong soldiers did not leave a trail of stragglers, whereas a poor unit had many "fall out." The difference in the good unit was that when one soldier gave up through fatigue, the entire unit or at least a portion of it would circle around, bring him back in, and provide the weary one with the strength he needed to continue by exhortation and encouragement. This is the pressing need forgotten today by those who would turn the church into nothing more than a worship center or a convert-producing factory! It makes all the difference when the ministers of God's Word are involved enough in believers' lives to give encouragement when needed. It makes all the difference when a congregation is knit together in love in the midst of afflictions so as "to establish and exhort" one another in the faith.

A Community Standing Firm for Victory

What is our goal in tending to our own faith and that of others in the midst of affliction? The answer is implied by Paul's concern that his labor would not "be in vain" through his readers' fall into unbelief (1 Thess. 3:5). Paul is more explicit in verse 8 when he rejoices to learn that "you are standing fast in the Lord." This tells us that our simple goal is to stand firm in our faith. Later, Paul would state the same goal of spiritual warfare in his letter to the Ephesians: "Finally, be strong in the Lord and in the strength of his might. Put on the whole armor of God, that you may be able to stand against the schemes of the devil" (Eph. 6:10–11).

In the end, we can be certain that the devil will be destroyed. Romans 16:20 proclaims, "The God of peace will soon crush Satan under your feet." Crushing Satan is God's job, not ours. Our job, set forth so clearly to the Thessalonians, is to be a community knit together by love and strengthened through faith so as to stand firm in victory. Our goal is not to root the devil and his minions out of this world—nor can we—although we should take advantage of every opportunity to thwart Satan's influence, especially by proclaiming the gospel. Our ultimate goal as Christians is, by all the means of God's appointment, simply to stand firm.

Do you realize what a victory it is for you to commit yourself to the worship of God and to obeying Jesus Christ? Do you realize what a blow it is to Satan and his realm every time a Bible study or children's Sunday school class meets? Every time a mother prays for her children or a father opens the Scriptures on the kitchen table, Satan is cast down by God. When you refuse to believe the lie that says that sin is good, and when you are inspired to love others sacrificially or to speak the gospel to an unbeliever, thrones and dominions topple in the spiritual realm. If Christians simply do not give in to the agenda of the world, but hold fast through faith to God's Word, to biblical godliness, and to gospel mission, then Satan cannot win. "Therefore, my beloved brothers," Paul wrote to the Corinthians, "be steadfast, immovable, always abounding in the work of the Lord, knowing that in the Lord your labor is not in vain" (1 Cor. 15:58).

Our goal is stated in Ephesians 6:13: "having done all, to stand firm." In light of the completed Bible, Paul's readers today can imagine the scene so brilliantly depicted in Revelation:

> A great multitude that no one could number, from every nation, from all tribes and peoples and languages, standing before the throne and before the Lamb, clothed in white robes, with palm branches in their hands, and crying out with a loud voice, "Salvation belongs to our God who sits on the throne, and to the Lamb!" (Rev. 7:9–10)

What does it take to stand in that glorious assembly? The angel told John, "They have washed their robes and made them white in the blood of the Lamb" (Rev. 7:14). This focus on the cross explains why, having so loved the Thessalonian converts, Paul was zealous to establish and encourage their faith in Jesus. The only way that anyone will triumph in the battle of this life is through faith in the blood of Christ to wash away our sins. Have you trusted Christ? If not, you have no hope of standing in God's grace now or in his glory in the age to come. But if you have trusted in Christ and continue to trust him, then you should never serve the devil through sin, but stand against him in the power of the Holy Spirit. Then, after all the toil and strife of this battle-scarred world, we will stand together in the glorious company of God's redeemed, no longer wearing armor but clothed only in white. We will be a garland crown to grace the head of the triumphant Jesus. Then the battle will be behind us and we will be safe amid the glories of God with great joy. When the trials of this life have been conquered through faith in Jesus, it will be said of us:

> They are before the throne of God,
>> and serve him day and night in his temple;
>> and he who sits on the throne will shelter them with his presence.
> They shall hunger no more, neither thirst anymore;
>> the sun shall not strike them,
>> nor any scorching heat. . . .
> And God will wipe away every tear from their eyes. (Rev. 7:15–17)

10

NOW WE LIVE

1 Thessalonians 3:6—10

> *For this reason, brothers, in all our distress and affliction we have been comforted about you through your faith. For now we live, if you are standing fast in the Lord. (1 Thess. 3:7–8)*

vangelical Christians today are living in what might be termed a Corinthian-church culture. Our attitude toward church growth and success is similar to that which was confronted and corrected by the apostle Paul in his letter to the ancient Corinthians. Their pride and joy was in an abundance of spiritual gifts and leaders with dynamic personalities. Paul therefore began 1 Corinthians by noting that they were "in every way . . . enriched . . . in all speech and all knowledge—. . . not lacking in any spiritual gift" (1 Cor. 1:5–7). He went on to point out that by reveling in gifts, they had become divided into personality-driven factions (vv. 12–13). This same tendency is pronounced in American evangelicalism, which is structured not so much around doctrinal commitments as it is around personality-driven ministries.

In contrast to the shallow and superficial Corinthians, the apostle Paul did not rely on dynamism but on biblical faithfulness. He was less concerned about spiritual gifts and more concerned about a biblical philosophy of ministry.

One of the most valuable portions of Paul's writings on ministry is found in the fourth chapter of 2 Corinthians, in which he sets forth his commitment to preach God's Word faithfully while relying on the power of the Holy Spirit. Churches today would likely make a deeper and longer-lasting impact if they gave heed to the principle that Paul set forth in 2 Corinthians 4:2: "We have renounced disgraceful, underhanded ways. We refuse to practice cunning or to tamper with God's word, but by the open statement of the truth we would commend ourselves to everyone's conscience in the sight of God."

First Thessalonians was written by Paul early in his first visit to Corinth, so in all likelihood he was starting to wrestle with these problems when he wrote this letter. It is no surprise, then, that so much of 1 Thessalonians focuses on Paul's understanding of a true ministry and his aspirations for his own proclamation of God's Word. This long section from 1 Thessalonians 2:1 to 3:10 is exceedingly valuable in developing a biblical approach to gospel ministry. The final section of this material, 3:6–10, is especially valuable as Paul sums up his thoughts about a true ministry as he has sought to offer it to his dearly loved friends in Thessalonica. In these verses, we see what according to the apostle are the true goals and biblical methods of gospel ministry, as well as the causes of rejoicing for those ministering in Christ's name.

The Goals of Ministry

The background for this material is the report recently given to Paul by his young protégé Timothy. Paul had sent him to Thessalonica to check on the believers whom they had been forced to leave behind. Paul wrote: "When we could bear it no longer, we were willing to be left behind at Athens alone, and we sent Timothy, our brother and God's coworker in the gospel of Christ, to establish and exhort you in your faith" (1 Thess. 3:1–2). In verse 6, Paul added that now "Timothy has come to us from you, and has brought us the good news of your faith and love and reported that you always remember us kindly and long to see us, as we long to see you." It seems that Timothy had just arrived and delivered his news to Paul, and the apostle was so excited that he fired off this letter to express his joy and thanksgiving.

Particularly noteworthy is the news that gave the apostle such pleasure. What was Paul hoping to hear from Timothy about the Thessalonians, so that when he received this news he was so thrilled? He states that it was "the good news of your faith and love." These, then, were the goals of Paul's ministry among the Thessalonians, and following in the apostolic pattern they should be the goals of any true gospel ministry today.

A study of Paul's letters will show that the graces of faith and love were not just his desire for this particular church, but also his consistent goal in all the other places where he ministered. We know this because of the frequency with which Paul wrote of faith and love in his other letters. In his later pastoral letter to Timothy, when his younger colleague was pastoring the important church in Ephesus, Paul stated: "The aim of our charge is love that issues from a pure heart and a good conscience and a sincere faith" (1 Tim. 1:5). To Philemon, Paul rejoiced: "because I hear of your love and of the faith that you have toward the Lord Jesus and for all the saints" (Philem. 5). One of Paul's strongest expressions of these ministry goals is found in Galatians 5:6: "For in Christ Jesus neither circumcision nor uncircumcision counts for anything, but only faith working through love."

In his excitement, Paul makes no mention of the numerical size of the Thessalonian church, although it is generally good when a church is growing in numbers. He makes no mention of the church's outward circumstances, except to note how bad they are. What Paul highlights with great excitement and joy is the Thessalonians' faith in Christ and love for one another. According to John Calvin: "In these two words he comprehends briefly the entire sum of true piety."[1] Leon Morris adds: "Just as faith is the characteristic attitude of the Christian toward God, so is love his characteristic attitude toward man."[2]

According to Paul, then, what should we aim for in the Christian nurture of our children? The answer: growth in faith in God and love for others. What should be our goal in the discipleship of new believers? According to Paul, it is faith and love. How should we evaluate our own growth in grace? These two graces—faith and love—are the two issues on which my entire life depends. What is my life about? Is my life as a Christian defined by outward achievements, success in ministry, or the opinion of others about me? All these goals involve factors largely outside my control. Instead, my

1. John Calvin, *Commentaries*, 22 vols. (1854; repr., Grand Rapids: Baker, 2009), 21:268.
2. Leon Morris, *The First and Second Epistles to the Thessalonians*, New International Commentary on the New Testament (Grand Rapids: Eerdmans, 1959), 106.

life is about faith and love: the goal of my growth in Christ is to learn to trust God more fully and to love others more genuinely. This is the true measure of a Christian man or woman: his or her faith toward Christ and love toward others. The same dynamics provide the apostolic measure of a healthy church.

So significant was the news of the Thessalonians' faith and love that Paul says that it provided comfort to him at a time when he was suffering distress in ministry: "For this reason, brothers, in all our distress and affliction we have been comforted about you through your faith" (1 Thess. 3:7). This comfort stemmed in part from the news that the Thessalonians remembered him with fondness and had not been turned against him by slander: "You always remember us kindly and long to see us, as we long to see you" (v. 6). Andrew Young observes: "News of this sort—of lasting life changes in those we serve in the gospel—is one of the greatest encouragements to press on in difficult times. . . . The recollection of what God has done through us is often enough to keep us at our post and revive our flagging spirits."[3]

THE METHODS OF MINISTRY

Paul's ministry benefited greatly from a clear and biblical understanding of the goals for which he was aiming: faith and love. He also had a clear understanding of the biblical methods of ministry. The Westminster Confession of Faith identifies three means of grace through which God promises to bless our faith, and through faith to accomplish our growth in love. Primary among these means of grace is God's Word, by which alone faith is brought to life by the work of the Holy Spirit (see Rom. 10:17). To God's Word we add prayer and the sacraments as means by which faith "is increased and strengthened" (WCF 14.1). Two of these means of grace—God's Word and prayer—are frequently mentioned in 1 Thessalonians, and the sacraments are strongly related to the third ministry emphasis in this passage: the fellowship of believers.

It is abundantly clear in all of Paul's writings that his first calling as an apostle and pastor was to the teaching and preaching ministry of God's Word. A compelling example is Paul's meeting with the Ephesian elders for the last time, an event recorded in Acts chapter 20. In describing his

3. Andrew W. Young, *Let's Study 1 & 2 Thessalonians* (Edinburgh: Banner of Truth, 2001), 53.

ministry, he claimed, "I did not shrink from declaring to you anything that was profitable, and teaching you in public and from house to house[;] . . . I did not shrink from declaring to you the whole counsel of God" (Acts 20:20, 27). Notice that Paul taught the Bible systematically, not merely focusing on certain messages that he liked to emphasize, but instructing the Ephesians in the whole range of biblical doctrine.

In 1 Thessalonians, Paul has repeatedly stressed the priority of God's Word, having rejoiced that "you received the word in much affliction, with the joy of the Holy Spirit" (1 Thess. 1:6). In 3:10, Paul relates his intense desire to "see you face to face and supply what is lacking in your faith," by which he evidently means that he longs to resume his teaching of God's Word so as to bring the Thessalonians into a sounder grasp of saving truth. Since Paul was hindered from going to Thessalonica, one purpose of this letter was to give an advance installment of his teaching, much of which focused on the biblical doctrine of the return of Christ and the day of the Lord. It is obvious that believers today need instruction from the Bible on these and all other doctrinal topics.

The priority that Paul put on the ministry of God's Word applies equally to believers today. We are to study our Bibles daily, seeking not only exposure to the Scriptures but a systematic understanding of Bible doctrine. Sound doctrine is not a matter for only pastors and elders. All Christians are to be sound theologians, understanding the basics of biblical truth in all its main topics. In his letter to the Romans, Paul made this the first imperative for a godly life: "Do not be conformed to this world, but be transformed by the renewal of your mind" (Rom. 12:2). This transformation takes place through the serious study of the Bible. Donald Grey Barnhouse thus remarked:

> It is the Word of God that can establish the Christian and give him strength to overcome the old forces and to live the new. It can never be done in any other way. . . . You cannot find even one Christian on this earth who has developed into strength of wisdom and witness in the Lord who has attained it by any other means than study and meditation in the Word of God. The Lord Jesus said, "Sanctify them through the truth: thy word is truth" (John 17:17).[4]

Are you committed in a serious way to studying God's Word? If not, your faith can hardly be expected to grow, since you are neglecting God's

---

4. Donald Grey Barnhouse, *Exposition of Bible Doctrines Taking the Epistle to the Romans as a Point of Departure*, 10 vols. (Grand Rapids: Eerdmans, 1952), 1:137–38.

chief provision for the strengthening of your precious faith. There is hardly anything more important to Christian growth than a strong commitment to studying God's Word, both in private and in attendance on faithful preaching in a sound church.

Second, Paul shows his typical commitment to the ministry of prayer. He asks, "What thanksgiving can we return to God for you, for all the joy that we feel for your sake before our God, as we pray most earnestly night and day . . . ?" (1 Thess. 3:9–10). Responding to Timothy's good news by giving thanks to God in prayer, Paul shows that he credits God for the Thessalonians' growing faith and love, relying not on any earthly device but on the power of God through the Word and prayer. In order to fulfill his ministry, Paul needs God's help; here he asks God to remove obstacles in the way of his return to the Thessalonians, "that we may see you face to face" (v. 9).

Moreover, Paul's expression "and supply what is lacking in your faith" may apply as much to his ministry of prayer as to his ministry of the Word. The word for *supply* was also used to mean "mend," "straighten out," or "set in order." Paul's point was simply that he was aware that as new believers in a difficult situation, the Thessalonians had weaknesses to be shored up, vulnerabilities to be protected, and areas of ignorance that needed instruction. Unable at present to meet these needs personally, Paul did the best thing possible: he prayed for his Christian friends with respect to their spiritual needs.

We should likewise pray for the church and for our Christian comrades, asking God to supply what is lacking for growth in faith and love. As a veteran minister who knew well the weakness of the flesh and the real threats to salvation, Paul prayed "earnestly" and with great frequency, so that his converts might be fully established and start to grow.

Third, Paul speaks throughout this passage about the value of Christian fellowship. Indeed, the reason he had sent Timothy to Thessalonica was to ensure that fellowship was not broken between Paul's band of ministers and the congregation that they had left behind. Paul alludes to his personal relationship with them throughout this passage, writing not merely in the abstract but in terms of *us* and *you*. Young observes: "True Christian ministry is never impersonal or mechanically task-oriented. It takes place in the context of loving personal relationships formed through costly self-giving."[5] Part of the normal fellowship that Christians should enjoy is shared

5. Young, *Let's Study 1 & 2 Thessalonians*, 52.

101

communion in the Lord's Supper. Paul saw this sacrament as fostering and protecting the fellowship of the church. To the Corinthians, he wrote: "The bread that we break, is it not a participation in the body of Christ? Because there is one bread, we who are many are one body, for we all partake of the one bread" (1 Cor. 10:16–17).

It is especially new converts like the Thessalonians who benefit greatly from encouraging Christian fellowship. I well remember when I was a new Christian how uplifting it was to be in the company of fellow believers who prayed for me and exhorted me to godliness. Many of my first lessons as a believer were received through friends who took an interest in my spiritual growth. Studies show that for youths in the church, one of the most important factors in their growth as believers is their participation in the fellowship of godly peers. Likewise, young Christians entering college or a new workplace should waste no time in locating other Christians for fellowship. The Puritan Thomas Watson urged the same for believers of all kinds: "Associate with sanctified persons. They may, by their counsel, prayers, and holy example, be a means to make you holy. As the communion of saints is in our creed, so it should be in our company. 'He that walketh with the wise shall be wise' (Prov. 13:20)."[6]

REJOICING IN MINISTRY

If we possess an approach to ministry that aims for the proper biblical goals of faith and love and employs the biblical methods of God's Word, prayer, and stimulating Christian fellowship, it is very likely that we will be blessed with reasons to rejoice, despite the many inevitable hardships. In this, Paul is our example as he followed the example of Christ (1 Thess. 1:3). His ministry in Corinth endured great "distress and affliction" (3:7), to such an extent that Acts 18:9–10 records that the exalted Jesus encouraged Paul with a special vision. Yet in the midst of these losses, Paul was compensated in ministry by the joy of the Lord's blessings. Paul is able to rejoice, exclaiming, "For now we live" because of what the Lord had done and was continuing to do through his ministry (1 Thess. 3:8).

The first and primary blessing that Paul mentions is the joy of learning that fellow believers are persevering in faith toward salvation. Paul's concern

6. Thomas Watson, *A Body of Divinity* (Edinburgh: Banner of Truth, 1958), 249.

over this reminds us that any professing believer's continuance in faith is far from automatic. Today's practice of assuring a new convert that he or she possesses the certainty of eternal life, without stressing the need for a costly perseverance in following Jesus, is totally at odds with the biblical pattern. Ben Witherington comments: "Paul did not believe that one's faith comes prepackaged and complete at the point of conversion. It is rather a living thing that grows or shrinks, can be little or great, can be enhanced or diminished, and can even be said to be brought to completion."[7]

Paul already knew, and would come to know even better, the bitter reality of apostasy, especially in times of strong persecution. The sheer power displayed among the early Christians sometimes attracted people with ulterior motives that would be proved only over time, just as the many blessings of Christian community and worship today will attract false professors with ulterior motives. Later in Paul's ministry, he would trust a colleague named Demas and would include him in his pastoral greetings to the Colossians, writing that "Luke the beloved physician greets you, as does Demas" (Col. 4:14). In his last letter, however, Paul will lament that "Demas, in love with this present world, has deserted me" (2 Tim. 4:10). Paul knew that it requires the supernatural provision of God to keep anyone secure in the faith, which is why he prayed for his converts and exercised such motherly anxiety over their salvation. G. K. Beale writes: "He cannot thank God enough for the Thessalonians' life of faith. He thankfully acknowledges that the readers' standing in the Lord is due to the Lord's all-powerful and gracious work in their hearts."[8] Likewise, there is hardly a greater cause for joy—a delight that sustains us in ministry—than to gain fresh evidence of the continuing faith of those we have loved and whose faith we have nurtured, whether they are converts who came to Christ under our ministry, children we have raised, or old friends who have supported us in times past. In my travels in ministry, I have had the occasion to note the joy of dinner-table conversations regarding the continuing faith and growth of those who are loved and remembered by old friends. To continue in the faith is to give ongoing proof of the reality of Christ's supernatural work for the salvation of our souls.

7. Ben Witherington III, *1–2 Thessalonians: A Socio-Rhetorical Commentary* (Grand Rapids: Eerdmans, 2006), 96.
8. G. K. Beale, *1–2 Thessalonians*, IVP New Testament Commentary Series (Downers Grove, IL: InterVarsity Press, 2003), 106.

A second cause for rejoicing takes place whenever the bonds of Christian love and fellowship are kept strong. It is obvious how important this was to the apostle. Along with his great relief over the continuing faith of the Thessalonians was the report that "you always remember us kindly and long to see us, as we long to see you" (1 Thess. 3:6).

Pastors not only should love their congregations, praying regularly and fervently for them, but also should prize the love that is returned by those they serve. There are occasions when it is virtually a pastor's duty to make himself obnoxious to wayward Christians and hard-hearted congregations. Paul did not shrink from this duty, especially in connection with the Corinthian church that he was founding at this time. But mutual love and close fellowship are of great value to the work of the gospel, and many prayers and much labor should be spent in this cause. Church members should prize the unity and feeling of loving joy within the church, and should loathe the thought of saying or doing anything that might injure the bonds of fellowship within the body of Christ. How much better for us to set aside preferences and debatable opinions rather than to diminish the joy-producing bonds of unity and love among the body of believers! Paul sometimes fretted over the slander and propaganda committed against him, and he could heartily express his thanks to God that such propaganda had not turned the Thessalonians' hearts against him.

Third, Paul rejoices at the inestimable privilege of his access in the presence of God for worship and prayer. He writes of "all the joy that we feel for your sake before our God" (1 Thess. 3:9). Do you realize the enormous blessing of having access to the presence of God? When you come to worship, do you thank God that he receives you, together with all the church, into his holy and loving presence, where a fountain of eternal life is found, so that you might praise and commune with him? Do you realize, as Paul did, what an overwhelming privilege it is to be able to come before the throne of grace with petitions that will be received into the loving hands of God himself? "For what thanksgiving can we return to God," Paul asks, for the staggering blessings that compensate a Christian for all the pains, anxieties, and distresses involved in a life of ministry (v. 9)? How foolish we are to take this privilege lightly—a privilege secured for us by the pains of God's Son on the cross. And we are equally foolish if we neglect the gathering of God's people for worship and the blessing of corporate and private prayer, through which God's mighty power is secured for our salvation and the salvation of those we love!

Get a Life!

A slang expression current today shows dismay over those who have devoted their lives to things that really are not worthwhile. "Get a life!" we say, when someone is obviously wasting his or her time or passions. To a worldly outsider, this slur might have been directed against the apostle Paul. After all, this brilliant, able man was not pursuing the things that matter in the world—money, earthly power, prestige, or pleasure. People would have seen the "distress and affliction" that he suffered, including public persecution, and wondered what could make a person take up such a life. Paul's answer is given in our passage. His exclamation "For now we live" reveals the surpassing joy experienced by those who yield their lives in service to Jesus Christ. Paul's exclamation challenges us to get a life like his. G. K. Beale summarizes: "His perspective on living is the opposite of ancient and modern unbelieving hedonists who say 'Let us eat and drink, for tomorrow we die' (1 Cor. 15:32). His understanding of a fulfilling life differs not only from modern conceptions but also from those within some sectors of the contemporary church that focus on styles of management or marketing to pump new life into the church."[9]

What are you doing to seek significance and meaning? Are you seeking it in the workplace? It is good to use our talents and training, especially if we can do work of value to others. Are you seeking fulfillment in relationships? The love we experience in family, marriage, and friendships is valuable and worthwhile. But these and other earthly fulfillments do not compare with the purpose and meaning of offering your life in service to the reigning Jesus Christ. So how can you get a life like Paul's—one that will have great troubles and anxiety but will cause you to abound in thankful praise to God? The answer can be found all around, in the lives of your fellow Christians, who need your ministry, encouragement, and prayers, and in the lost multitudes of unbelievers who perish without a witness to the gospel of Jesus Christ. Will you offer yourself to be used by Christ for the blessing and salvation of others?

If you do, you will really live, both in this world and in the age to come when the glory of a true Christian ministry will be fully seen.

---

9. Ibid., 103.

11

An Apostolic Pastoral Prayer

1 Thessalonians 3:11–13

Now may our God and Father himself, and our Lord Jesus,
direct our way to you, and may the Lord make you increase and
abound in love for one another and for all, as we do for you.
(1 Thess. 3:11–12)

*A*ny study of Paul's letters will reveal his intense commitment to prayer. A Christian's reliance on prayer—or lack of reliance—tells us much about his or her relationship with God. This is especially true for those engaged in Christian ministry. Charles Spurgeon wrote: "If you are a genuine minister of God you will stand as a priest before the Lord, spiritually wearing the ephod and the breastplate whereon you bear the names of [your] children . . . pleading for them within the veil."[1] Ministers who seldom pray for their spiritual charges, or parents who seldom pray for their children, reveal either a callous indifference to the souls of those under their care or a foolish reliance on human strength.

It also tells us much about a person to discover the *contents* of his or her

1. Charles Haddon Spurgeon, *Lectures to My Students* (Grand Rapids: Zondervan, 1985), 47.

prayers. Whereas many of us pray primarily for ourselves and our material needs, Paul prayed almost exclusively for others and for spiritual priorities. Richard Mayhue summarizes Paul's prayers as "directed to God; . . . focused on others; . . . spiritual in content; and [acknowledging] his utter dependence on God."[2] These petitions show that Paul not only preached salvation by grace, but also depended on that very grace to enable him to be used for the salvation of others.

Paul's prayers in 1 Thessalonians condense his most fervent desires for the members of that beloved church, focusing on requests for God's power to give strength to their faith and bring them to increasing maturity as Christians. Chapter 3 concludes its discussion of Paul's approach to ministry by disclosing his prayer wishes in such a way as to display some of his key views, including the apostle's view of God, ministry, and the Christian life.

PAUL'S VIEW OF GOD

What does Paul's prayer tell us about his view of God? The first thing we should notice is Paul's belief concerning the nature of God and the relationship between God the Father and Jesus Christ. Paul writes: "Now may our God and Father himself, and our Lord Jesus, direct our way to you" (1 Thess. 3:11). While not explicitly stating the doctrine of the Trinity, Paul's prayer contains the substance of the doctrine. Notice that Paul believes in and prays to a single God. In the Greek text, verse 11 begins with the singular pronoun *he*.[3] Moreover, the verb with which Paul asks for God to "direct" him is a masculine singular verb. Therefore, we should probably translate verse 11 as saying, "Now may he direct our way to you." Paul is praying to God in the singular, but then defines that singular God as "our God and Father . . . and our Lord Jesus." He understands that the one God exists in multiple persons.

Furthermore, it is clear that Paul prays to Jesus in just the same way that he prays to the Father, joining them together as the objects of his petition.

2. Richard Mayhue, *1 & 2 Thessalonians: Triumphs and Trials of a Consecrated Church* (Ross-shire, UK: Christian Focus, 1999), 105.
3. According to William Hendriksen, "the pronoun *he* refer[s] to the combination," including both Father and Son as one God. *1 and 2 Thessalonians*, New Testament Commentary (Grand Rapids: Baker, 1974), 90. See also G. K. Beale, *1–2 Thessalonians*, IVP New Testament Commentary Series (Downers Grove, IL: InterVarsity Press, 2003), 108.

Paul's prayer shows that he considers Jesus to be equal to the Father in dignity and power as God. Andrew Young comments: "Such consideration would be possible only if he understood that Jesus was essentially one in nature with the Father." This view of Christ's deity is heightened by Paul's assigning of the title *Lord* to Jesus in the context of his unity with the Father. So potent is the evidence of this passage that Athanasius argued from verse 13 for the deity of Christ in the Council of Nicaea (A.D. 325). The great church father pointed out that the pronoun *he* refers to the Father and Son in combination. Paul refers to both persons together when he writes: "so that he may establish your hearts blameless" (1 Thess. 3:13).[4]

In addition, Paul believed not only that the Father and Son are one in nature as God but also that they are unified in purpose and will. The Father is every bit as loving toward believers as Jesus is, and the two are working in concert for the salvation of the church. That Paul should so clearly express a unity of nature and purpose between the Father and Christ at such an early point in his ministry shows that the deity of Christ was basic and foundational to Christian dogma from the very beginning. This truth was not the result of doctrinal innovation or development at a later point in the life of the church, as is so often asserted by skeptics of orthodox Christian teaching.

Paul's prayer shows not only his belief in the deity of Christ but also his certainty about the sovereignty of God. His first request is for God to "direct our way to you," which suggests that the apostle was counting on God to intervene sovereignly in human affairs so as to permit Paul's return to Thessalonica. Young writes that he "believed that God's control over the events of life extended even to the practicalities of travel plans and consequently thought it both right and necessary to pray about such things."[5] Paul did not think God was too busy managing the universe to help in his affairs. It was because Paul relied on God's sovereignty that he practiced Proverbs 16:3: "Commit your work to the LORD, and your plans will be established."

Finally, Paul understood that believers have a personal relationship with God through Jesus Christ. "Now may *our* God . . . direct our way to you" (1 Thess. 3:11), he writes, indicating his access to the Father as a dearly beloved child. God is Father in his nature, but only those who believe on Jesus gain the right to be considered his children (see John 1:12).

---

4. Andrew W. Young, *Let's Study 1 & 2 Thessalonians* (Edinburgh: Banner of Truth, 2001), 57.
5. Ibid.

Thus, in Paul's prayer we see a basic theology that is essential to Christian faith and life. There is one God in three persons (in a moment, we will see how the Spirit also figures into this prayer), God is the Sovereign to whom we may pray, and God receives believers in Jesus as dearly beloved children who may refer to him as "our God."

PAUL'S VIEW OF MINISTRY

Paul's prayer wishes reveal not only his understanding of God but also his views regarding Christian ministry and service. Paul believed in God's sovereignty, and he knew that God's sovereign grace was necessary for the successful ministry of the gospel.

We earlier learned that, concerned about his readers' faith, Paul had greatly wanted to return to Thessalonica but was hindered by Satan (1 Thess. 2:18). In other words, Paul's human attempts to serve God were overthrown by stronger spiritual opposition. Anyone who seeks to serve Christ as a pastor or witness will find that this still happens today. So how did Paul expect to overcome obstacles and accomplish important things for the Lord? The answer is that he called on the Lord to make provision for his ministry needs. His prayer asks God to "direct our way" back to the believers (3:11), essentially praying for the Lord to open up a pathway that did not then exist. This did not mean that Paul abdicated his own responsibility to plan and labor in ministry, but rather that he relied on God to orchestrate ministry opportunities that Paul himself could never produce. We know that God answered this prayer at a later time of his choosing, since Acts 20:1–4 speaks of Paul's later returning to Macedonia and interacting with key Thessalonian leaders.

Servants of God today need to learn this same lesson. Christians who are effective in evangelism have learned to pray for God to provide them with opportunities to speak about Jesus along with the words to speak when the opportunities arrive. Pastors who find their preaching effective in people's lives are those who pray for God's power on his Word and who are prayed for by their congregations. Churches that dynamically serve the gospel have learned to pray for the needed provision to expand their ministry. On a personal level, marriages and families who enjoy a close spiritual bond are those who pray for God to grant this very thing. Christ's promise is above all

109

found true of those who apply it in their service to the Lord and his gospel: "Ask, and it will be given to you; seek, and you will find; knock, and it will be opened to you" (Luke 11:9).

Paul not only prayed for openings to his own ministry, but also petitioned God to intervene directly in the lives of his people. He dearly sought to return to minister in Thessalonica, but in the meantime he asked God to minister personally to them: "and may the Lord make you increase and abound in love" (1 Thess. 3:12). Paul fully realized that their spiritual growth was not in his hands but in God's. This is how his prayer incorporates the person of the Holy Spirit, since Paul knows that it is the Holy Spirit who will cause love to abound in God's people. A similar passage in Ephesians 3:16–17 specifies that God strengthens his people "through his Spirit in your inner being," so that believers are "rooted and grounded in love."

In noting his utter dependence on God's provision, in terms both of sovereign provision and of the Spirit's work in the lives of believers, Paul repeats the emphasis on love that has characterized this epistle. Previously, he highlighted faith and love together as the key goals of ministry (1 Thess. 3:6). Here, he mentions only love, as the fruit that includes the root and stem of faith: "May the Lord make you increase and abound in love" (v. 12).

The most potent expression of our salvation is the love of God working in and through our lives. One way to see the significance of Christian love is to watch believers who are involved in the care of foster children. D. A. Carson writes about Christian friends who took in twin eighteen-month-old boys who were going to stay, they thought, for just a few weeks until they could be placed in a more permanent setting. The first night, the little boys were crying in their cribs, as you would expect, only they were not making the slightest sound. It turned out that at one of their previous nine foster homes, they had been beaten for crying. An expert who was sent out to evaluate them concluded that the twins were hopelessly damaged emotionally and intellectually. As a result, the Christian couple decided to keep the boys until a good adoptive family could be found. Two years later, when another expert evaluated the boys, no evidence of emotional damage at all could be found. What had cured the little children's hearts? The answer: Love—tender, careful, Christian love.[6]

6. D. A. Carson, *A Call to Spiritual Reformation* (Grand Rapids: Baker, 1992), 196.

Love literally works miracles. This is true not merely for emotionally scarred children, but for all of us who are crippled and twisted by sin—our own and others'. God takes us into his family as spiritual infants, and as we "comprehend . . . what is the breadth and length and height and depth" of Christ's love on the cross, coming "to know the love of Christ that surpasses knowledge," we are "filled with all the fullness of God" (Eph. 3:18–19).

It is our experience of God's love through Jesus Christ that causes believers to "increase and abound in love for one another and for all" (1 Thess. 3:12). Because of God's love for us, we "should be so full of love for others that [we] cannot contain it."[7] As we grow in our experience of God's grace, Christians are to "increase and abound in love" toward others. "Walk in love," Paul urged the Ephesians, "as Christ loved us and gave himself up for us, a fragrant offering and sacrifice to God" (Eph. 5:2). Naturally, this love will be directed "for one another." Love among Christians is expressed in ministry to practical needs, fellowship in service, encouragement in trials, the mutual bearing of burdens (Gal. 6:2), and mutual prayers for God's power and help.

Christian love is not to be restricted to fellow believers, however, since Paul encourages us to increase in love "for all." Jesus commanded us to love our enemies, pray for our persecutors, and greet all people kindly (Matt. 5:43–47). Of course, our understanding of love may differ from what unbelievers desire, since we will pray for their salvation through faith in Christ and in some cases for God to thwart their evil designs—petitions that seek their ultimate good out of love.

Finally, Paul notes the importance of his own example in Christian ministry. He asks God to supernaturally intervene in providing opportunities to minister and prays for God's Spirit to increase the love among God's people. Meanwhile, as the Spirit works in his own life, Paul can set an example of faith and love for the church, just as all Christian leaders should do in the home and church today. Under loving and godly leadership and by God's power, the Christian community is "the school in which we learn to love" as "love is commanded and modeled, . . . lived out and practiced."[8] In this way, our growth in God's grace is measured in our expanded capacity to love others, even those who do not act lovingly toward us.

7. Tim Shenton, *Opening Up 1 Thessalonians* (Leominster, UK: Day One, 2006), 70.
8. Beale, *1–2 Thessalonians*, 109.

111

Paul's View of the Christian Life

In addition to showing the apostle's view of God and of ministry, Paul's prayer requests show his understanding of the Christian life. As the apostle sees it, Christians live with a focus on the future in Christ. Thus, he prays that God will "establish your hearts blameless in holiness before our God and Father, at the coming of our Lord Jesus with all his saints" (1 Thess. 3:13).

Notice the way that Paul anchors the Christian life in the future, so that our present experience is pulled in the direction of Christ's second coming. Andrew Young writes: "The Christian has been called by God 'into his kingdom and glory' (2:12), and it is that future hope that dominates the terrain of Paul's thinking."[9]

Paul establishes a link between love and holiness that seasoned believers will recognize from their own experience. He prays for God's love to fortify our hearts so that we are stimulated toward a changed life, desiring to please the Lord as a way of showing gratitude. Moreover, our love for others causes us to become serious about repenting of our sins. For this reason, one of the best ways to advance your sanctification—your progress in holiness—is to become involved in ministry toward others. Realizing that our attitude, speech, and lifestyle are making an impact on those we love—whether for good or for ill—will strongly motivate us to press on in godliness through God's Word, prayer, and our striving against sin. Love—Christ's love for us and our love for others—strengthens our hearts so that our selfish desires decrease and our character and habits are molded after the pattern of Christ.

Paul prays for God to establish our hearts "blameless in holiness before our God and Father" (1 Thess. 3:13). When he says that we are to be blameless, this does not mean that we can attain a perfect state of sinlessness, since that is impossible in this life (see Phil. 3:12; 1 John 1:8). He means, rather, that our record of conduct should be that of a godly life. In 1 Thessalonians 2:10, Paul described himself and his associates as "holy and righteous and blameless" in their "conduct toward you believers." In saying this, he did not mean that he had never sinned, but rather that his behavior had been consistent with godliness. Holiness pertains to our inward character and purity before the Lord. Christians have been made holy by the regenerating

9. Young, *Let's Study 1 & 2 Thessalonians*, 59.

work of the Holy Spirit; in an objective sense, we have been set apart for the service of God. This is why Paul would so often address the readers of his letters as "saints," that is, "holy ones." Having been set apart as holy, we are called to holiness in character and conduct. Peter charged his readers similarly: "As he who called you is holy, you also be holy in all your conduct, since it is written, 'You shall be holy, for I am holy'" (1 Peter 1:15–16, quoting Lev. 11:44).

Paul emphasizes that it is only God's work in us that enables us to make progress in holiness. This is why he prays for *God* to "establish your hearts blameless in holiness" (1 Thess. 3:13). At the same time, we are responsible to respond to God's work in striving after holiness. "Work out your own salvation with fear and trembling," the apostle says elsewhere, "for it is God who works in you, both to will and to work for his good pleasure" (Phil. 2:12–13). Paul added to that exhortation a compelling charge to holiness similar to the one in our passage from 1 Thessalonians:

> Be blameless and innocent, children of God without blemish in the midst of a crooked and twisted generation, among whom you shine as lights in the world, holding fast to the word of life, so that in the day of Christ I may be proud that I did not run in vain or labor in vain. (Phil. 2:15–16)

Looking forward to the coming of Christ, Paul states that only holiness can give us a confident expectation of salvation on the great day when Christ returns. He prays that the Lord "may establish your hearts blameless in holiness before our God and Father, at the coming of our Lord Jesus with all his saints" (1 Thess. 3:13). This blameless and holy life does not procure our salvation, but rather proves it. Practical evidence of a changed life grants us assurance of faith now, since, as Jesus said, "the tree is known by its fruit" (Matt. 12:33). Likewise, on the day of Christ's return, holiness will attest to the reality of the faith by which we are saved. Jesus taught this concept in his parable of the ten virgins. Only the five virgins who kept oil in their lamps were ready to meet the bridegroom when he came suddenly in the night. Jesus urged, "Watch therefore, for you know neither the day nor the hour" (25:13).

When Paul speaks of "the coming of our Lord Jesus with all his saints," he is perhaps suggesting a further motivation for holiness. Scholars debate whether the expression "with all his holy ones" (NIV) refers to the angels that will attend Christ's return or to the holy believers who had previously died and whose souls had gone to the presence of Christ in heaven. The context—in which Paul so often uses the idea of holiness to describe believers, and in which he will later state that Christ "will bring with him those who have fallen asleep" (1 Thess. 4:14)—strongly suggests that Paul at least includes the spirits of believers in heaven. If so, then he motivates his readers to increasing holiness by reminding them that in Christ they are destined for perfect holiness when they are glorified together with other Christians in the final resurrection. That resurrection will consummate our holiness, but only if there is a holiness in us to be brought to perfection! This is why the author of Hebrews frankly states the vital necessity of our possessing holiness in some real measure, referring to "the holiness without which no one will see the Lord" (Heb. 12:14).

THE SCAFFOLDING REMOVED

In 1994, a celebration was held at Westminster Abbey in London to celebrate the 350th anniversary of the Westminster Confession of Faith. One of the speakers was Eric Alexander, who spoke about Paul and the early Christians as they faced persecution and difficulty. He pointed out that their knowledge of what God was doing in history and for their own salvation "injected a certainty into their tentative, weak, poor faith. It gave many of them a security in a desperately insecure world. Were we more heavenly-minded in our living, it would do the same for us."[10]

Alexander went on to ask a series of pointed questions to make us think about our lives. He asked: "What is the really important thing that is happening in the world in our generation? Where are the really significant events taking place? What is the most important thing? Where do you need to look in the modern world to see the most significant event from a divine perspective? Where is the focus of God's activity in history?" How would you answer those questions? What would you identify as the great marvel of our time, the most interesting thing that demands our attention today? Alexander gave his answer:

10. Eric Alexander, "The Application of Redemption," in *To Glorify and Enjoy God: A Commemoration of the 350th Anniversary of the Westminster Assembly*, ed. John L. Carson and David W. Hall (Edinburgh: Banner of Truth, 1994), 245.

The most significant thing happening in history is the calling, redeeming, and perfecting of the people of God. God is building the church of Jesus Christ. The rest of history is simply a stage God erects for that purpose. He is calling out a people. He is perfecting them. He is changing them. History's great climax comes when God brings down the curtain on this bankrupt world and the Lord Jesus Christ arrives in his infinite glory. The rest of history is simply the scaffolding for the real work.[11]

Alexander finished by remembering the last time he had been in London. At the time, Westminster Abbey had been covered in scaffolding as workers were cleaning and beautifying it. "One could not see its true beauty," he noted, "but one was aware that something of great significance was happening behind that scaffolding. Something of majestic beauty was to be revealed." Drawing on this image, he applied it to our lives and to the church, in much the same way that Paul prayed for God to cause our awareness of our future in Christ to spur us on to holiness:

There will come a day, when God will pull down the scaffolding of world history. Do you know what he will be pointing to when he says to the whole creation, "There is my masterpiece?" He will be pointing to the church of Jesus Christ. In the forefront of it all will be the Lord Jesus himself who will come and say, "Here am I, and the children you have given me, perfected in the beauty of holiness."

That is the day for which we are laboring. In that day, we shall be resurrected. . . . We need to live for that day—the day when God will manifest his glory in his people. If we live for that day, it will change our living and it will change our serving. God grant it, as we say, "even so, come Lord Jesus."[12]

11. Ibid.
12. Ibid., 245–46.

12

SOVEREIGNTY AND SANCTIFICATION

1 Thessalonians 4:1—8

For this is the will of God, your sanctification. (1 Thess. 4:3)

T he famous first question and answer of the Westminster Shorter Catechism asks, "What is the chief end of man?" and answers, "Man's chief end is to glorify God, and to enjoy him for ever." It is seldom appreciated that the point of the second part of that answer— "to enjoy him for ever"—pertains to sanctification. To better access the original intent, we might say that our chief end is "to glorify God and to enjoy pleasing him forever."

Paul made a similar point in the fourth chapter of 1 Thessalonians: "Finally, then, brothers, we ask and urge you in the Lord Jesus, that as you received from us how you ought to walk and to please God, just as you are doing, that you do so more and more" (1 Thess. 4:1). G. K. Beale comments, "Whether in the ancient world or today, the chief end of humanity has often been to take pleasure in this life. In contrast, our passage begins by affirming the opposite: humanity's chief goal ought to be to take pleasure in pleasing God."[1] As Paul states it, sanctification is not aimed primarily toward our

1. G. K. Beale, *1–2 Thessalonians*, IVP New Testament Commentary Series (Downers Grove, IL: InterVarsity Press, 2003), 114.

own well-being or glory. Rather, the first goal of our sanctification, as with all other things, is to give God pleasure and to manifest his glory.

SANCTIFICATION BIBLICALLY DEFINED

Sanctification denotes the process of becoming holy. *Sanctus*, being the Latin word for *holy*, is joined to the Latin verb *facare*, which means "to make." Therefore, sanctification is the process by which believers in Christ are made holy. Paul describes this process in verse 1 as a walk, by which he means an entire lifestyle: "how you ought to walk and to please God."

God is holy in that he is utterly different from and higher than any other being. God's holiness especially involves his moral purity. It is because of his holiness that we take pleasure in pleasing God by being holy. God's holiness defines our *method* as well as our *goal* in sanctification. As God is separate from sin, we also separate ourselves from sin and sinfulness, having different values and desires from the nonbelieving world around us. Paul later emphasizes: "Abstain from every form of evil" (1 Thess. 5:22). Sanctification has not only a goal and a method, but also an *attitude*. Our attitude in pursuing holiness is to oppose sin and evil and to pursue godliness. The Bible describes sanctification as a *process*, a progressive work by which our lifestyle becomes more and more pleasing to God: "that you do so more and more" (4:1).

Paul singles out the need for Christians to be morally pure with respect to the sexual perversity of the world: "For this is the will of God, your sanctification: that you abstain from sexual immorality; that each one of you know how to control his own body in holiness and honor, not in the passion of lust like the Gentiles who do not know God" (1 Thess. 4:3–5). Apparently, Paul focuses on sexual purity not merely because this is one of God's moral expectations, but also because this was a sin to which the Christians in Thessalonica were tempted. Christians are to be different especially in those areas where their own generation is most debased, and where the world's influence will be strongest.

Paul's exhortation to purity provides an example of how sanctification involves both a negative abstention from sin and a positive exhibition of godliness. The apostle does not merely tell believers to abstain from sexual sin but also asserts that "each one of you [should] know how to control his own body in holiness and honor" (1 Thess. 4:4). This self-control extends to every area of life: our sexuality, our treatment of others, our use of money, our conduct in the workplace, and so forth. Not only are we not to fall into worldly patterns of sin, but we are also to honor God with conduct that will please and glorify him in every aspect of life. Paul states this positive approach to sanctification in verse 7: "For God has not called us for impurity, but in holiness."

Finally, note that sanctification is expressed *physically*. Holiness is rooted in our hearts, but always expressed in our actions. Notice how concrete is Paul's view of holiness and how bodily is its fulfillment. The problem with the pagans was their sensual outlook toward everything. By contrast, Christians are to live "not in the passion of lust like the Gentiles who do not know God" (1 Thess. 4:5). In every way, the unbelievers' lives were idolatrous, in service of debased passions and lusts. As Christians, knowing God, we are to use our bodies in honorable ways in accordance with God's law, with self-control and purity.

SANCTIFICATION: GOD'S SOVEREIGN WILL

With this biblical introduction to sanctification—that its *goal* is to take pleasure in pleasing God, its *method* is to be separate from impurity and sin, its *attitude* is both negative toward sin and positive toward godliness, and its expression is concrete and *physical*—we may now consider Paul's link between sanctification and the sovereignty of God. Some complain that a high view of God's sovereignty stands in the way of holy living. Just as people wrongly complain that the doctrine of predestination discourages evangelism, they also argue that God's sovereignty cuts off our motivation to holiness. "If God is sovereign and has chosen me to salvation," they argue, "then why should I bother living a holy life?"

First Thessalonians 4:1–8 sets forth three responses, each of which shows that divine sovereignty in fact promotes rather than deters sanctification. The biblical view centers holiness on God's sovereign will, which Paul explains in these words: "For this is the will of God, your sanctification" (v. 3). A high view of God's sovereignty promotes our zeal for holiness. Because God has ordained our sanctification, Christians therefore know that we will and must be holy.

The idea of holiness is often found in close proximity to the Bible's statements of God's sovereign grace. Romans 8:29 teaches, "For those whom [God] foreknew he also predestined to be conformed to the image of his Son." The goal of predestination is not merely salvation in general terms but specifically in terms of Christlike holiness. Equally pointed is Ephesians 1:4: "He chose us in [Christ] before the foundation of the world, that we should be holy and blameless before him." When the objection is made that sovereign grace inhibits a motivation for the difficult work of sanctification, Paul's answer is that we are sovereignly saved to holiness. Holiness is the mark of the elect, so that we are not warranted in thinking ourselves set apart for salvation unless a noticeable work of sanctification is taking place in our lives. Beale comments, "Those who do not break off from their former pagan ways of living should not be considered truly Christian and should certainly not be given assurance that their faith is genuine."[2]

A humble believer asks, "How can someone like me expect to be holy?" The Bible answers, "Because it is God's sovereign will for you. In Christ, you have a new identity: you are a holy one." Realizing God's calling and God's will, we are emboldened to a more active faith that is energetic in sanctification.

SANCTIFICATION: GOD'S SOVEREIGN REIGN

There is a second way in which a high view of God's sovereignty aids in the pursuit of holiness. We tend to think of God's sovereignty in terms of his *ultimate control* of all things. Yet we should also think of his *complete reign* as our Lord. God is sovereign over his kingdom, so that to be saved is to become his willing subject and to submit in everything to his rule. To know God as sovereign is to acknowledge his rights as King, including our duty to obey his Word.

We see this way of thinking in 1 Thessalonians 4:6: "that no one transgress and wrong his brother in this matter, because the Lord is an avenger in all these things, as we told you beforehand and solemnly warned you." Paul's point is that adultery is not only sinful uncleanness but also a transgression of our brother's rights. Gene Green comments, "What many would view in our day as a strictly personal issue is understood by the apostle as a com-

2. Ibid., 122.

munity issue that has eternal consequences."[3] We can expect the Lord—Paul means the exalted Lord Jesus as he reigns over God's kingdom—to make amends for our transgression by punishing the offender.

Paul's point is that Christians should realize that our sins will bring divine displeasure, with resulting retribution. He wrote in Galatians, "Do not be deceived: God is not mocked, for whatever one sows, that will he also reap. For the one who sows to his own flesh will from the flesh reap corruption, but the one who sows to the Spirit will from the Spirit reap eternal life" (Gal. 6:7–8). Because the Lord sovereignly reigns over his people, we know that sin will have negative consequences, just as we will not fail to be blessed through obedience to God's will. The writer of Hebrews pointed out God's sovereign rule in his teaching on the Lord's fatherly discipline. If we grow slack in pursuing holiness, God is likely to discipline us through circumstances designed to gain our attention. Hebrews 12:10 teaches, "He disciplines us for our good, that we may share his holiness."

Moreover, if God is sovereign over his people, then we are to derive our standards and values from God's Word rather than from worldly society. Paul expresses himself in this very way, emphasizing that Christians have commands from our Sovereign Lord: "For you know what instructions we gave you through the Lord Jesus" (1 Thess. 4:2). Greeks would not have been troubled if the Christians had followed the same loose sexual standards customary to that society. The same is increasingly true in America today. The very ideas of modesty and shame are but dim memories to many. It simply does not occur to most Americans that a couple would not enjoy sexual union during or shortly after their first date. For one to remain a virgin through high school graduation is to be subjected to incredulous mockery (even though statistics show that many teenagers are not, in fact, sexually active). So why should Christians be different? Because we know that God is sovereign and that his rule establishes our moral obligations.

Furthermore, when we realize that Christ is sovereign, and that we are humble servants of his glorious kingdom, then the last thing we will seek is to transgress his royal laws. Obedience to God's Word will then be the watchword of our ministries and our lives. We will reason, "If Christ is going

---

3. Gene L. Green, *The Letters to the Thessalonians*, Pillar New Testament Commentary (Grand Rapids: Eerdmans, 2002), 196.

to reign through my ministry, then my ministry must be like his—it must be true and humble and godly in accordance with God's Word." "If Christ is going to honor my life, then it will be in response to my life's honoring him," we will reason (see 1 Sam. 2:30). In these ways, a high view of God's sovereignty in reigning over his holy kingdom promotes the very sanctification that, according to Paul, is God's will for us.

SANCTIFICATION: GOD'S SOVEREIGN RESOURCES

Paul's teaching in this passage concludes with a statement so important that if we fail to note it, our view of sanctification will be greatly diminished. Here is the apostle's third reason why God's sovereignty promotes rather than deters sanctification: "Therefore whoever disregards this, disregards not man but God, who gives his Holy Spirit to you" (1 Thess. 4:8). As usual, Paul's view of sanctification is strongly Trinitarian: sanctification is the will of God the Father, through the rule of God the Son, and by the power of God the Spirit, whom God gives through Jesus Christ. This mention of the Holy Spirit as a divine gift assures us that God's sovereignty provides us with the resources we need for sanctification.

Whenever God's sovereignty is denied, or when a man-centered emphasis prevails, we will often see counterfeit holiness in the place of the genuine article. The Pharisees provide a classic example: Jesus declared that they cleaned the outside of the cup but left the inside filthy and rotten (Matt. 23:25). Something similar takes place today among legalists who replace biblical holiness with a shallow list of dos and don'ts that codify extrabiblical requirements. It is true, as we have noted, that sanctification involves rejecting sin and worldliness. Yet problems arise when holiness fails to penetrate deeply into our lives, or into what Jesus called "the weightier matters of the law" (v. 23). Although we do not divorce our spouses, we do not really love, honor, and cherish them. Although we may tithe of our income, like the Pharisees we may derive more pride than joy from the exercise. So on it goes. Pharisees looked on others with contempt because they performed a few outward acts of piety. Modern-day legalists may cultivate very little love and may completely miss the point of a life consecrated to God's glory, all the while feeling that they are holy because they vote correctly and avoid restaurants that serve alcohol.

121

How different Christianity looks when it is empowered not by human legalism but by the indwelling power of the Holy Spirit, whose work produces a supernatural holiness. Paul thus prayed for the Ephesians to "know what is the hope to which he has called you, what are the riches of his glorious inheritance in the saints, and what is the immeasurable greatness of his power toward us who believe" (Eph. 1:18–19). The power that Christians may access through faith is nothing less than "his great might that he worked in Christ when he raised him from the dead and seated him at his right hand in the heavenly places" (vv. 19–20). In other words, the same power that raised Jesus from death is able to raise us up from lives of selfishness, hatred, and sin. The power to which Paul referred was the Holy Spirit, as he made clear in Romans 8:11: "If the Spirit of him who raised Jesus from the dead dwells in you, he who raised Christ Jesus from the dead will also give life to your mortal bodies through his Spirit who dwells in you."

A high view of God's sovereignty fuels a high aspiration for personal holiness precisely because it relies on the power that God has promised in this regard. Paul says that by the ministry of the Holy Spirit, believers are being "transformed into [Christ's] image from one degree of glory to another" (2 Cor. 3:18). This is what gives us confidence that we can overcome our besetting sins: God will give us the Holy Spirit to overcome them. This is what makes us believe that we can display the fruit of the Spirit in ever-increasing measure: God has the power to bring holiness to life in our hearts. It is God's sovereign will that we should be holy; it is the rule of Christ's reign that we should obey God's Word; and it is the work of the Holy Spirit in us that empowers us to ever-higher degrees of holy living.

In addition to human-empowered legalism, there is a second feature of man-centered sanctification for us to avoid: a reliance on techniques for personal growth. Evangelical bookstores abound today with five steps for this and seven steps for that. We are fasting and touching prayer cloths; some even attempt to turn Jewish or Buddhist practices into Christian disciplines. There are, of course, necessary Christian activities, such as those of Bible study, prayer, and observing the sacraments. But we must not forget that even biblically mandated means of grace such as God's Word, prayer, and worship give power only as God sovereignly causes them to do so. Therefore, we direct our hearts toward God as the One who conveys the grace that we seek.

Important as Bible study and preaching are, we should never seek blessing from these activities themselves, but rather from God as we sit before his sovereign Word. As vital as prayer is, we must open our hearts to God and direct our thoughts to his throne if we expect to receive his peace. Finally, we must never think that merely having water poured over our heads or that taking the bread and the cup into our mouths provides us with any real grace. Instead, baptism and the Lord's Supper convey grace to us as our hearts receive Christ in faith as his saving work is sacramentally administered.

It is because of God's sovereign resource that Paul warns that to disregard God's call to holiness is to disregard "not man but God, who gives his Holy Spirit to you" (1 Thess. 4:8). Since God has made such rich provision for our sanctification, what an affront it is to him when we refuse his mighty aid, relying on earthly techniques and continuing to serve our sinful desires.

CALVINISM'S RECORD IN HISTORY

As we have studied the sovereignty of God in sanctification—seeing that holiness is God's sovereign will for us, that God's sovereign rulership demands holiness, and that God's Holy Spirit sovereignly empowers a supernatural holiness—we may conclude by inquiring into the record of history with respect to those who believed in the sovereignty of God in their sanctification. Philip Ryken tackles this question in a chapter entitled "What Calvinism Does in History," referring to the system of doctrine noted for emphasizing God's sovereignty. In addition to considering the biblical evidence, Ryken writes, "it may prove useful to consider the influence [that the belief in God's sovereignty] has had on Christian history. If Calvinism is biblical, then we should expect to discover that wherever and whenever these doctrines have come under assault, the church has suffered spiritual, moral, and social decline."[4] At the same time, if Reformed doctrines such as the sovereignty of God are biblical, we would expect spiritual power to flourish where and when these doctrines are fervently advanced.

As Ryken shows, this is precisely the record of church history. First, he points to the record of Geneva in the time of John Calvin. It was a city known for moral debauchery, including drunkenness, gambling, prostitution, and

4. James Montgomery Boice and Philip Graham Ryken, *The Doctrines of Grace* (Wheaton, IL: Crossway, 2002), 39.

widespread adultery. Dishonest business practices were common, and blasphemy was publicly practiced. This was the situation in 1536 when young John Calvin began preaching in Geneva. At first, his ministry was unpopular and his demand for biblical obedience resulted in his dismissal. When the city had deteriorated in his absence, however, Calvin was summoned to return. He preached twice on Sunday and several times during the week, teaching the Holy Scriptures verse by verse, chapter by chapter, and book by book. The hallmark of his teaching—expounding the Bible—bore witness to God's sovereignty over all things. Did "the Calvinist system of doctrine with its undying passion to see God glorified in all of life"[5] produce moral laxity? Not at all. The effect was exactly the opposite. Ryken explains:

> Daily exposure to Calvin's sound exposition of the Bible transformed the mind and heart of Geneva. The citizens embraced their election as the people of God and their calling to build a holy city. Their motto became *post tenebras lux*—"after darkness, light." As they learned to worship the God of grace, . . . Geneva became a happier city. It also became a more wholesome city.[6]

Another community of Christians noted for their devotion to God's sovereignty was the Puritans in seventeenth-century England and Scotland. The Puritan passion was to worship God according to his Word, both in the services of the church and in all of life. These Puritans were spiritual descendants of Calvin's Geneva, having been inspired by their countrymen who fled persecution to Geneva and who returned with a commitment to the sovereignty and glory of God. The Puritans were committed Calvinists, as is seen in the Westminster Confession of Faith and Catechisms. We ask, then, whether their emphasis on God's sovereignty made them lax in the matter of holiness.

The very name *Puritan* bears testimony that this was not the case. The name was meant as an insult by those who despised their devotion to the detailed obedience of God's Word. The Puritan attitude toward life was summarized by Benjamin Wadsworth: "Every Christian should do all he can to promote the glory of God, and the welfare of those about him."[7] The

5. Ibid., 44.
6. Ibid., 42.
7. Quoted in ibid., 46.

Puritans were hard workers, since they believed that Christ was sovereign not only over religious work but over all work. They placed a high value on marriage, the home, and education. They were known for their charity, believing that wealth was to be used for the good of society and not for personal pleasure. As Ryken wrote, "The Puritan mind was a God-centered mind, and the result was a God-glorifying life."[8]

Perhaps the greatest American Calvinist was Jonathan Edwards, a true heir of John Calvin and a latter-day Puritan. In his book *The End for Which God Created the World*, written in 1765, Edwards argued that God's ultimate purpose is to display his glory in all his works. It is little wonder, then, that in addition to being his generation's greatest theologian, Edwards was blessed by God with being a principal instrument by which the Great Awakening brought revival to America.

Meanwhile, our own day is one in which the full acknowledgment of God's sovereignty is uncommon among evangelical Christians. Would anyone seriously argue that ours is an age of great holiness? Would anyone suggest that there is a widespread passion to please God in accordance with his Word? Would anyone argue that we are benefiting from a strong wind of God's power, so that God's Word is strongly impacting society? Is it not instead the case that at this very moment when God's sovereignty is most strongly compromised and neglected, the church is stained by sin, shattered by division, and so weak that, far from shaping society, the church is instead being strongly reshaped by the world? Might it be that we need a theological repentance, whereby we humble ourselves before a mighty, sovereign God?

And what about Reformed Christians: those who explicitly believe and even defend the doctrines associated with God's sovereignty? Do we live with a commitment for God to be pleased through our holy lives? Have we committed ourselves to Christ's sovereign reign, as our Master and Lord? Do we rely, with expectant faith, on the sovereign power of the Spirit of holiness? By regaining not mere doctrinal assent to God's sovereignty but an actual vision of glorifying and pleasing our sovereign God, we may learn anew his will for our lives. For, as Paul declared, "this is the will of God, your sanctification" (1 Thess. 4:3).

8. Ibid., 48.

13

SEXUAL PURITY

1 Thessalonians 4:3–8

For this is the will of God, your sanctification: that you abstain
from sexual immorality, that each one of you know how to
control his own body in holiness and honor,
not in the passion of lust. (1 Thess. 4:3–5)

*I*n previous times, virginity was considered a touchstone of virtue. Chastity was publicly commended. Community pressure was exerted on the unmarried to be sexually pure and on the married to be sexually faithful. Public scorn was heaped on the sexually scandalous, especially on "loose women." Weddings were designed to celebrate the virginity of the couple, especially the bride. It was widely believed that chastity was essential to the preservation of healthy marriages, which is the basic building block of human society, and thereby to the health of the family and the raising of children.

A cultural earthquake regarding sexual purity has taken place in recent decades. Whereas Lady Diana Spencer's virginity was a matter of public importance before her 1981 royal wedding to England's Prince Charles, the question was deemed strictly private and ultimately irrelevant before the 2011 marriage between Prince William and Kate Middleton, who had admittedly been living together for several years. In America, the sexual attitude is symbolized by the popular entertainers Sonny and Cher Bono, a successful music and television couple. In 1969 their only child was born, a daughter named, ironically enough, Chastity. Before the child was school-age, however, Sonny and Cher had broken up in a divorce that involved mutual infidelity. In 2010, the thirty-one-year-old Chastity changed her name to Chaz and legally changed gender after a series of medical operations. Taking her/his experience as a metaphor, we should not be surprised that in a society where sexual purity is neither honored nor demanded, our basic human identity is ultimately compromised and confused.

Sexual sin is not a new problem to have suddenly befallen the human race, of course. The world in which Christianity began was awash in sexual corruption. In the face of widespread sexual promiscuity, the apostles were nonetheless resolute in setting forth God's demand for sexual purity among his people. One clear example is seen in the apostle Paul's teaching: "For this is the will of God, your sanctification: that you abstain from sexual immorality" (1 Thess. 4:3).

WHAT IS SEXUAL PURITY?

The apostle's teaching requires us, first, to define sexual immorality. Paul employs the word *porneia*, which signifies all sexual intercourse outside marriage and thus encompasses both adultery and fornication. Adultery is sexual intercourse in violation of one's marriage vows, while fornication is sexual intercourse between those not married.

The Bible makes it clear, however, that sexual sin includes more than physical acts of illicit sexual contact. Jesus taught that "everyone who looks at a woman with lustful intent has already committed adultery with her in his heart" (Matt. 5:28). Sexual impurity therefore encompasses not only our behavior but also our thoughts, both of which are to be pure. This is why Paul urged the Ephesians that sexual impurity "must not even be named among you." There should be "no filthiness nor foolish talk nor crude joking" (Eph. 5:3–4), an emphasis that shows how alien all sexual immorality ought to be among Christ's followers.

The priority placed on sexual purity in Paul's writings is not incidental. In cataloguing sins from which Christians are to flee, he typically lists sexual sins first. In Ephesians 5:3, Paul begins his teaching on sanctification with this priority. In Galatians 5:19, Paul lists "the works of the flesh" that must be shunned, starting with "sexual immorality, impurity, sensuality." He wrote to the Colossians, "Put to death therefore what is earthly in you," and then applied this immediately to "sexual immorality, impurity, passion" (Col. 3:5). Sexual purity was regarded by the apostles as so integral to Christian holiness that the first council of the church, the Jerusalem Council of Acts 15, emphasized that converts to Christ must "abstain from the things polluted by idols, and from sexual immorality" (Acts 15:20).

There are two evident reasons for this emphasis on sexual purity. The first reason is that sexual sins impact us more deeply and intimately than other sins. Contrary to the ethos of our times, in which sex is considered to be merely physical and recreational, sexual intimacy instead is deeply spiritual and significantly shapes the way in which our souls relate to our own bodies. Paul wrote: "Every other sin a person commits is outside the body, but the sexually immoral person sins against his own body" (1 Cor. 6:18). All sins are equally wrong and bring guilt, but sexual sin "wage[s] war against [the] soul" (1 Peter 2:11) and thus strikes deeply against the holiness to which Christians are called.

The second reason for the biblical emphasis against sexual sins was their prevalence in the society in which the apostles ministered. It is easy to suggest that our own times are as debauched as the ancient Greco-Roman world, but this is not yet quite true. We may lament eroding Christian values of sexual purity, but the people of Corinth (from which Paul was writing) and Thessalonica (to which he was writing) had never been impacted by Christian ethics at all. Every kind of sexual indecency was rampant in that world, especially in major cities. John MacArthur comments that Thessalonica "was rife with such sinful practices as fornication, adultery, homosexuality (including pedophilia), transvestism (men dressing like women), and a wide variety of pornographic and erotic perversions, all done with a seared conscience and society's acceptance."[1]

In such a culture, it was inevitable that ideas about marriage and sexuality would be grossly unbiblical. The Greeks generally considered it unreasonable to expect a man to restrict his sexual passions to the monogamous bond of marriage, so mistresses were commonplace. As is generally true today, whatever shred of expectation there was for sexual purity was placed solely on women, especially wives. As for men, many of whom in the ancient

---

1. John MacArthur, *1 & 2 Thessalonians* (Chicago: Moody, 2002), 102.

world owned women slaves, it was simply inconceivable that they should be expected to show sexual restraint.

We can see why Paul would prioritize sexual purity for Christians who had been converted out of such a society. Many new believers would have possessed mistresses, and many of the women would have practiced harlotry. Yet Paul insisted that union with Christ through faith required a complete and radical break with these practices and called believers to a holy use of their bodies. The context in which Christians live today might not be as thoroughly debauched as Paul's time, but all the trends are moving fast in that direction. It is just as urgent today, therefore, that followers of Jesus take a stance toward sexuality that is radically opposed to the wickedness around us and that honors our holy relationship with God.

In emphasizing sexual purity, it is important to note that Christians do not regard sex itself as impure. Sex is God's good gift designed to serve the spiritual, emotional, and physical bond of a man and woman in the holy union of marriage. Christians oppose sexual sin not because we have a low view of sex but because we have a high one. We care about chastity not because we think that sex is dirty but because it is holy. Realizing this reminds Christians that we must not only oppose the immoral values of pagan society, but also serve that society with a countercultural message of purity and love. J. I. Packer writes: "Our benighted society urgently needs recalling to the noble and ennobling view of sex which Scripture implied and the seventh commandment assumes: namely, that sex is for fully and permanently committed relationships, which . . . prepare us for and help us into that which is their archetype"[2]—namely, "the love and delight of knowing God."[3] Therefore, when it comes to sexual purity, Christians do more than defend traditional notions of marriage and morality; "our concerns are rooted in creation, redemption, and a knowledge of God."[4]

HOW TO BE SEXUALLY PURE

Paul's brief instruction in this passage may offer the clearest primer on sexual purity in all of Scripture. He begins by asserting the rule of Christian

2. J. I. Packer, *Growing in Christ* (Wheaton, IL: Crossway, 2007), 94.
3. James H. Grant Jr., *1 & 2 Thessalonians: The Hope of Salvation* (Wheaton, IL: Crossway, 2011), 95.
4. Ibid.

sexual conduct: "abstain from sexual immorality" (1 Thess. 4:3). This is not a relative but an absolute standard of sexual purity, calling not for moderation but abstention. Similarly, Peter said: "Beloved, I urge you as sojourners and exiles to abstain from the passions of the flesh, which wage war against your soul" (1 Peter 2:11).

Having stated the rule, Paul proceeds to give two perspectives on the *how* of sexual purity. The first is a positive call for sexual self-control: "that each one of you know how to control his own body in holiness and honor" (1 Thess. 4:4).

A translation matter causes commentators to take this verse in two different ways. The first interpretation is that given by the English Standard Version, namely, that Paul calls believers to exercise self-control over their bodies. A second interpretation notes that the Greek word *skeuos* is better translated as "vessel" than as "body" and is sometimes used to denote a man's wife (see 1 Peter 3:7). Moreover, the verb *ktaomai* normally means not "to control" but "to acquire." Therefore, many scholars regard 1 Thessalonians 4:4 as teaching that a man must learn to acquire a wife so as to avoid sexual sin. While the scholars are divided, I think the first interpretation is better, since the verb can mean not only "to acquire" but also "to gain mastery," and Paul's main point of teaching sexual purity more naturally speaks to the believer's own "vessel" or body. Moreover, in this view, Paul's teaching more naturally applies to women as well as to men, as it should.

Paul is urging Christians, therefore, to learn to exercise control over their sexual passions, just as with all other bodily cravings and desires. In a world that says, "If it feels good, do it," Christians realize that sensual pleasure is not the key to happiness. In a culture that prioritizes immediate gratification, Christians realize that good things are enjoyed and preserved only in their proper place and setting. In a world that urges us to define our own morality, Christians embrace their allegiance to a loving Lord who calls us to "holiness and honor" (1 Thess. 4:4). These two words mark out the Christian aim in sexual self-control: not to abhor sex but to retain its holiness and to grant it the honor it merits, along with the honor that our bodies and the bodies of others deserve. John Stott speaks of holiness as referring to the *context* of sex and honor as the *style* of sex. He writes: "There is a world of difference between lust and love, between dishonourable sexual practices which use the partner and true love-making which honours the partner, between the selfish desire to possess and the unselfish desire to love, cherish and respect."[5] The practice of sex in the holy context of marriage glorifies God and takes the form of mutual honor and ministry within a covenant bond of love.

Throughout Christian history, there have been believers who tried to attain sexual self-control through asceticism—an absolute denial and rejection of bodily desires—even to the point of seeking to destroy the sex drive. It was this attitude that led to the Roman Catholic Church's unbiblical requirement for priests and nuns to take a vow of celibacy. The problem with this approach is that our sexual desires were given by God for our good. When Paul speaks of the spiritual use of celibacy, he makes it strictly voluntary and usually short-term (see 1 Cor. 7:5). This fact that sexuality is good highlights one of the challenges to sexual purity: unlike sins such as pride, hatred, and greed, which believers should utterly put to death, sexual sins involve the misuse of something precious that should be properly cultivated and preserved.

In pursuing sexual self-control, we inevitably return to God's provision of marriage. The best way for most adults to practice sexual purity is to enter into marriage, one of the purposes of which is to provide a context for sexual love. Paul was one of the relatively few people who enjoy the gift of singleness, part of which is an unusual absence of sexual desires. Not many people have this gift, however, so Paul urges that "if they cannot exercise self-control, they should marry. For it is better to marry than to burn with passion" (1 Cor. 7:9). He summarizes: "Because of the temptation to sexual immorality, each man should have his own wife and each woman her own husband. The husband should give to his wife her conjugal rights, and likewise the wife to her husband" (vv. 2–3). This does not mean that marriage exists solely or even mainly to gratify sexual urges. It does mean that marriage is God's provision for the satisfaction of healthy sexual desires, just as sex is one of God's provisions for a loving marriage.

Seeing the role of marriage in sexual purity returns us to the alternative translation of 1 Thessalonians 4:4, namely, that Paul teaches each Christian man "to acquire his own wife." Whether or not this is a correct translation, it is good and biblical counsel. We live in a society where many young adults

5. John R. W. Stott, *The Message of 1 & 2 Thessalonians*, The Bible Speaks Today (Downers Grove, IL: InterVarsity Press, 1994), 85.

are so committed to selfishness and immaturity that they do not entertain marriage until their late twenties or early thirties. Among other problems, this approach virtually guarantees sexual impurity. God said, "It is not good that the man should be alone" (Gen. 2:18), and this is true physically, emotionally, and especially sexually. Our aim in raising Christian children, therefore, should be for our young men and women to be mature and responsible enough in their early adult years—their early twenties at least—that if God leads and provides, they are ready to enter into godly and loving marriage. A commitment to sexual self-control greatly motivates believers to marry and preserves Christians from the emotional and spiritual harm that so many experience through sexual immorality in various forms.

Having noted the value of marriage, John Stott, who remained single his entire life, adds a special comment for those who are single and thus lack the proper context for expressing love sexually: "We too must accept this apostolic teaching, however hard it may seem, as God's good purpose both for us and for society. We shall not become a bundle of frustrations and inhibitions if we embrace God's standard, but only if we rebel against it. . . . It is possible for human sexual energy to be redirected . . . both into affectionate relationships with friends of both sexes and into the loving service of others."[6]

Sexual abstinence results, first, from control over our bodies, to which Paul adds, second, the biblical requirement for Christians to flee sexual temptation. The Old Testament believer Joseph set the example when he "fled" from Potiphar's wife "and got out of the house" (Gen. 39:12). Likewise, Paul says, Christians must flee "the passion of lust," which characterizes "the Gentiles who do not know God" (1 Thess. 4:5). Here is the Christian response to all sexual temptation, involving both sexual union outside marriage and lustful sins such as pornography. Whereas the ungodly give themselves over to such passions, the Christian resists impure desires.

In his letter to the Romans, having called believers to shun "sexual immorality and sensuality," Paul adds: "Put on the Lord Jesus Christ, and make no provision for the flesh, to gratify its desires" (Rom. 13:13–14). This means that Christians are to starve sin and guard against likely temptations. In a hypersensualized society such as Paul's and ours, Christian men must control their eyes, saying with Job 31:1, "I have made a covenant with my

6. Ibid., 84.

eyes; how then could I gaze at a virgin?" Christian men should also not be found in places where sexual temptation is likely to strike. For Christian women, sexual purity calls for avoiding unsound relationships and situations that might lead to sexual compromise. It also means modesty in dress and sexual presentation, so as not to tempt their brothers in Christ. In his culture, Paul was calling Christians to disassociate from idolatrous temple festivals, cult prostitution, and all adulterous practices. In the cultural context of Christians today, we must be willing to shun not only places where sexual temptation is rampant—certain kinds of nightclubs, for instance—but also video entertainment that seeks to normalize sexual indecency. Through a combination of self-control, usually involving the right enjoyment of sex in marriage, and a shunning of indecent practices and sensual temptations, Christians are to live in a chaste and pure way for the glory of Christ in the midst of a dark and decadent world.

REASONS AND MOTIVES FOR SEXUAL PURITY

Paul not only calls believers to sexual purity, urging self-control and warning against lustful passions, but also supplies a number of reasons for believers to take this command very seriously.

Paul's first reason for sexual purity is one of the most important: because believers know the true and living God. This divine knowledge contrasts with the Gentiles, "who do not know God" (1 Thess. 4:5). Gene Green comments, "What determines the sexual conduct of the pagans is their desire to satisfy their sexual passions, but the guide to Christian sexuality is knowing God and longing to serve him."[7]

By joining sexual immorality with ignorance of God, Paul links with his more extensive teaching in Romans 1. There, Paul argues that unbelievers really do know God because of the way that nature reveals him to everyone. Nonetheless, "they did not honor him as God or give thanks to him, but they became futile in their thinking, and their foolish hearts were darkened" (Rom. 1:21). As a result of this idolatry, "God gave them up in the lusts of their hearts to impurity, to the dishonoring of their bodies among themselves, because they exchanged the truth about God for a lie"

---

7. Gene L. Green, *The Letters to the Thessalonians*, Pillar New Testament Commentary (Grand Rapids: Eerdmans, 2002), 195.

(vv. 24–25). If sexual impurity, especially homosexuality, is therefore a sign of God's judgment on those who have rejected the truth of God, sexual sin is the last thing that should characterize those who know God and live in light of his truth. According to the Bible, wherever the knowledge of God flourishes, there results a flowering of purity, holiness, and honor (see 1 Cor. 6:11; 1 Peter 4:3–4).

Second, Christians are motivated to sexual purity because of their loving obligations to others. Paul alludes to this in verse 6: "that no one transgress and wrong his brother in this matter." Whereas our licentious society defines sex as an exclusively private matter, the truth is that many people are deeply affected by each sexual sin. A woman who steals a husband breaks up his marriage and family. A man who seduces a single woman robs her future husband of the purity that she ought to offer him. A middle-aged man or a teenager who plugs his heart into pornographic images diminishes his capacity to love real people. Sexual sin inevitably involves spouses, parents, children, siblings, friends, and fellow Christians. Because sexuality is a covenantal and societal matter, Hebrews 13:4 commands: "Let marriage be held in honor among all, and let the marriage bed be undefiled."

It is in part because of the way that sexual impurity injures others that God is sure to "judge the sexually immoral and adulterous" (Heb. 13:4). This supplies Paul's third motive for sexual purity: "because the Lord is an avenger in all these things, as we told you beforehand and solemnly warned you" (1 Thess. 4:6). Not only does sexual sin bring its own ill effects, but God punishes people who indulge in it. Sexual impurity will damage a marriage, perhaps leading to divorce; promiscuity transmits numerous diseases; sometimes believers may be disciplined by withdrawal of God's outward blessing or even by suffering an untimely death. If unrepented, sexual sin will strip a believer of assurance of salvation and lead to a lessening of his or her heavenly reward (1 Cor. 3:12–15; 2 Cor. 5:10). G. K. Beale points out the stark language of the New Testament and notes that "those who do not break off from their former pagan ways of living should not be considered truly Christian . . . . Such people who confess to be Christians but live like Gentiles will be judged like unbelieving Gentiles (Eph. 5:3–6; Col. 3:5–6)."[8]

A fourth motivation for Christians' sexual purity is our awareness that

---

8. G. K. Beale, *1–2 Thessalonians*, IVP New Testament Commentary Series (Downers Grove, IL: InterVarsity Press, 2003), 42.

"God has not called us for impurity, but in holiness" (1 Thess. 4:7). I mentioned earlier that our generation needs an example of holiness in sexuality. Christians are called to provide this example to our children, who should pattern their sexual expectations not on images from the media or self-indulgent examples from society, but on the loving model of the way their parents act toward each other and the purity that has attracted their hearts through the holy lives of believers in the church. James Grant writes to men: "We must fight this fight for the sake of our wife, for the sake of our children, and for the sake of the gospel."[9] It is God who has called his people to holiness, which is why Paul adds that "whoever disregards this, disregards not man but God" (1 Thess. 4:8).

Finally, Christians are to take seriously our calling to sexual purity because we have been empowered to holiness by the Spirit of Christ who lives within us. What a difference it makes that Paul concludes by saying that God "gives his Holy Spirit to you" (1 Thess. 4:8). This means not only that we *must not* live in sexual sin but also that we *need not* give in to such temptations, since God's Holy Spirit is within us and is ready to provide God's power in answer to prayer. Whereas the world scoffs at even the possibility of virginity before marriage and faithfulness between a husband and wife, God gives us his own Spirit of holiness. Being joined to Christ in faith, indwelt by his Holy Spirit, and called to an eternal relationship of love with our wonderful Savior and Lord, Christians have every reason to live "in holiness and honor" and "not in the passion of lust like the Gentiles" (vv. 4–5). To do otherwise is to "grieve the Holy Spirit" (Eph. 4:30), wounding God as well as ourselves. "He who is joined to the Lord becomes one spirit with him," Paul urges us. He therefore adds: "Flee from sexual immorality. . . . Do you not know that your body is a temple of the Holy Spirit within you, whom you have from God? You are not your own, for you were bought with a price. So glorify God in your body" (1 Cor. 6:17–20).

For Christ's Sake

Ultimately, Christians maintain sexual purity for the same reason that a bride preserves her purity in anticipation of her wedding. Christians have turned from the world in order to give our love in holiness to Jesus Christ.

9. Grant, *1 & 2 Thessalonians*, 96.

In fact, it is through the gospel ministry of his Holy Spirit, granting power to God's Word and to prayer, that Christ himself labors to sanctify his bride, "having cleansed her by the washing of water with the word, so that he might present the church to himself in splendor, without spot or wrinkle or any such thing, that she might be holy and without blemish" (Eph. 5:26–27).

Does this mean that Christians will be free from all sexual sin, not only in action but also in thought and desire? The answer is No, since in this matter as in so many others the teaching of John is sadly true: "If we say we have no sin, we deceive ourselves, and the truth is not in us" (1 John 1:8). If we fall, we may confess our sexual sin and turn in faith to Christ, who "is faithful and just to forgive us our sins and to cleanse us from all unrighteousness" (v. 9). Christ has power not only to forgive but actually to cleanse our souls, restoring to our spirits a purity that our bodies may have lost. Experiencing this by Christ's grace, for Christ's sake we will apply ourselves with zeal in a holy battle for sexual purity, which Christ so fervently desires and our generation so greatly needs to see in the lives of people who know God. Having committed ourselves "to walk and to please God" in sexual purity, we will aim to "do so more and more" (1 Thess. 4:1). For the sake of Jesus, our loving Lord, we will "abstain," we will learn to control our bodies "in holiness and honor, not in the passion of lusts," we will resolve not to "transgress and wrong" our brother, and we will remember that "God is an avenger in all these things," as the Bible has told us. For this is the will of God, who has "not called us for impurity, but in holiness," and who richly "gives his Holy Spirit" (vv. 6–8).

14

CONCERNING BROTHERLY LOVE

1 Thessalonians 4:9–12

Now concerning brotherly love you have no need for anyone to write to you, for you yourselves have been taught by God to love one another. (1 Thess. 4:9)

The famous Archbishop Ussher was once shipwrecked off the coast of Ireland. Destitute of supplies, he wandered into the house of a local clergyman. The minister was suspicious of the disheveled man who claimed to be a bishop and hesitated to offer him aid. To test the stranger, the clergyman asked, "How many commandments are there?" Ussher replied, "I can at once satisfy you that I am not an imposter, as you think, for there are eleven commandments." Hearing this, the reluctant man answered, "No, there are only ten commandments." Only if Ussher could prove an eleventh commandment, he said, would he offer any help. The archbishop then asked for a Bible, and turning to John 13:34, he read Jesus' words to his disciples: "A new commandment I give to you, that you love one another." Corrected and convicted by Jesus' words, the man immediately received Ussher and provided all that he needed.[1]

1. Tim Shenton, *Opening Up 1 Thessalonians* (Leominster, UK: Day One, 2006), 82–83.

Years after Christ had spoken the new commandment, his servant the apostle Paul was writing to a group of Christians whom he had been forced to leave behind. In his exhortation, Paul first challenged them to lead holy lives, especially as it concerned sexual purity. Then he reminded the Thessalonians that Christian holiness is never a cold formalism but is always joined to the virtue of Christian love. To chastity, he wrote, they must add charity.

One theologian who wrote much about Christian love was Francis Schaeffer. Schaeffer was known as a powerful defender of Christian doctrine, yet at the same time he strove to maintain love within the body of believers. He wrote:

> Through the centuries men have displayed many different symbols to show that they are Christians. They have worn marks in the lapels of their coats, hung chains about their necks, even had special haircuts. . . . But there is a much better sign . . . . It is a universal mark that is to last through all ages of the church until Jesus comes back.[2]

That mark is love among Christians, and Schaeffer proved this with Jesus' teaching in John 13:35: "By this all people will know that you are my disciples, if you have love for one another." This statement contains a condition, an *if* (if we love one another), followed by a result, a *then* (that people will identify us as disciples of Jesus). Schaeffer therefore set forth love as the priority for the church: "Evangelism is a calling, but not the first calling. Building congregations is a calling, but not the first calling. A Christian's first call is to . . . return to the first commandment to love God, to love the brotherhood, and then to love one's neighbor as himself."[3]

TAUGHT TO LOVE

The apostle Paul's teaching on Christian love agrees wholeheartedly with Schaeffer's emphasis. He wrote to the Thessalonians: "Now concerning brotherly love you have no need for anyone to write to you, for you yourselves have been taught by God to love one another" (1 Thess. 4:9). There are

2. Francis A. Schaeffer, *The Mark of the Christian*, vol. 4 of *The Complete Works of Francis A. Schaeffer* (Wheaton, IL: Crossway, 1982), 183.
3. Francis A. Schaeffer, *Genesis in Space & Time*, vol. 1 of *The Complete Works of Francis A. Schaeffer*, 85.

several ways to take Paul's statement that they do not need to be reminded about love. He might mean that they had learned about the priority of love from God's Word or that Paul had made this emphasis clear during his time among them. Paul probably means, however, that the work of God in their souls that prompted them to love fellow Christians was integral to their salvation. The expression "taught by God" reflects Jeremiah's language in foretelling the new covenant in Christ: "I will put my law within them, and I will write it on their hearts" (Jer. 31:33). According to John Calvin, Paul meant "that love was engraven upon their hearts, so that there was no need of letters written on paper . . . , but that their hearts were framed for love."[4]

Paul wrote in Romans 5:5 that "God's love has been poured into our hearts through the Holy Spirit who has been given to us." Loving others is an outflow of our relationship with God, who imparts his own love to us by the indwelling Holy Spirit. Because faith in Christ brings believers into the family of God, we feel "brotherly love" for one another that is analogous to the natural loyalty and affection of earthly family members. This love is so closely tied to Christian regeneration that the Bible makes it a test of true faith. John wrote: "Whoever loves has been born of God and knows God. Anyone who does not love does not know God, because God is love" (1 John 4:7–8).

Seeing the priority that Paul places on love should prompt us to consider our own hearts. Have our hearts been "framed for love" by God? Have we felt God's love poured into us as we believed the gospel? If not, we might still be seeking to approach God by our own works instead of relying on the finished work of Jesus Christ, God's chief gift of love. If we think little of the cross of Christ, we are likely to feel little love from God and have little love for him and others. But if we stand before the atoning sacrifice of God's perfect Son, seeing how Jesus gave himself in love so that we might be saved, it is simply impossible that we would be unmoved and unchanged by love. This is why Paul does not need to say that God taught Christians "concerning" love but has taught us "to love one another" (1 Thess. 4:9).

Paul is comforted to know not only that his readers have been taught to love by God, but also that they have a strong track record of brotherly love: "for that indeed is what you are doing to all the brothers throughout Macedonia" (1 Thess. 4:10). Since theirs was the leading city of a highly

4. John Calvin, *Commentaries*, 22 vols. (1854; repr., Grand Rapids: Baker, 2009), 21:276–77.

populated region, the Thessalonian Christians had frequent contact with merchants, farmers, and traders. They had taken advantage of opportunities to spread the gospel and had prayed for friends and acquaintances. As the gospel advanced, they had shown hospitality to fellow believers and helped to provide for their needs as they became known. In this way, God had used their fervor for Jesus Christ to set an example for other new converts (1:7) and to cause the gospel message to sound forth throughout their region (v. 8).

This was Paul's idea of a good church: a body of Christians filled with faith in Jesus Christ and overflowing with God's love for one another. So what should a good church like this do when commended for brotherly love? And what should be done by a Christian who has received God's love in faith and has started spreading that love through acts of mercy, service, and witness to others? According to Paul, the thing for such Christians to do is more of it! "We urge you, brothers, to do this more and more," he writes (1 Thess. 4:10).

Part of what makes Christianity so exciting is our awareness that there is always so much more of God's glory in which to find delight. There is more for us to know of the grace, goodness, and majesty of God. There is a more intimate relationship with the Savior awaiting us. And there is more of the wonderful grace of Christian love for us to embrace and share. Having been taught by God to love one another, we will "do this more and more."

Andrew Young points out that Christian love may grow in a number of directions: "It may grow in breadth as it reaches out to embrace more of our fellow Christians. It may grow in depth as it enters more deeply into the hurts and joys of others. And it may grow in length as it forbears more patiently and forgives more heartily. A commitment to love others well will cause us to grow more and more in this grace."[5] When we think in these terms, most Christians will realize that we have been only wading in the shallow waters of the love that God has for us to know and to show. God invites us farther out into the depths, which we first experience in his boundless love for us in Christ and then are called to share more and more deeply with more and more people.

QUIET LOVE

When studying Paul's letters, we are frequently reminded that they were written to actual people with real problems. Therefore, while Paul's teaching

---

5. Andrew W. Young, *Let's Study 1 & 2 Thessalonians* (Edinburgh: Banner of Truth, 2001), 73.

is grounded on universal truths about God and salvation, the letters apply the gospel in particular ways that fit the local needs of Paul's readers. His exhortations in 1 and 2 Thessalonians are prime examples of this principle. In the final chapter of 2 Thessalonians, Paul highlights a concern about some who were "walking in idleness" (2 Thess. 3:6; cf. 3:11). The Greek word *ataktos* may mean "disorderly," "irresponsible," or "lazy." Either such persons had entered into the church community or else some members of the church had fallen into this vice. It is possible that this happened as a self-serving response to the generosity of Christians who possessed means, so that the very love that Paul commended was being taken advantage of. Whatever the cause of this idleness, the result was that these people had become "busybodies" (3:11) who were not only using up resources but making themselves a nuisance to others.

Anticipating this problem, Paul amplifies his teaching on Christian love by urging his readers "to aspire to live quietly, and to mind your own affairs" (1 Thess. 4:11). Paul sees Christian love as a quiet love that avoids meddling in and disturbing the lives of others.

Paul's expression seems to involve an oxymoron, since he first uses a word that means "to strive with ambition" (Greek *philotimeisthai*, 1 Thess. 4:11). Normally, such striving involves a great outward display of energy (see Rom. 15:20; 2 Cor. 5:9). Here, however, Paul tells us to be ambitious in the pursuit of quietness. The Greek word for *quietly* (*asuxazo*) is the same term used in 1 Peter 3:4 when that apostle commended to Christian wives "the imperishable beauty of a gentle and quiet spirit." Christians, Paul means, should have a great ambition to lead steady, sober, useful lives that call attention not to themselves but to the grace of God in Christ.

Paul's statement not only challenges Christians but also points out a blessing that we enjoy. Christians can be content with who we are in Christ and do not have to make ourselves out to be something we are not. We do not need to make a fuss to draw attention or seek vain plaudits to prove the value of our lives. To be sure, there is an important place for ambition in the Christian life! We are to have "ambition to preach the gospel" (Rom. 15:20) and be "zealous for good works" (Titus 2:14). We should be eager in service (Phil. 2:28) and in spiritual attainments (1 Cor. 14:12). Yet we can do all this within a quiet life that avoids making difficulties for others.

How different this ambition is from the spirit of the world, which abhors the very thought of being quiet. A Christian leads a life that includes space for meditation and prayer. He may be content with an occupation that few consider glamorous but that allows him to provide for his family and do good in the world. Such a believer need not lie awake at night dreaming of being a fighter pilot or a star athlete, but may live quietly and unnoticed by the world yet aware that God delights in the humble service he offers in the name of Christ. A woman may give up career prospects to nurture the precious souls of her children in the home, not bothered by the scorn heaped on such domestic servitude by a self-centered society. The mere fact that we are Christians and members of Christ's glorious church fills us with awe for "the glory which shall be revealed in us" (Rom. 8:18 NKJV). We may "aspire to live quietly," so long as we are living fruitfully for Jesus within the providential setting of our lives.

One intended result of this quiet life is that loving Christians would "mind your own affairs" (1 Thess. 4:11). We may infer from this statement that Paul was concerned that some in this young church were quick to point out the errors in others' lives and to demand conformity to a long list of items that had little to do with serving Christ. Martin Luther wrote harshly of such people:

> They have the notion that they must control everything and superintend and criticize what others do. These are malignant persons. They stir up nothing but mischief and have no grace to do anything good, even though in other respects they may have excellent gifts. For they do not use their talents in their calling or in the service of their neighbor; they use them only for their own glory and advantage.[6]

When it comes to assessing others, Christians should labor to mind our own business. Paul once wrote, "Who are you to pass judgment on the servant of another? It is before his own master that he stands or falls" (Rom. 14:4). There, the issue concerned the eating of foods sacrificed to idols: Paul insisted that this was a matter for the individual conscience. In similar matters of varying opinions and individual prudence where obvious sin is not involved—such as styles of dress, books and movies, attitudes toward the moderate use of alcohol, and the choice of recreational activities, to name a

---

6. Martin Luther, *What Luther Says*, comp. Ewald M. Plass (St. Louis: Concordia, 1959), 1497.

few examples—Christians should exercise charity toward others and a wise love that knows how and when to respect privacy. We have plenty to do with our own business, and can afford to look graciously on the judgment calls that our fellow Christians make.

In warning us to mind our own business, Paul is not giving us an excuse to neglect the needs of others. When it comes to suffering, sickness, poverty, and affliction, our brothers' and sisters' concerns *are* our business. The same is true for fellow Christians who are wandering from the faith or falling into flagrant sin. Hebrews 3:13 urges us to "exhort one another every day, . . . that none of you may be hardened by the deceitfulness of sin." Usually, the harmful busybody and the useless idler are the same person. In 2 Thessalonians 3:11, Paul says that those who "walk in idleness, not busy at work," are the very people guilty of being "busybodies." Alexander Maclaren laments that "nothing dries up sympathy and practical help more surely than a gossiping temper, which is perpetually buzzing about other people's concerns, and knows everybody's circumstances and duties better than its own."[7] On the other hand, those who are most closely engaged in meeting real needs—physical, emotional, and spiritual—are least disturbed by individual differences and are most eager to cover a multitude of sins with Christlike love (1 Peter 4:8).

Busy Love

In calling Christians to brotherly love, Paul envisions a quiet love that is also a busy love. In addition to living quietly and minding their own affairs, the Thessalonians should "work with your hands, as we instructed you, so that you may walk properly before outsiders and be dependent on no one" (1 Thess. 4:11–12).

This verse has played an important role in developing a Christian view of work. Most Greeks thought that manual labor was unworthy of a cultivated person. Physical work was what slaves were for! In contrast, the Bible endorses the nobility of honest work of all kinds. Paul's example as a tentmaker underscored this point, since the hands that held the apostolic pen were calloused with the daily hard work by which Paul met his own needs. Paul was not glorifying manual labor over other forms of work, but since many of the

7. Alexander Maclaren, *Expositions of Holy Scripture*, 17 vols. (Grand Rapids: Baker, 1974), 15:186.

converts hailed from the working class, he was quick to affirm the importance and dignity of all honest labor, including work that some considered menial.

Given Paul's emphasis in these letters on the return of Christ, it is possible that some believers were so focused on waiting for the second coming that they stopped working and made themselves a burden to others. Yet Christ's own teaching states that when he returns, he wants to find his people busy! In his parable of the talents, Jesus said that he will ask us to show the work we have done on his behalf. If we have worked hard and profitably at what the Lord has given us to do, he will respond, "Well done, good and faithful servant. You have been faithful over a little; I will set you over much" (Matt. 25:21, 23). This work should be thought of as including both spiritual and temporal labor, which so often work together to advance Christ's kingdom. Along these lines, Martin Luther is said to have remarked that if he knew that the world would end tomorrow, today he would plant a tree. He meant that an awareness of Christ's return, the final judgment, and the transformation of all things in the end should not cause us to neglect the world and our duties in it but should cause us to cheerfully serve in all the various callings that we have received from the Lord.

Paul cites two reasons why it is important for Christians to work hard. The first is "so that you may walk properly before outsiders" (1 Thess. 4:12). For Christians to be lazy or wrongly depend on others only disgraces the gospel that we proclaim to the world. This is why Christians who run businesses should make a special point of providing high-quality goods and services and treating customers with honesty and care. By contrast, able-bodied men who are not working hard to provide for themselves and their families are a disgrace to God's people. Paul wrote scathingly in 1 Timothy 5:8: "If anyone does not provide for his relatives, and especially for members of his household, he has denied the faith and is worse than an unbeliever." In 2 Thessalonians 3:10, he commanded, "If anyone is not willing to work, let him not eat." Since Christianity "makes people better citizens and neighbors, better parents and relatives," unbelievers "should be able to look at the way Christians work and live and go away respecting them deeply."[8]

Paul's second reason for Christians to work hard is so that they can "be dependent on no one" (1 Thess. 4:12). Believers should provide for themselves so as not to burden other believers. This exhortation does not apply to those

8. Young, *Let's Study 1 & 2 Thessalonians*, 76.

who are unable to work because of illness, injury, or honest unemployment. The New Testament makes it plain that Christians are to provide for fellow Christians in legitimate need. But because there will often be many such needs, Christians should do their best not to burden the church and to contribute to the assistance of others. Love does not take advantage of Christian generosity but works hard so as to contribute to those with true needs. Paul saw such a desire as evidence of gospel change in our lives: "Let the thief no longer steal, but rather let him labor, doing honest work with his own hands, so that he may have something to share with anyone in need" (Eph. 4:28).

REVEALING LOVE

It is obvious that Paul considered the love of God at work in his people to be an important witness to the world. We may therefore conclude that the apostle urged the Christians to increase in a love that not only was *quiet* and *busy* but also bore witness to the gospel of Jesus Christ. Our love is thus to be a *revealing* love. According to church history, this is precisely what happened. Writing in the late second century, Tertullian of Carthage explained the spread of Christianity by the power of its love. "See, they say, how they love one another," Tertullian wrote, "for themselves are animated by mutual hatred; how they are ready even to die for one another, for they themselves will sooner put to death."[9]

Not only did the early Christians display love for one another, but as they were sprinkled throughout society in their various workplaces, they also spread the same love to the world. Tom Nelson writes:

> The Thessalonian believers did not become a monastic community or pull up stakes and head out en masse as Christian missionaries. These first-century believers saw their gospel stewardship through the lens of their vocations and stations in life. Having embraced the gospel, they were honoring Christ in the various vocations and stations of life they were in when they were called. The gospel was spreading like wildfire throughout the increasingly mobile Roman world, which was brimming with economic activity . . . , as these Christians were faithful to their callings to these arenas.[10]

9. Tertullian, *Apology*, 39.7, in *Ante-Nicene Fathers*, ed. Alexander Roberts and James Donaldson, 10 vols. (1885; repr., Peabody, MA: Hendrickson, 1999), 3:46.
10. Tom Nelson, *Work Matters: Connecting Sunday Worship to Monday Work* (Wheaton, IL: Crossway, 2011), 192.

The record of the early Christians brings us back to the importance of Archbishop Ussher's "eleventh commandment." Our witness to Christ in the world requires a verbal testimony to his gospel and obedience to his command: "Just as I have loved you, you also are to love one another" (John 13:34).

The kind of witness that Paul envisioned was given by an evangelist named Jakov before the fall of the Communist regime in Yugoslavia. The formal church there had been a pawn to the cruel tyrants, so that Jakov had a hard time getting people to listen to his claims about the love of Christ. Once, an old man named Cimmerman sharply upbraided Jakov about the terrible record of those who called themselves Christians. "They wear those elaborate coats and caps and crosses," he exclaimed, "signifying a heavenly commission, but their evil designs and lives I cannot ignore." Jakov defended true Christianity by comparing the situation to a man who stole Cimmerman's coat, put it on, broke into a bank, and ran off into the distance. "What would you say to them if they came to your house and accused you of breaking into the bank?" he asked. Cimmerman responded angrily, and Jakov went on to continue his work. Ravi Zacharias concludes the story:

> Jakov continued to return to the village periodically just to befriend Cimmerman, encourage him, and share the love of Christ with him. Finally one day Cimmerman asked, "How does one become a Christian?" and Jakov taught him the simple steps of repentance for sin and of trust in the work of Jesus Christ and gently pointed him to the Shepherd of his soul. Cimmerman bent his knee on the soil with his head bowed and surrendered his life to Christ. As he rose to his feet, wiping his tears, he embraced Jakov and said, "Thank you for being in my life." And then he pointed to the heavens and whispered, "You wear His coat very well."[11]

On the basis of Christ's teaching, Francis Schaeffer reminded us that the mark of the Christian is not worn on our lapels or hung on chains around our necks. The mark of the Christian before the world is the love that God has spread into our hearts, starting with our Christian brothers and sisters. We know that we can never be saved by our own loving works, but are forgiven only by the love of Christ, who died for our

---

11. Ravi Zacharias, *Can Man Live without God?* (Dallas: Word, 1994), 102.

sins on the cross. But as we tell the world about God's love for sinners in Christ, remembering the important testimony of Christ's love working in and through us, what an incentive we have to take up Paul's exhortation concerning brotherly love: "we urge you, brothers, to do this more and more" (1 Thess. 4:10).

15

THE COMING OF THE LORD

1 Thessalonians 4:13–18

For the Lord himself will descend from heaven with a cry of
command, with the voice of an archangel, and with the sound
of the trumpet of God. And the dead in Christ will rise first.
(1 Thess. 4:16)

*T*o be a Christian is to hold a particular understanding of
history. This point was made by Augustine of Hippo in his
great book *The City of God*. The Greco-Roman world in
which Augustine lived viewed history as a circular process without end.
Most non-Christians in the ancient world believed that the same things
would happen over and over without any ultimate meaning. Augustine
pointed out that the incarnation of God's Son and his atoning death on
the cross were nonrepeatable events showing that history moved forward
according to God's redemptive plan. Today, the secular humanist believes
in "progress," trusting man's ingenuity to solve problems and open up
new horizons of opportunity. Instead, the Bible-believer holds that history is racing toward the second coming of Jesus Christ, after which the
Lord will judge the world and God's eternal purposes of salvation will
be fulfilled. These differing views of history produce different kinds of

lives, a point that highlights the importance of biblical eschatology to the Christian.

Eschatology: Controversial but Important

The Greek word *eschatos* means "last," so eschatology is simply the study of the last things. According to the Bible, believers need to know where history is going, in terms of both our personal histories beyond the grave and God's plan for the future of the world. Geerhardus Vos asserted: "Ours is a religion whose centre of gravity lies beyond the grave in the world to come."[1] Christians are pulled forward, Paul said, by "our blessed hope, the appearing of the glory of our great God and Savior Jesus Christ" (Titus 2:13).

The importance of understanding Christ's return is seen in the example of the apostle Paul. It is evident that Paul highlighted teaching about Christ's return during his short stay in Thessalonica. When news later reached the apostle that the new believers were confused on this subject, he provided extensive information in both of his letters to them. "We do not want you to be uninformed, brothers" (1 Thess. 4:13), Paul wrote. Likewise, there is no reason for believers today to be uninformed about Christ's second coming.

The apparent difficulty in understanding the Bible's eschatology, however, deters many Christians from even trying. In previous centuries, many commentators declined to write about the book of Revelation and similar portions of the Bible, considering them hopelessly obscure (Martin Luther and John Calvin are notable examples). Fifty years ago, Leon Morris expressed concern over "the comparative neglect of the doctrine"[2] of Christ's return.

Few observers would make the same claim today, especially as a result of a lucrative cottage industry of end-times fascination. Speculative and fictional books such as *Left Behind* have topped the best-seller charts.[3] End-times fervor was especially high during the years leading up to the new millennium in the year 2000. When I was preparing to enter seminary in the early 1990s, one Christian friend tried to dissuade me, on the grounds

1. Geerhardus Vos, *Grace and Glory* (Grand Rapids: Reformed Press, 1922; repr., Edinburgh: Banner of Truth, 1994), 165.
2. Leon Morris, *The First and Second Epistles to the Thessalonians*, New International Commentary on the New Testament (Grand Rapids: Eerdmans, 1959), 136.
3. Tim LaHaye and Jerry B. Jenkins, *Left Behind: A Novel of the Earth's Last Days* (Wheaton, IL: Tyndale House, 1995).

that the world was certain to end within a few years—he employed impressive charts to prove this—and that I was going to waste my remaining time with my nose in books. More recently, Harold Camping predicted Christ's return for October 21, 2011. When that date passed without the end of the world, the television news showed Camping's dismayed followers, some of whom had sold their possessions to spread his false prophecy. In reaction to this kind of controversy, some believers are wearied by disputed details of Christ's return and embarrassed by the hysteria so often associated with eschatology. As a result, they are accepting a relative ignorance on the subject and churches are once again neglecting to teach on Christ's return.

Yet despite the error and hysteria sometimes attached to the subject, the coming of the Lord is a truth that Christians should labor to understand. Christ's second coming is, as Cornelis P. Venema puts it, "the great centerpiece of biblical hope and expectation for the future."[4] Moreover, the Bible's teaching is not as obscure on this subject as many would have it. Among our most important resources on Christ's return are Paul's letters to the Thessalonians. His remarkably clear teaching touches on Christ's return to earth, the rapture of the church, the resurrection of the dead, the final judgment and eternal punishment in hell, the coming Antichrist, the millennial question, and the eternal age of glory. As we study the final section of 1 Thessalonians and then the first two chapters of 2 Thessalonians, we will consider each of these matters, as well as Paul's applications on how our knowledge of future history should shape our present lives.

CHRIST'S PERSONAL RETURN

At the heart of Paul's eschatology are his statements regarding the "coming of the Lord" (1 Thess. 4:15). Focusing on the event itself, Paul highlights three features of the second coming. The first feature is *the personal return of the Lord Jesus Christ to earth*. Paul writes, "For the Lord himself will descend from heaven" (v. 16). Liberal scholars have viewed the personal return of Christ as "mythical" and "untenable" and have therefore recast the second coming as an existential symbol for the believer's spiritual enlightenment.[5]

---

4. Cornelis P. Venema, *The Promise of the Future* (Edinburgh: Banner of Truth, 2000), 79.

5. Rudolf Bultmann, "New Testament and Mythology," in *Kerygma and Myth*, ed. H. W. Bartsch (New York: Harper and Row, 1961), 4–5.

Yet the Bible teaches a literal, bodily return of the same Jesus Christ who died on the cross for our sins, rose from the grave, and then ascended into heaven. Acts 1:9 relates that two angels appeared to the disciples who had watched Jesus ascend. "This Jesus, who was taken up from you into heaven," they said, "will come in the same way as you saw him go into heaven" (Acts 1:11). Paul tells us that this promise will be fulfilled when Jesus physically returns on the clouds to the very world he departed.

The Greek word that Paul used for Christ's *coming* is *parousia*, which describes the arrival of a person. The word is used about the coming of Paul's helpers in 1 Corinthians 16:17 and even about the coming "lawless one" in 2 Thessalonians 2:9, but is most frequently employed for the return of Christ (sixteen times in the New Testament). When used with the definite article, *the parousia* is practically a technical term for "the great event anticipated by believers, when Christ the King returns to judge the living and the dead and complete his work of bringing all things into subjection to the Father."[6]

When we speak of Christ's return, it is important to remember the important ways in which Christ is near to his people during this current age, even as we await his return. In other words, in anticipating Christ's coming, we must avoid the mistake of neglecting Christ's presence with us now. The very language of "second coming" stresses that Christ has come before, and the implications of his first coming are essential for Christians. In the final words of Matthew's Gospel, for instance, the departing Jesus emphasized not his return but his abiding presence: "Behold, I am with you always, to the end of the age" (Matt. 28:20). Question 47 of the Heidelberg Catechism asks, "Then, is not Christ with us unto the end of the world?" The answer makes a careful distinction: "As a man, he is no longer on earth, but in his divinity, majesty, grace, and Spirit, he is never absent from us."

How is Christ near to us, even after he has physically departed? Christ is with his people as his Spirit ministers through God's Word, prayer, and the sacraments so as to save us through faith. On the night of his arrest, Jesus promised Peter: "Simon, Simon, behold, Satan demanded to . . . sift you like wheat, but I have prayed for you that your faith may not fail" (Luke 22:31–32). As believers now face similar threats to our salvation, we may have the same comfort that Peter possessed in Christ's saving presence. Jesus

6. Venema, *The Promise of the Future*, 82.

went so far as to tell his disciples that "it is to your advantage that I go away" (John 16:7), since once in heaven our Lord would send his Holy Spirit to us.

Yet how much better it will be when Christ returns. If his departure did not impoverish his people, Christ's return will enrich us even more. Therefore, while Christ's first coming was an advancement in salvation and his ascension to heaven was a further improvement to our situation, his glorious return will complete our salvation and bring into our experience the fullness of our hope in Christ. Hebrews 9:28 tells us: "Christ, having been offered once to bear the sins of many, will appear a second time, not to deal with sin but to save those who are eagerly waiting for him." Jesus put it in comforting terms when addressing his disciples' sadness over his looming departure: "If I go and prepare a place for you, I will come again and will take you to myself, that where I am you may be also" (John 14:3).

CHRIST'S VISIBLE, GLORIOUS RETURN

Paul's second emphasis regarding Christ's return is *the visible manifestation of his glory*. He writes: "For the Lord himself will descend from heaven with a cry of command, with the voice of an archangel, and with the sound of the trumpet of God" (1 Thess. 4:16).

This description rules out any idea of a hidden or invisible return of Christ. In Paul's clearest teaching of what is often called the *rapture*—a word that describes God's people as being "caught up"—Christ's return is anything but secret: "the dead in Christ will rise first. Then we who are alive, who are left, will be caught up together with them in the clouds to meet the Lord in the air" (1 Thess. 4:16–17). The visible nature of this event is amplified in related descriptions of Christ's return. Revelation 1:7 explains, "Behold, he is coming with the clouds, and every eye will see him." And Jesus taught: "They will see the Son of Man coming on the clouds of heaven with power and great glory" (Matt. 24:30).

Paul's description in 1 Thessalonians 4:16 emphasizes not only the visible but also the audible nature of Christ's coming: "The Lord himself will descend from heaven with a cry of command, with the voice of an archangel, and with the sound of the trumpet of God." The last thing that could be said about this future event is that it will be secret! This opposes popular views of the rapture that predict Jesus' coming to earth secretly to gather his people, only to depart with them for a tribulation period. It is clear in

Paul's description that when Christ comes to take his people forever (he concludes: "so we will always be with the Lord," v. 17), this event involves the visible, audible display of Christ's glory to all the earth. Jesus taught, "For as the lightning comes from the east and shines as far as the west, so will be the coming of the Son of Man" (Matt. 24:27).

Another word used to describe Christ's coming is *apocalypse*, which means "the revealing of things hidden." When Christ returns, the glory and majesty that were denied to him during his first coming will be fully manifest before all creation. Paul speaks this way in 2 Thessalonians 1:7, referring to the time "when the Lord Jesus is *revealed* from heaven with his mighty angels."

A third term that Paul uses is *epiphaneia*, which means "appearing." In Titus 2:13, he speaks of "the *appearing* of the glory of our great God and Savior Jesus Christ." These ideas are present in Paul's description of Christ as "descend[ing] . . . in the clouds" (1 Thess. 4:16–17). In his divine glory, the Son of Man will be revealed before all eyes, just as Jesus foretold his "coming in clouds with great power and glory" (Mark 13:26).

As the New Testament tells it, the problem with our present world is that it does not recognize the glory and majesty of Christ as God's Son and our Savior. This is a problem that believers sometimes feel, since we perceive Christ's glory and power only by faith, never by sight. Hebrews 2:7–9 addressed this problem. In his ascension, Christ was "crowned . . . with glory and honor," with "everything in subjection under his feet." The problem is that "at present, we do not yet see everything in subjection to him." It is not apparent or manifest in our outward experience that Christ is Lord over all, though by faith we know that he is "crowned with glory and honor because of the suffering of death." When Jesus returns, however, what was disclosed only to faith will be made manifest to all by sight. Then, Paul foretells, "at the name of Jesus every knee [will] bow, in heaven and on earth and under the earth, and every tongue confess that Jesus Christ is Lord, to the glory of God the Father" (Phil. 2:10–11).

CHRIST'S HISTORY-CONCLUDING RETURN

It is clear from Paul's teaching that *Christ's return will conclude and culminate all of history*. In addition to being a personal, visibly glorious return, the second coming will be Christ's history-concluding return.

In this respect, we should note that the coming and appearing of Christ in glory is not an event that *precedes* the final episode of God's plan for history but is rather an event that *brings about* the end of history. This rules out, again, an idea of the rapture in which Christ returns only to depart so that more history can be played out, since the return that Paul describes actually ends history. It also rules out the premillennial view of eschatology, the view that there will be a thousand-year period after Christ returns, during which God fulfills his purpose for the people of Israel, and after which occurs the final crisis of history. Instead, the return of Christ *is* the final crisis of history and the last day of which Scripture so frequently speaks. The return of Christ does not usher in additional phases of history, but is simultaneously the end of this present age and the consummation of the eternal age that is to come.

Consider, for instance, how Paul unites the visible return of Christ with the resurrection of the dead: "The Lord himself will descend from heaven with a cry of command, with the voice of an archangel, and with the sound of the trumpet of God. And the dead in Christ will rise first" (1 Thess. 4:16). In 2 Thessalonians, Paul joins Christ's return with the final judgment: "When the Lord Jesus is revealed from heaven with his mighty angels," he will inflict "vengeance on those who do not know God and on those who do not obey the gospel of our Lord Jesus" (2 Thess. 1:7–8; cf. vv. 9–10). So the same event in which Christ gathers his people, who "meet the Lord in the air" (1 Thess. 4:17), is also the event that includes the resurrection and final judgment. This agrees completely with Jesus' description in Matthew 25:31–32: "When the Son of Man comes in his glory, and all the angels with him, then he will sit on his glorious throne. Before him will be gathered all the nations, and he will separate people one from another as a shepherd separates the sheep from the goats." According to Jesus, the sheep are then summoned to "inherit the kingdom prepared for you from the foundation of the world" (Matt. 25:34). In this same vein, Paul concludes 1 Thessalonians 4:17 by assuring his readers that Christ's coming will bring them into the eternal glory for which they have been waiting: "and so we will always be with the Lord." These statements make it plain that Christ's return concludes this present age. Venema comments on the significance of this realization:

> When believers today expectantly look to the future, anticipating the return
> of Christ, they should do so as those who are convinced this will mark the

end of the present period of history and inaugurate the final state. All that believers hope for in respect to the future finds its focus in this consummating event, an event that will fulfill all the promises of God that have their "yes" and "amen" in Christ.[7]

What are the final results of history that are brought about by the coming of the Lord? The first is the judgment of all people who have ever lived. We confess this in the Apostles' Creed: Christ "sitteth on the right hand of God the Father Almighty; from thence he shall come to judge the quick and the dead." Paul's description of Christ's return includes a summons to this judgment, as the Lord descends "with a cry of command, with the voice of an archangel, and with the sound of the trumpet of God," as Christ appears "in the clouds" (1 Thess. 4:16–17). These phenomena—angel cries, trumpet blasts, and clouds of glory—frequently occur in the Bible in the context of God's judgment. When God gave the law to Moses on Mount Sinai, he came to a mountain sheathed in clouds and shaking with trumpet blasts (Ex. 19:16–19). Christ the Lord will return to judge the nations according to that same law. Revelation chapters 8–10 pictures mighty angels coming to earth, wrapped in clouds and blowing trumpets, signaling God's wrath upon the earth. G. C. Berkouwer comments that the coming of Christ "is the hour of giving account (1 Pet. 4:5). . . . It is the day that will disclose everything: 'each man's work will become manifest' (1 Cor. 3:13). It is the Lord in His coming, 'who will bring to light the things now hidden in darkness and will disclose the purposes of the heart' (1 Cor. 4:5)."[8]

The second result of Christ's return may be regarded as the reverse side of the final judgment, namely, the deliverance and vindication of those made righteous in Christ. The blowing of trumpets in the Bible signals not only God's judgment but also the gathering of God's people for salvation. William Hendriksen notes how the prophets spoke of blasting trumpets "as a signal of Jehovah's coming to rescue his people from hostile oppression (Zeph. 1:16; Zech. 9:14)." Just as Leviticus 25 called for the sounding of trumpets on the Day of Jubilee, signaling release from bondage and liberty for God's people, "so also this final trumpet-blast, the signal for the dead to arise, for the living to be changed, and for all the elect to be gathered from the four

7. Ibid., 95.
8. G. C. Berkouwer, *The Return of Christ* (Grand Rapids: Eerdmans, 1972), 156.

winds (Matt. 24:31) to meet the Lord . . . , proclaim[s] liberty throughout the universe for all the children of God."[9]

Third, Christ's return culminates history by fulfilling God's sovereign purpose in the eternal kingdom of Christ. This purpose was revealed to Daniel when he saw Christ as "a son of man" who came "with the clouds of heaven" to the "Ancient of Days" in order to receive "dominion and glory and a kingdom." The angel told Daniel that this begins an eternal reign: "His dominion is an everlasting dominion, which shall not pass away, and his kingdom one that shall not be destroyed" (Dan. 7:13–14). The same purpose for history is revealed in Revelation 11:15: "Then the seventh angel blew his trumpet, and there were loud voices in heaven, saying, 'The kingdom of the world has become the kingdom of our Lord and of his Christ, and he shall reign forever and ever.'" In Revelation 19:6–7, an angel assembles the guests for the marriage feast of the Lamb of God. That feast involved a festal chorus: "Hallelujah! For the Lord our God the Almighty reigns. Let us rejoice and exult and give him the glory, for the marriage of the Lamb has come, and his Bride has made herself ready." As Christians live in a world that flouts the rule of Christ's gospel reign, how glorious is our knowledge that his return will bring the fulfillment of God's purpose to exalt his Son as sovereign over all. When he comes, Paul wrote to the Philippians, every knee will bow and "every tongue confess that Jesus Christ is Lord, to the glory of God the Father" (Phil. 2:10–11).

CHRIST'S COMFORTING, IMPLORING RETURN

The purpose of this study has been to introduce Paul's teaching on Christ's second coming in his letters to the Thessalonians, which we will examine in greater detail as we continue working through the apostle's text. Paul will make his own applications to the particular situation of his readers, starting with their need to understand the death of believers in light of Christ's coming. In concluding this introductory study, however, we can make a few applications that flow generally from Paul's teaching on the second coming of Christ.

9. William Hendriksen, *1 and 2 Thessalonians*, New Testament Commentary (Grand Rapids: Baker, 1974), 117.

The first application is that we should receive and teach the second coming as a message of comfort for all who have trusted in Jesus for salvation. It is true that when our Lord returns, there will be a final judgment of all sin. But having trusted in Christ for our forgiveness and justification, we rejoice that "there is therefore now no condemnation for those who are in Christ Jesus" (Rom. 8:1). The Lord who comes in glory is the Savior who first came in humiliation and made atonement for our sins by his death. Christ's nail-scarred hands will hold the royal scepter, and his justice will demand our justification on the basis of his redeeming work. Berkouwer writes: "The believer knows of the ultimate revelation before the judgment seat, and he does not fear it. The wonderful message of the gospel of the *parousia* removes the possibility of sudden terror, and preaches instead a confidence for the last day. This is indeed a message of comfort."[10]

For this reason, Christ's return should not be taught to frighten Christians but to comfort us regarding the glorious salvation that will soon arrive in the coming of the One who loves us. The second coming should not be spoken of to our children in order to "scare them straight." The fear of being "left behind" should not cause believers to dread Christ's return. Rather, Paul says, in the trials and struggles of this present life of faith, we are "waiting for our blessed hope, the appearing of the glory of our great God and Savior Jesus Christ" (Titus 2:13). It is true that the New Testament warns believers to be awake and ready, but Paul asserts that by trusting in Christ, all believers can be confident in the day of his coming: "For God has not destined us for wrath, but to obtain salvation through our Lord Jesus Christ, who died for us so that whether we are awake or asleep we might live with him" (1 Thess. 5:9–10). Instead of dreading Christ's return, as so many believers have been made to do in recent years, we should take up the plea of the first Christians: "Come, Lord Jesus!"—to which our Savior answers, "Surely I am coming soon" (Rev. 22:20).

Second, since the coming of Christ will bring us into his presence in order to share his glory, Christians should begin glorying in Jesus now. One of the chief problems with so much end-times fervor today is that attention is devoted to practically everything except to Christ himself. Eschatologically speculative Christians rack their brains searching the newspapers for signs of the end instead of directing our hearts to our Lord, who will soon come

10. Berkouwer, *The Return of Christ*, 157.

and take us into his glory. Paul sums up his message of Christ's return with these words: "and so we will always be with the Lord. Therefore encourage one another with these words" (1 Thess. 4:17–18). Encouraged with the thought of being with Christ, let us treasure our present communion with him, the One who is near to his people in his Word, in the secret place of prayer, and at the communion table of his covenant meal. Let Christ's presence through the Holy Spirit be the glory of our church and our dearest treasure while we await the greater glory of his coming with the clouds.

Third, the return of Christ calls Christians to readiness in the midst of this "present evil age" (Gal. 1:4). Hebrews 4:3 warns us that there is no salvation apart from following Christ, since only "we who have believed [will] enter that rest." Meanwhile, believers who might be tempted to despair because of persecution, or led astray by the temptations of sin, or distracted by the siren songs of this world, "are encouraged by the prospect of Christ's return, when he will grant them relief from their present distress and victory over their enemies, who are also his."[11] Believers know that Christ is returning to receive us into his love forever, so we anxiously await that day, "prepared as a bride adorned for her husband" (Rev. 21:2).

Finally, the coming of the Lord presents a fearful prospect of judgment and condemnation for all whose sins have not been forgiven through the blood of Christ. The Lord will return, Paul warns, "in flaming fire, inflicting vengeance on those who do not know God and on those who do not obey the gospel of our Lord Jesus" (2 Thess. 1:8).

Knowing this, Christ's people urgently pray and tell others the good news of salvation from sin through faith in Jesus Christ. We declare the return of the great Judge, whose sword is sharp and whose books document every deed. We hold forth the grace and mercy of Christ for all who repent and believe, declaring his own words that "whoever . . . believes him who sent me has eternal life. He does not come into judgment, but has passed from death to life" (John 5:24). Therefore, we appeal to all who have not believed and thus face the prospect of eternal judgment in the coming of the Lord. Paul wrote: "In Christ God was reconciling the world to himself, not counting their trespasses against them, and entrusting to us the message of reconciliation. . . . We implore you on behalf of Christ, be reconciled to God. . . . Behold, now is the favorable time; behold, now is the day of salvation" (2 Cor. 5:19–6:2).

11. Venema, *The Promise of the Future*, 86.

16

GRIEVING WITH HOPE

1 Thessalonians 4:13–14

*But we do not want you to be uninformed, brothers, about those
who are asleep, that you may not grieve as others do who have
no hope. For since we believe that Jesus died and rose again,
even so, through Jesus, God will bring with him those
who have fallen asleep.* (1 Thess. 4:13–14)

In 1899, two prominent men died. The first was Colonel Robert G. Ingersoll, for whom the Ingersoll lectures on immortality at Harvard University are named, and who gave his brilliant mind to the refutation of Christianity. Ingersoll died suddenly that year, leaving his unprepared family utterly devastated. So grief-stricken was his wife that she would not allow his body to be taken from their home until the health of the family required its removal. His remains were cremated, and his funeral service was such a scene of dismay and despair that even the newspapers of the day commented on it.

The other man who died that year was Dwight L. Moody, the great Christian evangelist. He had been declining for some time, and his family had gathered around his bed. On his last morning, his son heard him exclaim, "Earth is receding; heaven is opening; God is calling." "You are dreaming,

Father," said his son. But Moody replied, "No, Will, this is no dream. I have been within the gates. I have seen the children's faces." Moody seemed to revive but then started to slip away again. "Is this death?" he was heard to say. "This is not bad; there is no valley. This is bliss. This is glorious." By now his daughter had come, and she began to pray for him to recover. "No, no, Emma," he said. "Don't pray for that. God is calling. This is my coronation day. I have been looking forward to it." After Moody died, his funeral was a scene of triumph and joy. Those in attendance sang hymns of praise to God. "Where, O death, is your victory," they exclaimed through faith in Jesus Christ. "Where, O death, is your sting" (1 Cor. 15:55).[1]

COMBATTING IGNORANCE

In writing to the Thessalonian Christians, Paul expressed concern that they did not possess full confidence in victory over death. He therefore wrote to them: "But we do not want you to be uninformed, brothers, about those who are asleep, that you may not grieve as others do who have no hope" (1 Thess. 4:13).

Scholars explain the Thessalonian problem in various ways. One version states that they were concerned that believers who had died would not be able to participate in the joyous reception of Christ when he returned. Another version holds that the believers thought that the dead who missed Christ's return would have their resurrection delayed. The dispensational view holds that Paul's readers feared that they had all missed the rapture, since they associated their sufferings with the tribulation that dispensationalism says will occur after the removal of all Christians. The weakness of these views is that they cannot explain Paul's concern that the Thessalonians should not grieve their dead with the same hopelessness as unbelievers. The problem was not fears regarding the joy of witnessing Christ's return, the timing of the resurrection, or the sequence of the rapture, but rather the fear that only those who were alive when Christ returned would finally be saved. Being uninformed about the situation of Christians who have died, they were tempted to grieve for them without hope.

This problem shows that the early believers expected Christ's return at

---

1. Quoted in Richard D. Phillips, *Hebrews*, Reformed Expository Commentary (Phillipsburg, NJ: P&R Publishing, 2006), 467.

any moment. Perhaps Paul's teaching on this and other subjects had been cut short by his hasty departure, so that there were still errors and doubts. In the meantime, some of their number had died, perhaps by violent persecution, and they feared that one had to be alive when Christ returned to experience the resurrection. Leon Morris writes: "What a calamity to be robbed of that great triumph by failing to live out the few years intervening, and this after having passed out of the darkness of heathendom into the light of the gospel!"[2]

Paul's response to this problem, as with other problems of Christian experience, is instructive. He expressed his desire that "we do not want you to be uninformed, brothers" (1 Thess. 4:13). The answer to questions of doubt, confusion, or distress is the plain teaching of God's Word. So many problems in the experience of believers today likewise stem from ignorance of biblical truth, so that the great need of God's people is the careful teaching of Scripture. Weak believers may be attracted to worship that is as exciting as it is brief, but their true need is to benefit from a ministry like that of the apostle Paul, who declared "the whole counsel of God" (Acts 20:27) and educated believers in the whole range of God's truth. The way for Christians to be strong in faith was given by Peter at the end of his second epistle: "But grow in the grace and knowledge of our Lord and Savior Jesus Christ" (2 Peter 3:18).

The Christian Attitude to Death

Paul's remarks in this passage summarize the Bible's teaching on death. Twice he uses the analogy of sleep to describe believers who have died: "But we do not want you to be uninformed, brothers, about those who are asleep . . . . God will bring with him those who have fallen asleep" (1 Thess. 4:13–14).

This is one of several places where the Bible describes the death of God's people as *sleep*. The Old Testament spoke of believers' "going to rest with your fathers" (Deut. 31:16 NIV). Luke said that when the martyr Stephen died, "he fell asleep" (Acts 7:60). The analogy primarily describes the appearance of the

---

2. Leon Morris, *The First and Second Epistles to the Thessalonians*, New International Commentary on the New Testament (Grand Rapids: Eerdmans, 1959), 136. For a cogent assessment of the various opinions, see G. K. Beale, *1–2 Thessalonians*, IVP New Testament Commentary Series (Downers Grove, IL: InterVarsity Press, 2003), 131–32.

body in death, after the soul has departed. Anyone who has attended a funeral involving the viewing of the body understands why it is described as *sleeping*.

Yet *sleep* does speak to the Christian experience in death as well, distinguishing it from that death which truly is death. In 1 Thessalonians 4:14, Paul says that "Jesus died." On the cross, Christ experienced all that death fully is under the wrath of God: he did not sleep but truly and fully died. But when Jesus spoke of Lazarus, who had died in Christ, his sins forgiven and his salvation assured, he declared: "Our friend Lazarus has fallen asleep, but I go to awaken him" (John 11:11).

There are several ways in which *sleep* is a helpful description of Christian death. First, sleep does us no harm, and this can also be said about death in Christ. Psalm 121:7 declares, "The LORD will keep you from all evil; he will keep your life." This is true for believers not only in life but also in death, since verse 8 proclaims that God keeps our lives "from this time forth and forevermore." Paul said, "The sting of death is sin, and the power of sin is the law" (1 Cor. 15:56). Christ satisfied the law by imputing his own righteousness to believers and took away the sting of sin by suffering sin's punishment in our place. A. W. Pink explains: "He underwent the full horror that is death and in doing so transformed death, so that for his followers it is no more than sleep."[3]

Second, just as sleep is beneficial for the living, death also benefits the Christian. Sleep is often the best prescription for those ailing from sickness or fatigue. Sleep restores the body, and the sleep of death does more for the soul: it transforms us into glory, removing every vestige of sin and sorrow. John Owen explains: "When, at death, the soul departs from the body, it is immediately freed from all weakness, disability, darkness, doubts and fears . . . and being freed their souls flourish and expand to their fullest extent."[4] Matthew Henry adds:

> Being still in union with [Christ,] they sleep in his arms and are under his special care and protection. Their souls are in his presence, and their dust is under his care and power; so that they are not lost, nor are they losers, but great gainers by death, and their removal out of this world is into a better.[5]

---

3. Quoted in Leon Morris, *Reflections on the Gospel of John* (Peabody, MA: Hendrickson, 2000), 407.
4. John Owen, *The Glory of Christ*, abr. R. J. K. Law (Edinburgh: Banner of Truth, 1987), 124.
5. Matthew Henry, *Commentary on the Whole Bible*, 6 vols. (Peabody, MA: Hendrickson, n.d.), 5:632.

This teaching refutes the idea of *soul sleep*, which claims that believers enter an unconscious state in death until Christ returns. Instead, the Bible teaches that our conscious selves will be awake in the glory of the Lord while our bodies sleep in the grave, awaiting their summons to resurrection. The Westminster Confession of Faith explains: "The souls of the righteous, being then made perfect in holiness, are received into the highest heavens, where they behold the face of God, in light and glory, waiting for the full redemption of their bodies" (WCF 32.1). This is why Paul wrote: "For to me to live is Christ, and to die is gain," adding, "My desire is to depart and be with Christ" (Phil. 1:21–23). This expresses the present gain and blessing that comes to Christians through death. Eric Alexander suggests that believers should therefore not speak of "sudden death," but rather of "sudden glory" for those who die trusting in Jesus.[6]

Third, like sleep, the death of a Christian is temporary. Winston Churchill expressed this conviction through his funeral. It was a sad occasion for Britain, the end of an era. Many eyes were weeping at St. Paul's Cathedral in London as the bugler sounded the slow, mournful notes of taps, evoking the sadness of death. But no sooner had the last note drifted away than the bugler played again. The tune was reveille, the notes with which soldiers are called to a new day. Churchill thus reminded his mourners that death leads to a new morning. Christians can likewise know that the sleep of our own deaths will end when a trumpet call summons us to greet our returning Lord.

Understanding the Bible's teaching, however, does not completely spare Christians from the grief of death. Death remains a fearful enemy that has invaded God's garden. Being informed of our hope keeps believers from grieving in ignorance, but it does not relieve all the suffering of grief over those who have departed from us. Here, Jesus' example at the tomb of his friend Lazarus is instructive. Jesus knew the answer of his resurrection: in fact, Jesus knew that in just minutes he was going to call Lazarus back to life. Still, standing before the horror of the grave, "Jesus wept" (John 11:35). So, too, believers grieve, often with great suffering over the presence of our enemy and the departure of those we love, even while we are sustained through faith in the life-giving promises of God's Word.

This hope enables Christians to come alongside grieving friends not only with the truth of God's Word but also with tears that flow from Christ's

6. Eric J. Alexander, *Our Great God and Saviour* (Edinburgh: Banner of Truth, 2010), 121.

heart. A notable example was provided by the famous Southern theologian Robert L. Dabney, who suffered grievously when his two young sons died, one after the other. Despite his faith, Dabney struggled emotionally over such great sorrow. Some years later, he visited a couple whose only child was sick and dying. "An eyewitness reported that Dabney gently walked through the house to the back parlor where the child was lying. The mother was on her knees near the child. Dabney . . . walked to the bed, knelt beside the mother, and gave way to a flood of tears. Then he offered a prayer for the parents and the boy—a prayer that could only have come from one capable of empathizing with the family's affliction." After the child had died and was buried, "the mother reported that Dr. Dabney's visit did her more good than all the visits and prayers of all other friends."[7]

The Christian Hope in Death

If Christians do "not grieve as others do who have no hope," how do unbelievers respond to the tragedy of death? Many answers are found in the inscriptions and writings of ancient pagan unbelievers. A popular inscription on Latin tombstones reflects the attitude of many today: "I was not; I became; I am not; I care not." A letter has survived from a woman named Irene to grieving friends. It reads: "I was as sorry and wept over the departed one as I wept for Didymas. . . . But nevertheless against such things one can do nothing. Therefore comfort ye one another."[8] Yet Irene had no comfort to give, believing that nothing could be done to overturn the tragedy of death. Geoffrey Wilson concludes: "The finality of death filled the heathen with a feeling of blank despair. It was a sorrow which was unrelieved by any hope of a future reunion with their loved one." In contrast to countless unbelieving writings that speak of death as a final end, a Christian inscription in one ancient catacomb speaks for all believers: "Alexander is not dead, but he lives above the stars and his body rests in this tomb."[9]

What are the biblical truths that give believers such hope in the face of death? Paul provides these truths in 1 Thessalonians 4:14: "For since we

7. James W. Bruce III, *From Grief to Glory* (Wheaton, IL: Crossway, 2002), 61–62.
8. Quoted in William Barclay, *The Letters to the Philippians, Colossians, and Thessalonians* (Louisville: Westminster, 1975), 203.
9. Quoted in Geoffrey B. Wilson, *New Testament Commentaries*, 2 vols. (Edinburgh: Banner of Truth, 2005), 2:166–67.

believe that Jesus died and rose again, even so, through Jesus, God will bring with him those who have fallen asleep." Christ performs three great works—two of which have already happened, and one for which we await—that give hope to believers in the grief of death.

The first cause for our hope is the sin-atoning death of Jesus Christ: "We believe that Jesus died" (1 Thess. 4:14). The source of our chief fear in death—God's just judgment of our sin and the eternal punishment it deserves—has already been removed by Jesus, who bore that punishment in the place of all who believe in him. Jesus taught, "Truly, truly, I say to you, whoever hears my word and believes him who sent me . . . does not come into judgment, but has passed from death to life" (John 5:24).

The Bible teaches that the very Lord who will return to judge the living and the dead is the Savior who died on the cross for the sins of his people. When Jesus raises his hand in judicial authority over the assembled human race, believers will rejoice to see on his hands the marks by which their own sins were forgiven forever. Moreover, dying believers know that the grave into which their bodies must be laid has already been consecrated by the body that Jesus offered for us. Because "we believe that Jesus died," we know that sinners are reconciled to God by the grace that sent Jesus to the grave on our behalf. Therefore, we know that the words of Psalm 116:15 will apply to us: "Precious in the sight of the Lord is the death of his saints."

The second cause for the Christian hope in death is the resurrection of Jesus Christ: "We believe that Jesus died and rose again" (1 Thess. 4:14). Christ has conquered death by his own resurrection, and in this way has guaranteed the resurrection of all who confess their sins and trust in him. The resurrection proves to believers that our Savior still lives and reigns with power to complete our salvation. Paul further stated in 1 Corinthians 15:20 that Christ's resurrection is proof that all his people will likewise be raised from the dead: "Christ has been raised from the dead, the firstfruits of those who have fallen asleep." This means that the future resurrection of all believers is the continuation of Christ's resurrection conquest of death. His resurrection was the firstfruits, and the resurrection of all Christians will be the full harvest. "Each in his own order," Paul wrote: "Christ the firstfruits, then at his coming those who belong to Christ" (v. 23). Thomas Watson explained:

> Christ did not rise from the dead as a private person, but as the public head of the church; and the head being raised, the rest of the body shall not always lie in the grave. . . . As the first-fruits is a sure evidence that the harvest is coming, so the resurrection of Christ is a sure evidence of the rising of our bodies from the grave. Christ cannot be perfect as he is Christ mystical, unless his members are raised with him.[10]

Finally, and as the conclusion of his sequence, Paul asserts that Christ, having died and risen from the grave, will return with all the souls under his care: "We believe that Jesus died and rose again, even so, through Jesus, God will bring with him those who have fallen asleep" (1 Thess. 4:14). Since the souls of sleeping believers are present with the Lord (2 Cor. 5:8), it follows that his return includes their return to earth. J. Philip Arthur thus writes that Christ's return "will not be a solitary return; he will be escorted by an enormous multitude, for he 'will bring with him those who sleep in Jesus.'"[11] Therefore, when a fellow believer dies, Christians should never say, "We will never see him again!" Instead, Christians should rejoice in the certain hope that we will see beloved Christians when Christ returns, when together with Jesus all the people of God in heaven will join those on earth for the resurrection glory of the Lord.

There is some question about the precise meaning of the expression "through Jesus" (1 Thess. 4:14). Paul says that "through Jesus, God will bring with him those who have fallen asleep." This suggests that it is the Father who ensures that believers who have died will come back for the resurrection, and that God accomplishes this "through Jesus" and his mighty saving work. Some commentators hold instead that believers return "with Jesus" or that the resurrection and rapture are accomplished "through Jesus" in his return. Whatever the precise arrangement of Paul's argument, his main point is clearly made: believers who die in Christ through faith will return with Christ, by the Father's will, to participate in his second coming and join their resurrected bodies in the glory of the Lord.

The comfort that Paul offers differs absolutely from the hopeless grief of the unbelieving world. Unlike the ancient Irene, who vainly urged comfort while admitting that nothing could be done, Paul urges the believers to

10. Thomas Watson, *A Body of Divinity* (Edinburgh: Banner of Truth, 1958), 306.
11. J. Philip Arthur, *Patience of Hope: 1 and 2 Thessalonians Simply Explained*, Wellwyn Commentary Series (Ross-shire, UK: Evangelical Press, 1996), 66.

166

"encourage one another with these words" (1 Thess. 4:18). This encouragement rests on the solid foundation of what God has done and will yet do: "For since we believe that Jesus died and rose again, even so, through Jesus, God will bring with him those who have fallen asleep" (v. 14).

Hope Even in Grief

Our knowledge of the present glory of believers who have died and the future glory for all who believe in Jesus should shape our grief so that we are not overcome but are encouraged by hope.

Earlier, I mentioned the grief of Robert L. Dabney after the death of his sons. Dabney was a brilliant teacher of the very doctrines that Paul brought to the minds of the grieving Thessalonians. Yet he admitted that he struggled to apply them with complete comfort to his own sorrow-filled heart. Dabney wrestled over the death of his first son, Jimmy, in a poem entitled "Tried, but Comforted," expressing both his struggle and the comfort that he ultimately received from the truth of God's Word:

Five summers bright our noble boy
Was lent us for our household joy;
Then came the fated, wintry hour
Of death, and blighted our sweet flower.

They told me, "Weep not, for thy gem
Is fixed in Christ's own diadem;
His speedy feet the race have run,
The foe have 'scaped, the goal have won."

. . . .

Then, thus I heard their anthem flow:
"Praise Him, all creatures here below;
Praise Him above, ye heavenly host;
Praise Father, Son, and Holy Ghost."

But how, I said, can this sad heart
In joyful praises bear its part?
It hath no joy; it naught can do
But mourn its loss and tell its woe.

167

And then I thought, What if thy lost
Is now among that heavenly host,
And with the angel choir doth sing,
"Glory to Thee, Eternal King"?

. . . .

Oh! that for once mine ear might hear
That tiny voice, so high, so clear,
Singing Emmanuel's name among
Those louder strains, that mightier throng.

Oh! that but once mine eyes could see
That smile which here was wont to be
The sunshine of my heart, made bright
With Jesus' love, with Heaven's light.

Then would my burdened heart, I know,
With none but tears of joy o'erflow.

Having comforted himself with the hope of glory into which he had
committed his dear, departed son, Dabney could embrace the challenge of
faith during this present life. The poem concludes with words of advice to
all Christians who grieve the bitterness of loss while looking with hope to
the coming of Christ:

'Tis not for sight and sense to know
Those scenes of glory here below;
But be it ours to walk by faith
And credit what our Savior saith.

Let patience work till we be meet
To dwell in bliss at Jesus' feet;
Then death, once dreaded, friendly come,
And bear us to our lost one's home.

Then shall that glorious hour repay
The woes of all that dreary way,
And I shall hear forever more
My seraph boy his God adore.

Yea, he shall teach this voice to raise,
As angels taught him, Heaven's lays;
And I, who once his steps did lead,
Shall follow him to Christ, our Head.[12]

ALIVE IN CHRIST

Everything that Paul wrote of our hope in death and that Robert Dabney gained for his comfort in grief is true only in the way that Paul insisted in 1 Thessalonians 4:14: "through Jesus." It is only those who have "died to sin" (Rom. 6:2), confessing their guilt and turning to Jesus for forgiveness and new life, who now can be "alive to God in Christ" (v. 11), with the sure hope of a resurrection to come. It is Dwight L. Moody, who lived by faith in Christ, who was able to die in faith with hope and joy, in contrast to Robert Ingersoll, who did not live in faith and therefore could not find any hope in death. Since it is "through Jesus" that God brings souls back from heaven for a resurrection into glory, it is urgent that sinners come now to Jesus in faith to receive eternal life. To those who believe in him—and to these only—Jesus spoke words of consolation and hope: "I am the resurrection and the life," adding, "Whoever believes in me, though he die, yet shall he live" (John 11:25). Paul anticipates this resurrection life when he concludes: "And so we will always be with the Lord" (1 Thess. 4:17). This is our hope as well, if only we come to Jesus for salvation now, humbling ourselves in faith and adoring him as Lord, seeking the eternal life he grants to all who call on his name and believe in him.

12. Quoted in Bruce, *From Grief to Glory*, 62–64.

17

THE RESURRECTION
OF THE DEAD

1 Thessalonians 4:14—17

*For the Lord himself will descend from heaven with a cry of
command, with the voice of an archangel, and with the sound
of the trumpet of God. And the dead in Christ will rise first.*
(1 Thess. 4:16)

Many recipes contain a secret ingredient without which
the dish is not properly prepared. For instance, without
oregano your spaghetti sauce isn't really Italian. A chef
can bake apples in a pie, but without cinnamon it isn't apple pie. Put meat,
tomatoes, and onions in a broth, but it still won't be chili until you add the
cumin.

In a similar way, the gospel contains a secret ingredient, apart from which
our salvation falls short of the genuine article. All Christians know that
Christ forgives our sin so that when we die, we go to heaven. But fewer Christians realize that "going to heaven when we die" is not our final blessing. For
after believers have gone to heaven, the day will come when Christ returns
to earth and his people will be raised in the glory of the final resurrection.

According to Paul, this is the hope that sustains God's people in the trials of this life. "The sufferings of this present time are not worth comparing with the glory that is to be revealed to us," he writes. We wait now with hope for "the redemption of our bodies," when we will finally "obtain the freedom of the glory of the children of God" (Rom. 8:18–23). How bland the Christian hope must be—like apple pie without cinnamon—if we forget the resurrection of the dead!

The resurrection is absolutely necessary for our salvation. Without the resurrection of the body, Christians may be forgiven of our sins, but we are not delivered from the futility of our present mortal existence. If the dead are not raised, then despite our justification through faith in Christ, our sanctification will never be complete and we will remain eternally unfit for the glories of Christ's kingdom. "I tell you this, brothers," Paul wrote: "flesh and blood cannot inherit the kingdom of God, nor does the perishable inherit the imperishable" (1 Cor. 15:50). This is why he was so determined to inform his readers of the resurrection, the knowledge of which brings spice to our present lives of faith: "For the Lord himself will descend from heaven with a cry of command, with the voice of an archangel, and with the sound of the trumpet of God. And the dead in Christ will rise first" (1 Thess. 4:16).

Paul's teaching on Christ's return in 1 Thessalonians 4 is an eschatological treasure trove. While addressing the salvation of believers who have died, Paul gives straightforward teaching about Christ's return, life after death, the rapture, and the resurrection of the dead. Each of these topics is worthy of study from this vital passage. In considering the resurrection, we will ask a number of important questions, receiving answers that will not leave us uninformed (1 Thess. 4:13), but will encourage us with the apostle's words (v. 18).

WHAT IS THE RESURRECTION OF THE DEAD?

The first question to ask is: What is the resurrection of the dead? The Greek word for resurrection is anastasis, which comes from a verb that means "to raise up." The resurrection, then, is the raising of our bodies after we have died. The Westminster Confession states that "the dead shall be raised up, with the selfsame bodies, and none other . . . , which shall be united again to their souls forever" (WCF 32.2).

171

It is important to note the bodily nature of the resurrection, because this truth has often been neglected or assailed. The ancient Greeks tended to view the body as ignoble and unworthy, so that in the ancient mystery religions, salvation involved an escape from the body. But the Bible values the body as God's good creation, and Christian salvation positively affects our bodies, both now and forever. Christians are not to be radical ascetics who harmfully deny the body (1 Tim. 4:3–5) or libertines who sinfully misuse the body. Paul reasons: "Do you not know that your body is a temple of the Holy Spirit[?] . . . So glorify God in your body" (1 Cor. 6:19–20). Cornelis P. Venema writes: "The same Lord who forgives all our sins is the One who 'heals all our diseases', including that sickness of body and soul that leads to death (Ps. 103:3). Thus no biblical picture of the believer's future may fail to include as a central part the promise of the resurrection of the body."[1]

The Bible states many times that the final resurrection pertains to our bodies. David wrote in Psalm 16:9–10 that "my whole being rejoices; my flesh also dwells secure. For you will not abandon my soul to Sheol, or let your holy one see corruption." Job exclaimed in wonder: "For I know that my Redeemer lives, and at the last he will stand upon the earth. And after my skin has been thus destroyed, yet in my flesh I shall see God" (Job 19:25–26). Paul teaches that "since we believe that Jesus died and rose again, even so, through Jesus, God will bring with him those who have fallen asleep" (1 Thess. 4:14). By *even so*, Paul means "in the same way," so that Christ's bodily resurrection was the forerunner of that resurrection for which believers hope.

There is a vital difference between the future resurrection and the way in which the dead were resuscitated during Jesus' ministry. When Jesus called Lazarus back from the grave, for instance, Lazarus received his old body back to life, with all its flaws, limitations, and mortality. Before long, Lazarus would die again. But the future resurrection will involve the eternally glorious transformation of the bodies of Christ's people. The prototype we have is the resurrected body of Jesus. It was a true body, capable of being touched and of eating and drinking (Luke 24:39–43), but also capable of appearing and disappearing and passing through locked doors (John 20:19), as well as shining with the glorious light of heaven (Acts 9:3). This is pre-

1. Cornelis P. Venema, *The Promise of the Future* (Edinburgh: Banner of Truth, 2000), 365.

cisely the kind of body that believers will inherit in the resurrection, since Paul states that Christ "will transform our lowly body to be like his glorious body" (Phil. 3:21).

In the future resurrection, our same bodies that lived and died will be raised. The body is not simply replaced with a new body but is changed into a glorified body suitable for the new heavens and new earth in which Christ will reign forever in glory. Geerhardus Vos writes: "There is not a simple return of what was lost in death; the organism is returned endowed and equipped with new powers[;] . . . there are added faculties and qualities which should be regarded as super-normal from the standpoint of the present state of existence."[2] Thus, we see that while we tend to look forward to the entry of our souls into heaven, the Bible emphasizes the resurrection as a greater blessing awaiting both the living and the dead with the return of Christ. N. T. Wright observes: "Resurrection is something new, something the dead do *not* presently enjoy; it will be life *after* 'life after death.' "[3]

Realizing that our bodies will be raised and glorified should transform how Christians think about our present lives. The resurrection conveys dignity to the most humble Christian soul and body, both of which are destined to "shine like the brightness of the sky above" (Dan. 12:3). Our bodies are holy to the Lord. Reminding us that our bodies are united with Christ "in a resurrection like his," Paul urged, "Let not sin therefore reign in your mortal body, to make you obey its passions" (Rom. 6:5, 12). The next time you are tempted to use your body to sin, remember that it is intended by God to be transformed for a holy eternal existence.

The resurrection of the dead is a great comfort to those who grieve the loss of loved ones, or who face the ravaging of their own bodies as death approaches. Ultimately sin and death will claim nothing from anyone who has trusted in Christ: the very body of every believer will be redeemed and brought to glory. What hope this gives as we grieve the loss of a father, whose voice once instructed us, knowing that we will hear that same voice singing praises to Christ in glory; or a mother, whose hands so tenderly ministered to our needs and will yet again clasp us in renewed strength. So Paul exulted, "God raised the Lord and will also raise us up by his power" (1 Cor. 6:14).

2. Geerhardus Vos, *The Pauline Eschatology* (Princeton, NJ: Princeton University Press, 1930; repr., Phillipsburg, NJ: P&R Publishing, 1994), 154–55.

3. N. T. Wright, *The Resurrection of the Son of God* (Minneapolis: Fortress, 2003), 215.

WHO WILL BE RAISED FROM THE DEAD?

A second question asks: *Who* will be raised from the dead? The Bible's answer is that everyone who has ever lived will be raised in the body on the last day when Jesus returns. Paul speaks of the "dead in Christ" as rising when Jesus returns (1 Thess. 4:16), but the Bible elsewhere informs us that all will be resurrected to stand in their bodies before the final judgment, receiving either eternal punishment or reward. The angel spoke of this to Daniel in the Old Testament: "Many of those who sleep in the dust of the earth shall awake, some to everlasting life, and some to shame and everlasting contempt" (Dan. 12:2). Jesus was even more emphatic, teaching that "an hour is coming when all who are in the tombs will hear his voice and come out, those who have done good to the resurrection of life, and those who have done evil to the resurrection of judgment" (John 5:28–29).

It is clear in these statements that while believers and unbelievers will alike be raised, they will experience radically different results. Jesus taught that on the day of judgment he will "separate people one from another as a shepherd separates the sheep from the goats" (Matt. 25:32). This indicates that there will be a tangible difference between the resurrection of the godly and the ungodly. To his justified people, on his right hand, Jesus will declare, "Come, you who are blessed by my Father, inherit the kingdom prepared for you from the foundation of the world" (v. 34). It will be exactly the opposite for the ungodly: "Then he will say to those on his left, 'Depart from me, you cursed, into the eternal fire prepared for the devil and his angels'" (v. 41).

The final judgment that immediately follows the resurrection should worry unbelievers greatly. God has told us in the Bible how history will end. In this present age, there is no outward difference between those who believe in Christ and those who deny him. And when the two are compared in this world, unbelievers often seem to come out ahead. Even Christians sometimes wonder what difference it makes to follow Christ, given how things often turn out in this world. Asaph felt this way in Psalm 73, "until," he said, "I discerned their end" (Ps. 73:17). Then Asaph remembered that for the ungodly, despite whatever pleasures the present may hold, at the final judgment "they are destroyed in a moment, swept away utterly by terrors!" (v. 19).

The Bible declares a resurrection judgment to those who have not believed and therefore still bear the wrath of God for their sins. Samuel Waldron explains: "Though the unjust are raised, theirs is a very strange and paradoxical resurrection. Though they are raised physically, they are not raised to 'life,' but to 'death.' In the highest sense, theirs is not a resurrection—a restoration to true life—at all."[4] It is by God's mercy that this warning is given now, so that we may turn in faith to Jesus Christ, who died for the forgiveness of sins. "Believe in the Lord Jesus," the Bible says, "and you will be saved" (Acts 16:31).

The coming resurrection not only warns unbelievers to turn in faith to Christ, but also challenges believers in their attitude toward all other people. In his famous essay "The Weight of Glory," C. S. Lewis urged us to remember the eternal significance of every person we will ever know:

> The dullest and most uninteresting person you can talk to may one day be a creature which, if you saw it now, you would be strongly tempted to worship, or else a horror and a corruption such as you now meet, if at all, only in a nightmare. . . . It is with the awe and the circumspection proper to them, that we should conduct all our dealings with one another, all friendships, all loves, all play, all politics. There are no *ordinary* people. You have never talked to a mere mortal. . . . But it is immortals whom we joke with, work with, marry, snub, and exploit—immortal horrors or everlasting splendours.[5]

WHEN WILL THE DEAD BE RAISED?

If Paul tells us what the resurrection is and who will be raised, we necessarily wonder *when* the dead will be raised. His clear answer is that the resurrection of the dead will occur when Jesus returns from heaven to earth in all his glory: "For the Lord himself will descend from heaven with a cry of command, with the voice of an archangel, and with the sound of the trumpet of God. And the dead in Christ will rise first" (1 Thess. 4:16).

Passage after passage in the Bible tells us that the resurrection will take place when Christ returns, as the immediate precursor to the final judgment of all mankind. Jesus combines these three events—return, resurrection,

4. Samuel E. Waldron, *The End Times Made Simple* (Amityville, NY: Calvary Press, 2003), 209.
5. C. S. Lewis, *The Weight of Glory and Other Addresses* (New York: Macmillan, 1980), 18–19.

The Resurrection of the Dead

and judgment—in Matthew 25:31–32: "When the Son of Man comes in his glory, and all the angels with him, then he will sit on his glorious throne. Before him will be gathered all the nations." Jesus said that "all who are in the tombs will *hear his voice* and come out" (John 5:28–29), a description echoed in Paul's statement that Christ will return "with a cry of command" (1 Thess. 4:16). Elsewhere, Paul again joined Christ's return with the resurrection: "each in his own order: Christ the firstfruits, then *at his coming* those who belong to Christ" (1 Cor. 15:23).

According to premillennialism, there will be two distinct resurrections: the raising of the godly before a literal thousand-year reign of Christ and then the resurrection of the ungodly after Christ's millennial reign on earth. This is supposedly supported by Paul's statement in 1 Thessalonians 4:16 that "the dead in Christ will rise first." The problem with this interpretation is that Paul is not comparing the resurrection of the just to that of the unjust, but rather is comparing the resurrection of the dead to the transformation of believers who are still living when Christ returns. We can see Paul's point if we keep reading into verse 17: "And the dead in Christ will rise first. Then we who are alive, who are left, will be caught up together with them." Paul is not describing, first, the believers' resurrection and, second, the unbelievers' resurrection. Rather, he speaks of those who are dead in Christ and then those believers who are still living.

As we have seen, the Bible clearly teaches that the resurrection is a single event involving both the just and the unjust at the time of Christ's return. Revelation 20 informs us that at the end of the millennium, which is best understood as the present gospel age (a view known as *amillennialism*), all mankind—saved and unsaved—will stand before Jesus to be separated in the judgment. John saw this in his revelation of glory: "I saw the dead, great and small, standing before the throne, and books were opened. Then another book was opened, which is the book of life. And the dead were judged by what was written in the books, according to what they had done" (Rev. 20:12). Here is fulfilled the scene prophesied in Daniel 12:2, in which the godly and the ungodly stand in one judgment. Two books are present in this judgment—one condemning sin and the other recording salvation—because of the two kinds of people who are raised: "Those who sleep in the dust of the earth shall awake, some to everlasting life, and some to shame and everlasting contempt."

HOW WILL THE DEAD BE RAISED?

A fourth question that we should ask about the resurrection is *how* the dead will be raised. This question may be approached in two ways: first, asking, "By what power does the resurrection take place?" Paul answers in 1 Thessalonians 4:16 by pointing to emblems of divine authority and power: "For the Lord himself will descend from heaven with a cry of command, with the voice of an archangel, and with the sound of the trumpet of God. And the dead in Christ will rise first." Here, God's sovereign power is symbolized in Christ's return by the call of the archangel and the trumpet blast of God. Just as Jesus often used external signs to make obvious the divine nature of his miracles, Wilhelmus à Brakel explains: "This resurrection will not have a natural cause—as if those bodies could again be brought to life after a period of time by certain motions, changes, and transformations. This can neither be accomplished by an angel nor any other creature. Rather, this is a work of omnipotence and will therefore be performed by God, the Creator of heaven and earth."[6]

Jesus said that "the Father raises the dead and gives them life" (John 5:21). Realizing this divine cause for the resurrection should relieve any concerns over how bodies long decayed or otherwise damaged can ever be raised. To be sure, belief in the resurrection evokes respect for the bodies of the dead, which is why Christian faith has historically resulted in a strong preference for burial over cremation.[7] But just as God created all things out of nothing, no barriers can thwart the Almighty in raising our bodies to glory on the last day.

A second way to approach the *how* of the resurrection concerns the nature of our transformation: How will believers be changed when our bodies are raised? This matter is most fully addressed by Paul in the fifteenth chapter of 1 Corinthians: "Someone will ask, 'How are the dead raised? With what kind of body do they come?'" (1 Cor. 15:35). The apostle answers by outlining four dimensions to the transformation of the believer's body in the resurrection.

First, the resurrected body is *imperishable* so as to partake forever in the reign of Christ: "What is sown is perishable; what is raised is imperishable"

6. Wilhelmus à Brakel, *The Christian's Reasonable Service*, 4 vols. (Grand Rapids: Reformation Heritage, 1995), 4:328.

7. See Richard D. Phillips, "Is Cremation Appropriate for Christians?," available at http://www.tenth.org/resource-library/articles/is-cremation-appropriate-for-christians.

(1 Cor. 15:42). Our current bodies are prone to disease and decay, our natural beauty fades over time, and ultimately the body gives way to death. But in the resurrection "the mortal puts on immortality," so that "death is swallowed up in victory" (v. 54).

Second, the resurrection body is *glorious*: "It is sown in dishonor; it is raised in glory" (1 Cor. 15:43). The term *dishonor* is usually used by Paul with reference to the disgrace of sin, to which our bodies have been corrupted in their present desires (see Rom. 1:26; 2 Cor. 6:8; 11:21). But in the resurrection, our bodies will shine in the glory of perfect holiness.

Third, the resurrection body is *mighty*: it "is sown in weakness" but "raised in power" (1 Cor. 15:43). Unlike our current condition that so often falls short of what we desire, the resurrection body "serves God tirelessly and powerfully in the redeemed creation."[8]

Finally, whereas we presently inhabit "a natural body," the resurrection body is *spiritual* in nature: "It is raised a spiritual body" (1 Cor. 15:44). This statement does not mean that the resurrection body lacks material substance, but rather that it is ideally designed for the spiritual life in the age of glory with Christ. As an imperishable, glorious, powerful, and spiritual body, the resurrection body will be, as John Owen writes, "a blessed instrument for the soul's highest and most spiritual activities."[9]

WHY WILL THE DEAD BE RAISED?

This study of Paul's teaching on the resurrection leaves two vital questions unanswered. A fifth question is: *Why* will the dead be raised? The best answer for the *why* of salvation is always this: that God may be glorified in the mighty working of his grace. We see Christ glorified as he descends on the clouds before all the earth (1 Thess. 4:17). Describing a similar scene, when Christ ascended into heaven, Daniel said: "To him was given dominion and glory and a kingdom, that all peoples, nations, and languages should serve him; his dominion is an everlasting dominion, which shall not pass away, and his kingdom one that shall not be destroyed" (Dan. 7:14). Thoughts of Christ's return should likewise expand our notions of the majesty of our Lord and the grandeur of his saving work. Responding to this same scene,

8. Waldron, *The End Times Made Simple*, 213.
9. John Owen, *The Glory of Christ* (Edinburgh: Banner of Truth, 1994), 125.

the angelic powers in heaven "fell on their faces and worshiped God, saying, 'We give thanks to you, Lord God Almighty, who is and who was, for you have taken your great power and begun to reign'" (Rev. 11:16–17).

There is another reason why the dead are raised on the last day, a reason given by Paul at the end of 1 Thessalonians 4:17: "And so we will always be with the Lord." The eternal age of glory is designed to fulfill the covenant purpose of God: "Behold, the dwelling place of God is with man. He will dwell with them, and they will be his people, and God himself will be with them as their God" (Rev. 21:3). God's purpose in salvation is "to purify for himself a people for his own possession" (Titus 2:14). Yet we cannot be forever with the Lord unless we are first made like the Lord, at least as far as this is possible for mere creatures. Thus, the final stage and climax of God's saving purpose in all of history is the resurrection of his people, who are vindicated in the final judgment and gathered into a perfect, eternal communion with Christ so that "we will always be with the Lord."

According to Paul, knowing about our future glory in communion with God is the encouragement designed to keep us going through the hard times of this present life of faith. Paul never tells believers that God has promised to make us winners now, with everything going smoothly in a carefree present life. Instead, the apostle admits the tribulation of our present life of faith and points ahead for encouragement to the glory yet to be revealed: "For this light momentary affliction is preparing for us an eternal weight of glory beyond all comparison" (2 Cor. 4:17). This is why Christians today need to be biblically informed about Christ's return and the resurrection of the dead, so that our hope may be fulfilled in the promise of Christ's return. This is how even a most afflicted saint such as Job could lift up his head rejoicing in the midst of great sorrows: "For I know that my Redeemer lives, and at the last he will stand upon the earth. And after my skin has been thus destroyed, yet in my flesh I shall see God . . . . My heart faints within me!" (Job 19:25–27).

HOW DO WE KNOW THAT WE WILL BE RAISED?

This leaves one last, vitally important question: *How do we know* that we will be raised? How can we be sure that there will be a resurrection of all the dead on the last day, the just into glory and the unjust into eternal

179

death? Paul gives the answer in 1 Thessalonians 4:15: "For this we declare to you by a word from the Lord."

Paul does not seem to be referring to any statement of Christ's that is known to us, so this is probably a revelation given directly by the risen Jesus to the apostle. What matters is Paul's reminder that the Bible is God's revealed Word of truth. Who else knows what God has planned for the future but God himself? Where else can we learn about life beyond the grave and the end to the history of the world than from the One who is the Alpha and Omega of all things? Why, then, should we appeal to the fancies of men or charlatan spiritualists, who cannot penetrate beyond the grave and do not know the future plans of God, when we have "a word from the Lord" to tell us the future? If the Bible is true, as it can be shown to be by its many proofs, then God's Word is the message to which we must affix our hopes and commit our hearts in faith.

There is one last way to consider the resurrection. The vital question is not merely how I can know that there will be a future resurrection. The more important question is how I can know that in that resurrection I will be raised to the glory of eternal life, rather than to the condemnation of eternal punishment that I deserve for my sins. The answer to this vital question is found in our stance toward Jesus Christ now. According to Jesus, those who are raised for vindication in the final judgment are those who were chosen by God in sovereign grace and thus trusted in Christ for salvation. "All that the Father gives me will come to me, and whoever comes to me I will never cast out," Jesus declared (John 6:37). "And this is the will of him who sent me, that I should lose nothing of all that he has given me, but raise it up on the last day" (v. 39). Who are the people who were given to Jesus by the Father and will be received by him in glorious joy on the day of his coming? Jesus answered in a way that sets before our feet today the very matter that will decide our eternal destiny then: "For this is the will of my Father, that everyone who looks on the Son and believes in him should have eternal life, and I will raise him up on the last day" (v. 40). Learning about the future from God's Word, we have the ultimate application as it concerns our faith in Christ now. Paul stated the matter succinctly in his second letter to the Corinthians: "Behold, now is the favorable time; behold, now is the day of salvation" (2 Cor. 6:2).

18

MEETING THE LORD IN THE AIR

1 Thessalonians 4:16–18

Then we who are alive, who are left, will be caught up together
with them in the clouds to meet the Lord in the air, and so we
will always be with the Lord. (1 Thess. 4:17)

S ince the 1970 publication of Hal Lindsey's best-selling book *The Late Great Planet Earth*, dramatic images of the rapture have dominated evangelical thinking. Lindsey described his idea of the rapture in the words of a fictional reporter: "There I was, driving down the freeway and all of a sudden the place went crazy[:] . . . cars going in all directions . . . and not one of them had a driver." A sports journalist noted: "Only one minute to go and they fumbled—our quarterback recovered—he was about a yard from the goal when—zap—no more quarterback—completely gone, just like that!" A United Nations spokesman announced to "all peace-loving people of the world that we are making every human effort to assist those nations whose leaders have disappeared."[1] Images like these have been replayed in Christian novels and movies, depicting believers as suddenly vanishing without a trace. The moral is clearly stated in youth-camp and revival sermons: when Christ returns, don't be left behind through sin or unbelief!

1. Hal Lindsey, *The Late Great Planet Earth* (Grand Rapids: Zondervan, 1970), 136.

The term *rapture* comes from the Latin word *rapio*, which the Vulgate translation employed for the Greek word *harpazo*, which Paul uses in 1 Thessalonians 4:17. The apostle says that believers "will be caught up" to meet the Lord when he returns. Whereas allusions to the rapture may be seen in other Bible passages, the event is directly stated only in this verse, which explains that when Christ returns and "the dead in Christ" have been raised, then "we who are alive, who are left, will be caught up together with them in the clouds to meet the Lord in the air" (vv. 16–17).

EVALUATING THE "SECRET" RAPTURE

The understanding taught in Lindsey's popular book and accepted by many evangelicals today is a view that was virtually unknown before the mid-nineteenth century. This doctrine, which is called the *secret rapture*, teaches that Christ's second coming will take place in two stages, one before and one after a seven-year period of tribulation. The first stage of Christ's return is a secret rapture because only believers are aware that it is happening (except for the cars that crash without drivers and athletes who disappear from football games!). The secret rapture removes all Christians so that they will not suffer the tribulation prophesied in the Bible. For this reason, the *secret rapture* is also called the *pretribulation rapture*, language that is a standard feature of dispensational premillennialism. This teaching holds that after the Christians are removed and a seven-year tribulation is completed, Christ will come in visible glory to judge his enemies and inaugurate a literal thousand-year reign on the earth, after which comes the final judgment and the eternal state.

Teachers of the pretribulation, secret rapture will usually admit that the key features of their doctrine are not found in 1 Thessalonians 4:17, the only verse in the Bible to describe the rapture directly. For instance, John MacArthur writes that "no solitary text of Scripture makes the entire case for the pretribulation Rapture."[2] This being true, advocates of this view

---

2. John MacArthur, *1 & 2 Thessalonians* (Chicago: Moody, 2002), 135. Noted books advancing the dispensational view include Charles C. Ryrie, *Dispensationalism* (Chicago: Moody, 2007); and J. Dwight Pentecost, *Thy Kingdom Come: Tracing God's Kingdom Program and Covenant Promises throughout History* (Grand Rapids: Kregel, 1995). Noted books critically evaluating dispensationalism include Keith A. Mathison, *Wrongly Dividing the People of God* (Phillipsburg, NJ: P&R Publishing, 1995), and Vern Sheridan Poythress, *Understanding Dispensationalists* (Phillipsburg, NJ: P&R Publishing, 1993).

make their case not on the direct teaching of any Bible passage but from inferences taken from Scripture on the basis of a presupposed system of doctrine.

On what basis, for instance, is it claimed that Christ's return will take place in two or more events separated by many years? The primary reason is that dispensational teaching presumes that God has separate agendas for the people of Israel and the Christian church. Believing this, the church age is seen as ending with the rapture, after which God resumes his work for the saving of ethnic Israel. Hence, the separation of Israel and the church yields a two-stage return of Christ. Arguments are then marshaled to defend this scheme. Primary among them is the observation that some descriptions of Christ's return include the judgment of the wicked, whereas others do not, which is taken to prove that there are two different stages in Christ's return. Since Christ's first return is not seen to involve a worldwide judgment, this rapture is described as secret. Presuming as well that Christians do not endure the end-times tribulation, this secret rapture occurs before the dreadful events that presage Christ's final return.

Taken together, these assertions combine to form a unified system of teaching. It is not one, however, that can survive careful biblical scrutiny. For starters, the key supposition that Israel and the church represent different plans of God is contrary to the New Testament's whole way of thinking. Over and over again, the New Testament uses Old Testament images for Israel in describing the church, thus identifying the old covenant and new covenant people of God as one people. In Romans 11, Paul describes Gentile Christians with the Old Testament symbol of Israel as an olive tree: "You, although a wild olive shoot, were grafted in among the others and now share in the nourishing root of the olive tree" (Rom. 11:17). This teaches not that Gentile Christians form a different work in God's saving plan but rather that they have been organically joined to God's redeeming work for Israel. Hebrews 12:22 appropriates Israel's exodus imagery in describing the gathering of Christians for worship: "You have come to Mount Zion and to the city of the living God, the heavenly Jerusalem." One of the more potent proofs of the unity between Israel and the church is the cloud imagery that Paul uses in 1 Thessalonians 4:17. The glory cloud led Israel through the exodus into the Promised Land, and in Christ's coming the same cloud will escort his people into the promised final glory. It is this kind of covenant theology that led Paul to write to Gentile Christians: "Peace and mercy . . . upon the Israel of God" (Gal. 6:16).

Just as the Bible does not separate Israel and the church, so also the two-stage return of Christ is not supported by Scripture. It is true that different versions of Christ's return present different elements, for the simple reason that individual passages are making particular points. At the end of 1 Thessalonians 4, Paul addressed concerns regarding believers who have died, so his answer focuses on how Christ's return involves their resurrection. There was no reason, in making this point, to mention the judgment of the ungodly. As Paul continues in chapter 5, however, he addresses a different question, one pertaining to the timing of Christ's coming. Here, he does mention Christ's judgment on the wicked: "Sudden destruction will come upon them" (1 Thess. 5:3). Remembering that the original manuscripts did not include chapter divisions, and reading the passage in its plain sense, we find no reason to take Paul as describing two different events, one without judgment and the other with judgment. Other key passages, such as Matthew 24:29–44, present Christ's return as a single event featuring both the judgment of unbelievers (vv. 30, 38–39) and the gathering of Christ's people (vv. 31, 40–41). The strong parallels between Paul's teaching in 1 Thessalonians and Jesus' teaching in Matthew 24 indicate that Paul likewise envisions a single coming of the Lord in both judgment and salvation.[3]

It is even more obvious that the coming of Christ as described by Paul is anything but a secret. In fact, it is mystifying how believers who claim a literal interpretation of the Bible, as dispensationalists do, can describe as secret an event that is announced "with a cry of command, with the voice of an archangel, and with the sound of the trumpet of God" (1 Thess. 4:16). Leon Morris argues, "It is difficult to see how [Paul] could more plainly describe something that is open and public."[4] Kim Riddlebarger agrees: "The whole thrust of the three-fold announcement is that God himself will proclaim the return of Jesus Christ so loudly that the whole earth will hear."[5] The images in so much popular Christian literature of unbelievers' searching for

3. See G. K. Beale, *1–2 Thessalonians*, IVP New Testament Commentary Series (Downers Grove, IL: InterVarsity Press, 2003), 136–38.

4. Leon Morris, *The First and Second Epistles to the Thessalonians*, New International Commentary on the New Testament (Grand Rapids: Eerdmans, 1959), 145.

5. Kim Riddlebarger, *The Case for Amillennialism* (Grand Rapids: Baker, 2003), 143.

missing Christians with no idea that Christ has come are utterly contrary to the Bible's depiction.

Moreover, the doctrine that Christians are raptured before the great tribulation is thoroughly refuted by any number of Bible verses that warn Christians to be prepared to endure these very trials. In his teaching on his return in Matthew 24, Jesus warns believers not to be deceived by false christs and then warns that "they will deliver you up to tribulation and put you to death, and you will be hated by all nations for my name's sake" (Matt. 24:9). Jesus says nothing about believers' being removed before this tribulation, but warns them instead to endure it without falling away: "The one who endures to the end will be saved" (v. 13). Furthermore, Jesus' statement that "for the sake of the elect those days will be cut short" (v. 22) makes little sense if his people have previously been removed from the earth. Only when a prior grid is presupposed can a natural reading of the New Testament yield a pretribulational removal of Christ's people.

It should be stressed that the secret rapture is believed almost exclusively by Christians who hold a high view of the Bible's authority and are courageously devoted to Jesus. The point of assessing and critiquing their teaching is not to mock them but rightly to handle the Word of Truth. Riddlebarger's summary is offered in this spirit of respectful disagreement: "The dispensational theory of the secret rapture cannot be justified from the Scriptures. The Bible teaches that though there are different aspects involved, they are all part of one event—the blessed hope—when Jesus Christ will come again on the last day to judge the world, raise the dead, and make all things new."[6]

The Triumphant Conqueror

The widespread prevalence of "secret rapture" teaching has made it necessary to critique its distortion of the Bible. But we have not yet answered this question: What is the rapture? If there are not two different events in Christ's return, if it is not secret, and if it is not designed to remove Christians before a period of tribulation, then what *does* Paul teach about Christ's coming to rapture his church?

6. Ibid., 145.

One valuable clue to understanding Paul's meaning is to recognize the cultural and political background in which he was writing. Scholars agree that the word *parousia*, which Paul uses for Christ's "coming" (1 Thess. 4:15), was widely used in the Roman world to describe formal visitations of the emperor or other high officials to a city.[7] This connection is strengthened by Paul's use of the Greek word *apantesin* to say that believers will "meet" the Lord in the air (v. 17). Gene Green comments that this word "was almost a technical term that described the custom of sending a delegation outside the city to receive a dignitary who was on the way to town."[8] There can be little question that Paul's Thessalonian readers would have understood his terminology in this way, since their own recent history included visitations by prominent leaders such as Pompey the Great and Octavian Caesar. In his sermon on this text, the ancient preacher John Chrysostom understood Paul's meaning in just this way: "For when a king drives into a city, those who are honorable go out to meet him; but the condemned await the judge within."[9]

Understood this way, Paul depicts the return of Christ as the coming of a great king, a conquering emperor returning to his capital to celebrate a triumphal parade. The hero appeared outside the gate with his army, and his supporters joyously went out from the city to meet him. One custom was for loyal subjects to present the emperor with a crown to wear while in their city, an idea that Paul employed when he described the faithful believers as his "crown of boasting before our Lord Jesus at his coming" (1 Thess. 2:19). Then, with all his loyal people around him, the triumphal ruler entered the city in order to take up his rule and bask in his people's praise. When Julius Caesar returned from his victories in 49 B.C., Cicero wrote, "Just imagine what a royal welcome (*apantesis*) he is receiving from the towns, what honors are paid to him."[10] How much greater will be the glory of Christ when he comes, not to remove his adoring people from the earth but to bring them with him into the creation that he comes to reclaim and fill with his glory.

---

7. See, for instance, Herman Ridderbos, *Paul: An Outline of His Theology* (Grand Rapids: Eerdmans, 1975), 536–37.

8. Gene L. Green, *The Letters to the Thessalonians*, Pillar New Testament Commentary (Grand Rapids: Eerdmans, 2002), 226.

9. Quoted in Peter Gorday, ed., *Colossians, 1–2 Thessalonians, 1–2 Timothy, Titus, Philemon*, Ancient Christian Commentary on Scripture, New Testament 9 (Downers Grove, IL: InterVarsity Press, 2000), 90.

10. Quoted in Ben Witherington III, *1–2 Thessalonians: A Socio-Rhetorical Commentary* (Grand Rapids: Eerdmans, 2006), 138.

TO MEET THE LORD IN THE AIR

If the imperial visitation provides a background for Paul's description of Christ's return, how should we understand the details of his rapture teaching? What does it mean for believers to be "caught up . . . in the clouds" and "to meet the Lord in the air" (1 Thess. 4:17)?

Paul's statement that believers will be "caught up" gives us the word *rapture* (Greek *harpazo*). Elsewhere this same Greek word is used of the taking of a kingdom by force (Matt. 11:12), a wolf's snatching sheep (John 10:12), and the deacon Philip's being torn away from the Ethiopian eunuch (Acts 8:39). These examples make the point of the suddenness by which Christ draws his people in sovereign power. John MacArthur describes it as "a strong, irresistible, even violent act. . . . It is when living believers are caught up so that they are transformed and receive their glorified bodies."[11]

The question is raised as to whether Paul means for us to envision a literal lifting up of believers into the atmosphere. Critical scholars such as N. T. Wright bemoan the "astonishing literalness in popular fundamentalism" that sees Paul as envisaging "Christians flying around in mid-air on clouds."[12] It is true that Paul employs apocalyptic language here that is elsewhere meant symbolically, but it is also true that 1 Thessalonians is a letter that is otherwise taken in a straightforward, literal sense. The best way to understand Paul's teaching, then, is to note the symbolism he employs and then to understand his description in as literal a manner as possible.

The worldwide nature of the rapture, which requires that "every eye will see him" (Rev. 1:7), seems to preclude us from thinking of Christ's appearing over London, New York City, our own hometown, or any other localized area. At the same time, when Jesus ascended into heaven, the disciples did see him rising up through the sky. The angels who appeared said that he would return "in the same way as you saw him go into heaven" (Acts 1:11). There is undoubtedly great mystery about this event from our present perspective; it is a supernatural intervention beyond our previous experience. G. K. Beale writes: "The old-world reality will be ripped away, and the dimension of the new, eternal reality will appear along with Christ's 'presence.' . . . Just as one can lay flat a map of the whole world and see it all at one glance, so Christ

11. MacArthur, *1 & 2 Thessalonians*, 134–35.
12. N. T. Wright, *The Resurrection of the Son of God* (Minneapolis: Fortress, 2003), 215.

will appear and be able to behold humanity at one glance and they him. . . . A new dimension will break into the old physical dimension . . . . God and the Lamb will form a 'tabernacling' presence over all redeemed believers."[13]

The imagery of clouds has a rich background in the Bible. Elijah was translated to heaven in a cloud of glory, as Jesus was in his ascension. On the Mount of Transfiguration, "a cloud came" and overshadowed Jesus, Moses, and Elijah (Luke 9:34), and when Solomon dedicated the temple of Mount Zion, "a cloud filled the house of the LORD" with the "glory of the LORD" (1 Kings 8:10–11). As we noted earlier, the glory cloud led Israel through the exodus wilderness, and in the rapture that same cloud will reappear to escort Christ's people into the final glory. Herman Ridderbos thus states that the cloud in Paul's rapture vision "constitutes the manifestation of the glory of Christ, in which his own are permitted to participate."[14] Here biblical symbolism and literal interpretation meet, for while we should understand the symbolism of clouds as the Son of Man's chariot, there is no reason for believers to doubt that in the supernatural cataclysm of Christ's return we will literally see the *shekinah* glory and be caught up into it.

Just as the cloud has a symbolic significance, the same is true of the "air" where believers will meet the Lord. The air is the region between heaven and earth. It is significant that believers are not caught up to meet Christ in heaven but in the airy outskirts of earth, for Christ will have returned from heaven to redeem the earth in glory (Rom. 8:22–23). The air is sometimes compared to the realm of spiritual powers, as when Paul described Satan as "the prince of the power of the air" (Eph. 2:2). But evil will no longer hold sway in the air, for there Christ will be revealed as the triumphant Savior and Lord over all.

Furthermore, we should consider Paul's statement that "we who are alive, who are left," will experience the rapture (1 Thess. 4:17). This refers to Christians who are living when Christ returns, in contrast with "the dead in Christ" who are first raised (1 Thess. 4:16). It is worth noting that Paul's language is exactly opposite of the "left behind" fantasy portrayals, in which it is the ungodly who are left behind. For Paul, it is "we who . . . are left." This lines up with Jesus' teaching on the second coming in Matthew 24, where he compares his return to Noah's flood. In that earlier judgment, the wicked

13. Beale, *1–2 Thessalonians*, 138–39.
14. Ridderbos, *Paul*, 535.

were swept away and believers were left behind on the earth, emerging from Noah's ark into a new and cleansed world. Jesus said that something similar will happen in his second coming: "Then two men will be in the field; one will be taken and one left. Two women will be grinding at the mill; one will be taken and one left" (Matt. 24:40–41). This does not depict a two-stage coming of Christ but rather two fates on the day of judgment. Paul employs the same language, in which those "left behind" are not the ones who miss out on the rapture, but rather are those left behind from the cleansing judgment in Christ's return. Our fervent desire as Christians is to be left behind after Christ's cataclysmic judgment so that we may "always be with the Lord" (1 Thess. 4:17).

FOREVER WITH THE LORD

Paul's teaching of the rapture has several implications, the first of which may be regarded as political. As Paul adapts the political customs of the Roman Empire in his rapture teaching, he makes a statement about worldly powers and the sovereignty of Christ.

We have noted how Paul's terms *parousia* and *apantesis* had a political meaning in the Roman world. Another word was equally claimed by both Christ and Caesar: the word *kurios*, which means "lord." We know from church history that the early Christians refused to ascribe ultimate lord-ship to the emperor, many of them suffering death rather than bowing to Caesar's image and saying, "*Caesar estin kurios*," "Caesar is Lord." With his information about Christ's appearing as Lord over all, Paul is challenging Caesar's sovereignty and urging his converts not to grant ultimate allegiance to the secular state. To be sure, Paul taught believers to obey rulers placed over them (Rom. 13:1–5), but only with the clear understanding that the highest authority belongs to Christ. N. T. Wright has aptly expressed Paul's intent: "Jesus was Lord . . . and Caesar was not. . . . Paul's answer to Caesar's empire is the empire of Jesus."[15]

Christians who face persecution today should remember, therefore, that history will end with Christ's triumph, in which his glory will seize all the "air time" and his ultimate authority will be displayed for all to see. In

15. N. T. Wright, "Paul's Gospel and Caesar's Empire," in *Paul and Politics: Ekklesia, Israel, Imperium, Interpretation*, ed. R. A. Horsley (Harrisburg, PA: Trinity, 2000), 182–83.

America today, few Christians have been persecuted, yet an increasingly militant government makes growing claims on our consciences. Courts threaten Christians for refusing to permit sexual deviancy on their campuses or among their employees. Recently, a court case challenging the right of denominations to enforce the biblical morality of their ministers went all the way to the Supreme Court before being defeated. Most recently, the federal government has pressured Christian businesses and colleges to include abortion funding as part of their medical insurance. Must Christians yield to Caesar in the church and in matters of Christian conscience where Jesus alone should rule? Paul answers by showing us how history will end, with the power and authority of Christ placing all else under his feet. At his sovereign return, all who trusted him and obeyed his Word will meet him in the air, joining the triumphant Lord as he manifests his uncontested reign over the entire universe.

Paul's vision not only shows the true power in the universe but also provides a vision of glory that should motivate us to persevere through tribulation. It is said that when a Roman conqueror rode through the capital city in his triumph, a slave was assigned to ride behind him on his chariot, both to hold a golden laurel wreath over his head and to whisper in his ear that all glory is fleeting. So it is for all the fame, fortune, and glory that men and women sell themselves to gain in this present world. But in the return of Christ, there will be a glory that is not fleeting. Then "the earth will be filled with the knowledge of the glory of the Lord as the waters cover the sea" (Hab. 2:14). Here is a glory beyond all imagining, providing us with ample incentive to persevere in the midst of earthly troubles, in the deadly persecutions that our Christian brothers and sisters are suffering now around the globe, and even in the great tribulation that is foretold before the coming of the Lord. As the exalted Jesus declared in Revelation 3:21: "The one who conquers, I will grant him to sit with me on my throne, as I also conquered and sat down with my Father on his throne."

Finally, as Paul urges us to "encourage one another with these words" (1 Thess. 4:18), we focus on his concluding statement: "and so we will always be with the Lord" (v. 17). The souls of Christians who die go immediately to "be with Christ" (Phil. 1:23) in heaven. Those who have trusted Christ in this life, loved the Lord, and served his gospel "will be caught up together" (1 Thess. 4:17) and thus will be with the Lord forever. Death will bring no final loss to those of us who live in Christ now and reign with him then. We will together enjoy the perfect fellowship for which we have so longed in this life, each of us joined together in love by the great love of Christ that will be our all in all.

ENCOURAGED BY THESE WORDS

What an encouragement Christians receive now from the knowledge of Christ's glorious, saving return. First, we have a strong incentive *to live as followers of Christ*. This world, with its temptations to sin, is seen passing swiftly away. The reality that is found in Christ will soon appear forever, so that wise believers are glad to live now for his sake. Second, we are greatly emboldened *to witness the gospel of Christ* to a lost and dying world. Jesus said, "All authority in heaven and on earth has been given to me. Go therefore and make disciples of all nations, baptizing them in the name of the Father and of the Son and of the Holy Spirit" (Matt. 28:18–19). Third, Christ's coming encourages us *to labor for building up the church and advancing the kingdom of Christ*. Jesus urges us to "seek first the kingdom of God" (6:33). "Blessed is that servant," he says, "whom his master will find [serving] when he comes" (Luke 12:43). Fourth, we are encouraged *to love one another as Jesus has loved us*, realizing that we will be caught up in order to be together forever with the Lord. The relationships that we forge now in Christian worship, fellowship, and service will literally last forever. And the most valuable thing that you and I will ever behold before seeing Jesus in glory is one another: precious saints purchased with the blood of Christ.

Finally, Paul's teaching urges everyone *to come to Christ in saving faith*. The encouragement of which he spoke is valid only for those who have believed in Jesus. What will become of those who refuse Jesus now and thus remain guilty of their sins on the day of his coming? One hymn laments their fate: "The day of grace is past and gone; trembling they stand before the throne, all unprepared to meet him." How much better to be forgiven of our sins now so as to anticipate Christ's return with joy! Then we will sing with joy: "Beneath his cross I view the day when heav'n and earth shall pass away, and thus prepare to meet him."[16]

16. William B. Collyer, "Great God, What Do I See and Hear!" (1812).

When Jesus returns, with heaven and earth passing away, those who are caught up in the air to meet him will return with him to the new heavens and the new earth. How many people close their hearts, fearing that they will lose the world if they put their faith in Christ! In the end, however, the very opposite will be true. Christians do, in many respects, lose this present world, especially its sinful pleasures, when they give their allegiance to Christ. But when he returns, they will be left when all others are taken away in judgment, to meet him in the splendor of his glory. Then, believers in Christ will gain the new world together with him. Trusting in his promise, we call to him now, together with all the rest of his adoring people, saying, "Amen. Come, Lord Jesus!" (Rev. 22:20).

19

LIKE A THIEF IN THE NIGHT

1 Thessalonians 5:1—4

For you yourselves are fully aware that the day of the Lord will
come like a thief in the night. While people are saying, "There
is peace and security," then sudden destruction will come upon
them as labor pains come upon a pregnant woman,
and they will not escape. (1 Thess. 5:2–3)

Stephanie and Ray left the suburbs for a safer home in the country after being burglarized while on vacation. A visit from ex-convicts Matt Johnston and Jon Douglas Rainey, however, proved that Stephanie and Ray were no more safe in the country than they had been closer to town. Johnston and Rainey were hosts of the Discovery Channel show *It Takes a Thief,* and the ease with which they broke in and stole valuable property week after week before a national audience shows how vulnerable anyone is to a trained and motivated burglar. Their example shows why the expression "a thief in the night" is one that evokes fear and dread.

THE DAY OF THE LORD

It seems from Paul's letter that the Thessalonian Christians were worried about what might occur to them on some dark night. Having earlier addressed their concern about the destiny of believers who had died, Paul now responds to their concerns about the timing of Christ's return. "Now concerning the times and the seasons, brothers," he writes, "you have no need to have anything written to you" (1 Thess. 5:1). The two words for "times and seasons" (*chronos* and *kairos*) correspond roughly to "length of time" and "sequence of events." The Thessalonians were concerned, we may infer, about the timing of Christ's return, lest they be unprepared when Jesus came. Paul responded that he had covered this topic thoroughly during his time among them: "You have no need to have anything written to you. For you yourselves are fully aware that the day of the Lord will come like a thief in the night" (1 Thess. 5:2).

Before we criticize these early believers for fretting over a matter about which they had already been taught, we should realize the sober nature of the subject. In 1 Thessalonians 4:15, Paul had written about "the coming of the Lord." Now he describes the same event with the designation "the day of the Lord." If we understand the meaning of this term, we will better understand their concern about the timing and sequence of events in its coming.

"The day of the Lord" is an expression with its origin in the prophetic writings, signifying the coming of God to judge his enemies in fiery wrath. The eighth century B.C. prophet Amos warned of God's coming to the wicked people of Samaria: "Is not the day of the LORD darkness, and not light, and gloom with no brightness in it?" (Amos 5:20). The day of the Lord is the time of reckoning for sinners who transgress God's law and enemies who oppress God's people. Ezekiel wrote: "It will be a day of clouds, a time of doom for the nations" (Ezek. 30:3). In the Old Testament, "the day of the Lord" referred to a complex of events in which God broke into history to judge his enemies and save his people, pointing forward to the great day of the Lord when Christ returns. Andrew Young described it as "a day of wrath and destruction for rebellious individuals and nations, and at the same time a day of salvation and deliverance for his people."[1]

Dispensational scholars seek to distinguish between "the day of Christ," which brings deliverance to the church, and "the day of the Lord" as a cataclysmic judgment. This distinction is mandated by the pretribulation eschatology that requires a two-stage return, with Christ's first removing his church and then later returning to judge the earth before his millennial

1. Andrew W. Young, *Let's Study 1 & 2 Thessalonians* (Edinburgh: Banner of Truth, 2001), 87.

rule. This theory becomes particularly strained, however, when it seeks to differentiate between "the day of the Lord" and "the day of Christ" (Phil. 1:10), or even "the day of the Lord Jesus" (1 Cor. 5:5 NKJV). This arbitrary distinction is most clearly refuted in 2 Thessalonians 2:1–2, where Paul speaks of "the coming of our Lord Jesus Christ" as "the day of the Lord," showing that they are in fact one and the same event (see also 2 Thess. 1:6–7). The apostle Peter states that the day of the Lord is not merely one among many steps along the way to the end but is the climactic event to end all history: "But the day of the Lord will come like a thief, and then the heavens will pass away with a roar, and the heavenly bodies will be burned up and dissolved, and the earth and the works that are done on it will be exposed" (2 Peter 3:10).

The Bible's teaching on the day of the Lord tells us that history is moving forward to a great reckoning for all the evil on the earth and to salvation for the people of God. This contrasts with the prevailing unbelief of our day, based on the theory of evolution, which holds that history has neither a goal nor any meaning. As Ravi Zacharias writes, "A philosophy of meaninglessness is an unavoidable consequence of the antitheistic starting point."[2] The Bible teaches the opposite. Just as history had its beginning in God's sovereign act of creation, it will conclude in the sovereign return of the Lord, the day when man's apparent sway is brought to an end and God's sovereign purposes are unveiled as being fully achieved. John Lillie writes: "Now it is man's day—the day of man's ambition—man's pleasures—man's judging—man's glory; and 'God is not in all his thoughts' (Ps. 10:4). How great the change from this to 'the day of the Lord'! Then 'the lofty looks of man shall be humbled, and the haughtiness of men shall be bowed down; and the Lord alone shall be exalted in that day.'"[3]

Since the day of the Lord will culminate God's purpose for history, Christians must not shrink from declaring this important Bible truth. To be sure, there are better and worse ways to declare the day of the Lord. When I ministered in Philadelphia, a woman came almost every day to the train station with a large placard depicting the human race in flames and called sinners to escape God's judgment. In all the days I walked past the woman and her

---

2. Ravi Zacharias, *Can Man Live without God?* (Dallas: Word, 1994), xvii.
3. John Lillie, *Lectures on Paul's Epistles to the Thessalonians*, Tentmaker Classic Commentaries (1860; repr., Stoke-on-Trent, UK: Tentmaker Publications, 2007), 210–11.

sign, I never saw anyone stop to discuss the topic, despite the accuracy of her message. Yet we must avoid the opposite extreme of neglecting to tell the world about the day of the Lord. It is evident that Paul had given priority to this doctrine while in Thessalonica. Like Paul, we need to combine our witness to God's coming judgment with a declaration of God's grace and mercy through Jesus, who came to die for sin and whose return is the believer's "blessed hope, the appearing of the glory of our great God and Savior Jesus Christ" (Titus 2:13).

CHRIST'S UNFORESEEN RETURN

The Thessalonians were asking about "times and seasons" because they were concerned to be prepared for God's judgment. John Stott comments, "They thought they could most easily get ready for Christ's coming in judgment if they could know when he would arrive."[4] The problem with this approach, Paul replied, is that "the day of the Lord will come like a thief in the night" (1 Thess. 5:2).

The point of this analogy is that the Lord's return will arrive at a time and in a way unforeseen by the world. The problem with thieves is that they do not announce their coming, but wait for an unexpected opportunity. Here Paul is reproducing the teaching of Jesus on his own return: "But concerning that day or that hour, no one knows, not even the angels in heaven, nor the Son, but only the Father" (Mark 13:32). Unfortunately, this plain teaching has not kept history from being littered with those claiming to know when Christ will return. In 1833, William Miller published his belief that Christ would return in 1843. When that year passed, the date was reset for April 18, 1844, and then again for October 22, 1844, with thousands of followers anxiously awaiting the end of the world, many of them having sold their possessions. After "the Great Disappointment," when this date passed, various theories were offered, one of them spawning the Seventh-day Adventist movement that continues to thrive today. G. K. Beale notes a similar occurrence when a group of Korean Christians so strongly expected Christ's return in October 1992 that they sold their homes and goods. In the despair that overcame them when Christ failed to meet their schedule, some of them took their

4. John R. W. Stott, *The Message of 1 & 2 Thessalonians*, The Bible Speaks Today (Downers Grove, IL: InterVarsity Press, 1994), 108.

own lives.[5] Beale notes that "without exception, the expectations of each of these groups throughout history have been dashed."[6] Today "The Rapture Index" can be accessed on the Internet, offering advance warning of Christ's return by means of a point scale for activities associated with the end of the world. The website describes itself as "a Dow Jones Industrial Average of end time activity," and a "prophetic speedometer. The higher the number, the faster we're moving towards the occurrence of pre-tribulation rapture."[7]

While both Jesus and Paul emphasized the unforeseen nature of the Lord's coming, the Bible also displays an expectation of its nearness. Isaiah warned wicked Jerusalem of an onslaught from the north as an unforeseen day of the Lord that would come soon: "Wail, for the day of the LORD is near; as destruction from the Almighty it will come!" (Isa. 13:6). Ezekiel later gave a similar warning related to Nebuchadnezzar's destruction of Jerusalem: "Wail, 'Alas for the day!' For the day is near, the day of the LORD is near" (Ezek. 30:2–3). Zephaniah added: "The great day of the LORD is near, near and hastening fast" (Zeph. 1:14). What was said of these earlier, more limited judgments is all the more true of the great and final day of the Lord in the coming of Jesus Christ. Even if it should turn out that Christ returns at some far distant date in the future, the reality of death makes it certain that judgment is near to everyone who lives and breathes at this very moment. Hebrews 9:27 reminds us that "it is appointed for man to die once, and after that comes judgment."

Some scholars have made much of Paul's use of the first-person plural in speaking of his expectation of Christ's coming: "We who are alive, who are left, will be caught up together with them in the clouds to meet the Lord in the air, and so we will always be with the Lord" (1 Thess. 4:17). The claim is made that Paul erroneously believed that Christ would return during his own lifetime and was disappointed by his mistake. This idea is refuted by Paul's own teaching that no one knows the time of Christ's return. Yet the apostle's urgency does point out that the Christian attitude toward the day of the Lord ought always to be one of excited expectation. Anthony Hoekema explains: "The believer should live in constant, joyful expectation of Christ's

5. G. K. Beale, *1–2 Thessalonians*, IVP New Testament Commentary Series (Downers Grove, IL: InterVarsity Press, 2003), 142.
6. Ibid.
7. http://raptureready.com/rap2.html (viewed February 4, 2012). The rapture index was then at a nearly all-time high of 180, which led the index to warn: "Fasten your seatbelts."

return; though he does not know the exact time of it, he should always be ready for it."[8] In the second-to-last verse of the entire Bible, Jesus himself declared: "Surely I am coming soon." The expectant believer answers, "Amen. Come, Lord Jesus!" (Rev. 22:20).

SUDDEN DESTRUCTION

As Paul and other biblical writers explain it, the result of Christ's unforeseen coming will be sudden destruction on those who were unprepared: "While people are saying, 'There is peace and security,' then sudden destruction will come upon them as labor pains come upon a pregnant woman, and they will not escape" (1 Thess. 5:3). Here, the apostle mirrors the earlier teaching of Jesus, who compared the world at his return to the unprepared world on the brink of Noah's flood: "For as were the days of Noah, so will be the coming of the Son of Man. For as in those days before the flood they were eating and drinking, marrying and giving in marriage, until the day when Noah entered the ark, and they were unaware until the flood came and swept them all away, so will be the coming of the Son of Man" (Matt. 24:37–39).

Jesus was not teaching that there is something wrong with eating, drinking, or marrying. His point was that the worldly will be oblivious to the demands of God and to their danger as rebels against God's rule. They will be concerned about their own affairs: their pleasures, ambitions, and worldly pursuits. Just as worldly preoccupation keeps so many men and women from thinking about God and eternity now, the same attitude will expose the ungodly to destruction on the day of the Lord when it suddenly comes, completely unforeseen, like a thief in the night.

In virtually every judgment recorded in the Bible, worldly unbelievers, having turned from the light of God's Word, were completely in the dark about the devastation about to strike them. While Jeremiah was foretelling Jerusalem's destruction, the false prophets were telling the people: "You shall not see the sword, nor shall you have famine" (Jer. 14:13). "Peace, peace," they cried, but there was no peace (6:14). The prophets of secular unbelief take the same stance today in mocking the Bible's claims of coming judgment. Ben Witherington argues that "there is peace and security" was probably a political slogan frequently heard in the Roman Empire of Paul's day, just

8. Anthony A. Hoekema, *The Bible and the Future* (Grand Rapids: Eerdmans, 1979), 126.

as similar slogans are often trumpeted in our elections today. If this was the boast of the Roman Empire in the first century, then "Paul must have thought 'What foolish slogans and vain hopes when the day of the Lord is coming.'"[9] Likewise, Christians today should not be caught up in the utopian promises of any political party or social movement, knowing as we do that every endeavor of man is crippled by sinful corruption and believing the Bible's claim that only the return of Christ will bring true "peace and security" to those who hope in him.

Yet as Jesus notes in Matthew 24:37–39, the most complete blindfold is not secularist dogma but the combination of worldly materialism and sensualism. Tim Shenton writes: "Unbelievers only believe what they can see. As they cannot see the judgment of God approaching, they dismiss it as fantasy and scaremongering. . . . They are deaf to the warnings of God, absorbed in their own selfishness, and utterly blind to the judgment that is hanging over them."[10] This situation again highlights the necessity of Christians' speaking the truth boldly about the day of the Lord and the judgment of God.

The Bible clearly states that the sudden judgment on the day of the Lord will involve utter ruin and devastation. Peter foretold a cataclysmic cleansing of the world in fire: "The day of the Lord will come like a thief, and then the heavens will pass away with a roar, and the heavenly bodies will be burned up and dissolved, and the earth and the works that are done on it will be exposed" (2 Peter 3:10). Revelation 6:15–17 presents a similar picture of supernatural upheaval, in which the dismayed ungodly seek to hide "themselves in the caves and among the rocks of the mountains, calling to the mountains and rocks, 'Fall on us and hide us from the face of him who is seated on the throne, and from the wrath of the Lamb, for the great day of their wrath has come, and who can stand?'" On that day, all the treasures gained by a world of sin will be lost, replaced by the wretched prospect of "eternal destruction, away from the presence of the Lord and from the glory of his might, when he comes on that day to be glorified in his saints" (2 Thess. 1:9–10).

Jesus cited Noah's flood as a type of the future judgment. People were leading their self-centered lives, oblivious to God's wrath, when the flood

9. Ben Witherington III, *1–2 Thessalonians: A Socio-Rhetorical Commentary* (Grand Rapids: Eerdmans, 2006), 147.
10. Tim Shenton, *Opening Up 1 Thessalonians* (Leominster, UK: Day One, 2006), 95–96.

struck them suddenly and swept virtually the entire race away in watery wrath. Jesus said: "So will be the coming of the Son of Man. Then two men will be in the field; one will be taken and one left. Two women will be grinding at the mill; one will be taken and one left" (Matt. 24:39–41). The future judgment of the day of the Lord will bring similar disaster, only by fire instead of by rain and water. In this connection, it should be pointed out that in Noah's flood, those who were "left behind" were the godly remnant whom God saved. As mentioned in the previous chapter, one of the curiosities of recent end-times speculation is the reversal of this biblical pattern, so that Christians dread above all things being "left behind." As Paul stated clearly in 1 Thessalonians 4:17, it is "we who are alive, who are left," who join the Lord in his return and enjoy an everlasting bliss with him.

We have noted that the day of the Lord will be unforeseen and sudden, but Paul adds that it will also be unavoidable. There will be no escape on the day of the Lord. He makes this point by making reference to a pregnant woman in birth pangs: "sudden destruction will come upon them as labor pains come upon a pregnant woman, and they will not escape" (1 Thess. 5:3). Daunting as labor is today, in the ancient world it involved dreadful suffering and serious danger to the delivering mother. The point is that once the contractions begin, the painful labor is inescapable and irreversible. Likewise, once the judgment of God has come, there will then be no chance of escaping divine wrath and destruction. J. Philip Arthur notes: "Once the end of all things is upon us, it will be too late for those who are not prepared to escape the inevitable outcome."[11]

READINESS ON THAT DAY

Realizing that once the day of the Lord has appeared it will be too late to get ready brings us back to the anxiety of the Thessalonians. They were concerned to be ready for Christ's coming and therefore wondered about the "times and the seasons" of this great event. Paul answered that the way to be prepared for Christ's coming is not to know the date—which no one can know—but to prepare ourselves in advance. The way to be ready for

11. J. Philip Arthur, *Patience of Hope: 1 and 2 Thessalonians Simply Explained*, Wellwyn Commentary Series (Ross-shire, UK: Evangelical Press, 1996), 75.

the day of the Lord is to act now on the offer of salvation granted to sinners through the saving work of Jesus Christ.

One of the unfortunate features of much end-times teaching is the notion that Christians must ready themselves in some special way beyond trusting in the gospel. Shock-sermons are given to youths, suggesting that if caught in some sinful act when Jesus returns, they may join the ranks of those swept away for judgment. The biblical calling to readiness is often taken to involve some special intensity beyond that of simple Christian faith. The promises of Jesus Christ, however, assure us that readiness for the day of the Lord may be achieved now simply by turning to him for forgiveness and eternal life. Jesus preached: "Truly, truly, I say to you, whoever hears my word and believes him who sent me has eternal life. He does not come into judgment, but has passed from death to life" (John 5:24). John 3:36 contrasts the danger of unbelief with the readiness of simple faith in Jesus: "Whoever believes in the Son has eternal life; whoever does not obey the Son shall not see life, but the wrath of God remains on him."

To be sure, those who prepare for the last day by believing in Jesus not only receive forgiveness of sin and justification through faith alone, but also are regenerated so that they increasingly are "dead to sin and alive to God in Christ Jesus" (Rom. 6:11). Paul therefore writes: "But you are not in darkness, brothers, for that day to surprise you like a thief" (1 Thess. 5:4). Unpreparedness for the day of the Lord is a feature of life in the darkness of sin and unbelief, whereas readiness characterizes those who live in light of Christ. The believer's readiness for Christ's coming does not consist in additionally meritorious fervor, but through the salvation that every sinner receives when he or she turns to Christ in saving faith. In other words, while believers look with dismay on the world's giddy blindness of coming judgment, we may be certain of our own readiness right now simply by trusting Christ for our salvation and surrendering our lives to the Savior who one day will come as Lord both to judge the wicked world and to complete the salvation of all who trust in him.

BELIEVERS ON TIPTOE

For all who have stepped out of darkness into the light by trusting Jesus, Paul has an all-important statement that completely changes our attitude toward the coming of Christ. "But you are not in darkness, brothers," he remarks, "for that day to surprise you like a thief" (1 Thess. 5:4). Everything that Paul has said about the unbelieving world is reversed when it comes to Christ's believing people. Jesus' coming is unforeseen by the world. But far from being surprised, the believer lives every day in joyful expectation of the Lord's day. Christ will come to the unbeliever like a thief in the night, breaking into a life that the person had deemed secure and stripping away all that he or she had trusted and loved. To the believer, who has primarily sought for treasures not in this world but in heaven, the coming of the Lord unlocks our inheritance. Romans 8:17 says that believers are "heirs of God and fellow heirs with Christ, provided we suffer with him in order that we may also be glorified with him." The day of the Lord brings destruction and defeat to all the evil, worldly powers, but the believer looks forward to Christ's coming as our day of vindication, deliverance, and glorification. Though the ungodly will "suffer the punishment of eternal destruction," Christ "comes on that day to be glorified in his saints, and to be marveled at among all who have believed" (2 Thess. 1:9–10).

According to Paul, not only believers but also "the creation itself will be set free from its bondage to corruption and obtain the freedom of the glory of the children of God" (Rom. 8:21). The day of the Lord is the creation's own deliverance from the curse of mankind's sin. Therefore, Paul exclaims, "the creation waits with eager longing for the revealing of the sons of God" (v. 19). Eric Alexander points out two things in this statement. The first is that the longing creation sets an example for everyone who has readied himself or herself for Christ's coming by trusting in Jesus for salvation. As the creation expresses "eager longing" for that coming day, so believers ought to live in conscious expectation of the coming day of Christ's glory in us and our glory in him. Second, Alexander points out that "eager longing" falls short of expressing Paul's true point about the creation's attitude. He writes:

> The language expresses the idea of someone standing on tiptoe—the kind of thing people do when they are waiting for somebody to arrive at an airport or a train station. There are crowds of people there. So when somebody is waiting for a friend, perhaps a fiancée, he is on tiptoe, peering over people, waiting. This is how creation is pictured. The whole cosmos is standing on tiptoe, groaning, waiting for the liberation of the glory of the people of God.[12]

12. Eric J. Alexander, *Our Great God and Saviour* (Edinburgh: Banner of Truth, 2010), 120.

The example of creation is given for us to emulate as we anticipate the coming of Christ. The day of the Lord is not unforeseen to those who have received God's Word in faith. Christ does not come like a thief in the night, but like a long-awaited king whose triumph will inaugurate our own liberation and glory. We look for his coming as a bride prepares for the coming of her beloved groom, to whisk her away on a wonderful adventure. Therefore, we wait on tiptoe, casting our glance constantly on the clouds for a gleam of the glory of the Son of Man. Alexander concludes: "So we should set our hearts on that day and walk through this world as men and women who eagerly—like the creation itself which is here teaching us a lesson—wait for the day of God."[13]

13. Ibid., 121.

20

VICTORS VALIANT

1 Thessalonians 5:4–8

*For you are all children of light, children of the day. We are not
of the night or of the darkness. So then let us not sleep, as others
do, but let us keep awake and be sober. (1 Thess. 5:5–6)*

*I*n 1969, Bo Schembechler was appointed head football coach
at the University of Michigan. One of college football's most
storied programs, the Michigan Wolverines had languished
in mediocrity for over a decade. Schembechler arrived with an intensity
that shocked his players, and almost half of them quit during his demanding first training camp. Schembechler's philosophy was not based merely
on individual expectations, however, but even more on a commitment to
teamwork. He expressed his winning philosophy in a memorable speech
on "The Team":

> We want the Big Ten championship and we're gonna win it as a team . . . The
> Team. The Team, the Team. . . . We're gonna play together as a team. We're
> gonna believe in each other, we're not gonna criticize each other, we're not
> gonna talk about each other, we're gonna encourage each other. And when
> we play as a team, when the old season is over, you and I know, it's gonna
> be Michigan again.

Not only was Schembechler a legendary football coach, but the apostle Paul would have agreed with his priority on teamwork. In his first letter to the Thessalonians, Paul responded to their challenges with a similar emphasis. At the end of chapter 4, Paul gave clear teaching about Christ's second coming and urged, "Therefore encourage one another with these words" (1 Thess. 4:18). In chapter 5, Paul addressed concerns about the timing of Christ's return, concluding with a similar charge: "Therefore encourage one another and build one another up, just as you are doing" (5:11).

According to the apostle, the Christian strategy for enduring in faith through trials is to strengthen one another with biblical truth. This is Christian teamwork in the church and home. How is the Christian family to endure against cultural attacks? By the husband's encouraging his wife and the parents' encouraging their children with biblical truths. How are Christians to minister to those faltering or discouraged? With the encouragement of biblical truth. We are to take a team approach in the Christian life, not tearing each other down but building each other up with the truths of God's Word.

CHILDREN OF LIGHT

The truth that Paul wants to impress on the minds of his Thessalonian readers concerns their relationship with Christ. The way to be prepared for Jesus' coming, he says, is to have our heads clear about what it means to be joined to Christ in salvation. Paul writes: "But you are not in darkness, brothers, for that day to surprise you like a thief. For you are all children of light, children of the day. We are not of the night or of the darkness" (1 Thess. 5:4–5).

To describe the Christian's situation, Paul employs the familiar biblical image of light. Believing in Jesus, the Christian no longer lives in the darkness but belongs to the realm of the light of Christ. This image has a number of facets, each of which is relevant to the believer. First, light *reveals*, whereas darkness leaves us in ignorance. Christians, therefore, are those who have seen the light of the truth of Christ and have come to know him as God's Son and as Savior (see Isa. 9:2). Christians no longer live in ignorance of the great truths about God and man, sin and salvation, and Christ's first and second comings. Second, light *warms*, which refers to the spiritual transformation of the heart that has been touched by the grace of Jesus. In darkness, our hearts were cold toward God. But now that Christ's light has shone on us, our affections are warmed toward the things of God (John 12:46). Third, light *conveys and stimulates life*. We were once dead to God when we lived in darkness, but now we are alive and responsive to his Word. Just as sunlight causes plants to reach up toward the sky, God's light draws us upward to heaven. Fourth, light *guides* us in the way we should go. The darkness of unbelief is the realm of stumbling, but Psalm 119:105 says, "Your word is a lamp to my feet and a light to my path." Similarly, Jesus asserted, "I am the light of the world. Whoever follows me will not walk in darkness" (John 8:12).

Paul's point is that Christians should not be unprepared for Christ's coming, since we now belong to the light. By calling us "children of light," he means that the blessings of God's light have come to distinguish us and characterize our lives. We belong to and are being transformed by the light of Christ. This truth applies not only to some believers but by definition to all who come to Christ in faith. Paul proclaims that "you are *all* children of light, children of the day" (1 Thess. 5:5). Christians have gained knowledge of truth, have been warmed to God's ways, have received spiritual life, and are guided by the light of God's Word. John described Jesus as "the light of men" (John 1:4). Therefore, the day of the Lord should never come upon us as a "surprise," like "a thief" (1 Thess. 5:4), since we have been looking forward to and preparing for that bright day.

Verses 4 and 5 present one of the Bible's main principles for Christian living and sanctification, namely, that Christian living arises out of Christian thinking. We observed earlier that Christians are to persevere in faith by encouraging one another in biblical truth. Paul now explains how this works: God's Word is taught to us, we begin thinking in light of God's Word, and by God's grace this new thinking yields a new and godly lifestyle. Jesus mandated this process of transformation by illumination when he prayed to the Father, "Sanctify them in the truth; your word is truth" (John 17:17).

This knowledge-based approach to sanctification mirrors Paul's teaching in the book of Romans. Paul had taught the doctrine of justification through faith in Christ alone, apart from works. This raised a question whether Christians may continue to live sinfully, since we are saved by

God's grace as a free gift. Paul answered that no Christian who really thinks about salvation can draw such a conclusion: "How can we who died to sin still live in it?" he asked (Rom. 6:2). Paul argued that as Christians, we have died to sin in Christ and have been raised in Christ to righteousness. This being the case, Paul wrote, "reckon yourselves to be dead indeed to sin, but alive to God in Christ Jesus our Lord" (Rom. 6:11 NKJV). When Paul said "reckon yourselves," he employed an accounting term (*logizomai*), saying that just as we record financial transactions in our bank accounts, we must also take spiritual stock of our lives and take note of the radical change that has come through faith in Christ. James Montgomery Boice writes: "A holy life comes from *knowing* . . . that you can't go back, that you have died to sin and been made alive to God."[1] The result of such biblical thinking will be a transformed lifestyle befitting our relationship with the Lord: "Let not sin therefore reign in your mortal body, to make you obey its passions . . . , but present . . . your members to God as instruments for righteousness" (Rom. 6:12–13).

Using the imagery of light and darkness, Paul pressed this same case upon the Thessalonians: "For you are all children of light, children of the day. We are not of the night or of the darkness" (1 Thess. 5:5). Reckoning what we have been given and have been made in Christ, we should live accordingly as we prepare for his return.

Staying Awake

Having expressed his principle of reckoning who and what we are in Christ—children of light—Paul makes the application in terms of how we should therefore live in anticipation of Christ's return. He focuses on three aspects of Christian readiness that will enable us to persevere in faith until the coming of Jesus to save us.

Paul's first application is that since believers no longer belong to the darkness but are children of light, we should stay awake and not slumber: "So then let us not sleep, as others do, but let us keep awake" (1 Thess. 5:6). Being children of the light, Christians should not engage in the nighttime activities of darkness. Those in the dark are asleep to God, unaware of what is happening in the world, and unresponsive to the call of the gospel.

1. James Montgomery Boice, *Romans*, 4 vols. (Grand Rapids: Baker, 1992), 2:656.

The children of light, in contrast, are to be awake to God's plan and alive to God's calling.

The Bible provides a number of illustrations of believers who have fallen asleep. We think of the three disciples who were summoned to watch and pray with Jesus in the garden of Gethsemane. Jesus returned and found them sleeping. "Could you not watch with me one hour?" he asked (Matt. 26:40). Likewise, Christians are to be watchful during the significant events of our times. Are we to be obliviously prayerless as the great work of the gospel goes forth today? Should we not be watching and praying for missionaries, church-planters, parents raising Christian children, evangelists reaching their neighbors, and Christian leaders trying to stand for truth in our society? Should we not similarly be praying to God about the decline of our culture and the advance of sin tendencies that the Bible abhors? When it comes to watchfulness and prayer, the evidence today suggests that many Christians are asleep, hardly responsive to the spiritual challenges of our time. Jesus warned, "Watch and pray that you may not enter into temptation" (v. 41).

A second biblical example of a sleeping believer was Samson, who lost his strength as his hair was cut in the night. Samson had once been a mighty foe of the Philistine enemy. But he took his rest and made his peace with the world around him, settling into the arms of a Philistine named Delilah, who betrayed him. Samson's slumber cannot be blamed on Delilah, however: Samson put himself to sleep spiritually by violating his covenant with the Lord. Once asleep, he awoke to his danger too late, realizing only then what he had lost through his alliance with the world. How many Christians today are asleep to the influences of popular culture, so that like Samson we become prisoners of worldly thinking and acting and so lose our usefulness to the cause of Christ?

A third example was given by Jesus in his parable of the tares and the wheat. A man sowed good seed in his field, "but while his men were sleeping, his enemy came and sowed weeds among the wheat and went away" (Matt. 13:24–25). Likewise, in the tolerant spirit that grips the church today, there is little doctrinal vigilance over our churches and ministries. Christians are asleep to the threat of an active enemy who seeks to undermine and infiltrate the works of Christ's kingdom so that we squander the gains given to us by God and lack the spiritual power to prevail in dangerous times. Charles Spurgeon lamented, "Those who ought to have been watchmen, and to have guarded the field, slept, and so the enemy had ample time to enter and scatter tares among the wheat."[2]

When Paul says that Christians should not sleep "as others do," he notes that sleeping is the normal state of the unbelieving world, insensitive to the warnings of God's wrath and the offer of God's salvation in the gospel. John Lillie writes: "However wide awake they fancy themselves to be, however knowing and sagacious, they are really, as to all highest things—things of the soul, of eternity, of God—in a state of slumber; of habitual, deep, lethargic sleep. . . . They are alike insensible to the obligation of present duty, and secure as to the approach of danger."[3] Are you slumbering in the blissful folly of unbelief? If you are, the Bible offers you examples not merely of temporal loss but of eternal doom in God's coming judgment. Sisera, the enemy of God's people, was sleeping in his tent when Jael drove the spike through his skull (Judg. 4:21). Yet those who cry out to God for mercy will be saved. The prophet Jonah slept in the hold of the ship while the tempest raged above. For his hardness of heart toward God, Jonah was thrown overboard to die beneath the waves. God had mercy on the prophet by sending the great fish to bring him to salvation. If you are now asleep to your need for the gospel, God's Word and the prayers of Christ's people provide the only hope that you will be saved by awakening to faith.

Perhaps the most relevant biblical illustration of our need to stay awake is Jesus' parable of the ten virgins waiting for the coming bridegroom. Five virgins were wise and "took flasks of oil with their lamps," whereas the five foolish virgins "took no oil with them" (Matt. 25:2–3). The bridegroom was delayed, and when he arrived, only the five wise virgins had oil left to light their lamps. Furthermore, only "those who were ready went in with him to the marriage feast, and the door was shut" (v. 10). In the Bible, oil often stands for the ministry of the Holy Spirit. Thus, the emphasis in the parable is on the Spirit's work in enabling us to believe the gospel and respond with a life of faith. If we neglect our faith and fall into unbelief, then like the foolish virgins we may be caught unawares by Christ's coming. "Watch therefore," Jesus said, "for you know neither the day nor the hour" (v. 13).

2. Charles H. Spurgeon, *Metropolitan Tabernacle Pulpit*, 63 vols. (Pasadena, TX: Pilgrim, 1971), 17:653.
3. John Lillie, *Lectures on Paul's Epistles to the Thessalonians*, Tentmaker Classic Commentaries (1860; repr., Stoke-on-Trent, UK: Tentmaker Publications, 2007), 221.

STAYING SOBER

In addition to staying awake, Christians maintain their readiness for Christ's return by staying sober: "For those who sleep, sleep at night, and those who get drunk, are drunk at night. But since we belong to the day, let us be sober" (1 Thess. 5:7–8). This application is a companion to the previous one: since Christians belong to the day, they should not be characterized by practices that take place during the night. Among these nighttime practices is a lifestyle that is inebriated with earthly pleasures and sin.

Underlining Paul's teaching here is the realization that "there are certain kinds of conduct which are appropriate enough in the sons of night, but quite unbefitting to Christians."[4] Most obvious, here, is the fact that being drunk from alcohol or drugs, along with related forms of sensual revelry, is inexcusable in a follower of Jesus. When I was a college professor, a Christian student once gave in to his roommate and went out drinking and carousing. In the morning, he was chagrined to discover that even his unbelieving friends expressed their disgust: after all, he was supposed to be a Christian! In Ephesians 2:2–3, Paul described spiritually dead unbelievers as "following the course of this world, . . . carrying out the desires of the body and the mind," and thus identifying themselves as "children of wrath." Obviously, the children of light, who are "destined . . . to obtain salvation" (1 Thess. 5:9), should not embrace a similarly drunken pattern of life.

We should understand Paul's call to sober living to involve more than drunkenness on alcohol or drugs. Today, this calling extends to the whole realm of entertainments of which Christians may imbibe, including movies and music that promote a sensual, self-absorbed lifestyle and glorify values that are contrary to God's Word. In the workplace, Christians can become drunk with academic prestige, political power, or financial success. G. K. Beale explains: "To be drunk spiritually is to imbibe too much of the world's way of looking at things and not enough of the way God views reality. To be intoxicated with the world's wine is to be numbed to feeling any fear in the present of a coming judgment."[5]

4. Leon Morris, *The First and Second Epistles to the Thessalonians*, New International Commentary on the New Testament (Grand Rapids: Eerdmans, 1959), 157.
5. G. K. Beale, *1–2 Thessalonians*, IVP New Testament Commentary Series (Downers Grove, IL: InterVarsity Press, 2003), 147.

Paul's emphasis on sober living, repeated twice in these verses, could indicate that this was a problem among the Thessalonian new believers. Given our similarly intoxicated culture today, many young believers and new converts will likewise need to seek God's power to start living a sober life that no longer indulges in the kinds of worldly recreations that deaden us to the things of God.

In his letter to the Romans, Paul spoke similarly about sobriety: "The night is far gone; the day is at hand. . . . Let us walk properly as in the daytime, not in orgies and drunkenness, not in sexual immorality and sensuality, not in quarreling and jealousy" (Rom. 13:12–13). Here, Paul defines sobriety in terms of rejecting drunkenness, pursuing sexual purity and modesty, and living peaceably with others. He summed up his appeal in Romans 13:14 by exhorting his readers to "make no provision for the flesh, to gratify its desires." How essential it is for all Christians to realize as soon as possible our call to separation from the drunken ways of the world. Andrew Young writes: "Christians are not to be like others. As unpopular as it may be to stand apart from the crowd, we need to do so. . . . Ours is not to be a lifestyle of slumber and drunkenness, but by contrast, we are to be self-controlled and alert."[6]

READY AND ARMED

Paul's first two applications were negative in principle: "Let us not sleep . . . [or] get drunk" (1 Thess. 5:6–7). The third application is active and positive, calling for Christians to arm themselves with biblical virtues: "having put on the breastplate of faith and love, and for a helmet the hope of salvation" (5:8).

Paul presents here for the first time in his writings an analogy that he will continue to develop in his later epistles, especially in Ephesians 6. He imagines Christians as preparing themselves for life in the same way that a soldier puts on his armor before heading into battle. John Calvin notes that Paul therefore understands that "the life of Christians is like a perpetual warfare . . . . He would have us, therefore, be diligently prepared and on the alert for resistance."[7] It is not enough for Christians merely to say No to sin

---

6. Andrew W. Young, *Let's Study 1 & 2 Thessalonians* (Edinburgh: Banner of Truth, 2001), 92.

7. John Calvin, *Calvin's Commentaries*, 22 vols. (1854; repr., Grand Rapids: Baker, 2009), 21:289.

and worldliness; we must also actively cultivate faith, love, and hope in order to be guarded from threats that would endanger our salvation.

The three virtues noted by Paul have recurred throughout this letter as the chief Christian resources: faith, love, and hope. The apostle thanked God in 1 Thessalonians 1:3 for the believers' "work of faith and labor of love and steadfastness of hope in our Lord Jesus Christ." In 3:6, Paul rejoiced at Timothy's "good news of your faith and love." Now, he urges the Thessalonians to keep themselves ready for the coming of Christ by putting on these same virtues to defend themselves for salvation.

The two pieces of armor that Paul cites here are those that protect the vital areas of the heart and the head. The soldier's chest was protected in battle by a breastplate, and Paul urges Christians to "put on the breastplate of faith and love" (1 Thess. 5:8). In Ephesians 6:14, Paul speaks of putting on "the breastplate of righteousness." These descriptions go together—"faith and love" on the one hand and "righteousness" on the other—because faith and love are the means by which righteousness is received and then practiced. We are forgiven our sins and justified before God through faith in Jesus Christ (Gal. 2:16). Having believed, we then pursue a practical righteousness by leading a life of love—love for God and love for one another as outlined in God's holy law.

The breastplate was the primary and most important piece in any panoply of armor, and likewise faith and love are at the center of Christian life and readiness. As Paul wrote to the Galatians, what really matters is "faith working through love" (Gal. 5:6). Christians should therefore put on faith by devoting ourselves to God's Word and prayer, and then train ourselves to exercise our faith in loving obedience to God and loving service to others. With this armor, Christians fight to win in the warfare of this darkened age.

Added to the breastplate that guards the vital organs is the helmet that protects the head: "and for a helmet the hope of salvation" (1 Thess. 5:8). According to Paul, the Christian who possesses a biblical hope for salvation is able to think clearly and resist blows that would daze him or her into unbelief or folly. We ground our hope in God's sovereignty over history—a history that is defined by Christ's saving death for our sins and that will conclude in Christ's saving return. When life comes crashing down on a believer's head, the Christian's helmet—his or her hope of salvation—imparts "a calm assurance in the midst of all trials and perils."[8] We are confident

8. Lillie, *Thessalonians*, 228.

that whatever may happen, Christ is certain to save us in the end, and this hope enables us to think clearly amid the tumults of this world.

As an illustration of this helmet of salvation, John Lillie cites the example of the first Christian martyr, Stephen, who rejoiced to see Christ standing to receive him even "as he sank beneath the blows of his murderers," praying aloud for Christ to forgive his persecutors.[9] "I see the heavens opened, and the Son of Man standing at the right hand of God," Stephen cried with joy (Acts 7:56). Paul himself would face martyrdom with a bold calmness, confident of his salvation in the face of death:

> I am already being poured out as a drink offering, and the time of my departure has come. I have fought the good fight, I have finished the race, I have kept the faith. Henceforth there is laid up for me the crown of righteousness, which the Lord, the righteous judge, will award to me on that Day, and not only to me but also to all who have loved his appearing. (2 Tim. 4:6–8)

The helmet of salvation will deliver us not only from worldly threats but also from a misguided dread of Christ's second coming, as many Christians have sadly been led to do. For Paul and the early believers, Christ's return was the hope for which they fervently longed. We are to live in readiness for that day, not suspending our lives and gazing at the sky in trepidation, but awake, sober, and armed with faith, love, and Christian hope. G. K. Beale writes: "The way to be ready for the last advent is to live a life of trust in God and his promises."[10] If we trust in the work that Christ has done for our salvation, dying on the cross for our sins; if we cultivate a love for God and for one another according to God's Word; and if we look in hope for Christ's coming to bring us with him into glory, we will be guarded for salvation and crowned with the grace to stand without fear before a dark and wicked world that can be awakened to the gospel only by the witness that we are emboldened to give.

HAIL TO THE VICTORS!

Paul makes it clear that Christians should expect struggle and difficulty as we await the return of our Lord. Some may wonder whether it is worth all

9. Ibid.
10. Beale, *1–2 Thessalonians*, 149.

the effort of staying awake, keeping sober, and arming ourselves with faith, love, and hope. Can we expect to prevail? Jesus answers, "In the world you will have tribulation. But take heart; I have overcome the world" (John 16:33).

I mentioned how Bo Schembechler challenged Michigan football players with high expectations and rigorous demands, with nearly half his players quitting the team. During that first training camp, Bo strolled into the locker room one day and nailed a sign to the wall that remains there still. It reads, "Those Who Stay Will Be Champions!" That promise was kept throughout Schembechler's tenure as Michigan football coach. Not one class of his recruits who stayed for four years failed to be conference champions at least once, and their collective efforts established a tradition of victory. If Bo Schembechler was able to keep his promise to make his teams champions, how much more able is Jesus Christ to promise eternal glory and salvation to all who persevere through faith, love, and hope in him. Paul urges believers to remind each other of such truths: "Therefore encourage one another with these words" (1 Thess. 4:18).

The Michigan fight song exclaims, "Hail to the Victors Valiant! Hail to the conquering heroes!" How much more honor will accrue to all who answer the call of Christ for salvation, who are made righteous with God through faith in him, and who persevere in love and hope to the end! William Walsham How wrote of the great day to come when the valiant children of light will be hailed as victors:

> But lo! there breaks a yet more glorious day;
> The saints triumphant rise in bright array;
> The King of glory passes on his way.
> Alleluia! Alleluia!

That is the glorious hope of all who trust in Christ. Our calling now is worthy of that glorious end:

> O may thy soldiers faithful, true, and bold
> Fight as the saints who nobly fought of old,
> And win with them the victor's crown of gold.
> Alleluia! Alleluia![11]

11. William Walsham How, "For All the Saints" (1864).

21

DESTINED FOR SALVATION

1 Thessalonians 5:9–11

For God has not destined us for wrath, but to obtain salvation
through our Lord Jesus Christ, who died for us so that whether
we are awake or asleep we might live with him. (1 Thess. 5:9–10)

John Duncan is regarded as one of the holiest men that Scotland produced in the nineteenth century. His vast learning in ancient languages earned him the nickname *Rabbi*, but it was his fervent piety that gained the affection of the young men whom he helped to prepare for the ministry. One former student remembered, "When we looked at 'the Rabbi' we all felt and were wont to say, 'There is the best evidence of Christianity, and especially the best evidence that there is such a thing as living personal godliness; there is a man who walks closely with God, who actually knows what it is to enjoy the light of God's countenance.' "[1] Despite this accolade, Duncan is also remembered for his lifelong struggle to gain assurance of salvation, a struggle that absorbed a considerable portion of his spiritual energy and deprived him of much joy. For all his evidences of saving faith, Duncan lived in nearly perpetual want

1. Quoted in John E. Marshall, "Rabbi Duncan and the Problem of Assurance," in *Life and Writings* (Edinburgh: Banner of Truth, 2005), 207.

of assurance and approached death or the thought of Christ's return with great trepidation.

The apostle Paul was concerned that a similar problem not rob the Thessalonians' joy over the coming return of Jesus Christ. It is true that Christ will return to the unbelieving and unexpecting world "like a thief in the night" (1 Thess. 5:2), removing all its treasures and consigning impenitent sinners to eternal punishment. "But you are not in darkness, brothers," Paul assured the believers, "for that day to surprise you like a thief" (v. 4).

If the unbeliever's problem is a false assurance, the believer's calling is to embrace the joy of true assurance through faith in Jesus. Paul thus urges Christians to put on the hope of salvation like a helmet to crown and protect the head (1 Thess. 5:8). But what is the true ground of assurance of salvation? Paul points his struggling friends to the gospel truths that he had preached to them: salvation from sin, salvation to new life, and salvation by God's sovereign grace. He writes, "For God has not destined us for wrath, but to obtain salvation through our Lord Jesus Christ, who died for us so that whether we are awake or asleep we might live with him" (1 Thess. 5:9–10).

SALVATION FROM SIN

According to Paul, his readers should look with confidence to the return of Christ because they had been saved from sin: "For God has not destined us for wrath" (1 Thess. 5:9). In saying this, the apostle makes the important assumption that punishment for sin is the chief threat to our eternal well-being. The gospel that Paul preached, therefore, and that we should believe and preach today, is a gospel of salvation from the ruinous effects of sin.

In particular, Paul considers salvation from sin in terms of deliverance from the wrath of God. Our problem, he indicates, is not merely that sin harms us but that God will punish us in anger for our sins against his law. This being the problem, Paul's good news to believers in Jesus is that "God has not destined us for wrath."

Non-Christians have always objected to the idea of God's anger for our sins, but more recently even evangelical Christians have sought to turn down the heat on God's wrath against sin. To some, the idea of God's being angry about anything seems incompatible with the biblical teaching about his love and grace. For instance, self-acclaimed evangelicals Joel Green and Mark Baker have written, "The Scriptures as a whole provide no ground for a portrait of an angry God needing to be appeased in atoning sacrifice."[2] These scholars complain that the idea of God's being wrathful toward sinners suggests "a God from whom we need to be saved!"[3] Yet this is precisely Paul's point when he encourages believers that through their faith they have been delivered from God's wrathful punishment for sin. Apart from Christ, God's wrath is our chief problem.

To be sure, divine wrath can be wrongly presented. God should never be described as vindictive or sadistic in punishing sin. J. I. Packer rightly describes the biblical teaching of divine wrath as "*righteous* anger—the *right* reaction of moral perfection in the Creator towards moral perversity in the creature." Far from questioning God's wrath, Packer says, "the thing that would be morally doubtful would be for Him *not* to show His wrath in this way. God is not *just* . . . unless He inflicts upon all sin and wrongdoing the penalty it deserves."[4] The problem of sin lies not in God's wrath *against* it but rather our guilt *for* it. It is obvious from Paul's teaching that to lack the salvation offered in Jesus Christ is to remain under God's wrath in the guilt of our sin. But to be saved is to be delivered from the divine wrath that we have deserved as sinners.

It is remarkable that Bible scholars should deny the idea of God's wrath, since the Bible includes literally hundreds of references to it. In fact, this teaching is so important to the gospel that we must not shrink from proclaiming it to non-Christians. Moreover, our own gratitude for salvation should include thanksgiving for deliverance from the wrath that we have deserved. Benjamin Warfield writes: "It is clear that before all else [Paul] is impressed with the fact that the wrath of God hangs imminent over mankind, and that the great black cloud of sin rests loweringly over the entire world. It is because of this sense of sin that the need of deliverance looms so big in his mind; and that it is such good news, such glad tidings to his heart that Jesus is our deliverer from the coming wrath—that in His death

---

2. Joel B. Green and Mark D. Baker, *Recovering the Scandal of the Cross: Atonement in New Testament and Contemporary Contexts* (Downers Grove, IL: InterVarsity Press, 2000), 51.

3. Ibid., 150.

4. J. I. Packer, "The Heart of the Gospel," in J. I. Packer and Mark Dever, *In My Place Condemned He Stood: Celebrating the Glory of the Atonement* (Wheaton, IL: Crossway, 2007), 35.

and resurrection we have salvation from the wrath that otherwise would be appointed to us."[5]

Christians must persist in teaching God's final judgment in wrath for the simple reason that Warfield has stated: it is the great peril hanging over the heads of all mankind. But we must also proclaim God's wrathful judgment in order to restrain the wickedness of men in the present time. Miroslav Volf came to this conclusion during the years of bloody civil war in the Balkans. He came to see that the doctrine of final judgment is a necessary restraint on human violence: "The certainty of God's just judgment at the end of history is [necessary for] the renunciation of violence in the middle of [history]." If there is no judgment, why not crush anyone you can? Why not plunder and enslave? Volf saw terrible things during civil war in his homeland. He realized that a God who was not angry at injustice and did not finally end it "would not be worthy of our worship."[6] The holy justice of God demands punishment for impenitent sinners. A loving God can be filled with wrath, not despite his love but because of it. It is right to be angry in the presence of injustice and violence toward loved ones, and Christians have a duty to declare both the guilt of sin and the wrath of God against it.

The question may be raised as to how a holy God delivers sinners from his wrath. Paul answers that believers "obtain salvation through our Lord Jesus Christ, who died for us" (1 Thess. 5:9–10). Christians are saved from God's wrath because Jesus "died for us."

In these words we hear the heart of Paul's gospel: "Jesus . . . died for us." The *us* that Paul refers to is believers in Christ, who have confessed the guilt of their sin and sought forgiveness by trusting Christ's death. Paul speaks of Christ's death in a way that implies penal substitutionary atonement—the evangelical doctrine that Jesus died in our place to pay the penalty for our sins. The apostle teaches that Jesus' death had the effect of saving us from God's wrath. We are not saved simply by having our hearts warmed by a demonstration of God's love or by receiving an inspiring example to follow. Jesus died to save us from God's wrath, substituting himself as a sacrifice in our place. This is why, when the famous

5. Benjamin B. Warfield, *The Power of God unto Salvation* (Vestavia Hills, AL: Solid Ground, 2004), 190.

6. Miroslav Volf, *Exclusion and Embrace: A Theological Exploration of Identity, Otherness, and Reconciliation* (Nashville: Abingdon Press, 1996), 301–4.

theologian Karl Barth was asked to name the most important word in the Bible, his audience was surprised. They were expecting him to reply with *love* or *grace*. Instead, Barth answered, *"Huper,"* the Greek preposition that Paul uses in 1 Thessalonians 5:10 to say that Jesus died "for" us.[7] *Huper* means "on behalf of" or "in the place of." The heart of the good news of salvation from sin and wrath is that Jesus died on our behalf and in our place, receiving in his body and spirit the just and wrathful punishment that we deserved for our sins.

Paul's point in the context of our passage is that his readers should not fear the return of Jesus and the final judgment he will bring, since Christians have been saved from God's wrath by Jesus' sin-atoning death on the cross. Christ's people, for whom he died, will not be destroyed in his coming but will be saved to the uttermost. Christ's second coming will consummate the salvation he purchased in his first coming at such great cost to himself. As Paul sees it, therefore, joyful Christians—those who are most assured of salvation and who most eagerly await Christ's return—are those most willing to see the truth of their sin so as to be most fervently reliant on the finished work of Christ's death.

Yet there is a way that sin can be emphasized so as to destroy a Christian's hope and joy, and this seems to have been the problem paralyzing Rabbi John Duncan. One biographer described him as "a truly humble man, whose desire was to behold by faith the face of his Saviour."[8] Yet Duncan feared that his remaining sin nullified his faith, and thus he exhausted himself seeking proofs of a nearly sinless piety. His mistake was to seek assurance of salvation in his own spiritual performance, with the result that the traces of sin in his life drove him to a terror of the God he really loved. Instead of looking inside ourselves for a hope of salvation, Paul urges his readers to look away to Jesus Christ, who died for our sins on the cross. The words "[he] died for us" are to be a helmet of salvation hope, so that our heads are lifted in joyful expectation of Christ's return as the beloved Savior in whose favor we are certain. Am I a sinner? Yes, but he died for me! Is my life still tainted by sin? Certainly, but he died for me! How can such a poor Christian as I hope for salvation in the end? Because Jesus died for me!

7. James Montgomery Boice, *Romans*, 4 vols. (Grand Rapids: Baker, 1992), 3:976.
8. Quoted in Marshall, "Rabbi Duncan and the Problem of Assurance," 207.

SALVATION TO NEW LIFE

Looking away from ourselves to Jesus does not mean, however, that Christ does nothing within us in salvation. According to Paul, the same gospel that delivers us from wrath also saves us to a new life: he "died for us so that . . . we might live with him" (1 Thess. 5:10). The words *so that* express a purpose clause: Jesus' death had the purpose not only of delivering us from wrath but also of enabling us to live for and with him. Paul expanded the same idea in 2 Corinthians 5:15: "He died . . . , that those who live might no longer live for themselves but for him who for their sake died and was raised."

According to the Bible, the Christian's new life begins at the moment of faith and salvation. Paul said that "if anyone is in Christ, he is a new creation. The old has passed away; behold, the new has come" (2 Cor. 5:17). As reborn believers, we are to pursue godliness and good works in keeping with our discipleship to Christ. Having been saved by grace and through faith, apart from works, we realize that "we are his workmanship, created in Christ Jesus for good works, which God prepared beforehand, that we should walk in them" (Eph. 2:10).

In discussing Christ's death, I noted the mistake of basing our acceptance with God on our spiritual performance instead of resting in Christ's finished work. Some people draw the mistaken conclusion that Christians should not seek moral and spiritual improvement and that to emphasize obedience to God's Word is a form of legalism. Yet this, too, deviates from the Bible's teaching.

Paul's formula in 1 Thessalonians 5:10—"[Jesus] died for us so that . . . we might live with him"—corresponds to the theological categories of justification and sanctification. Christians are saved by trusting in Christ, receiving from him two saving benefits—one legal, our justification before God, and one transformational, our sanctification—so that we are increasingly conformed to the moral and spiritual character of Jesus Christ. John Calvin described this as the *duplex gratia*—the double grace that Christians receive through union with Christ:

> By partaking of him, we principally receive a double grace (*duplex gratia*), namely, that being reconciled to God through Christ's blamelessness, we may have in heaven instead of a Judge a gracious Father; and secondly, that

sanctified by Christ's Spirit we may cultivate blamelessness and purity of life.[9]

Paul has emphasized these same dual aspects of salvation in 1 Thessalonians. In 5:9, he highlighted our salvation from God's wrath—this is justification. In 4:3, he stated that "this is the will of God, your sanctification." Therefore, to be saved is both to be justified—forgiven and accounted righteous in God's sight for Jesus' sake—and to be sanctified—increasingly transformed by God's grace—through our union with Christ in faith. Hugh Martin put together the dual grace of Christ by saying that salvation is both "Christ for us" and "we with Christ."[10] This is Paul's very point: Jesus "died for us" so that "we might live with him" (1 Thess. 5:10). These two connections—"for us" and "with him"—make up Christian salvation, through union with Christ in faith.

Earlier, I mentioned that Rabbi Duncan made the mistake of looking within himself for the ground of his salvation, when he should have looked away to Christ instead. There is, however, an important sense in which our changed lives encourage assurance of salvation. I look away to Christ and I see that he died to save believers. How do I know, then, that I believe? James asserted that we find proof of our faith in our works. He wrote, "Someone will say, 'You have faith and I have works.'" But James answered, "I will show you my faith by my works" (James 2:18). In saying this, James did not teach salvation by works but rather the necessity of works in demonstrating our faith. Likewise, Peter urged us to "supplement your faith" with virtues such as "knowledge, ... self-control, ... steadfastness, ... godliness, ... brotherly affection, ... [and] love." These evidences of a changed life confirm our salvation, making our "calling and election sure" (2 Peter 1:5–10). As Jesus said, "the tree is known by its fruit" (Matt. 12:33).

With this principle in mind, we may avoid a problem opposite from the one that plagued Rabbi Duncan but that accounts for the lack of assurance in many Christians today: having failed to pursue a godly life, they lack the inward signs of a true and saving faith. Within ourselves, we do not gain a basis for acceptance with God—this comes only at the cross of Christ—but we can see Jesus' fingerprints on our character and proof of his power in our

9. John Calvin, *Institutes of the Christian Religion*, ed. John T. McNeill, trans. Ford Lewis Battles (Philadelphia: Westminster, 1960), 3.11.1.

10. Hugh Martin, *Christ for Us* (Edinburgh: Banner of Truth, 1998).

changed and changing lives. Do you lack a joyful assurance of salvation? Do you find yourself fearing the return of Jesus to judge the world? Perhaps the way for you to increase in joy and peace is, first, to look to the cross where Christ took away your sins and, second, to apply yourself to a lifestyle of obedience, so that by living for and with Jesus you may gain assurance that you truly belong to him.

SALVATION BY SOVEREIGN GRACE

In encouraging his readers about their hope in Christ, Paul further appeals to the sovereignty of God. Believers can be sure of their salvation because "God has not destined us for wrath, but to obtain salvation through our Lord Jesus Christ" (1 Thess. 5:9). The believer's salvation ultimately rests not in time but in eternity, when God has destined—elsewhere, he will specify "predestined" (Rom. 8:29–30; Eph. 1:5)—his people to be saved.

The Bible teaches that the whole of our salvation rests on the saving decree of God in eternity past. According to Scripture, God did not simply ordain that those who believe will be saved, but selected persons for himself, sending his Son to die for their sins and then sovereignly bringing them to faith so that they receive eternal life. Paul proclaimed in Ephesians 1:4 that God "chose us in [Christ] before the foundation of the world, that we should be holy and blameless before him." God chose not merely the way of salvation in principle but actual people to be saved: "He predestined us for adoption as sons through Jesus Christ, according to the purpose of his will" (v. 5). Here is our deepest ground of assurance: as Calvin wrote, "there cannot . . . be a better assurance of salvation gathered, than from the decree of God."[11]

The sovereignty of God is not limited to the predestination of his people to come to faith for salvation. God is also sovereign in the perseverance of believers, so that we continue in faith until death or the return of Christ. Here is the concern pressing on the Thessalonians' minds: would life or death find them ready for Jesus' coming? Paul answers that since they believe in Jesus, they can trust that "God has not destined" them "for wrath, but to obtain salvation through our Lord Jesus Christ" (1 Thess. 5:9).

Paul acknowledges here the necessity of trusting in Christ for salvation. We "obtain salvation through our Lord Jesus Christ," that is, through faith

11. John Calvin, *Commentaries*, 22 vols. (1854; repr., Grand Rapids: Baker, 2009), 21:290.

in him. Yet this requirement for faith does not throw us back onto our own resources and strength, so that, like Rabbi Duncan, we should nervously sweat the return of Jesus, wondering whether we will measure up. Rather, the God who was sovereign in ordaining our salvation through faith is also sovereign in maintaining our salvation through faith. Peter wrote that "by God's power [we] are being guarded through faith for a salvation ready to be revealed in the last time" (1 Peter 1:5). Yes, perseverance is "through faith," so that Christians must continue believing in Jesus. Yet through faith we "are being guarded" by a sovereign God who has committed himself to our salvation in the return of Christ. Paul gave the same reassurance in Philippians 1:6: "He who began a good work in you will bring it to completion at the day of Jesus Christ." The apostle's concern for the Thessalonians' assurance led him to conclude his benediction on this same theme of God's sovereign, preserving grace: "He who calls you is faithful; he will surely do it" (1 Thess. 5:24).

With this promise in mind, we realize that when Paul says that Jesus "died for us so that . . . we might live with him" (1 Thess. 5:10), he is referring not only to the life that we begin in Christ now but also to the eternal life that we will enjoy with him after he returns. Paul comments that "whether we are awake or asleep" makes no difference. Here, he returns to the topic at the beginning of this section, using *sleep* as a metaphor for *death*. Whether we are living or have died when Christ returns, we will live forever with him in glory. How can we be so sure? Because he "died for us" according to God's sovereign will. Christ's death is the seal for believers that secures the entirety of our salvation. Because Jesus died and rose again to live and reign forever, Paul concludes that Christians have every reason to rejoice in the certainty of eternal life to come when Christ returns: "For I am sure that neither death nor life, nor angels nor rulers, nor things present nor things to come, nor powers, nor height nor depth, nor anything else in all creation, will be able to separate us from the love of God in Christ Jesus our Lord" (Rom. 8:38–39).

GOD'S PURPOSE, OUR CALLING

In his brief but potent application, Paul tells us simply that God's purpose should become the basis of our ministry in the church: "Therefore encourage one another and build one another up, just as you are doing" (1 Thess. 5:11).

We see in Paul's exhortation a threefold agenda in response to the saving message of God's salvation in Christ. First, we must receive the gospel in personal faith. This emphasis is clear in 1 Thessalonians 5:9, where Paul says that we are destined "to obtain salvation through our Lord Jesus Christ." The word for *obtain* (Greek *peripoieo*) means to "acquire" or "take possession of." This does not mean that Christians merit their salvation, but it does speak of actively believing so as to receive God's freely offered salvation in Jesus Christ. Here is the key for our salvation: we must personally believe in Jesus Christ, trusting his death for our sins, resting our hopes in his work of salvation, and living with him. God chose us "in [Christ]" (Eph. 1:4), so that we may "obtain salvation" by trusting in Jesus as Lord and Christ.

Second, having received salvation, we continue to serve God's purpose by encouraging one another with words of gospel truth. The Greek word *parakaleo* may be translated as either "comfort" or "exhort." The idea is coming alongside those in weakness, difficulty, or doubt so as to help one another to continue in faith. We exhort not to tear down but to "build one another up." Tim Shenton gives some examples: "They must allay each other's fears about missing out on eternal life, comfort the downcast who have lost loved ones, and exhort the careless to behave in a manner worthy of their calling."[12] Are you giving such comfort and exhortation as a friend, a spouse, a parent, or a fellow Christian? Each of us should prayerfully seek opportunities to encourage fellow believers with the precious truths of God's saving Word. Most Christians can remember a conversation—perhaps after church or in a gathering—in which another believer spoke words that made a real difference in our lives. We should be connected with one another so as to understand our trials and temptations, and each of us should be ready with a biblical word of encouragement to another Christian in need.

Third, when Paul speaks of exhorting others so as to build them up, this implies that Christians are to be growing spiritually. We are not to be like the tribes of Israel when they settled into the Promised Land of Canaan. They had defeated their major enemies but left pockets of resistance all around them. Instead of pressing forward with the conquest as God had commanded, they settled in and took it easy. Before long, they were interacting with the pagans and then intermarrying with them. Within just years of entering the Promised Land, the Israelites were defiled through idolatry

---

12. Tim Shenton, *Opening Up 1 Thessalonians* (Leominster, UK: Day One, 2006), 100.

and other sins and ultimately came under God's judgment. Let us not repeat their mistake, but build one another up, pressing forward together instead of going backward.

When Paul uses the phrase "just as you are doing" (1 Thess. 5:11), he acknowledges that his readers had started well in encouraging one another to Christian growth. J. Philip Arthur writes: "Let them go on from this good beginning; let each of them excel in the business of fortifying and building up his or her brothers and sisters. Modern Christians who respond to Paul's challenge can be sure that they are doing something to meet a real need."[13]

In reflecting on the life and struggles of John Duncan, it seems that this matter of spiritual growth may explain a large part of his torment in lack of assurance. Duncan received the nickname *Rabbi* because of his unrivaled scholarship in biblical languages. By his own admission, however, this scholarship occupied the bulk of his attention, and his intense academic habits kept him from a healthy participation in the life of the church. Fervently pursuing his work for the Lord, he spent little time with the Lord, especially in personal devotional reading of Scripture.[14] His mistake is highlighted by John Murray, who notes that Christian growth, like assurance, "is cultivated . . . through faithful and diligent use of the means of grace and devotion to the duties which devolve upon us in the family, the church, and the world."[15]

Duncan's mistake urges us to consider Paul's approach to being joyfully ready for Christ's return. We do not ready ourselves by engaging in vain speculation about world events and the return of Jesus. But we do cultivate a joyful assurance and hope by looking in faith to the cross, by responding to faith with good works and obedience, and then by taking our part in the body of God's people, in the family, the church and the world, building up one another with God's Word of truth, the same gospel message by which we received salvation "through our Lord Jesus Christ" (1 Thess. 5:9).

13. J. Philip Arthur, *Patience of Hope: 1 and 2 Thessalonians Simply Explained* (Darlington, UK: Evangelical Press, 1996), 78.

14. Richard D. Phillips, "Assured in Christ," in *Assured by God*, ed. Burk Parsons (Phillipsburg, NJ: P&R Publishing, 2006), 85.

15. John Murray, "The Assurance of Faith," in *Collected Writings of John Murray* (Edinburgh: Banner of Truth, 1977), 2:274.

22

THE CHURCH IMPERATIVE

1 Thessalonians 5:12—13

We ask you, brothers, to respect those who labor among you and are over you in the Lord and admonish you, and to esteem them very highly in love because of their work. (1 Thess. 5:12–13)

A frequent complaint about Christianity goes like this: "I love Jesus, but I hate the church." The reasons given for this statement usually reflect the reality that while God's Son is perfect, his disciples on earth are far from it. One example is a rap song by Jefferson Bethke, titled "Why I Hate Religion, but Love Jesus," which was posted on the Internet and was so popular that it quickly received almost twenty million viewings. Bethke rapped: "Religion might preach grace, but another thing they practice / Tend to ridicule God's people, they did it to John the Baptist . . . So for religion, no I hate it, in fact I literally resent it / Because when Jesus said it is finished, I believe he meant it."[1]

To oppose religion is not, of course, exactly to hate the church. Yet most people think of "organized religion" in terms of churches, and many can share church experiences that support Bethke's accusation of self-righ-

---

1. Jefferson Bethke, "Why I Hate Religion, but Love Jesus," available at https://www.youtube.com/watch?v=1IAhDGYlpqY.

teousness and hypocrisy. So is it right for Christians to love Jesus and hate the church? The person to ask is Jesus himself, who not only did not hate the church because of its admitted failings but "loved the church and gave himself up for her" (Eph. 5:25). Jesus called it "my church," which "I will build" (Matt. 16:18). According to the Bible, if we love Jesus, we must love the church, which comes from him, belongs to him, and is sanctified by his saving work.

Church Leadership and Authority

As we draw near to the end of 1 Thessalonians, which by all accounts is one of Paul's earliest letters, it becomes evident that the church was not some later addition to the original Christian movement but was integral to it from the very beginning. As Paul concludes this letter, he gives instructions strongly suggesting that he had established the converts in that city as an organized church. He begins: "We ask you, brothers, to respect those who labor among you and are over you in the Lord and admonish you, and to esteem them very highly in love because of their work" (1 Thess. 5:12–13).

This statement shows that Paul recognized official leaders among the believers in Thessalonica. Some scholars argue that this text does not prove the official status of these leaders, but in fact Paul's description closely corresponds to that of the office of elder. Acts 14:23 shows that from the very beginning, Paul "appointed elders" in the churches he founded and invested them with authority by "committ[ing] them to the Lord." It is clear from later letters that Paul and the other apostles institutionalized this practice. For instance, Paul instructed Titus to "appoint elders in every town as I directed you" (Titus 1:5). Apostolic churches such as the one in Thessalonica were organized under the spiritual leadership of a group of elders working together. Acts 20:4 mentions two Thessalonian men who likely were elders ("Aristarchus and Secundus"), and there were probably more.

The Greek word for *elder* is *presbuteros*, which gives us the English word *presbyterian*. Presbyterian churches are organized on the apostolic pattern of shared leadership by a plurality of elders. In contrast to Presbyterian rule are Congregationalism, in which rule of the church is invested in the entire body of church members, and Episcopalianism, in which a bishop exercises sole authority over a church or churches. Presbyterian churches usually distinguish between ruling and teaching elders, the latter of whom are often called *ordained ministers* or *pastors* in light of 1 Timothy 5:17, which notes that some elders are set apart to "labor in preaching and teaching." Despite this distinction, teaching and ruling elders share the office that authorizes them together to oversee a church.

First Thessalonians 5:12 identifies the work to which church leaders are called. Paul's description applies to all elders, but especially to ministers in their full-time calling to the church: they "labor among you," "are over you in the Lord," and "admonish you."

First, Paul says that church leaders "labor among you." Primarily, this statement notes the costly effort—even to the point of exhaustion—involved in providing spiritual leadership to the church. The Greek word *kopiao* often refers to hard manual labor, as when Paul used it to describe his own work as a tentmaker. This description makes the point that pastors should be expected to work hard in service of the church. Matthew Henry aptly remarks: "They are called labourers, and should not be loiterers."[2] Hard work is needed because there is so much important work in the church for ministers to do. John Stott notes: "Whether it is study and the preparation of sermons, or visiting the sick and counseling the disturbed, or instructing people for baptism and marriage, or being diligent in intercession—these things demand that we 'toil, striving with all the energy which [Christ] mightily inspires within' us (Col. 1:29, RSV)."[3] While few things that a pastor does are physically difficult, the spiritual demands and emotional anxieties involved in the work can even "sap the strength of someone with a robust constitution."[4] It is noteworthy that Paul elsewhere speaks of the "labor" of "preaching and teaching" God's Word (1 Tim. 5:17). This tells us that churches should expect pastors to work especially hard in preparing their sermons, which week in and week out demand the greatest exertions of those called to this holy work.

Paul specifies not only how hard pastors should work but also in what sphere: they labor "among you" (1 Thess. 5:12). As shepherds in Christ's fold, ministers have their occupation with the sheep. Hebrews 13:17 points out

2. Matthew Henry, *Commentary on the Whole Bible*, 6 vols. (Peabody, MA: Hendrickson, n.d.), 5:636.
3. John R. W. Stott, *The Message of 1 & 2 Thessalonians*, The Bible Speaks Today (Downers Grove, IL: InterVarsity Press, 1994), 119.
4. J. Philip Arthur, *Patience of Hope: 1 and 2 Thessalonians Simply Explained*, Wellwyn Commentary Series (Ross-shire, UK: Evangelical Press, 1996), 81.

that ministers "are keeping watch over your souls," an expression that speaks of staying up late at night with anxiety. This emphasis is especially telling in a time when ministers tend to be evaluated according to the numerical size of their churches. A more biblical approach would focus pastors on the spiritual maturity and health of their people instead of the mere size of their congregations. This focus of labor "among you" should not keep pastors from interacting in matters pertaining to the broader church as may be warranted, but it should preclude ordained ministers from becoming extensively involved in the political or business sphere.

Second, Paul emphasizes that church leaders "are over you in the Lord" (1 Thess. 5:12). Here, the Greek word *proistemi* conveys the idea of presiding over or having charge. In 1 Timothy 3:4, the same word has the idea of "manage," and in 1 Timothy 5:17 of "rule." Paul expressed a similar notion when he identified the eldership as "the office of overseer" (1 Tim. 3:1).[5] Therefore, elders and pastors are authority figures in and over the church. Unlike secular authorities, who rule over the affairs of the world, the elders of Christ's church wield a spiritual authority that is ministerial and declarative: it falls to the elders to wield what the Bible calls "the keys of the kingdom" (Matt. 16:19). They do this by admitting or barring persons from church membership and the sacraments and by declaring on Christ's behalf the truths of God's Word as they pertain to those within the realm of the church.

It makes all the difference that Paul specifies the elders' rule as being "in the Lord" (1 Thess. 5:12). Their pastoral authority comes from Christ and must be wielded on his behalf and in his name. Thus, Peter referred to elders as shepherds under "the chief Shepherd," to whom they will give an account when he returns (1 Peter 5:2–4). G. K. Beale specifies: "Church leaders are not autonomous sovereigns but represent Jesus' authority. They are commissioned by Christ to carry out their oversight of the flock according to his will and not their own."[6] Therefore, elders must seek from Jesus the same love that died for their sins, the same zeal for truth and holiness that guided Christ's ministry on earth, and the power that only he can give to

---

5. The Greek word for *overseer* is *episcope*, from which we get *Episcopal* today. Whereas modern Episcopalianism represents the sole role of the bishop, Titus 1:5–7 makes it clear that presbyter and overseer were one and the same office, both words describing the general biblical office of elder.

6. G. K. Beale, *1–2 Thessalonians*, IVP New Testament Commentary Series (Downers Grove, IL: InterVarsity Press, 2003), 161.

save the lost and sanctify the saints, along with an overarching zeal for the glory of Christ in the worship and life of the church.

It is essential that Christian leaders demonstrate that their authority is "in the Lord" by always explaining the biblical basis or logic behind actions that are taken. Church members will not always agree with judgments that are made, but they should be able to see that the elders are doing their best to act in accordance with Scripture. Another way for elders to demonstrate that their rule is on Christ's behalf is a willingness to sacrifice for the well-being of church members. Leon Morris writes: "This is not a cold, external authority, but one exercised in the warmth of Christian bonds. Being 'in the Lord' it is an authority to be exercised for the spiritual good of believers (2 Cor. 10:8), and not to give the office-bearers opportunity for lording it over them."[7]

Third, Paul says that church leaders are called to "admonish" (1 Thess. 5:12). Here, the Greek word *noutheteo* means to "rebuke" or "correct." This is not a harsh exercise of judgment, but a loving admonition of believers who are going astray in either doctrine or life. We gain a flavor for the style of reproof required of elders when we see in Paul's letters both a forthright boldness and a tender mildness in dealing with the wayward. For instance, Paul directed the Corinthians to cast out of the church a man who was persisting in gross sexual sin, even having a sexual affair with his father's wife. Paul ordered, "Let him who has done this be removed from among you" (1 Cor. 5:2). This action might convey the idea of harshness in Paul's church discipline, until we read its epilogue in Paul's follow-up letter. It seems that the man in question repented under the prescribed discipline, in which case Paul became a chief advocate for his loving embrace: "You should rather turn to forgive and comfort him, or he may be overwhelmed by excessive sorrow. So I beg you to reaffirm your love for him" (2 Cor. 2:6–8). Here we see a living example of how Paul later advised Timothy regarding the *how* of pastoral admonishment: "reprove, rebuke, and exhort, with complete patience and teaching" (2 Tim. 4:2).

A Mandate for Church Membership

One of the most important applications that we can make from Paul's teaching on church leaders is to realize that it entails a mandate for church

---

7. Leon Morris, *The First and Second Epistles to the Thessalonians*, New International Commentary on the New Testament (Grand Rapids: Eerdmans, 1959), 166.

membership. If the Lord has placed leaders over the church and called them to the triple function of laboring, ruling, and admonishing, then it follows that the Lord's people are to be organized in churches under this very kind of spiritual leadership.

Some people ask the question, "Why should I join the church?" There are a number of good answers. One is that God has organized human society in covenantal relationships, and Christians are to bond together as a covenant people in the Lord. This points to the analogy of the church as a family, with its associations of affection, loyalty, and commitment. Just as the family bond is a relationship based on blood unity, the church family expresses our unity in the Spirit of Christ. Many Christians who enter the church should find the kind of acceptance, honesty, and ministry that they have never known in their natural families, and should gain the opportunity to provide warm and affectionate family love to others.

Another reason why church membership is essential is our calling together to the work of the Lord. Jesus' Great Commission charges us not merely to make casual believers or fickle spiritual consumers. Instead, Jesus gave his followers a commission that can be fulfilled only in the context of a faithful church: "Go therefore and make disciples of all nations, baptizing them in the name of the Father and of the Son and of the Holy Spirit, teaching them to observe all that I have commanded you" (Matt. 28:19–20). Christ's command to baptize is especially telling, since this sacrament serves to initiate new members into the church.

A third mandate for church members flows from Paul's teaching in 1 Thessalonians 5:12. Believers young and old need to be placed under spiritual authority that is exercised on Christ's behalf. We are not free agents with respect to our faith and Christian service, but sheep under the careful oversight of Christ's appointed shepherds. Occasionally, I interact with Christians who lament significant personal and moral problems. I ask, "Are you members in a church where you trust the elders, who exercise faithful Christian oversight and discipline?" Often, I am told, "No, we don't believe in that," or "We have chosen our church based on the kind of music we like." This attitude becomes a major problem when sin and temptation enter into people's lives and relationships and there is no spiritual authority willing or able to call them to biblical repentance. One sad tendency today is for churches to outsource pastoral care to paid, independent Christian counselors. While many of these counselors are loving and skilled servants of the Lord, they lack the authority needed to demand real and difficult change or impose the sanctions of church discipline as they may be needed. For this reason, the kind of specialized skill that counselors often provide is best organized as part of a pastoral staff under ministerial authority.

By using Paul's outline of the leader's duties as a guide, we can see what church membership requires. First, Christians must be willing to wholeheartedly support and eagerly receive the labor of their leaders. They should open their lives to the ministry of their pastors and elders, regularly attending worship services and other activities and coming to them for counsel when important and difficult decisions need to be made. They should seek biblical advice and prayer for needed changes in their lives. Above all, they should open their minds and hearts to the faithful preaching and teaching of God's Word. If Christians are served by pastors and elders who are laboring hard for their well-being, how important it is that they should make every effort to benefit from those vitally important labors!

It is important that preachers clearly teach and explain God's Word in their pulpit ministry. When the preacher sets forth the Scripture in this manner, Christians in the pew are to receive that instruction as the very Word of God in all its authority to inform their faith, motivate their worship, and shape their lives. This does not mean that church members should fear to ask questions, seek clarification, or even test a sermon against the standard of Scripture—any faithful pastor delights to receive such responses. It does mean, however, that when the teaching of Scripture is made clear through the pastor's ministry, church members should grant that teaching all the authority and reverence due to God himself. The Puritan Thomas Watson wrote: "How does [Christ] speak but by his ministers? As a king speaks by his ambassadors. Know, that in every sermon preached, God calls to you; and to refuse the message we bring, is to refuse God himself."[8] This claim can be made only when a pulpit ministry is clearly faithful to God's Word, which deserves the most fervent and careful attention of church members.

Tim Shenton tells of a missionary translator who was struggling to find the word to use for *obedience* in the native language. As he arrived home, he whistled for his dog, who came running at full speed. An old native, watching, smiled and said, "Your dog is all ear." Shenton writes: "Immediately the

---

8. Thomas Watson, *A Body of Divinity* (Edinburgh: Banner of Truth, 1958), 221.

missionary knew that the word obedience should be translated 'all ear.'"[9] Likewise, church members should be "all ears" when the Bible is preached in the church.

Second, as the elders are to exercise authority, church members must submit to this authority. Sometimes this will mean cheerfully accepting decisions that are not fully understood, but that involve the elders' spiritual judgment according to Scripture. There undoubtedly are cases when church elders act abusively or unbiblically, in which case concerns should be broached to their own fellow overseers (presuming that they have them). And sometimes, sadly, it will be necessary for Christians to separate from a church because of unbiblical priorities or untrustworthy leadership. But it should be the norm for Christ's people to respond submissively to the authority placed over them by Christ himself through obedience to his Word. I am often astonished at how ready church members are to elect men of spiritual quality and judgment to serve as their leaders, and then to jump to the worst possible conclusions when those same leaders make decisions after hours of prayer and scriptural deliberation! Paul had this very kind of unruly Christian in mind when he urged the Thessalonians "to respect those who labor among you and are over you in the Lord" and "esteem them very highly in love because of their work" (1 Thess. 5:12–13).

Third, and perhaps most difficult of all, church members should humbly respond to pastoral rebuke and admonishment, whether it is given to the whole church from the pulpit or in private from the pastor or a group of elders. Christians should place themselves under spiritual authority that they trust. Then, when those leaders bring matters of sin or duty to a member's attention, their admonishment should be accepted and given the most urgent attention and prayer. Whether men are reproved by the elders for the failure to provide for or lead their families, wives are reproved for rebellion against their husbands, or children are reproved for disrespect to their parents, Christian families are greatly bolstered by the admonishing ministry of the elders. When church members fall into open sin or fail in their obligations to attend worship or support the church's work, pastoral reproof should bring them back to their calling. Especially in the exercise of formal church discipline—which is probably the most daunting, exhausting, and heart-wrenching of all the work performed by elders—members

9. Tim Shenton, *Opening Up 1 Thessalonians* (Leominster, UK: Day One, 2006), 102–3.

should tremble to be barred from the sacraments of Christ or, even worse, excommunicated from the body of Christ's people by faithful shepherds who speak and act in Christ's own name.

When Hebrews 13:17 calls for obedience to church leaders, the author gives this reason: "for they are keeping watch over your souls." Many Christians have security companies that watch over their homes and possessions. When such a company calls for new locks or windows, the homeowner dutifully responds. Others have financial experts who watch over their money, and when a stockbroker recommends a sale of stock, the action is immediately taken. Pastors and elders watch over the immortal souls of God's people. How eagerly should submission be given, especially on clear biblical grounds, when the church leaders admonish us, calling for change or increased motivation for the well-being of our souls!

SUPPORTING CHURCH LEADERS

In 1 Thessalonians 5:13, Paul adds a word about the importance of Christians' support and encouragement of pastors and elders. This charge has three components, the first of which is to appreciate and respect church leaders. Paul began verse 12 this way: "We ask you, brothers, to respect those who labor among you." The word *respect* is the Greek word *know* and involves the ideas of both personal acquaintance and acknowledgment. In verse 13 he adds a charge for Christians "to esteem them very highly."

The point is not for Christians to be cringingly deferential like serfs before their lords, but respectfully appreciative like children with their fathers. A pastor friend related to me his experience during a home visit when a man verbally abused him and spoke in highly disrespectful tones. The pastor's chief lament over the situation was for the grave injury done to the man's sons, who sat watching. "How will those boys ever respect the ministry of God's Word," he wondered, "seeing their father's ill-treatment of a man called to the ministry of the gospel?"

Paul says that Christians should do more than show normal respect to their pastors; they should "esteem them very highly," the idea being that of special honor due to the holy office of the minister and elder. It is this biblical mandate that has prompted ordained ministers to receive the title *Reverend*, in keeping with Paul's emphasis in 1 Timothy 5:17: "Let the elders who rule well be considered worthy of double honor, especially those who labor in preaching and teaching." The issue is not the granting of social prestige, still less of celebrity status, but rather the spiritual submission to biblical authority that will enable the pastor to fulfill his God-given role in the lives of Christ's people.

In addition to respect, Paul would have Christians grant loving affection to their spiritual leaders: "Esteem them very highly in love because of their work" (1 Thess. 5:13). A faithful pastor labors intensely and prayerfully for the spiritual well-being of his flock; one of the chief blessings that compensates for many trials is the loving appreciation and affection of the people. This loving esteem includes providing generously for their material needs and praying for God to protect and bless their ministry (see 1 Cor. 9:9–14; Eph. 6:18–20).

One challenge to achieving this ideal is that the longer we know pastors and elders, the more we become aware of their defects and failings. Over time, it is inevitable that a pastor is going to let virtually everyone down. The anniversary of a death will be forgotten; wrong, though well-meant, words will be spoken; or providentially the pastor will be unavailable at a time when he is truly needed. In urging for pastors to be loved, however, Paul appeals not to their merits but to their work. Matthew Henry comments: "They must esteem their ministers highly in love; they should greatly value the office of the ministry, honour and love the persons of their ministers, and show their esteem and affection in all proper ways, and this is for their work's sake, because their business is to promote the honour of Christ and the welfare of men's souls."[10]

Finally, church members support their pastors and elders by placing a priority on the peace and unity of the church: "Be at peace among yourselves" (1 Thess. 5:13). Few things distract and discourage a pastor more greatly than when church members level needless complaints against fellow believers or disturb the church with quarrels and strife. Being peaceable also implies a willing support of decisions made by church leaders. John Calvin noted the spiritual importance of good relations in the church: "For Paul, in my opinion, had in view to oppose the artifices of Satan, who ceases not to use every endeavor to stir up quarrels, or disagreements, or enmities, between people and pastor." How great is the advantage to the enemy of Christ's people

10. Henry, *Commentary*, 5:636.

when "this desire for the cultivation of peace, which Paul recommends so strongly, is not exercised as it ought."[11]

THE BLESSED CHURCH

Everything that Paul has taught about church leadership and membership must be applied in careful biblical balance. Leaders are to oversee, not dominate or stifle. Authority is to be "in the Lord" and not in the flesh. Church members are to respect but not to worship their pastors. Christians are to obey and follow their leaders, but leaders are to teach and make decisions in keeping with Scripture. Members are to love church leaders not so much for their gifts—which may result in division or favoritism—but for their work on Christ's behalf. This need for balance and the difficulty of achieving it ought to persuade every Christian of the great need that we have for prayer, both for ourselves and for the church to which we belong.

Yet no matter how poorly we may succeed in achieving the biblical standard of church leadership and membership, we should never hate but always love the church. John MacArthur writes: "The church is the most blessed institution on earth, the only one built by the Lord Jesus Christ Himself . . . , the only institution He promised to eternally bless . . . , and the one about which He declared 'the gates of Hades will not overpower it.'"[12] For these reasons, in response to our relationship through faith with Jesus himself, Christians should treasure the church, pray for the church, and bind together in the church for the worship and work that is designed by God to bring glory to Christ and the gospel of salvation to the world.

---

11. John Calvin, *Commentaries*, 22 vols. (1854; repr., Grand Rapids: Baker, 2009), 21:293.
12. John MacArthur, *1 & 2 Thessalonians* (Chicago: Moody, 2002), 165–66.

23

A CALL TO MINISTRY

1 Thessalonians 5:13–15

*And we urge you, brothers, admonish the idle, encourage
the fainthearted, help the weak, be patient with them all.*
(1 Thess. 5:14)

A dispute that arises from time to time among Christians has
to do with the relationship between the law and the gospel,
or, to put it differently, between justification and sanctification. Sound Christians note the distinction between these doctrinal
matters. The law is what God commands us to do, and the gospel is what
God promises in order to save us. Justification is God's declaring sinners
forgiven and righteous through faith in Jesus. Sanctification is the process
by which justified believers become holy in practical ways.

In our studies of 1 Thessalonians, we have had several occasions to
note that while these doctrines are distinct, they must never be separated.
Throughout this letter, Paul celebrates the faith of the Thessalonians, through
which they are justified (1 Thess. 1:3, 8). This emphasis on faith does not
deter Paul, however, from also urging good works. In believing, they had
"turned . . . from idols to serve the living and true God" (v. 9). Having been
justified through faith, the believers are reminded by Paul that "this is the
will of God, your sanctification" (4:3).

Seeing that the law and the gospel, faith and works, and justification and sanctification are always intended to go together, Christians should not be surprised to receive not only promises but also exhortations in the Bible. Thus, when Paul issues commands to believers, he has not descended into legalism. Rather, he is reminding us that faith in Jesus involves getting up from the place of our sin and following him, just as Jesus himself so often commanded, "Come, follow me."

In the concluding section of 1 Thessalonians, Paul exhorts the believers in the church in their shared discipleship to Christ, charging them with three categories of attitude and action. The first of these categories deals with their relationships, involving respect for their leaders, mutual ministry among believers, and good deeds for even their enemies (1 Thess. 5:12–15). Second, the Thessalonians are exhorted with respect to their piety, which should be filled with joy and thanksgiving (vv. 16–18). Third, they are charged to be receptive to God's revealed Word (vv. 19–22). In all these matters, Christians are to respond to Christ's grace not only by trusting him but also by following his example of ministry, godliness, and zeal.

A BIBLICAL BALANCE FOR MINISTRY

The first set of Paul's exhortations pertains to the believers' duty to minister to one another. This is an important point of emphasis, especially since in the previous verses Paul had given prominence to the authority of church leaders. It is vital that the church have a balanced relationship between its official ministers and the rank-and-file members, or, as it is sometimes put, between the clergy and the laity. Errors in this matter have often crippled the church and brought needless strife.

The first error is called *clericalism*. This is the view that all ministry is performed by the ordained ministers, who are paid to do it, while the members are merely to follow in a docile manner. Historically, this approach is represented by the priests of the Roman Catholic Church, although it is found among Protestants as well. Many ministers promote this view by wanting to be in charge of everything and sometimes by holding their church in actual tyranny. The church is impoverished under this approach, because while Christ has distributed gifts to all believers, only a small few are permitted to exercise them. In his first epistle, Peter warned pastors to be "not domineering over those in your charge" (1 Peter 5:3), which is the case under clericalism.

A second error, *anticlericalism*, runs to the other extreme. Here, the church strips ministers of their authority or even does away with them, ignoring the fact that Christ has appointed pastors and teachers to lead and serve his flock. The book of Acts shows that Paul appointed elders in each of his churches and entrusted these men to train and lead Christ's people (Acts 14:23; 20:17). The Pastoral Epistles specifically command the appointment of leaders, whose qualifications are clearly laid out (1 Tim. 3:1–13; Titus 1:5–9). Furthermore, Paul calls for gifted teachers to be set aside for full-time teaching and pastoral work (1 Cor. 9:4–14; 1 Tim. 5:17).

The true model for ministry is neither clericalism nor anticlericalism, but is the *dual* approach to ministry explained by Paul in Ephesians 4:11–12. He pointed out that Christ appointed pastors and teachers for the church. Their role is "to equip the saints for the work of ministry, for building up the body of Christ." Ministry therefore starts with the teaching of God's Word by faithful and gifted pastors. This does not replace but inspires other ministries in the church and provides the biblical understanding and motivation that the people need. John Stott sees this well portrayed by a church bulletin he once saw. It was an Anglican church, so the bulletin listed the rector and then gave his name. Next came the associate rector and then the assistant rector with their names. But finally came the following: "Ministers: the entire congregation."[1] This captures Paul's emphasis and Christ's design for the building of his church.

MINISTERING TO NEEDS

If Ephesians 4:12 calls for all Christians to engage in ministry, 1 Thessalonians 5:14 works out some of the details: "And we urge you, brothers, admonish the idle, encourage the fainthearted, help the weak, be patient with them all." These charges are not given to the leaders, but to the rank-and-file Christians, who are commanded to care for one another. Paul cites three groups that need attention from fellow Christians: the idle, the fainthearted, and the weak.

1. John R. W. Stott, *The Message of 1 & 2 Thessalonians*, The Bible Speaks Today (Downers Grove, IL: InterVarsity Press, 1994), 168.

First, Paul identifies church members who are "idle." Many commentators point out that the Greek word *ataktos* has a broader meaning along the lines of "unruly" or "apathetic." This is a word used in the military for a soldier who has stepped out of rank. In this sense, Paul is describing a wide variety of unruly Christians who are not living up to their responsibility as church members.

It seems likely, however, that Paul has a specific kind of unruliness in mind, namely, the sin of idleness. Not only has he mentioned this problem in this letter already (1 Thess. 4:11), but in 2 Thessalonians 3:6 and 11 Paul addresses idleness again, using this same word: "For we hear that some among you walk in idleness, not busy at work, but busybodies." This problem might have been related to confusion over the return of Christ, so that some believers abandoned their earthly duties to wait for Jesus' coming. For this or other reasons, "there were some at Thessalonica who had ceased to work and were imposing on the generosity of others."[2] In this way, the gospel was disgraced as Christians neglected their duties in the family and society.

A similar situation occurs in churches today when believers engage in an idle lifestyle of recreation and especially when Christians neglect important duties. It is true that Christian salvation offers believers liberty, but this freedom is never to be used irresponsibly or for self-indulgence. There may be fully employable fathers who refuse to work hard to provide for their families, mothers who neglect the needs of the home and of children, or students who are too busy socializing to put in the study needed for decent grades. There are, of course, unusual situations in which faithful believers need understanding and encouragement. But when Christians are simply neglecting their duties, they should be appropriately reproved by fellow Christians.

Years ago when I was a college professor, a student who was the leader of a Christian discipleship group was failing my class. When I summoned him to my office, he suggested that as a fellow believer I would understand that Bible study was more important than academic work. I answered that if he did not improve his grades, I would not only fail him but also ensure that he was removed from his Christian leadership position. When he expressed shock at this reply, I pointed out from passages such as the one before us that

2. Leon Morris, *The First and Second Epistles to the Thessalonians*, New International Commentary on the New Testament (Grand Rapids: Eerdmans, 1959), 168.

a Christian witness is disgraced by neglect of duty. In response to my rebuke, and suddenly aware that I would not give him special treatment as a fellow believer, he managed to put in the work necessary to improve his grade.

A second kind of person who needs attention is the "fainthearted" (1 Thess. 5:14). In contrast to the slacker, Paul here addresses the needs of those who are easily discouraged. While some Christians boldly embrace the dangers and challenges of following Jesus in this world, others are easily made to tremble, especially in a situation like that at Thessalonica, in which the church faced serious and painful persecution. The literal meaning of the Greek term *oligopsukos* is "little-souled." Some Christians merit this description nearly all the time, but virtually all of us will fall into this condition at least some of the time. The proper ministry response from Christian friends is encouragement: "encourage the fainthearted" (v. 14). This ministry may include reminders of biblical promises, support in prayer, and examples of others who struggled but continued in salvation.

One of the best biblical examples of this kind of encouragement was given by Jonathan, the beloved covenant friend of David. Jonathan came to David at a time when his friend was deeply disheartened over the ceaseless malice of Israel's King Saul, who happened to be Jonathan's father. Jonathan encouraged David, first, by making the effort to spend time with him. According to 1 Samuel 23:16, he further "strengthened [David's] hand in God." This expression tells how Jonathan restored David's confidence in the Lord: primarily by reminding him of God's promises for his eventual success. In most cases, the greatest helps that a Christian friend can give are encouraging truths taken from the Bible and wisely applied to the needy soul.

Third, Paul urges Christians to "help the weak." This term probably applies to those who find it difficult to abandon sin and resist worldly pressures. Paul's letters reveal how uncompromising the apostle was in demanding that Christians turn away from patterns of sin. Yet at the same time, he urges Christians never to abandon believers who are weak, yet still trying to do better. The word for *help* literally means "to lay hold of," with the idea of not letting them go. This should be our response to Christians who fall prey to substance abuse or are entangled in ungodly relationships, and who thus require close accountability and constant support. Leon Morris writes: "It is good for weak souls to know that there are others who are with them, who will cleave to them in the difficult moment, who will not forsake them[;] . . . the weak are not to be simply abandoned, but made to feel that they belong, that they have strong comrades in Christ."[3]

Gene Green points out that Paul sometimes uses the word for *weak* to point out those with low social status or economic standing. In 1 Corinthians 1:26–29, the apostle states that it is God's design that many Christians will be such weak persons, since "God chose what is weak in the world to shame the strong." While Greco-Roman society held the weak in contempt, Christians were to reach out with help toward their brothers and sisters who were downcast in the world. Green argues that the Christian attitude to weakness is to take social action in aid of those who are poor or down-trodden: "Those whom society walks over and puts down are lifted up and given support by the church."[4]

In reflecting on these three categories of ministry, we find it obvious that a first step is to seek to understand the person and the situation. The "idle," "fainthearted," and "weak" may exhibit similar behavior. For instance, a believer who is out of work may put little effort into finding a job for any of these reasons. Yet there is a significant difference between them! Only through caring, personal involvement can we discern the difference and know how to minister appropriately. This need for personal care especially needs to be emphasized when it comes to admonishment: Paul's teaching does not grant a warrant to every church member to give a piece of his or her mind to everyone with whom he or she has a difference. Paul's approach to ministry calls us to enter into close personal relationships that will enable us to understand the heart, so that with prayerful wisdom we may know how best to constructively encourage and exhort.

To his varied counsel for ministry, Paul adds a vital note that applies to all situations and people: "Be patient with them all" (1 Thess. 5:14). Unless a wayward believer has hard-heartedly rejected all church authority and accountability, Christians should never give up but patiently bear with all manner of failings and weaknesses. Even in the case of those who turn away completely, we should continue to persevere in the patient ministry of intercessory prayer. In contrast to the irritable and impatient attitude that so often marks worldly relationships, Christians are to be mild and

---

3. Ibid., 169.
4. Gene L. Green, *The Letters to the Thessalonians*, Pillar New Testament Commentary (Grand Rapids: Eerdmans, 2002), 254.

long-suffering with one another. Jesus taught that if a brother sins as many as seven times in a day, and yet "turns to you seven times, saying, 'I repent,' you must forgive him" (Luke 17:4). His meaning was that we should never fail to bear with those in need of patient forgiveness, just as God patiently forgives all our sins through Christ's ministry of grace.

Doing Good, Not Evil

First Thessalonians 5:12–15 forms a unit focusing on the Christian attitude in a variety of relationships. Christians are to treat church leaders with respect and "esteem them very highly in love" (1 Thess. 5:13). Among their fellow believers, Christians are to minister to the needs around them with a balanced response of truth and love. Finally, Paul offers a word of exhortation concerning even the believers' enemies, which includes those violent persons who were persecuting this fledgling church. In this case, Paul charges them: "See that no one repays anyone evil for evil, but always seek to do good to one another and to everyone" (v. 15).

Paul's first point in this matter is that Christians must not retaliate for wrongs so as to seek to harm others. People outside the church—and sometimes within it—may deal out evil, but it should never be returned to them. Jesus taught: "Love your enemies and pray for those who persecute you, so that you may be sons of your Father who is in heaven. For he makes his sun rise on the evil and on the good, and sends rain on the just and on the unjust" (Matt. 5:44–45). The apostle Peter exhorted believers to adopt this attitude in direct imitation of Jesus' meek demeanor in taking up the cross: "When he was reviled, he did not revile in return; when he suffered, he did not threaten, but continued entrusting himself to him who judges justly" (1 Peter 2:23).

This precept does not preclude Christians from seeking lawful redress from the civil authorities who are appointed by God to this very end (see Rom. 13:3–4). Nor does it mean that we should not act in defense of others. Yet when it comes to merely personal injuries against ourselves, Christians are privileged to honor Jesus by "turning the cheek" and giving our cloak as well to the one who asks for our tunic (Matt. 5:39–40).

Not only are Christians not to retaliate in answer to evil, Paul urges, but they are to go to the other extreme by seeking all opportunities to do good:

"Always seek to do good to one another and to everyone" (1 Thess. 5:15). Here is an accurate depiction of true Christian liberty: since we have God to save us and meet all our needs, believers are freed from self-interested concern so as to devote ourselves to doing good to everyone else.

Two words in this verse highlight exactly what Paul means. He says to "always" do good, which means that this should be the settled policy of Christ's people in every situation and to all people. Moreover, he charges us to "pursue" good (NIV), using a word that means to "chase after" or "zealously hunt down" (Greek *dioko*). Paul therefore is not advising Christians to occasionally do something good but to make a habit of going out of our way in order to bless others. Leon Morris explains that Paul "is laying down goodness in the face of provocation to evil as a great general principle which must underlie the conduct of the Christian at all times."[5] Morris suggests that the extent to which the early Christians embraced this precept demonstrated not only their spiritual vitality but "that this was responsible in some measure for the impact the early Christians made on the men of their day."[6] If Christians today will commit ourselves to a similarly gracious attitude toward everyone, we may see an increase in our influence as well. William Barclay wrote: "When a church lives up to Paul's advice, it will indeed shine like a light in a dark place; it will have joy within itself and power to win others."[7]

MINISTRY IN IMITATION OF CHRIST

In one of his greatest summaries of the Christian life, Paul wrote to the Galatians, "I have been crucified with Christ. It is no longer I who live, but Christ who lives in me" (Gal. 2:20). If Christ lives in and through those who trust him, then we should expect to see their lives bear an increasing resemblance to the ministry of Christ. This resemblance is exactly what Paul has in mind as he sets forth the Christian calling to relationships of love and grace. Indeed, in considering Paul's charge to the early converts, we see a reflection of the very actions by which Christ brought salvation to our souls.

5. Morris, *First and Second Thessalonians*, 171.
6. Ibid., 170.
7. William Barclay, *The Letters to the Philippians, Colossians, and Thessalonians* (Louisville: Westminster, 1975), 207–8.

244

In 1 Thessalonians 5:12–13, Paul urges Christians to lovingly submit to their leaders. This reflects Jesus' humble submission to his heavenly Father and the zeal with which he obeyed the mission given to him in this world. Jesus told his disciples, "My food is to do the will of him who sent me and to accomplish his work" (John 4:34). Jesus was sent into the world by his Father on no less a mission than to deliver his people from sin by dying in their place on the cross. When Christians receive the biblical calling to submit and obey, they should remember the great submission of Christ on the cross. If Jesus was exalted by the Father for his humble obedience in bearing the cross, we should therefore be eager to do likewise. When Christians read in the Bible of how Jesus glorified God by doing good in the midst of unjust suffering, we should remember Peter's words in charging us to do likewise: "For to this you have been called, because Christ also suffered for you, leaving you an example, so that you might follow in his steps" (1 Peter 2:21).

We especially think of Jesus' example in light of Paul's urging us to ministry in the church. From this perspective, we realize that everything that Paul is asking us to do for the needy in our midst only mirrors the actions that Jesus took in saving our souls. For instance, Paul says to "admonish the idle." Were we not only idle in the things of God but active in pursuit of selfishness and sin? Jesus came warning us of God's judgment and the need of every sinner to be forgiven by God. To reject Jesus' salvation, he said, is to "die in your sin" (John 8:21). Jesus sent forth his gospel to rouse us from idleness toward the things of God, so that through faith we might embrace the gift of eternal life.

Paul urges believers to "encourage the fainthearted." There has never been greater encouragement than that given by Jesus in the Bible. He calls the weary, saying, "Come to me, all who labor and are heavy laden, and I will give you rest" (Matt. 11:28). He encourages the fearful who face tribulation, imploring, "Take heart; I have overcome the world" (John 16:33). Have you heard Jesus' invitation to be forgiven of your sins and then to receive the saving grace that he alone can give? He declares, "Truly, truly, I say to you, whoever hears my word and believes him who sent me has eternal life" (5:24). There is no greater encouragement to the fainthearted soul than to hear the call of Jesus, inviting you into the fullness of salvation through faith in him.

Finally, Paul tells us to "help the weak." This exhortation, above all the others, may be the most Christlike. Romans 5:6 reminds us that Christ did

245

not save us after we had already done something to save ourselves. Instead, it was "while we were still weak" that "Christ died for the ungodly." Did you imagine that it is only godly people whom Jesus saves—the kind of public Christian who seems to have it all together? Have you been thinking that you have already disqualified yourself from Christianity through your sin or unbelief? The Bible says that Jesus died for the weak and ungodly. Paul declares, "God shows his love for us in that while we were still sinners, Christ died for us" (v. 8).

Paul said that Christians should help the weak by laying hold of them and not letting them go. Jesus set the example: he laid hold of us even in our sin, taking our guilt to himself and bearing its penalty on the cross. If we believe in him—committing our soul to his salvation through simple faith—we can know that he will never let us go. "I will never leave you nor forsake you," he promised (Heb. 13:5). Since this is true, why should we ever let go of one another, however fainthearted or weak we might be? Even though, regrettably, we continue to fail, "the blood of Jesus . . . cleanses us from all sin." By trusting his grace together and walking in his light, we truly may "have fellowship with one another" (1 John 1:7).

24

THE SPIRIT OF JOY

1 Thessalonians 5:16—22

Rejoice always, pray without ceasing, give thanks in all circumstances; for this is the will of God in Christ Jesus for you.
(1 Thess. 5:16–18)

aving arrived in the final section of Paul's message to the Thessalonians before his benediction, we are prompted to ask a question: What is the purpose of the church? This question is closely linked to Paul's final exhortations, since from the beginning of this letter he has identified the Thessalonian congregation as a good church. Paul has not written to correct a major doctrinal error, as in Galatians, or to rebuke major moral lapses, as he will later do in 1 Corinthians. Instead, Paul has written to express his joy over the Thessalonians' faith, love, and hope, to address questions about Christ's second coming, and to deal with minor concerns. As he concludes his letter, he gives his general pastoral encouragement for them to press on and fulfill their calling together.

So what is the primary calling of the church? Some people say that the main purpose of the church is evangelism. After all, Jesus told the apostles to "go . . . and make disciples of all nations" (Matt. 28:19). Those who think this way look on the church as an army conquering the world through its witness. Others answer that the church's purpose is to do ministry in the world. Jesus rejoiced in Matthew 25, "I was hungry and you gave me food, I was thirsty and you gave me drink" (25:35). On this view, the church is mainly a social-service agency. Still others think of the church as a safe place where we can escape the damage occurring in our world. Those who think this way look on the church as a fortress and a refuge.

According to Paul, none of these is the primary calling of the church. Certainly, the church must evangelize, minister, and protect, but these are not God's main purposes for the church. According to Paul, the purpose of the church is that we, God's people, should grow spiritually so that we increasingly attain to Christlike holiness and maturity. This principle is perhaps most clearly expressed in the fourth chapter of Ephesians, a letter that is widely regarded as the most full and developed expression of Paul's pastoral philosophy. There, he writes that we are to attain "to mature manhood, to the measure of the stature of the fullness of Christ . . . . Speaking the truth in love, we are to grow up in every way into him who is the head, into Christ" (Eph. 4:13–15).

This definition challenges the kind of Christianity that is common today. For many church members, Christian faith resides in the background of their lives. They think little about the Bible or God or their own spiritual condition, and they draw from very little of the power for godliness that is available to them in Christ. For many, Christianity is mainly the comfort that we can dial 911 to heaven and make an emergency call when needed. Martyn Lloyd-Jones asks, "Is Christian truth something you like to have, and to know that it is there if you are taken desperately ill, or some loved one is taken ill, or if you are suddenly confronted by the loss of your income, or when some disaster takes place, or when you are on your death bed?"[1]

If this describes your Christianity, then you should realize that it is very far from the conception not only of Paul but also of Jesus Christ. "And this is eternal life," Jesus prayed, "that they know you, the only true God, and Jesus Christ whom you have sent" (John 17:3). The essence of salvation is knowing God in a personal relationship that grows continually in this life until, in eternity to come, we are "filled with all the fullness of God" (Eph. 3:19).

1. D. Martyn Lloyd-Jones, *The Unsearchable Riches of Christ: An Exposition of Ephesians 3* (Baker: Grand Rapids, 1998), 290–91.

A TRINITARIAN RELATIONSHIP WITH GOD

As Paul concludes his first letter to the Thessalonians, he is concerned to direct the new believers to a spiritual maturity in which their relationship to God has grown and been strengthened. Here, as elsewhere, Paul conceives of our relationship to God in terms of the doctrine of the Trinity. There is only one God, but God is known in three persons: Father, Son, and Holy Spirit. Paul's concluding exhortations clearly follow this biblical pattern: through our relationship with God the Son, believers are brought into communion with God the Father, through the power provided by God the Spirit (Eph. 2:18).

In 1 Thessalonians 5:14–15, the apostle calls believers to *enter sacrificially into the ministry of the Son.* To heed Paul's call to "admonish the idle, encourage the fainthearted, help the weak, be patient with them all" is to follow in the footsteps of Jesus, who began the Last Supper by donning a servant's towel and washing his disciples' feet. "I have given you an example," he said, "that you also should do just as I have done to you" (John 13:15). His example called them, as it calls us, to humble, personal, and sacrificial care for the well-being of others.

Paul's exhortations in 1 Thessalonians 5:16–22 open up further dimensions of the Trinity by teaching us how to relate to the Father and the Holy Spirit. The Bible teaches that while the Son accomplishes our salvation, the Father plays the role of ordaining his saving will for us. Paul describes in verses 16–18 "the will of God in Christ Jesus for you" in terms of *living consciously in the Father's love.* Moreover, the Holy Spirit has the role of applying God's saving work in our lives. Therefore, in verses 19–22, Paul urges us to *walk intentionally in step with the Holy Spirit.*

LIVING IN THE FATHER'S LOVE

Since our study of 1 Thessalonians 5:14–15 considered Paul's charge to imitate the servant ministry of God's Son, we progress in verse 16 to living consciously in the presence of the Father's love. Paul expresses this principle in terms of a threefold exhortation: "Rejoice always, pray without ceasing, give thanks in all circumstances; for this is the will of God in Christ Jesus for you" (1 Thess. 5:16–18). All three of these responses—joy, prayer, and thanksgiving—are by-products of a life consciously opened to the Father's love.

When speaking of Christian joy, we must first differentiate between true spiritual joy and the giddy emotionalism of the world. Unbelievers are happy when their circumstances are good. Christian joy, in contrast, does not depend on how well things are going, but is able to flourish even amid great afflictions. This was the setting in Thessalonica: it was to a persecuted church with many troubles that Paul gave his exhortation, "Rejoice always."

The commands of 1 Thessalonians 5:16–18 are very terse, lacking any development. This probably reflects the fact that Paul had recently spent time with the Thessalonians, so they could remember his more detailed teaching on subjects such as joy, prayer, and thanksgiving. Fortunately for us, Paul expands on these themes in his other letters, as do the other apostles in their writings, so we may consider his brief teaching in our passage in light of that broader instruction.

Speaking of joy, if pleasant circumstances are not the cause of a Christian's happiness, then what are the sources of our rejoicing? First, Christians rejoice in the Father's gift of his Son to be our Savior. The Christian says, "No matter what the world may do to me, God has given his Son Jesus for my salvation!" Paul reasoned this way in Romans 8:32, saying that since God "did not spare his own Son but gave him up for us all, how will he not also with him graciously give us all things?" John Lillie notes some of our reasons for rejoicing in Christ:

> What is there that our ruined nature needs, which it cannot find in Christ?—atoning blood, to cleanse from all sin—a righteousness, in which not even the eye of the Divine holiness can discern spot or blemish—subduing, renewing power, to form us into the Divine image—a Teacher, to instruct our ignorance—a Friend, to cheer us—a kindred High Priest, to intercede for us in the heavenly places, and reconcile us to God—a wise, faithful, gentle, almighty Shepherd, to lead us, and feed us, and guard us through the wilderness into the bright, spacious, ever fresh and unfading pastures of eternity.[2]

According to Peter, rejoicing in Jesus is one of the chief marks of a true Christian. He writes: "Though you do not now see him, you believe in him

---

2. John Lillie, *Lectures on Paul's Epistles to the Thessalonians*, Tentmaker Classic Commentaries (1860; repr., Stoke-on-Trent, UK: Tentmaker Publications, 2007), 261.

and rejoice with joy that is inexpressible and filled with glory" (1 Peter 1:8). Jesus spoke in the same emotional key when he said that "father Abraham rejoiced that he would see my day" (John 8:56). The angels who heralded Jesus' birth gave us an example of rejoicing by announcing "good news of great joy that will be for all the people" (Luke 2:10). Christians may and should rejoice in all settings for God's gift of his Son.

A second source of Christian joy is the relationship with the Father that Jesus has secured by his saving work—what Paul described in Romans 5:1 as "peace with God through our Lord Jesus Christ." The knowledge of God's sovereign care compensates for all manner of earthly troubles, so that Christians can rejoice even in the most barren times. Habakkuk memorably expressed this reality:

> Though the fig tree should not blossom,
>> nor fruit be on the vines,
> the produce of the olive fail
>> and the fields yield no food,
> the flock be cut off from the fold
>> and there be no herd in the stalls,
> yet I will rejoice in the Lord;
>> I will take joy in the God of my salvation.
> God, the Lord, is my strength;
>> he makes my feet like the deer's;
>> he makes me tread on my high places. (Hab. 3:17–19)

This example points out a third source of the believer's joy, namely, the Bible's testimony to God's saving promises. God's Word assures us that "for those who love God all things work together for good, for those who are called according to his purpose" (Rom. 8:28). Psalm 55:22 encourages us, "Cast your burden on the Lord, and he will sustain you; he will never permit the righteous to be moved." These and myriad other promises enable the Christian to "rejoice in the hope of the glory of God" and even to "rejoice in our sufferings" (Rom. 5:2–3).

In addition to joy, Christians are to live in an attitude of continual prayer. "Pray without ceasing," Paul says (1 Thess. 5:17). He is not suggesting that Christians drop all our other activities so as only to pray, but urges a heart that is always open to God. Paul advocates prayer not merely as an action but

251

also as an attitude. J. B. Lightfoot wrote: "It is not in the moving of the lips, but in the elevation of the heart to God, that the essence of prayer consists. Thus amidst the commonest duties and recreations of life it is still possible to be engaged in prayer."[3] The prayerful attitude that Paul seeks was lived by Enoch and Noah, who according to the Bible "walked with God" (Gen. 5:24; 6:9).

It is not difficult to see the relationship between rejoicing in the Lord and prayer, since Paul frequently connected them. In Romans 12:12, he wrote: "Rejoice in hope, be patient in tribulation, be constant in prayer." Similarly, in Philippians, when he commanded believers to "rejoice in the Lord always," he followed this command with an exhortation to prayer: "Do not be anxious about anything, but in everything by prayer and supplication with thanksgiving let your requests be made known to God" (Phil. 4:4, 6). Starting with the joy of knowing God, "believers are so to cultivate a spirit of constant prayerfulness that their whole lives will be permeated by the presence of God."[4]

The third leg of Paul's call to live in God's presence is to "give thanks in all circumstances" (1 Thess. 5:18). How are Christians to be thankful for trials and tribulations? The answer is that our faith turns us away from ourselves and onto God. Just as David faced giant Goliath without fear by his faith in God, Christians face all threats and dangers with gratitude to the God who they know is sovereignly ruling for his glory and our salvation.

The great Princeton theologian Benjamin Warfield told the story of a Christian man who traveled west during the days of the pioneers. One day he found himself in the middle of a gunfight in a wild western town. The whole town was in an uproar, but he saw one man who—despite all the commotion—remained calm, cool, and collected. The traveler was so amazed at the man's composure that he said to himself, "Now there is a man who knows his theology." At this he walked up to him and asked the first question in the Shorter Catechism, "What is the chief end of man?" The man answered correctly, "Man's chief end is to glorify God and to enjoy him forever." "Ah!" said he; "I knew you were a Shorter Catechism boy by your looks!" "Why that is just what I was thinking of you," was the rejoinder.

3. J. B. Lightfoot, *Notes on the Epistles of St. Paul* (Peabody, MA: Hendrickson, 1993), 81.
4. Geoffrey B. Wilson, *New Testament Commentaries*, 2 vols. (Edinburgh: Banner of Truth, 2005), 2:177–78.

Young people who are raised on the biblical truth of God's sovereignty as summarized in the Shorter Catechism grow up to be adults who possess confidence in God's working for his glory and our salvation.[5]

Thinking on this truth caused the Scottish preacher George Matheson to grow in spiritual maturity. Matheson had often trusted God to help him manage the near-blindness that he had suffered since childhood, but he could not remember ever thanking God for this dreadful affliction. Then he prayed: "My God, I have never thanked you for my 'thorn'. I have thanked you a thousand times for my roses, but never once for my 'thorn'. . . . Teach me the glory of my cross; teach me the value of my pain. Show me that my tears have made my rainbows."[6] Likewise, when we realize that God is sovereignly working in all our circumstances, knowing the faithfulness of his love, we will thank the Lord at all times.

Paul notes that these gracious responses to God's loving presence are "the will of God in Christ Jesus for you" (1 Thess. 5:18). God does not necessarily will that we should have good health or earthly riches, faithful friends or successful careers. God does something better than these things for us: he gives us his Son to be our Savior, and in his Word he promises us eternal life in glory. It is his will that we should grow into the maturity of joy, prayer, and thanksgiving, because of and "in Christ Jesus." God's grace is revealed to us in Christ, and the Holy Spirit's power for this spiritual transformation comes through faith in Jesus.

Knowing that these blessings are found in Christ Jesus warns us against directly seeking after joy, prayerfulness, or thanksgiving. We do not attain to joy by seeking to be happy, but by seeking Christ and by coming to God through the promises of his Word. We do not attain to prayer by means of rigorous schedules, but by realizing all that God is and has for us in Christ. We will become thankful not by means of reminders that we place on our desks but by coming to know God better and reflecting on everything that he has secured for us eternally in his Son. In short, it is through a worshiping heart that is directed to God that these graces arise in our souls. Psalm 16:8–9 declares: "I have set the LORD always before me; because he is at my right hand, I shall not be shaken. Therefore my heart is glad, and my whole

5. B. B. Warfield, "Is the Shorter Catechism Worth While?," in *Selected Shorter Writings of Benjamin B. Warfield*, ed. John E. Meeter (Phillipsburg, NJ: Presbyterian and Reformed, 1980), 1:383–84.
6. Quoted in Tim Shenton, *Opening Up 1 Thessalonians* (Leominster, UK: Day One, 2006), 109–10.

being rejoices." It is the trusting and worshiping heart, David asserts, that knows the joy of the Lord.

FUELING THE FLAME OF THE HOLY SPIRIT

Paul's final exhortations concern the believer's cooperation with the Holy Spirit's work in our lives. Just as Christians are to enter sacrificially into the servant ministry of the Son and live consciously in the Father's love, we are also to *fuel the flame of the Holy Spirit.*

Along these lines, Paul urges his readers, "Do not quench the Spirit" (1 Thess. 5:19). The ministry of the Holy Spirit is sometimes compared to a fire (Matt. 3:11; Acts 2:3), so resisting the Spirit's ministry is similar to dousing a fire with water or ashes. Presumably, this quenching takes place when believers crowd out God's Word, prayer, and corporate worship with earthly pursuits or sinful pleasures. The result is that the effects of the Spirit's work are diminished, like the flickering flames of a fire that has been deprived of oxygen. Leon Morris suggests problems that Paul had identified earlier in this letter: "Loafing, immorality, and other sins . . . will quench the Spirit in a man's life, and result in the loss of spiritual power and joy."[7]

Paul's particular concern focuses on neglecting or rejecting God's revealed Word. "Do not despise prophecies," he writes (1 Thess. 5:20). Paul occasionally mentions the New Testament prophets (1 Cor. 12:28; Eph. 3:5; 4:11). We remember that these early churches did not yet possess the written New Testament, so God provided prophets to declare God's Word concerning salvation in Jesus Christ. These prophets might also foretell future events, but their main job was to "forth-tell" the gospel: they were preachers of the New Testament message before that message was recorded in writing. These gifted men belonged to the foundation-laying era of the apostles, and once the canon of the Bible was completed, their foretelling function ceased in the church (see also Eph. 2:20).

Today, the analogy to prophecy is the preaching of God's Word. This means that to fuel the flame of God's Spirit, we must devote ourselves to the ministry of the Bible, in personal reading and especially in the preaching ministry of the church. Either the Word of God will shape our thinking

---

7. Leon Morris, *The First and Second Epistles to the Thessalonians*, New International Commentary on the New Testament (Grand Rapids: Eerdmans, 1959), 175.

or the message of the world will drown out God's voice and quench the ministry of God's Spirit.

Whenever we emphasize the importance of following teachers of God's Word, however, there is the serious danger of false teachers who lead many people astray. The New Testament frequently warns against wolves "in sheep's clothing" (Matt. 7:15)—false teachers who intentionally lead followers astray, along with self-serving religious charlatans (Phil. 3:18–19). Paul's ministry was frequently opposed by false teachers, many of whom were outwardly more impressive than he was (1 Cor. 2:1–4). It was important, therefore, for the Thessalonians to listen to true prophets and close their ears to false teachers. How could they tell the difference? Paul writes: "Test everything; hold fast what is good. Abstain from every form of evil" (1 Thess. 5:21–22).

We are living in a time when spirituality is big business and also when spiritual discernment among Christians is low. For this reason, one of the most dangerous places for an undiscerning believer is the average Christian bookstore. Whether it is mystical paganism dressed up in Christian garb or the lies of the so-called prosperity gospel, deadly false teaching is aggressively marketed by many Christian businessmen, most of whom are themselves unaware of the danger they are posing. In this kind of environment, the apostle John urges us: "Beloved, do not believe every spirit, but test the spirits to see whether they are from God, for many false prophets have gone out into the world" (1 John 4:1).

The way to test someone's teaching is to compare it with the written Word of God. This is what the Bereans had done during Paul's recent visit there to preach the gospel. Acts 17:11 commends the Bereans as being "more noble" than others, because "they received the word with all eagerness, examining the Scriptures daily to see if these things were so." Preachers are to base their messages on the Bible, proving their doctrine through straightforward appeals to Scripture and not with clever displays of logic or flights of emotion. Moreover, Jesus said that the personal character and conduct of teachers would reveal the soundness of their teaching: "You will recognize them by their fruits. . . . Every healthy tree bears good fruit, but the diseased tree bears bad fruit" (Matt. 7:16–17).

With careful attention to biblical faithfulness, and by keeping watch for the personal conduct of teachers and the spiritual quality of their ministry, believers cooperate with the Holy Spirit. "Test everything," Paul says, and "hold fast what is good." Paul's word for the idea of testing means to "prove" the soundness of metals. Like a goldsmith gazing intently on a bar of precious metal, believers are to examine teaching for its genuine biblical quality, taking from it "what is good" and true according to Scripture, and always being careful to "abstain from every form of evil" (1 Thess. 5:21–22). Whenever it is clear that teaching is promoting self-worship, malice, greed, sexual indecency, or falsehood, Christians are responsible to recognize violations of God's law and to flee from worldliness and sin.

In Galatians 5:25 (NIV), Paul wrote that believers are to "keep in step with the Spirit." The Spirit is, of course, the author of the Bible, having supernaturally inspired its human writers. The way to hear the Spirit today is not by opening our hearts to mystical impressions but by directing our minds to the pages of the Bible, where the Spirit of God speaks and gives life to God's people. We live in a day when worldly, sensual voices will soon quench the Holy Spirit's influence if we walk in a casual, careless manner. But if we give attention to the Bible and "keep in step" with the Spirit's application of Scripture to our lives, he will bear the good fruit by which God's ministry is known, the fruit of "love, joy, peace, patience, kindness, goodness, faithfulness, gentleness, self-control" (Gal. 5:22–23).

WEANED FROM EARTHLY THINGS

Paul's message to the Thessalonians is one that our generation of Christians greatly needs to hear. Having begun well in the faith, they are urged by Paul to grow up. He commends to us a *childlike* faith that receives God's true Word in simplicity and love (Matt. 18:3), but never a *childish* faith that is easily tossed back and forth by every fad and deceitful teaching (Eph. 4:14).

Yet this is the predominant situation in churches today. Os Guinness laments that "we are people with a true, sometimes a deep experience of God. But we are no longer a people of truth."[8] Pollster George Gallup cites "the glaring lack of knowledge about the Bible, basic doctrines, and the traditions of one's church . . . [and] the superficiality of faith, with many people not knowing what they believe, or why."[9] Such a church culture will

---

8. Os Guinness, *Fit Bodies, Fat Minds* (Grand Rapids: Baker, 1994), 38.
9. George Gallup Jr. and D. Michael Lindsay, *Surveying the Religious Landscape: Trends in U.S. Beliefs* (Harrisburg, PA: Morehouse, 1999), 4.

never impress unbelievers with the value of the Christian message, nor will it safeguard believers from the deadly worldly influences that seek to crowd out our faith, quench the Spirit's voice, and steal the joy that ought to be ours.

The first priority for the Thessalonians then and for us today is to return with new devotion to the sacred book. In the Bible, Christians meet with God so as to live consciously in the Father's love and walk intentionally in step with the Holy Spirit. Donald Grey Barnhouse testifies to what countless Christians have experienced through a devotion to God by means of his Spirit-inspired Word:

> It begins, as we read it, by being a book with cover and paper pages, overprinted with ink. Little by little, we forget the work of the printer and are brought into the presence of God Himself, the Author of the Book. We are brought face to face with Him and He speaks to us therein. . . . Our heart is then opened to the truth and becomes receptive to His grace. . . . From one end of the Bible to the other there are verses that now stand before me as bushes which burn, but which are not consumed, where once I put my shoes from off my feet and stood on holy ground. I can read these verses today and remember how the Lord spoke to me there in a time of need, how He drew me away from myself to follow Him, how He weaned me from earthly things to feed me with the living bread of Christ, how He cleansed me from sin, how He maintained me in Christ in a time of difficulty, and how He gave me the power to walk before Him in a way that was pleasing to Him.[10]

10. Donald Grey Barnhouse, *Exposition of Bible Doctrines Taking the Epistle to the Romans as a Point of Departure*, 10 vols. (Grand Rapids: Eerdmans, 1953), 2:156.

25

FAITHFUL TO SANCTIFY

1 Thessalonians 5:23–28

Now may the God of peace himself sanctify you completely . . . .
He who calls you is faithful; he will surely do it.
(1 Thess. 5:23–24)

n A.D. 405, a British monk by the name of Pelagius was living in Rome. When he came to that great city, Pelagius was disgusted by its moral corruption. He believed the problem was caused not merely by the wealth and power of the capital city, but also by the theology of grace being taught there. He was particularly offended by a popular book called *Confessions*, written a few years earlier by Aurelius Augustine. Augustine was a brilliant philosopher who had been converted to Christ through the preaching of Ambrose of Milan. Augustine's *Confessions* was a testimony to the grace of God that had changed his heart and broken the power of sin in his life.

Augustine's *Confessions* is noted for its famous prayers, many of which are frequently quoted today. In the book's opening chapter, he prayed, "You have made us for yourself, and our heart is restless until it rests in you."[1] Another famous prayer especially irked Pelagius. Augustine wrote: "I have no hope at all but in your great mercy. Grant what you command and command what

---

1. Augustine, *Confessions*, trans. Henry Chadwick (New York: Oxford University Press, 2009), 1.1.

you will."[2] His point was that God has the right to command whatever he desires, whether or not we are able to do it. In saving his people, however, God graciously grants the saving power that we need to obey him. Augustine's theology, drawn from that of the apostle Paul, taught that Christians are able to overcome sin only as God gives us grace to do so, which he freely does for those who ask.

When the Visigoth Alaric sacked Rome in A.D. 410, Pelagius fled to North Africa, where Augustine was bishop of Hippo. The two leaders entered into a conflict in which Augustine brilliantly articulated the biblical doctrine of salvation by grace alone. The main dispute concerned the state of human nature after Adam's fall. Pelagius held that the fall had not corrupted human nature but had merely set a tragic example that men have followed. Correspondingly, the gospel of Jesus Christ had corrected the fall merely with a good example to show what human nature can accomplish through free will. Augustine, in his *Anti-Pelagian Writings*, argued from Scripture that before salvation fallen man is in bondage to sin so that salvation can be caused only by God's sovereign grace. Philip Schaff states the difference between Augustine and Pelagius as concerning "whether redemption is chiefly a work of God or of man; whether man needs to be born anew, or merely improved. The soul of the Pelagian system is human freedom; the soul of the Augustinian is divine grace."[3] Augustine's arguments resulted in the condemnation of Pelagianism in the Council of Ephesus in 431 and set the table for the theology of later Protestant Reformers such as Martin Luther and John Calvin.

One passage that answers the Pelagian controversy is the benediction with which Paul closes his first letter to the Thessalonians. In chapter 5, Paul has given the believers a series of exhortations that would have made Pelagius proud. But on whose power does Paul depend for the sanctification that he desires to see? He answers, "Now may the God of peace himself sanctify you completely" (1 Thess. 5:23).

SANCTIFIED COMPLETELY

Paul concludes his letter with a prayer for the holiness of his readers. Earlier, the apostle wrote that "this is the will of God, your sanctification"

2. Ibid., 10.29.
3. Philip Schaff, *History of the Christian Church*, 8 vols. (1867; repr., Peabody, MA: Hendrickson, 2002), 3:787–88.

(1 Thess. 4:3). *Sanctification* refers to the process by which God's people are made like him in his holy nature. Thomas Watson explained: "A sanctified person bears not only God's name, but His image."[4] This is what God desires for all believers.

Paul declares that God is himself the source of our sanctification: "Now may the God of peace himself sanctify you" (1 Thess. 5:23). *Peace* is an attribute of God that Paul frequently notes in his benedictions (see Rom. 15:33; 16:20; 2 Cor. 13:11; Phil. 4:9). In speaking of our sanctification, we can see why he would refer to the peace of God, especially if we understand peace in its fullest sense of ultimate blessing and integrity. Ours is the God of *shalom*, the comprehensive well-being that describes God's own nature and that he gives to his people in Jesus Christ. John Stott writes that God "is the author of harmony," and "is himself the only perfectly integrated personality who exists."[5] Therefore, God does not delegate our sanctification to some other, but "the God of peace himself" takes up the work of our holiness. In this way, we see that holiness and peace are inseparable: believers cannot experience the peace of God except in the pursuit and experience of God's holiness. In linking the two, Paul shows that the only way to really be happy is to be holy.

Not only is God the One who sanctifies, but Paul further emphasizes how total and entire this sanctification is intended to be: "Now may the God of peace himself sanctify you completely" (1 Thess. 5:23).

Paul expresses this principle of entire sanctification in three ways. First, we are to be sanctified *completely*, combining the Greek word for *whole* with the word for *to the end* (Greek *holotelas*). We might regard this as the designed *extent* of our sanctification: it is to be finished and complete. While the best of Christians remain in this life only partially sanctified, with many sins and character defects, God's intention is for our sanctification to be brought to completion. Our holiness is ultimately to mirror God's own; Peter wrote: "As he who called you is holy, you also be holy in all your conduct" (1 Peter 1:15).

Continuing in making this point, Paul adds a second prayer item: "And may your whole spirit and soul and body be kept blameless at the coming

4. Thomas Watson, *A Body of Divinity* (Grand Rapids: Baker, 1958), 167.
5. John R. W. Stott, *The Message of 1 & 2 Thessalonians*, The Bible Speaks Today (Downers Grove, IL: InterVarsity Press, 1994), 132.

of our Lord Jesus Christ" (1 Thess. 5:23). This statement is considered important to the question whether man is composed of two parts (body and soul—called *dichotomy*) or of three parts (body, soul, and spirit—called *trichotomy*). Trichotomists claim this passage as proof of their doctrine. Yet Paul did not intend to define the parts of the human nature, any more than Jesus did when he said to love God "with all your heart and with all your soul and with all your mind and with all your strength" (Mark 12:30). In general, the Bible uses the terms *soul* and *spirit* interchangeably (see Luke 1:46-47) and presents man's nature in two parts: soul/spirit and body (see Matt. 10:28; Rom. 8:10; 2 Cor. 7:1).

Paul's point here in noting our "whole spirit and soul and body" is to show that in addition to being finished, our sanctification is to be *comprehensive*. We see this in the word *whole* that he applies to our inner and outer selves (Greek *holokleros*), meaning "in all the parts." No part of us will be left unsanctified: we are intended to be holy through and through. Note that Paul thus sees our holiness not only in terms of our inner spirits but also in terms of our bodies: in our thoughts, desires, and actions, we are to be holy.

Third, Paul writes that our sanctification is such that we are "kept blameless at the coming of our Lord Jesus Christ" (1 Thess. 5:23). The meaning of *blameless* (Greek *amemptos*) is "faultless" (Heb. 8:7) or "without blemish" (Phil. 2:15). Here we see the end product of our sanctification, our *blamelessness*, which takes place when Christ returns. Since Paul includes our bodies, along with our inner selves, he is referring to the resurrection of the dead. According to the Bible, when Christ returns, "the dead in Christ will rise" (1 Thess. 4:16). In 1 Corinthians 15, Paul notes that "we shall all be changed, in a moment, in the twinkling of an eye, at the last trumpet." He adds that "the dead will be raised imperishable, and we shall be changed" (1 Cor. 15:51-52). Here we see the completion of our sanctification, when in the resurrection our glorified souls will be reunited with our then-glorified bodies. It is after this that the final judgment takes place, in which all of Christ's people will stand "blameless" and justified. G. K. Beale writes that "we are perfected immediately before the final judgment and have nothing for which to be judged."[6]

6. G. K. Beale, *1-2 Thessalonians*, IVP New Testament Commentary Series (Downers Grove, IL: InterVarsity Press, 2003), 176.

Since it is only at "the coming of our Lord Jesus Christ" that believers are sanctified completely and wholly, so as to be without any blemish, it follows that this work is incomplete in this present life. Benjamin Warfield writes: "It is a thing not yet in possession but in petition. It is yet to come."[7] As perfect holiness is promised to believers, and as the apostle prays for this work in our lives, it follows that sanctification is the goal to which we should aim—a holiness that is finished, whole, and without blemish in the end. Joseph Carlyl writes: "Perfect holiness is the aim of the saints on earth, and it is the reward of the saints in heaven."[8] As followers of Christ, we are to pursue our daily lives with the aim of pleasing God in increasing holiness.

SANCTIFIED SOVEREIGNLY

Paul's doctrine of sanctification is a radical one, so we can understand why many Christians find it hard to believe that God intends complete holiness for us. It is probably in anticipating this kind of response that Paul continues to say that we are sanctified not only completely, but also *sovereignly* by God: "He who calls you is faithful; he will surely do it" (1 Thess. 5:24).

The apostle reminds us that our salvation begins with the call of God: "He who calls you." Paul himself was interrupted on the road to Damascus by the glorious appearing of Christ, who called him to faith and apostleship (Acts 22:6–10, 21). Likewise, Matthew was sitting at the tax collector's booth where he defrauded the people. Jesus approached, calling, "Follow me" (Matt. 9:9), and the tax collector began a new and holy life as a disciple of Christ. So it is, in one form or another, for everyone who comes to faith in Christ. Like Paul, Jesus emphasized the sovereignty of God in the divine call: "You did not choose me," he explained, "but I chose you" (John 15:16).

Paul adds that God is not only a sovereign caller to salvation but also a sovereign actor in sanctification: "He who calls you . . . will surely do it" (1 Thess. 5:24). In this way, Paul identifies God himself as the chief mover in the salvation of Christians. This makes sense when we see our present sanctification in light of our past and future. In our conversion, believers receive a *positional* sanctification as we are set apart for Christ through faith.

7. B. B. Warfield, *Faith and Life* (1916; repr., Edinburgh: Banner of Truth, 1974), 368–69.
8. Quoted in Tim Shenton, *Opening Up 1 Thessalonians* (Leominster, UK: Day One, 2006), 114.

In our glorification, Christians will all receive an *ultimate* sanctification, as we are brought into an eternal state of sinless glory in Christ. Linking these two—our conversion and our glorification—is our present *progressive* sanctification. The God who is the author and the finisher of our sanctification is also the doer of our sanctification now. This teaching should not be used to downplay the necessity of labor and activity on the part of the Christian, but rather grounds the challenging work of sanctification in the saving work of God. Paul put the two together in Philippians 2:12–13: "Work out your own salvation with fear and trembling, for it is God who works in you, both to will and to work for his good pleasure." Sanctification in the present involves our practical outworking of the holy life that God is working into us by the ministry of his Holy Spirit.

How can we know that the God who calls us will also do the work of sanctification within us? Paul answers: "He who calls you is faithful; he will surely do it" (1 Thess. 5:24). In calling us to salvation, God pledged to perfect in us the good work that he began. Paul writes in a similar vein to the Philippians: "He who began a good work in you will bring it to completion at the day of Jesus Christ" (Phil. 1:6). J. Philip Arthur writes: "Having begun a good work in a person's life there is no possibility that he will not honour his commitment and bring everything to a happy conclusion."[9]

There can hardly be sweeter music than this to the ears of Christians who know their own weakness and sin all too well. We sing with regret: "Prone to wander—Lord, I feel it—prone to leave the God I love."[10] How blessed it is, then, that Paul does not write to us, saying, "I know you can do it if you try hard enough," or even "You can do it because I and others are praying for you." Instead, Paul grounds our sanctification and perseverance in the only One who can grant real assurance: "He who calls you is faithful; he will surely do it." It is only the sovereignty of God in sanctification that enables redeemed sinners to rejoice: "For I am sure that neither death nor life, nor angels nor rulers, nor things present nor things to come, nor powers, nor height nor depth, nor anything else in all creation, will be able to separate us from the love of God in Christ Jesus our Lord" (Rom. 8:38–39).

9. J. Philip Arthur, *Patience of Hope: 1 and 2 Thessalonians Simply Explained*, Wellwyn Commentary Series (Ross-shire, UK: Evangelical Press, 1996), 92.

10. Robert Robinson, "Come, Thou Fount of Every Blessing" (1758).

SANCTIFIED MUTUALLY

God's sovereignty certainly does not rule out individual effort in our sanctification, which is why Paul proceeds to note the importance of our ministry to one another in pursuit of holiness. We are sanctified completely and sovereignly, Paul writes, and we are also sanctified *mutually*.

We see the mutuality of our sanctification in three exhortations, starting with a summons to prayer: "Brothers, pray for us" (1 Thess. 5:25). Paul's logic is obvious: if God is the One who sanctifies his people, then just as Paul has prayed for the Thessalonians, he would have them pray for him and for one another. Like us, Paul found himself in situations that he did not know how to handle (see 2 Cor. 7:8, for instance). "He was very conscious of his own limitations, and knew that his only hope was in God. So quite often we find him seeking the prayers of his converts as he does here."[11] The same is true for other apostles, who relied on prayer, as for Christians in general. The book of Acts records God's mighty acting in sending an angel to release Peter from prison (Acts 12:2–9). Thomas Watson comments: "The angel fetched Peter out of prison, but it was prayer that fetched the angel."[12]

There is a special need for preachers of God's Word to be aided by the prayers of God's people, which is why Paul so often sought prayer for both his personal needs and his ministry (see Eph. 6:19–20). Gardiner Spring wrote *A Plea to Pray for Pastors*, in which he urged:

> O it is at a fearful expense that ministers are ever allowed to enter the pulpit without being preceded, accompanied, and followed by the earnest prayers of the churches. It is not a marvel that the pulpit is so powerless, and ministers so often disheartened when there are so few to hold up their hands. The consequence of neglecting this duty is seen and felt in the spiritual declension of the churches, and it will be seen and felt in the everlasting perdition of men; while the consequences of regarding it would be the ingathering of multitudes into the kingdom of God, and new glories to the Lamb that was slain![13]

In addition to praying for one another, Paul urges the believers to loving fellowship in the church. He writes: "Greet all the brothers with a holy kiss"

---

11. Leon Morris, *The First and Second Epistles to the Thessalonians*, New International Commentary on the New Testament (Grand Rapids: Eerdmans, 1959), 183.

12. Quoted in Shenton, *Opening Up 1 Thessalonians*, 116.

13. Gardiner Spring, *A Plea to Pray for Pastors* (Amityville, NY: Calvary Press, 1991), 5.

(1 Thess. 5:26). It was the practice of early Christians to greet one another with a kiss—most likely on the cheek or the forehead—that expressed their loving brotherhood in Jesus Christ. This holy kiss is mentioned in writers of the second and third centuries (Justin Martyr and Tertullian, respectively) as continuing in the church. "By this kiss the early Christians expressed the intimate fellowship of the reconciled community."[14] Over time the practice took on a liturgical form, where it continues in the liturgy of the Eastern church, although most Western churches no longer practice holy kissing.

This exhortation points out the importance of what takes place not only during but also before and after the worship service. How wonderful it is to realize that in the church we enter into relationships that will literally last forever and engage in personal ministry that will make an eternity of difference. Whether it is a quiet, listening ear, a word of encouragement from experience or from the Bible, a welcoming smile to a visitor, or a helping hand to one in need, we are participating in God's sanctifying work that will ultimately be perfected in glory. Young girls address each other as *BFFs* ("best friends forever")—this is literally true of the friendships that we form among fellow Christians.

When Paul says to greet "all the brothers," we should note how the *all* urges us to make sure that none are left out, that none who need encouragement in godliness lack friendship, and that all who belong to Jesus through faith find a place to belong in his church as well. Depending on their cultural setting, believers in the West today are more likely to extend a handshake or a warm hug than a kiss in greeting one another. What truly matters is the love and mutual ministry that accompanies these greetings. John Lillie writes: "Forms may change; but the same spirit of brotherly love, and cordial recognition . . . , should ever characterize those who know the love of a common Saviour, and have thus entered into the communion of the saints."[15]

Third, Paul exhorts the Thessalonians that the ministry of God's Word must be honored in the life of the church: "I put you under oath before the Lord to have this letter read to all the brothers" (1 Thess. 5:27). The forcefulness with which the apostle speaks tells us about both the nature of his

14. D. K. McKim, "Kiss," in *The International Standard Bible Encyclopedia*, ed. Geoffrey W. Bromiley, 4 vols. (Grand Rapids: Eerdmans, 1986), 3:44.

15. John Lillie, *Lectures on Paul's Epistles to the Thessalonians*, Tentmaker Classic Commentaries (1860; repr., Stoke-on-Trent, UK: Tentmaker Publications, 2007), 310.

ministry and the priority he placed on God's Word. It was the practice in Jewish synagogues for the Scriptures to be read, and here Paul gives that same place to the reading of his own letter. Likewise, Peter described Paul's writings as "Scriptures" (2 Peter 3:16). More than simply validating his ministry, Paul's command signals how vital the reading of Scripture is to the sanctification of believers. "Sanctify them in the truth," Jesus prayed to the Father on the night of his arrest; "your word is truth" (John 17:17). John Calvin cited this text in condemning those church authorities that withhold the Scriptures from the people, calling them "more refractory than even devils themselves."[16] Then, it was Roman Catholic churches that sought to keep their people from the Bible. Today, it is evangelical churches that are so busy attracting large numbers with spiritual entertainment that little place is given to the sober reading and the careful exposition of God's Word. From the beginning of this letter, when Paul expressed thanks that they "received the word in much affliction, with the joy of the Holy Spirit" (1 Thess. 1:6), to here at the end, as he commands the public reading of his letter, Paul has emphasized the primacy of God's Word in the life of the church.

As we sum up Paul's exhortations concerning ministry to believers, we are struck by their correspondence to what the Reformed tradition describes as the three "means of grace" for ministry in the church. Especially when we note that greeting with a holy kiss was particularly associated with the Lord's Supper, we see that Paul urges the same three ministries that the Westminster Larger Catechism highlights as "ordinary means" of grace: God's Word, the sacraments, and prayer (WLC 154). Just as the church is given the purpose of building up believers in holiness, these three ministries are blessed by God with power to contribute mightily to the sanctification that will be perfected on the day of Christ's return.

SANCTIFIED GRACIOUSLY

Paul concludes this remarkable letter to the Thessalonians with a benediction focused on the grace of God in Christ. Following the apostolic example, many churches today conclude their worship services with a pastoral benediction taken from the Scriptures, the purpose of which is to offer a

16. John Calvin, *Commentaries*, 22 vols. (1854; repr., Grand Rapids: Baker, 2009), 21:306.

declaratory prayer for the blessings that God has promised to provide to those who trust in Jesus.

Paul began 1 Thessalonians with an appeal to "grace . . . and peace" (1 Thess. 1:1), so it is fitting that he concludes first with a reference to the God of peace and finally with a benediction on the grace of God in Christ: "The grace of our Lord Jesus Christ be with you" (5:28). This statement is no mere wish from Paul, but a declaration of what is certainly the case for those who have believed in Jesus. The final word that they need to hear from their pastor is the truth that the grace of Christ is with them. We need the same assurance of God's grace today—an assurance that comes through faith in Jesus Christ.

God's grace is his own favor—freely given to those who have deserved his wrath—because of the saving work of Jesus Christ for his people. At various points in this letter, Paul has pressed his readers to be serious about their growth in salvation, especially about their sanctification into increased holiness. Here at the end, he reminds them once again that this expectation is grounded in the grace that God provides through his Son. Whereas a Pelagius might write to say that there was no reason that they could not lead moral and upright lives in their own power, Paul is more candid in facing the debilitating effects of sin in our lives. Like Augustine after him, the apostle would have our last thoughts to center not on human free will or effort—which must fail us in this life—but on the divine grace that provides our sure hope of eternal life.

Warfield asks why, if God is the One who will sanctify us completely on the day of Christ's returning, he calls us to struggle in the pursuit of holiness—repenting of sin, praying for strength, looking to God daily in the trial of faith—throughout this present life.

> He could, no doubt, make the soul perfect in a moment, in the twinkling of an eye, just as He could give us each a perfect body at the very instant of our believing. He does not. The removal of the stains and effects of sin—in an evil heart and in a sick and dying body—is accomplished in a slow process. . . . We still struggle with the remainders of indwelling sin; though Jesus has bought for us the sanctifying operations of the Spirit. To us it is a weary process. But it is God's way. And He does all things well.[17]

17. Warfield, *Faith and Life*, 372.

If Paul's final words are any indication—and they must be—then God's purpose in our struggle for holiness is not just so that we might give up sinful things for him and offer good works in their stead, though this is part of what it means to love God. By concluding with grace, Paul suggests that God leaves us to struggle with holiness so that we might come to learn the reality and extent of his grace for us. He called us in grace to a patient, long-suffering, power-exhibiting process of sanctification. In this way, he gives each of us a personal experience of his grace. We are to learn not only how to be holy but also how gracious our God is to poor sinners whom he has saved. Our holiness, therefore, is to breathe the air and exude the aroma of God's grace, responding to him by singing: "Here's my heart, O take and seal it, seal it for thy courts above."[18]

Finally, Paul reminds us that God's grace is in "our Lord Jesus Christ" (1 Thess. 5:28). God wants us to understand his grace by appropriating the gift of his Son, Jesus Christ, to be our Savior and Lord. The process of becoming holy causes us to look frequently to the cross, where Jesus died for our sins. By facing our sins in practical ways, we realize how great was the love of Christ that willingly bore our penalty on the cross. We are to rely wholeheartedly on Christ's intercession for us in heaven (Rom. 8:34) and his power at work in our lives through the Holy Spirit whom he sends (Eph. 1:19–20). As a result, our holiness is to take on the lovely graciousness of the holiness of Christ. And relying wholly on God's grace in him, we are to learn to sing fervently the truth of Robert Robinson's words:

Jesus sought me when a stranger, wand'ring from the fold of God: he, to rescue me from danger, interposed his precious blood.

O to grace how great a debtor daily I'm constrained to be; let that grace now, like a fetter, bind my wand'ring heart to thee.[19]

18. Robinson, "Come, Thou Fount of Every Blessing."
19. Ibid.

2 Thessalonians

IN LIGHT OF CHRIST'S COMING

26

GROWING IN FAITH

2 Thessalonians 1:1–4

We ought always to give thanks to God for you, brothers, as is right, because your faith is growing abundantly, and the love of every one of you for one another is increasing. (2 Thess. 1:3)

he letters of the apostle Paul feature a significant and surprising doctrine of boasting. According to Paul, there is nothing wrong with a little bragging, so long as you boast about the right thing. So at the end of Galatians, he pledged his boast to the cross of Christ: "Far be it from me to boast except in the cross of our Lord Jesus Christ, by which the world has been crucified to me, and I to the world" (Gal. 6:14). And to the Corinthians he recalled the boasting advice of the prophet Jeremiah: "Let not the wise man boast in his wisdom, let not the mighty man boast in his might, let not the rich man boast in his riches, but let him who boasts boast in this, that he understands and knows me, that I am the LORD" (Jer. 9:23–24, quoted in 1 Cor. 1:31).

What we boast about reveals a great deal about the character of our religion. Churches in the West today increasingly take pride in the beauty of their buildings, the quality of their music, the dynamic personalities of their preachers, and above all their numerical size. More biblically minded

271

churches take satisfaction in doctrinal fidelity, commitment to world missions, and sound biblical leadership. Yet when Paul writes his second letter to the fledgling church in Thessalonica, he boasts in something more surprising. Having expressed his thanks for his readers' growing faith and increasing love, he writes: "We ourselves boast about . . . your steadfastness and faith in all your persecutions and in the afflictions that you are enduring" (2 Thess. 1:4). If we follow Paul's example, we will also make our boast in a faith that grows, loves, and perseveres under persecution.

PAUL'S SECOND LETTER TO THE THESSALONIANS

During the years A.D. 49–51, the world was powerfully shaken by Jesus Christ and the work of the Spirit, through the second missionary journey of the apostle Paul. One of Paul's stops was in the large and prosperous Macedonian city of Thessalonica (Acts 17:1–9). Preaching the gospel there, Paul assembled believers into a local church, which immediately suffered persecution. The apostle himself was forced to flee the city, journeying through Athens to Corinth. There, Paul received cherished news of the Thessalonians and wrote to express his thanks for their faith and give them continued teaching, especially on the doctrines of sanctification and the return of Christ. When Paul received a reply, he penned a second letter, probably within a few months of the first. Second Thessalonians thus completes the message of the first letter, centering on the church's continued persecution, additional teaching on Christ's return, and a forceful directive concerning members who refused to work.

Paul begins this letter in typical fashion, first identifying himself and his recipients, and then greeting them with an appeal to the grace and peace of God the Father and of Christ. "Paul, Silvanus, and Timothy," he begins, joining his message to the same assistants he mentioned in the first letter (which is one reason to suspect that this letter followed shortly after the first). He writes to "the church of the Thessalonians in God our Father and the Lord Jesus Christ" (2 Thess. 1:1). The way in which Paul closely identifies Jesus Christ with God the Father shows his belief in the deity of Jesus. Moreover, by referring to the church as being "in" the Father and Son, Paul notes a distinctive feature of the Christian faith. John MacArthur writes: "The truth that Christians are in personal, spiritual, and eternal union with

God is unique to Christianity; adherents of other religions do not speak of being *in* their god. But the Bible teaches that those who put their faith in Christ 'become partakers of the divine nature' (2 Peter 1:4), sharing eternal life with God through faith and identification with His Son."[1]

There is a subtle difference in how Paul describes God in this letter compared to 1 Thessalonians. In the previous letter, he wrote of "God the Father," whereas here he twice describes him as "God our Father" (2 Thess. 1:1–2). In the first instance, Paul emphasized God as the Father of Jesus Christ; now he emphasizes our adoption as God's children, so that God is not only Jesus' Father but ours as well. It is as beloved, adopted children that the believers are "in God our Father," through our faith in "the Lord Jesus Christ" (2 Thess. 1:1).

From this same union believers receive the two great blessings that Paul almost always mentions in the opening of his letters: grace and peace. The apostle continues: "Grace to you and peace from God our Father and the Lord Jesus Christ" (2 Thess. 1:2). This statement sums up the gospel that Paul preached. Grace is God's free gift of favor to those worthy of condemnation because of their sin. Grace flows from the Father in the form of his sovereign will to save his people into fellowship with himself. Grace is offered by God the Son on the basis of his redeeming work on the cross. As Paul wrote to the Ephesians, "by grace you have been saved through faith. And this is not your own doing; it is the gift of God, not a result of works, so that no one may boast" (Eph. 2:8–9). The result of God's grace in our lives is peace: the comprehensive blessing of peace with God through forgiveness of sin, God's peace at work in our hearts through the indwelling Holy Spirit, and peace with one another through the love that Christ gives to us.

A Growing Faith

Just as in his first letter, Paul follows his initial greeting with thanks to God for the faith of his readers. The difference in the second letter is that Paul highlights their *growing* faith: "We ought always to give thanks to God for you, brothers, as is right, because your faith is growing abundantly" (2 Thess. 1:3). A true faith in Jesus Christ is designed to grow exceedingly.

1. John MacArthur, *1 & 2 Thessalonians* (Chicago: Moody, 2002), 224.

Therefore, having been initially relieved to learn of the Thessalonians' faith, Paul is now delighted to learn that their faith is growing as it should.

Paul describes their faith with a complex verb (*huperauxanei*) that means to "superabound." J. B. Lightfoot describes this abundance as "an internal, organic growth, as of a tree."[2] Just as a healthy tree typically grows to its proper stature, a healthy faith in Christ grows in strength and capacity. Christian faith involves a personal relationship with God, and like all other relationships, it is able to grow or shrink. So important is our faith relationship with God that Paul feels obliged to thank God for the Thessalonians' growth: "We ought always to give thanks to God for you, brothers," he writes, "because your faith is growing abundantly" (2 Thess. 1:3).

In his spiritual classic *Pilgrim's Progress*, John Bunyan depicted the common problem of a weak faith by devoting a variety of characters to it. There was Mr. Ready-to-halt, who hobbled on crutches to the Celestial City. Mr. Fearing shrank back from the first appearance of trouble. Mr. Despondency and Miss Much-afraid were locked up in the dungeon of the Giant Despair. Mr. Feeble-mind was held in the cave of Giant Slay-good. Charles Spurgeon comments that Bunyan "put a great many of those characters in his book, because there are a great many of them. He has left us with . . . seven or eight graphic characters because he himself in his own time has been one of them, and he had known many others who had walked in the same path."[3]

Spurgeon also noted three "inconveniences of little faith," which supply reasons for us to grow our faith. First, he pointed out that little faith in Christ will gain little assurance of salvation. Notice that Spurgeon did not say that little faith will not save! Little faith *will* save the sinner, so long as it is true faith, because it lays hold of a strong Savior in Jesus Christ. Spurgeon writes: "When Christ counts up his jewels at the last day he will take to himself the little pearls as well as the great ones. . . . So will faith [be precious], be it never so little, if it be true faith. Christ will never lose even the smallest jewel of his crown. . . . Little-faith was bought with the blood of Christ, and he cost as much as Great-faith." The problem with little faith is that it seldom knows that these things are true. Spurgeon notes:

2. J. B. Lightfoot, *Notes on the Epistles of St. Paul* (Peabody, MA: Hendrickson, 1993), 98.
3. Charles Haddon Spurgeon, *The New Park Street Pulpit*, 6 vols. (Pasadena, TX: Pilgrim, 1975), 4:322.

Now Great-faith is sure of heaven, and he knows it. He climbs Pisgah's top, and views the landscape o'er; he drinks in the mysteries of paradise even before he enters within the pearly gates. He sees the streets that are paved with gold; he beholds the walls of the city, the foundations whereof are of precious stones; he hears the mystic music of the glorified, and begins to smell on earth the perfumes of heaven. But poor Little-faith can scarcely look at the sun; he very seldom sees the light; he gropes in the valley, and while all is safe he always thinks himself unsafe.[4]

A second inconvenience of little faith is that weak believers seldom attempt to do things for God. Despite God's promise that "my grace is sufficient for you" (2 Cor. 12:9), weak believers think that there is never sufficient grace for what needs to be done. Whereas a greater faith would like Samson take on an enemy with only the jawbone of a donkey, the one with little faith is not even aware of the victories that he has already won. Because of a faith that is hardly growing, those with little faith bear little fruit for God's glory and make little difference for the gospel.

Third, those with little faith are more apt to stumble when tempted to sin. When the devil offers the kingdoms of the world, a stronger faith answers that all things are already ours together with Christ (Rom. 8:32). A weak faith, however, is tempted to think of all that it has given up to follow Christ and thus succumb to worldly pleasures. Or perhaps Satan accuses God's people because of their sin, arguing that they must fail of salvation. A strong faith answers that "the blood of Jesus [God's] Son cleanses us from all sin" (1 John 1:7). But a weak faith trembles for fear of condemnation, forgetting that the Bible promises that there is "no condemnation for those who are in Christ Jesus" (Rom. 8:1). Spurgeon comments:

> Little-faith says, "I am not quite sure that I am a child of God, that I have a portion among them that are sanctified;" and he is very apt to fall into sin by reason of the littleness of his faith. . . . Beloved, you who are Little-faiths, I tell you it is inconvenient for you always to remain so; for you have many nights and few days. Your years are like Norwegian years—very long winters and very short summers.[5]

These reasons highlight the importance of a growing faith. Only a growing faith is able to heed Christ's command: "Rejoice in the Lord always; again

4. Ibid., 4:322–23.
5. Ibid., 4:324.

I will say, Rejoice" (Phil. 4:4). When fellow Christians see this joy in you, they will be able, like Paul, "to give thanks to God for you . . . because your faith is growing abundantly" (2 Thess. 1:3).

HOW TO GROW IN FAITH

The calling to grow in faith raises the question how this is to be done. Spurgeon answers, "If you would have your little faith grow into great faith, you must *feed* it well." Faith must be primarily fed on a steady diet of the Word of God: "Thou tellest me thou hast little faith. I ask thee whether thou art given to the meditation of God's Word, whether thou hast studied the promises, whether thou art wont to carry one of those sacred things about with thee every day?"[6] If you answer "No," then the lack of growth in your faith is not surprising. Psalm 1 promises that the one who meditates daily on God's Word is blessed with a growing faith: "His delight is in the law of the LORD, and on his law he meditates day and night. He is like a tree planted by streams of water that yields its fruit in its season, and its leaf does not wither" (Ps. 1:2–3). If your faith would be like a tree that grows tall and strong, you must have your roots in the water of life.

Second, faith grows through prayer in response to God's Word. Try God's promises and ask him to show their fulfillment in your own life. As an example, the Bible says that God's "power is made perfect in weakness" (2 Cor. 12:9). So ask God to exhibit his power in your weakness. Paul writes that "the peace of God, which surpasses all understanding," will guard the "hearts and . . . minds" of those who pray in Christ (Phil. 4:7). Ask God to grant that peace to your heart and mind. Jesus told us to pray, "Give us this day our daily bread" (Matt. 6:11). So ask God daily to provide for the things that you need. Not only will you find God faithful to his promises, but your faith in him will grow correspondingly.

Third, faith in Christ grows through association with godly fellowship. Spurgeon writes: "It is astonishing how young believers will get their faith refreshed by talking with old and advanced Christians." When those of little faith describe their spiritual troubles, they find that others have had the same difficulties and overcome them by trusting in Jesus. The veteran believer "will tell you what dangers he has passed, and of the sovereign

6. Ibid.

love that kept him; of the temptations that threatened to ensnare him, and of the wisdom that guided his feet; and he will tell you of his own weakness and God's omnipotence; of his own emptiness, and God's fullness; of his own changeableness, and God's immutability."[7] In fact, this kind of faith-building conversation is one of the primary callings of the church. Hebrews 3:13 directs believers to "exhort one another every day, as long as it is called 'today,' that none of you may be hardened by the deceitfulness of sin."

INCREASING IN LOVE

A further way for faith to grow is by being exercised in loving ministry to other people. Paul specifies this calling when he rejoices that "the love of every one of you for one another is increasing" (2 Thess. 1:3). Faith and love are so joined in Paul's letters that we can hardly claim the first without the evidence of the second. In his first letter to the Thessalonians, Paul praised their "work of faith and labor of love" (1 Thess. 1:3). Similarly, in Galatians 5:6 he wrote that what matters most in the Christian life is "faith working through love."

The importance of love was highlighted by a life philosophy that has made the rounds on the Internet in recent years. It is wrongly attributed to Charles Schulz, famous for his *Peanuts* cartoon, although we can well imagine that he would wish to have written it. First, readers are asked to name the five wealthiest people in the world, the last five winners of the Heisman Trophy, the last five Miss Americas, ten people who have won the Nobel or Pulitzer Prize, the last half-dozen Academy Award winners for best actor and actress, and the teams that won baseball's World Series over the last ten years. The point of these questions is to show that we remember few of these famous achievers because they are not important to our lives. Then readers are asked to name a different class of people: a few teachers who aided your journey through school, three friends who helped you in a difficult time, five people who have taught you something worthwhile, a few people who have made you feel appreciated and special, and five people you enjoy spending time with. These are questions for which we have answers! Why? Because the people who really make a difference in our lives are not

7. Ibid., 4:325.

those with the most impressive credentials, the most money, or the most notoriety, but the ones who most express their care through acts of love.

When Paul gave thanks for the Thessalonians' growing faith, he used a word for the kind of growth that a tree shows. Now, in praising their love, the apostle uses a verb (*pleonazo*) that signifies "a diffusive, or expansive character, as of a flood irrigating the land."[8] His emphasis is on the wide distribution of the Thessalonians' love: it is "the love of every one of you for one another" (2 Thess. 1:3). The urgency of this kind of love was specified by Jesus on the night of his arrest: "A new commandment I give to you, that you love one another: just as I have loved you, you also are to love one another" (John 13:34).

In creating his church, Jesus formed a new family that is to bear the marks of a community and not of a club. Philip Yancey pointed out that a club is a place where you choose the people with whom you will associate, whereas a community is a place where the person you least want to associate with may also live. By this definition, the church is a community, not a club. A true church will exhibit an attitude of love that is based on Christ's sacrificial love for us, not on the attractiveness of others. Moved by his Spirit, Christians will not turn away from difficult or needy people simply because of the effort that love requires in their case. Rather, we will see the ministry of fellowship and encouragement to be an essential part of our service to the Lord. In this way, marvels of grace have been seen in the transformed lives of broken sinners who would never thrive in anything less than a self-less community.

This is the problem with the "homogeneous unit principle" that is practiced by so many churches today in a quest for rapid numerical growth. The idea is to target a certain demographic group—usually upwardly mobile suburban whites or hip progressive young adults—and design everything according to their tastes: the building, the worship style, and even the minister. Churches that follow this approach can quickly grow to an enormous size. The problem is what they are designed to be: self-serving spiritual clubs, instead of the communities of grace that Jesus desires. Yancey asserts, "Anyone can form a club; it takes grace, shared vision, and hard work to form a community."[9]

8. Lightfoot, *Notes on the Epistles of St. Paul*, 98.
9. Philip Yancey, "Why I Don't Go to a Megachurch," *Christianity Today* (May 20, 1996): 80.

By means of their growing faith in Christ, Paul saw in Thessalonica something that J. Philip Arthur says "amounted to a miracle. The gospel had brought people together who would normally have avoided one another." Our prayer and desire today is that churches would enjoy a Christ-centered unity that draws people from a wide range of racial and socioeconomic backgrounds into the blessing of Christ. We practice an active gospel love when we deliberately cross boundaries in order to bring others to salvation. When a church practices the love of Christ, its own well-being and stability increases as well: "It is vital that Christians pray that love of this kind should permeate our churches to an increasing measure, for when love begins to diminish, friction increases and churches fall apart."[10]

SOMETHING TO BOAST ABOUT

The positive tone with which Paul writes once more to the Thessalonians is seen in his praise to God for their growing faith and increasing love. But his highest boast is seen in yet another fruit of a true and living faith in Christ. We have highlighted a number of ways that Christian faith grows. Faith in Christ grows on a diet of God's Word, through prayer, through godly company, and through exercise in works of love for all kinds of people. Moreover, Paul concludes, our faith in Christ will grow as we persevere in the midst of trials: "Therefore we ourselves boast about you in the churches of God for your steadfastness and faith in all your persecutions and in the afflictions that you are enduring" (2 Thess. 1:4).

I mentioned that Paul's letters provide a fertile theology of boasting. Christians are to boast in the cross of Christ (Gal. 6:14) and in knowing the Lord (1 Cor. 1:31). But Paul goes into unexpected regions of boasting when he brags about the persecutions that these young believers had endured. Steadfastness in affliction is not something that the world brags about, but Paul says that "in the churches of God" it is one of the most praiseworthy subjects. Whereas worldly thinking will lead us to glorify churches and Christians that enjoy the greatest outward success and never seem to suffer any difficulties, the spiritual thinking of true churches will glory in a faith that abounds under persecution for Christ. One fruit of this way of

10. J. Philip Arthur, *Patience of Hope: 1 and 2 Thessalonians Simply Explained*, Wellwyn Commentary Series (Ross-shire, UK: Evangelical Press, 1996), 102.

thinking will be a positive overall attitude toward world missions. Instead of merely thinking of churches in developing countries and persecuted regions as needing our help, we will more wisely look to them for inspiration, spiritual encouragement, and valued insights regarding the life of true and costly faith in Christ.

Likewise, the most valuable Christians are not those who make the biggest impact both in joining and in leaving their churches, but quiet members who stand fast in hard times. Arthur writes that Paul "prized Christians who could hold up when the going got rough because they knew that suffering was not a sign that the Lord had abandoned them, but proof positive that they were following in the steps the Master trod."[11] The afflicted Thessalonians could be encouraged that their example was making a difference by encouraging believers elsewhere of the sufficient grace of Christ.

One of the chief benefits of persecution is that it reveals the difference between true and false faith. In his parable of the soils, Jesus described the kind of faith that is like a seed that falls amid rocky ground and springs up quickly from the earth. Yet because such a person "has no root in himself," he professes faith for a while, but "when tribulation or persecution arises on account of the word, immediately he falls away" (Matt. 13:20–21). Since our response to opposition shows the real state of our faith, new believers who have been rejected by their friends, been ridiculed by their families, or, like Paul's Thessalonian readers, suffered violence and even death for Jesus gain the benefit of assurance that theirs is a true and saving faith.

The Christian under trial and persecution is called to "steadfastness," which involves both patience and perseverance. Although the Thessalonians were not able to make their afflictions cease, their faith enabled them to continue enduring the trials until the Lord removed them. For *steadfastness*, Paul uses the word *hupomoneis*, which combines the prefix *under* with the word *abide*. Their growing faith and increasing love enabled them to remain under the pressure of affliction, thus proving the reality of their salvation. In his letter to the church in Thyatira, Jesus spoke words of great joy to the hearts of all such believers: "I know your works, your love and faith and service and patient endurance" (Rev. 2:19). The perseverance of his people under the affliction of persecution, solely for his sake, is precious to the heart of Jesus and therefore worthy of boasting among the churches of Christ.

11. Ibid., 103.

Do you need encouragement in your life of faith? Perhaps you look at yourself and see little or nothing that the world would boast about. Be encouraged, then, if your faith is growing, if God is enabling you to spread Christ's love, and if you are patiently enduring difficulty for Jesus' sake. You, then, are like the believers to whom Paul wrote in 2 Thessalonians. Undoubtedly, some of them would have doubted their relationship to the Lord or his faithfulness to them because their outward circumstances were not improving. Paul wrote to show that we are obliged to praise God with thanksgiving whenever our faith is growing, our love is increasing, and we are remaining steadfast to Christ under affliction.

Love and steadfastness flow from a living and growing faith, so our calling is to strengthen our faith through God's Word, prayer, and godly fellowship. As our faith grows, our love will increase and we will gain strength to abide under persecution. Then we, too, will have something to boast about, together with the apostle John, who wrote: "This is the victory that has overcome the world—our faith" (1 John 5:4).

27

GOD'S RIGHTEOUS JUDGMENT

2 Thessalonians 1:5—8

> *God considers it just to repay with affliction those who afflict*
> *you, and to grant relief to you who are afflicted as well as*
> *to us, when the Lord Jesus is revealed from heaven*
> *with his mighty angels.* (2 Thess. 1:6–7)

*I*n 734 B.C., two historically important figures met outside the city of Jerusalem, "at the end of the conduit of the upper pool on the highway to the Washer's Field" (Isa. 7:3). One of them was Ahaz the son of Jotham, king of Judah, who was facing a looming national crisis. The problem was an alliance to his north, in which the nations of Israel and Syria were threatening an assault with overwhelming forces. The second figure was the great prophet Isaiah, sent by the Lord to summon King Ahaz to faith. Ahaz was at that time scheming to enter into an alliance with the warlike empire of Assyria, led by Tiglath-Pileser, to the north of Israel and Syria. The idea was to deflect Israel's and Syria's threat against Judah by arranging an even greater threat against them. The only problem was that in order to secure the alliance, Ahaz had to agree to worship the Assyrian gods. Isaiah warned about the disaster that this action would bring: "If you do not stand firm in your faith, you will not stand at all" (Isa. 7:9 NIV). Ahaz refused to believe, however, and the result of his appeal to worldly support brought calamity. Not only did the Assyrians defeat Ahaz's enemies, wiping out the Israelite capital Samaria in 722 B.C., but they also made Judah a vassal state required to pay tribute and to bring their idols into God's holy city.

The famous encounter between Isaiah and Ahaz is relevant to Paul's second letter to the Thessalonians, since he was concerned that they not fall prey to a similar mistake. The fledgling Christians had believed the gospel and trusted in Jesus. As a result, they immediately faced such violent opposition that some had been killed. It was essential for these Christians, therefore, to stand firm in their faith, relying on God to save them. If the Thessalonians sought a worldly solution to their problem, and especially if they betrayed their faith in Christ, the result would be an eternal disaster. In this situation, Paul reminds them that God's righteous judgment would destroy their enemies in due time and that their faith would ultimately win salvation when Christ returns.

God's Judgment Anticipated by Faith

One of the thoughts that undermines the faith of suffering believers is the idea that God doesn't care or is uninvolved in their trials. In Romans 8:32, Paul countered this harmful idea by pointing out that God has already acted decisively for us in sending his Son to die for our sins: "He who did not spare his own Son but gave him up for us all, how will he not also with him graciously give us all things?" Since the cross, God can never credibly be accused of remaining aloof from the trials of this world. In 2 Thessalonians 1:5, Paul advances another reason why they should never believe that God had abandoned them in their suffering. In verse 4, he had boasted about their "steadfastness and faith" in affliction. Now, he adds that this very faith is "evidence of the righteous judgment of God."

There are two ways in which Paul's statement may be taken. He may mean that by allowing the ungodly to persecute believers, God was making plain how certain it was that unbelievers would suffer his judgment. This was the view of John Calvin, who commented: "The injuries and persecutions which innocent and pious persons endure from the wicked and abandoned, shew clearly, as in a mirror, that God will one day be the judge of the world."[1] It

---

1. John Calvin, *Commentaries*, 22 vols. (1854; repr., Grand Rapids: Baker, 2009), 21:312.

is more likely, however, that when Paul speaks of the "evidence" of God's "righteous judgment," he is referring not to the persecution experienced by the believers but to their steadfast faith in enduring it (2 Thess. 1:4). The fact that they were continuing to trust the Lord while suffering was a sign that God was working in them and was on their side, thus anticipating the final judgment of his and their enemies. Suffering Christians sometimes ask, "Why isn't God doing something?" The first answer is that God has already done what is most needful in sending his Son to die for our sins. A second answer is that God is upholding our faith under trials so that we will be saved in the end.

Reading Paul's treatment of persecution introduces us to the Christian understanding of suffering and trials. The non-Christian regards suffering as an utter disaster to be avoided at nearly all costs. It is likely that some believers in Thessalonica were thinking this way. If God is sovereign, how could they be experiencing persecution? If God loves his children, how could he stand by while they suffer and even die? Andrew Young summarizes Paul's pastoral perspective in addressing this concern: "If they could only see their sufferings in the right way, they would realize that God was at work in what was happening to them. Far from letting them down, he was in fact preparing them for glory."[2]

The Bible teaches, first, that suffering is inevitable for the believer. The Christian is never promised a care-free life but is in fact promised trials and affliction. Earlier Paul had reminded the Thessalonians that "we are destined for this" kind of trouble (1 Thess. 3:3). Christians are destined for tribulation just as certainly as we are destined for glory, both of which result from our union with Christ. "If you were of the world," Jesus taught, "the world would love you as its own; but because you are not of the world, but I chose you out of the world, therefore the world hates you. . . . If they persecuted me, they will also persecute you" (John 15:19–20). Therefore, Peter wrote: "Beloved, do not be surprised at the fiery trial when it comes upon you to test you, as though something strange were happening to you. But rejoice insofar as you share Christ's sufferings, that you may also rejoice and be glad when his glory is revealed" (1 Peter 4:12–13). Every Christian is duly forewarned that trials are part and parcel of the Christian experience.

In addition to knowing that trials are inevitable, Christians also know that under God's control they are beneficial in preparing us for glory. Leon

2. Andrew W. Young, *Let's Study 1 & 2 Thessalonians* (Edinburgh: Banner of Truth, 2001), 128–29.

Morris explains: "In the good providence of God suffering is often the means of working out God's eternal purpose. It develops in the sufferers qualities of character. It teaches valuable lessons. . . . The very troubles and afflictions which the world heaps on the believer become, under God, the means of making him what he ought to be."[3] According to John Calvin, there are at least four ways in which suffering improves the character and faith of believers: it makes us long for heaven, stirs up our hope for Christ's return, destroys our longing for the things of this world, and teaches us to value the eternal life purchased by Jesus. Calvin writes: "In short, . . . believers are prepared and, as it were, polished under God's anvil . . . to renounce the world and to aim at God's heavenly kingdom."[4]

Given this understanding of afflictions and persecution, Paul writes to change his readers' attitude. They should realize not only that their steadfast faith anticipates God's judgment on their enemies, but also that they may be "considered worthy of the kingdom of God, for which you are also suffering" (2 Thess. 1:5). The point is not that enduring under suffering makes us worthy of Christ's kingdom, but rather that it reveals our membership in Christ, which is by God's grace and through faith. According to the Bible, faithful suffering for the kingdom is in fact necessary to mark those who will inherit his glory by God's grace. Elsewhere, Paul writes that believers are saved "if indeed you continue in the faith, stable and steadfast, not shifting from the hope of the gospel that you heard" (Col. 1:23). "For it has been granted to you," he adds, "that for the sake of Christ you should not only believe in him but also suffer for his sake" (Phil. 1:29). G. K. Beale thus observes: "One will not be able to enter the kingdom without the badge of enduring faith and its accompanying good works."[5]

Beale elaborates on the relationship between faith and perseverance by the analogy of a ticket that grants entry into a sporting event. A person who wants to attend a game pays money and receives a ticket. Beale asks, "Is it the money that provides access to the game or the ticket?" The answer is "Both!" "Ultimately, the money paid is what really gets you in, but you must

---

3. Leon Morris, *The First and Second Epistles to the Thessalonians*, New International Commentary on the New Testament (Grand Rapids: Eerdmans, 1959), 197–98.

4. Calvin, *Commentaries*, 21:314.

5. G. K. Beale, *1–2 Thessalonians*, IVP New Testament Commentary Series (Downers Grove, IL: InterVarsity Press, 2003), 184.

have the ticket as evidence that you really paid the price for the game."[6] It is not Christians who pay the price of their entry into heaven, but Jesus, who redeems us with his precious blood. The evidence of this payment, which is as necessary for heaven as a ticket to a football game, is an enduring faith that stands up under trial. This is why Paul urges the Thessalonians to rejoice in afflictions for Christ: "that you may be considered worthy of the kingdom of God" (2 Thess. 1:5).

Paul's teaching on persecution prompts a question about the church in our time: If being a Christian were made illegal by a hostile government, so that believers risked arrest by gathering for worship, how many of the people who fill evangelical churches today would still do so? There can be little doubt that the attendance in many churches, especially those that attract numbers by means of worldly entertainment, would plummet. Paul's teaching suggests that not all who profess Christ in times of ease will persevere under trials. He also asserts that those who do stand up for Christ despite suffering for the kingdom receive a testimony that they are saved and will inherit eternal life. In peaceful times, people come to church to make business contacts, find friends, obey family pressure, or just try it out.

What about you? Why do you come to church now? Would you identify yourself as a Christian if you could be persecuted for it? True Christians come to worship their Savior and Lord, to be fed by God's Word, and to gather in the assembly of the godly. No amount of persecution will keep them from these things, and in this way, they give evidence that they are those who really belong to Christ's kingdom and will be accepted on the day of his coming.

God's Judgment in Just Retribution

As Paul sees it, the key to enduring persecution is to understand God's righteous judgment. In 2 Thessalonians 1:5, he wanted his readers to see their steadfast faith as both evidence of God's faithfulness and proof of their right to enter Christ's kingdom. Continuing in verse 6, Paul turns to the other side of the coin, displaying God's avenging justice against the ungodly who persecute his church: "since indeed God considers it just to repay with affliction those who afflict you."

---

6. Ibid., 184–85.

Here Paul states the biblical principle of divine retribution for sin. Believers in Jesus rely on God's righteousness for our salvation: we know that God will keep his promises and that the payment that Jesus offered for our sins will be accepted. This same divine righteousness, however, ensures precise repayment for the sins of all those who do not receive Christ in faith. In particular, those who "afflict" God's people will be repaid by God "with affliction" in return. Leon Morris comments: "Just as it is true that it is a righteous thing with God to bring believers to salvation and blessing in His kingdom, so it is a righteous thing with Him to bring punishment to those who persist in courses of evil."[7] This is another answer to the question, "Why doesn't God do something?" God has done what we really need by sending Jesus to die for our sins and then upholding our faith under trials. God will do something further by executing righteous judgment on our wicked oppressors.

Final judgment is the Bible's solution to believers who resent the apparent unfairness of their own suffering and the apparent happiness of the wicked. One believer who struggled with this problem was Asaph, the author of Psalm 73. "As for me," he confided, "my feet had almost stumbled, my steps had nearly slipped. For I was envious of the arrogant when I saw the prosperity of the wicked" (Ps. 73:2–3). While he suffered for his faith in the Lord, he looked on the ungodly people who seemed so carefree and happy. So bitter was Asaph's heart toward God that the only thing that kept him from denying his faith was his concern not to depress other believers spiritually (v. 15). Asaph did one thing right, however. Eventually, he said, "I went into the sanctuary of God; then I discerned their end" (v. 17). The psalmist went to church, heard God's Word, and remembered that however happy unbelievers seem now, they are destined for eternal judgment. He observed: "Truly you set them in slippery places; you make them fall to ruin. How they are destroyed in a moment, swept away utterly by terrors!" (vv. 18–19).

Realizing this truth helped Asaph to restore his heart before the Lord, so that he concluded his song with soaring words of rejoicing, despite his ongoing trials: "My flesh and my heart may fail, but God is the strength of my heart and my portion forever" (Ps. 73:26). This is the attitude that Paul wants his readers to have, first realizing God's blessing on their faith and then recalling the judgment awaiting the wicked.

7. Morris, *First and Second Thessalonians*, 200.

When Christians point out God's righteous judgment of sinners, the question is sometimes raised as to how a loving God can treat people this way. Does not Paul himself write in Romans 5:8 that God loved us "while we were still sinners"? How can a God who loves sinners punish them with eternal afflictions? The Bible's answer is that God loved the world by sending his Son to die on the cross. Paul stated that "God shows his love for us in that . . . Christ died for us" (v. 8). John added: "In this is love, not that we have loved God but that he loved us." He then elaborated as to how God loved us: he "sent his Son to be the propitiation for our sins" (1 John 4:10). Paul specifies that God will judge "those who do not obey the gospel of our Lord Jesus" (2 Thess. 1:8). This shows that unbelievers who refuse to accept Jesus in faith are judged precisely for spurning the love that God offered them. Isaac Watts wrote that "love so amazing, so divine, demands my soul, my life, my all,"[8] yet the ungodly not only despise the love of God but persecute his people. Having rejected the only way of forgiveness and reconciliation with God, persistent unbelievers have no other option than to be repaid "with affliction" (2 Thess. 1:6).

GOD'S JUDGMENT IN THE APPEARING OF CHRIST

The inevitable question that suffering Christians will ask, especially under extreme duress, is *when* God will come to judge and repay their oppressors. Paul has reminded the suffering Thessalonians that God was already helping them by upholding their faith and that this help proved his final judgment of unbelief. But when will that final judgment actually take place? Paul's answer is that it will happen at the second coming of Christ: "when the Lord Jesus is revealed from heaven with his mighty angels" (2 Thess. 1:7). This is the second time that Paul has emphasized the return of Christ to the Thessalonians. In 1 Thessalonians 4:13–18, the apostle offered Christ's return as our hope for believers who have died. Now he comes back to Christ's return as the time when the ungodly are judged and the oppression of God's people comes to a final end.

When Paul spoke of Christ's return in 1 Thessalonians, he used the Greek word *parousia*, which indicated his "arrival." The apostle now employs the word *apocalypsis*, which means the "revelation" or the "unveiling" of Christ.

8. Isaac Watts, "When I Survey the Wondrous Cross" (1707).

The emphasis here is not on the entry of Christ to earth from heaven, but rather on the revealing to the world of the Christ who has been sovereign all the while. The same word would be used for the unveiling of a sculpture. The statue has been present all along, but under its cover no one noticed its glory and splendor. Likewise, Christ is reigning now from heaven for his church (Eph. 1:21). The problem is that the world rejects this truth and that Christ's own people often forget it. But like the statue that is revealed to sight when its covering is removed, at Christ's return his sovereign majesty will be displayed before all the world, the godly and ungodly alike. J. Philip Arthur writes:

> The unbelieving world has mocked the hope of Christians for years. Why put your trust in someone when you have no guarantee that he is even there? Believers for their part have had to live with the frustration that, though convinced of the reality of Jesus, they have not been able to silence the cynics. But scoffers will find that every taunt will die on their lips when the one who has been concealed stands revealed in all his splendor.[9]

Paul provides a stirring picture of Christ's glorious return, saying that he will be revealed "with his mighty angels in flaming fire" (2 Thess. 1:7–8). We are reminded of Jesus' remark before his arrest, when his glory as the Christ was so completely veiled to human sight that men thought it right to put him to death. When Peter sought to defend Jesus with a sword in the garden of Gethsemane, the Lord responded, "Do you think that I cannot appeal to my Father, and he will at once send me more than twelve legions of angels?" (Matt. 26:53). Jesus explained that the angels would be kept at bay in order for him to offer his blood as the Lamb of God who died for our sins.

The angelic host that so marveled in the Bethlehem sky when Jesus was born of the virgin Mary must have strained at the leash when Jesus forbade them to vent their fury at those who would nail him to the cross. But when his glory is unveiled in the second coming, that angel host will be set free to take "vengeance on those who do not know God and on those who do not obey the gospel of our Lord Jesus" (2 Thess. 1:8). The book of Revelation shows that angels will bring final judgment to the earth in the fires of God's

9. J. Philip Arthur, *Patience of Hope: 1 and 2 Thessalonians Simply Explained*, Wellwyn Commentary Series (Ross-shire, UK: Evangelical Press, 1996), 105.

wrath. John writes: "Then I heard a loud voice from the temple telling the seven angels, 'Go and pour out on the earth the seven bowls of the wrath of God'" (Rev. 16:1). The final bowl of wrath in Revelation is the very vengeance that Paul sees unleashed by angels when Jesus returns.

Whereas the appearing of Christ will spell doom for the unbelieving world in the righteous judgment of God, the same appearing will "grant relief to you who are afflicted as well as to us" (2 Thess. 1:7). In Mark 13:26–27, Jesus taught that in his return, "they will see the Son of Man coming in clouds with great power and glory. And then he will send out the angels and gather his elect from the four winds." Christ's coming will remove all suffering and affliction from his people and usher them into a glorious communion that will last forever. Jesus had told his disciples that "if I go and prepare a place for you, I will come again and will take you to myself, that where I am you may be also" (John 14:3). Believers will be greatly relieved to be taken by Jesus to the place that he has been preparing, but even more, filled with joy that he takes us to himself. The Scots Confession states: "The time of refreshing and restitution of all things shall come, so that those who from the beginning have suffered violence, injury, and wrong, for righteousness' sake, shall inherit that blessed immortality promised them from the beginning" (chap. 11).

Notice that Paul did not call his suffering friends to endure persecution while he enjoyed ease. Instead, Christ's coming will bring relief to them "as well as to us" (2 Thess. 1:7). The apostle led them into the communion of suffering with their Savior and knew firsthand the joyous anticipation of what he called "our blessed hope, the appearing of the glory of our great God and Savior Jesus Christ" (Titus 2:13). In fact, it is Jesus who first led the way in renouncing this world and enduring its scorn, so that Paul was willing to give up everything, "that I may know him and the power of his resurrection, and may share his sufferings, becoming like him in his death, that by any means possible I may attain the resurrection from the dead" (Phil. 3:10–11).

God's Judgment Determined by Faith or Unbelief

A generation after Isaiah met with such frustration in his meeting with King Ahaz, vainly urging him to trust the Lord in his trials rather than to appeal to the world and its powers, there was another meeting between the prophet and a new king, Ahaz's son Hezekiah. This time, the situation was even more dire. The Assyrians whom Ahaz had once hired were now besieging Jerusalem with a mighty army of a hundred eighty-five thousand mercenary warriors. This time, at the very place where Isaiah and his king had once stood, the herald of the Assyrian emperor now came to mock Hezekiah and his pretensions to faith in the Lord. This is what happens when a generation turns from the Lord to the world: from places once occupied by God's people—college professorships, church pulpits, and evangelical organizations—assaults are launched against Christ and his gospel. Thus it was that the Assyrian herald mocked Hezekiah and his God from "the conduit of the upper pool on the highway to the Washer's Field" (Isa. 36:2). "Do not let Hezekiah make you trust in the LORD by saying, 'The LORD will surely deliver us,'" he cried in ridicule (v. 15). Instead, he advised the worldly counsel of submission to false gods: "For thus says the king of Assyria: Make your peace with me and come out to me" (v. 16).

After receiving the Assyrian threats, Isaiah and Hezekiah met. As before, the prophet called on the king to face persecution by standing firm in his faith in God. Hezekiah believed, rejecting the Assyrian threats and entering the temple to offer his prayers to God. Hezekiah prayed, "O LORD our God, save us from his hand, that all the kingdoms of the earth may know that you alone are the LORD" (Isa. 37:20). In response, Scripture records that "the angel of the Lord went out and struck down a hundred and eighty-five thousand in the camp of the Assyrians. And when people arose early in the morning, behold, these were all dead bodies" (v. 36).

God's deliverance of Hezekiah and Jerusalem stands as an abiding testimony to his mighty power to save his people from any danger or affliction. Indeed, the destruction of the Assyrian host before Jerusalem's wall was a special foretaste of the great judgment that will come upon all the earth when Jesus is revealed in his sovereign majesty, "with his mighty angels in flaming fire" (2 Thess. 1:7–8). The world that is then judged will possess no excuse for the charge that they "do not know God," since they suppressed the truth of God "by their unrighteousness," in stubborn unbelief and hardened idolatry (Rom. 1:18). Though God sent his Son in saving grace, they would not submit to "obey the gospel of our Lord Jesus" (2 Thess. 1:8), and will thus receive righteous vengeance for their rebellious sin. Meanwhile, the beleaguered Christian people, though often afflicted, enduring suffering of one kind or another for the sake of Christ and his kingdom, will be gathered from the four corners of the earth to enter into the glory of their Lord.

On which side will you stand on that day? The answer is given now. Either, like Hezekiah, you open your heart to the worship of God and respond with an obedient faith to the gospel of his Son or else, like Ahaz, you shut your eyes to the glory of Christ that will be revealed on the day of his coming. "Behold, I am coming soon," Jesus says, "bringing my recompense with me, to repay everyone for what he has done" (Rev. 22:12). He adds, inviting us all to accept the salvation that is still offered to everyone in the world: "Blessed are those who wash their robes, so that they may have the right to the tree of life and that they may enter the city by the gates" (v. 14).

28

THE BIBLICAL DOCTRINE
OF HELL

2 Thessalonians 1:8–9

. . . inflicting vengeance on those who do not know God and
on those who do not obey the gospel of our Lord Jesus. They
will suffer the punishment of eternal destruction, away from
the presence of the Lord and from the glory of his might.
(2 Thess. 1:8–9)

Some years ago, one of the royal princesses of England was departing from a cathedral service and spoke to the dean. "Is it true, Dean," she asked, "that there is a place called hell?" The clergyman answered: "Ma'am, our Lord and his Apostles taught so, the Creeds affirm so, and the Church believes so." To this, the princess replied, "Why, then, in God's name, do you not tell us so?"[1]

The royal princess observed a very real phenomenon in churches today: the disappearance of hell. In older days, preachers such as Jonathan Edwards

---

1. Sinclair B. Ferguson, "Pastoral Theology: The Preacher and Hell," in *Hell under Fire: Modern Scholarship Reinvents Eternal Punishment*, ed. Christopher W. Morgan and Robert A. Peterson (Grand Rapids: Zondervan, 2004), 226.

spoke often of hell. "Consider that if once you get into hell, you'll never get out," Edwards pleaded. "They that go there return no more. Consider how dreadful it will be to suffer such an extremity forever."[2] A preacher who spoke this way today would be considered unbalanced by many of his hearers, even in supposedly Bible-believing churches. R. Albert Mohler writes: "The traditional doctrine of hell now bears the mark of *odium theologium*—a doctrine retained only by the most stalwart defenders of conservative theology . . . . The doctrine is routinely dismissed as an embarrassing artifact from an ancient age—a reminder of Christianity's rejected worldview."[3] In keeping with this spirit, it is no longer open deniers of the Bible who reject the doctrine of hell, but supposedly evangelical scholars as well. Some onlookers undoubtedly consider this development a sign of maturity on the part of professing believers.

The problem with such a revision of the doctrine of hell is the standing testimony of the Holy Scriptures. This point was made by J. Gresham Machen in a sermon on Matthew 10:28, the text in which Jesus said, "Do not fear those who kill the body but cannot kill the soul. Rather fear him who can destroy both soul and body in hell." Machen began by stating: "These words were not spoken by Jonathan Edwards. They were not spoken by Cotton Mather. They were not spoken by Calvin, or Augustine, or by Paul. But these words were spoken by Jesus."[4]

In keeping with the words of Jesus, the apostle Paul also taught about hell in his second letter to the Thessalonians. The context of his remarks was the suffering of the believers under persecution from the world. They were to be comforted by knowing that God would exact vengeance on their oppressors: "God considers it just to repay with affliction those who afflict you," Paul said, by "inflicting vengeance" through "the punishment of eternal destruction" (2 Thess. 1:6–9). Out of this pastoral concern for the perseverance of believers under persecution, the apostle provides some of the most potent teaching about hell that is found in all of Scripture.

2. Jonathan Edwards, "The Torments of Hell Are Exceedingly Great," in *The Works of Jonathan Edwards*, vol. 14, *Sermons and Discourses: 1723–1729*, ed. Kenneth P. Minkema (New Haven, CT: Yale University Press, 1997), 326.

3. R. Albert Mohler Jr., "Modern Theology: The Disappearance of Hell," in Morgan and Peterson, *Hell under Fire*, 16.

4. J. Gresham Machen, *God Transcendent* (1949; repr., Edinburgh: Banner of Truth, 1982), 28.

The Punishment for Rejecting God

The first thing for us to know about hell, Paul explains, is that it is God's just punishment on his enemies. Earlier, the apostle mentioned God's vengeance on "those who afflict you" (2 Thess. 1:6), speaking of his readers' persecutors. Now he broadens the scope, with God inflicting "vengeance on those who do not know God and on those who do not obey the gospel of our Lord Jesus" (v. 8). Some scholars think that Paul is setting forth two kinds of God's enemies: Gentile atheists and Jewish gospel-deniers. It is more likely, however, that Paul is setting forth the two sides of damning unbelief: rejecting the knowledge of God and refusing the gospel message of salvation.

We know from Romans chapter 1 that there is no one who truly does not know God. "For his invisible attributes, namely, his eternal power and divine nature, have been clearly perceived," Paul explains, "ever since the creation of the world, in the things that have been made" (Rom. 1:20). It is the designed purpose of nature to bear testimony to God, so that "what can be known about God is plain to them" (v. 19). How, then, can people "not know God"? The answer is that unbelievers willfully reject the knowledge of God that they have. "By their unrighteousness," Paul declares, they "suppress the truth" (v. 18). Moreover, "although they knew God, they did not honor him as God or give thanks to him," but instead "exchanged the glory of the immortal God for images" (vv. 21–23). For this grave sin of idolatry, God will punish those who have lived as practical atheists, whatever actual creed they might have professed.

Matters become worse when the unbeliever hears but rejects the gospel. God sent his own Son to bring salvation to rebel humanity. Those who despise the death of Jesus for sins, refusing to repent and believe, have grievously offended God and merited his just condemnation. Paul's description of unbelief as "not obey[ing] the gospel" reminds us that the message of Jesus is not merely a warmhearted invitation to sinners but also a sovereign summons to repent and believe.

The judgment of those who reject God and his gospel will involve God's full and just punishment that these sins deserve. The Bible makes it clear that God's judgment will condemn sinners not only for unbelief but also "according to what they had done" (Rev. 20:12). God will punish every last sin committed against his law. Still, Paul describes condemned sinners as "those who do not obey the gospel" (2 Thess. 1:8), since it was by refusing the gospel that they forfeited the only way of forgiveness for their sins. John 3:36 thus warns that "whoever does not obey the Son shall not see life, but the wrath of God remains on him."

The Punishment of Hell

In Paul's teaching about God's wrath in Romans 1, the apostle emphasized the way that sin is punished in this life, as God gives "them up to a debased mind to do what ought not to be done" (Rom 1:28; see also 1:24–26). Second Thessalonians differs by focusing on the judgment that God will inflict when Christ returns. Thus, 2 Thessalonians 1:8–9 provides some of the Bible's clearest teaching on the punishment of hell. In the Old Testament, the Hebrew word *sheol*, translated in Greek by the word *hades*, describes the place of the dead generally, regardless of their status before God. In the New Testament, however, *hades*, translated in English as *hell*, is used exclusively of the place of final, fiery judgment for unforgiven sinners.

We may summarize the Bible's teaching on the punishment of hell with three adjectives, the first of which is that it is an *eternal* punishment. Paul writes in 2 Thessalonians 1:9, "They will suffer the punishment of eternal destruction." The point is that sinners who rejected God and his gospel in this life will face in the afterlife an unending punishment for their transgressions.

The Bible's teaching on hell is so dreadful that even many devout Christians struggle to accept it. This is particularly true of the eternal nature of hell. One attempt to avoid this doctrine is called *Christian universalism*. This teaching holds that while a holy God must punish sin and therefore there is punishment in the afterlife, the love of God will eventually win through so that sooner or later every last person is brought into the blessedness of heaven. This view was advanced through Rob Bell's best-selling book, *Love Wins*. Bell looks on the gracious character of God revealed in the Bible and asserts "the belief that, given enough time, everybody will turn to God and find themselves in the joy and peace of God's presence. The love of God will melt every hard heart, and even the most 'depraved sinners' will eventually give up their resistance and turn to God."[5] According to Bell and others,

5. Rob Bell, *Love Wins: A Book about Heaven, Hell, and the Fate of Every Person Who Ever Lived* (San Francisco: HarperOne, 2011), 107.

there are "second chances" after death, so that many and perhaps all who rejected Christ in this life will eventually escape hell in order to spend eternity in heaven.

The problem with Christian universalism is the clear teaching of the Bible. Hebrews 9:27 rules out any second chance to believe the gospel after death: "It is appointed for man to die once, and after that comes judgment." Jesus frequently pressed the need to believe on him in this life, telling the religious leaders that "unless you believe that I am he you will die in your sins" (John 8:24). The urgency of Jesus' appeal would be pointless if dying in one's sin did not determine one's condemnation forever. Moreover, Paul says that those who suffer "eternal destruction" are cast out forever "away from the presence of the Lord" (2 Thess. 1:9). It is clear that such persons will never enter heaven, but suffer a permanent isolation from the blessing of God.

Another way to deny the eternal nature of hell is the teaching known as *annihilationism*. This theory holds that Paul's phrase "eternal destruction" means the complete eradication of the person. This interpretation is given to Jesus' warning that God "can destroy both soul and body in hell" (Matt. 10:28). The most famous evangelical proponent of this view was John Stott, who in his earlier years argued that in these verses, *destruction* means "an extinction of being." "It would seem strange," he wrote, "if people who are said to suffer destruction are in fact not destroyed."[6] A similar argument is made from the Bible verses that refer to the flames of hell: since fire consumes its victims, at some point they would seem to no longer exist.

Like Christian universalism, annihilationism is unable to sustain the critique of the whole Bible, despite its purported attempt to take biblical imagery seriously. It is true that Paul speaks of "eternal destruction," but "it does not follow that those who suffer destruction cease to exist."[7] Indeed, the word that Paul used for *destruction* (Greek *olethros*) does not "signify so much annihilation as the loss of all that is worthwhile, utter ruin"[8]—an apt description of the consequences of ending up in a fiery hell. Moreover, since the apostle describes unbelievers as being eternally separated from God's presence, they must not have ceased to exist. Furthermore, the word

6. David L. Edwards and John Stott, *Evangelical Essentials: A Liberal-Evangelical Dialogue* (London: Hodder & Stoughton, 1988), 315–16.

7. D. A. Carson, *The Gagging of God* (Grand Rapids: Zondervan, 1996), 522.

8. Leon Morris, *The First and Second Epistles to the Thessalonians*, New International Commentary on the New Testament (Grand Rapids: Eerdmans, 1959), 205.

that he uses to say that destruction is eternal is the same word used in the New Testament for eternal life, which every believer accepts as everlasting. Eternal destruction and eternal life are opposites (see Matt. 25:46). Just as eternal life is the blessed state of communion with God that goes on forever, so also hell is the cursed stated of exclusion from God's blessing that will never cease.

Not only does Paul teach that hell is eternal, but second, he describes it in terms of *conscious* punishment. When he says that the condemned are cast "away from the presence of the Lord and from the glory of his might" (2 Thess. 1:9), this implies a conscious experience of alienation. And when he warns that they will "suffer punishment," he uses an active verb (*tino*) that means that they will actively render payment for their sins. Revelation 20:10 tells us that in the final judgment, the devil is "thrown into the lake of fire and sulfur," there to be "tormented day and night forever and ever." Suffering can be described as "torment" only if it is consciously experienced. Revelation 20:15 adds that all whose names were not found in Christ's book of life were also "thrown into the lake of fire" to receive conscious punishment forever.

Sin deserves conscious eternal punishment because of the infinite offense given to the eternal God. It may also be argued that judgment involves conscious eternal torment because the damned remain eternally sinful people who keep on sinning against God. In the last book of the Bible, the angel says to John: "Let the evildoer still do evil, and the filthy still be filthy, and the righteous still do right, and the holy still be holy" (Rev. 22:11). This verse erects a parallel between the eternally holy state of those who are saved and the eternally evil state of the condemned. Revelation 16:21 explains that those suffering God's judgment "cursed God" for what they were suffering. It seems that hell involves eternal conscious hatred of God and a conscious corresponding punishment from God forever.

Third, we may summarize the Bible's teaching of hell by noting that in addition to eternal and conscious suffering, it involves the *bodily* punishment of those condemned by God. The Bible reveals that in the coming of Christ, all the dead—godly and ungodly—are resurrected so that souls are rejoined forever to their bodies to stand before the Lord (Rev. 20:12). Jesus will say to those who rejected God and despised his offer of mercy in the gospel: "Depart from me, you cursed, into the eternal fire prepared for the devil and his angels" (Matt. 25:41). By speaking of the fires of hell, the Bible plainly indicates bodily punishment for the ungodly. In fact, the clearest testimony to bodily torment in hell comes from Jesus himself (Matt. 5:22; 13:40–42; 18:8–9; 25:41; etc.), who warned that in hell "their worm does not die and the fire is not quenched" (Mark 9:48). John the Baptist alluded to Psalm 1 in saying of Jesus: "The chaff he will burn with unquenchable fire" (Matt. 3:12). Just as sin offers fleshly pleasures in this life, under God's judgment it yields the wages of fleshly pain in eternity.

Some people attempt to minimize the horror of hell's torment by arguing that fire is merely a symbol for hell's punishment. If that is so, however, the question must be raised as to what is being symbolized in this manner. James Montgomery Boice writes that "although the Bible uses imagery to portray the unimaginable, it does so precisely because the reality is unimaginable. That is, the suffering of the wicked in hell is so intense and so terrible that, if it is not actual physical suffering by fire, only such intense physical suffering can be used to describe it."[9] The very terror of the Bible's description of hell—an eternal, conscious, and bodily torment—should persuade us not to argue with God, but instead to fearfully believe what God has revealed to us about hell. Then we may turn to God, humbly seeking at whatever cost to avoid the suffering that he has warned us about in hell.

The Punishment of Separation from God

There is no sin in admitting to difficulty in accepting the Bible's teaching on hell. John Stott commented, "Emotionally, I find the concept [of hell] intolerable," but he added, "As a committed Evangelical, my question must be . . . not what does my heart tell me, but what does God's word say?"[10] Surely, a fully biblical position on hell will impact our hearts as well as our minds. In believing the biblical doctrine of hell, we should experience the tears shed by Jeremiah when he preached judgment on Israel and the broken heart of Jesus as he called out, "O Jerusalem, Jerusalem," and lamented the unbelief of the Jewish people (Matt. 23:37).

It is because of the heart's difficulty in accepting hell that so many Bible teachers seek a way to soften the blow. We have already noted that some

9. James Montgomery Boice, *The Parables of Jesus* (Chicago: Moody Press, 1983), 42.
10. Edwards and Stott, *Evangelical Essentials*, 314–15.

take the unbiblical path of universal salvation, whereas others take up the similarly unbiblical position of annihilation. A third attempt to turn down the fires on hell stems from a wrong interpretation of Paul's teaching in 2 Thessalonians 1:9, in which the apostle states that the condemned will be cast "away from the presence of the Lord." Based on this verse, Christians will often hear that hell is not so bad, since it "is only separation from God."

There are two major problems with this view. The first is that we have already seen that the Bible clearly teaches bodily torment in hell. But the larger problem is the use of the word *only* with respect to separation from God. In speaking this way, Paul was not intending to limit the dire nature of hell but to plumb the depths of hell's despair. If eternal destruction in hell is the opposite of eternal life in salvation, and if, as Jesus said, eternal life consists in knowing God (John 17:3), then being cast out from the Lord's presence is the very nadir of divine condemnation. G. K. Beale notes: "Thus, the punishment 'fits the crime,' in that those who refuse to know God (1:8) and want to be separate from him in this life will be punished by being separate from God in the next life."[11]

Paul's expression "away from the presence of the Lord" recalls the great Aaronic blessing of the old covenant: "The LORD bless you and keep you; the LORD make his face to shine upon you and be gracious to you; the LORD lift up his countenance upon you and give you peace" (Num. 6:24–26). This blessing is the highest expression of what any creature could desire, to be drawn near to the presence of God in intimate communion, understanding, and delight. This alone can satisfy our souls forever—to look into the glorious face of God, to know him and be known! Correspondingly, the greatest desolation possible is to be eternally and completely shut out from all communion with God, to have his face turned away forever. John Lillie therefore warns: "The day is coming, when to be for ever sundered from the Lord—to hear from his lips that one word: 'Depart from me'—will be found to comprise in it all elements of woe, the darkness and horror, the anguish and despair, of hell."[12]

Thus we see that to be condemned by God is to have the blessing he gave through Aaron reversed: "The Lord curse you and reject you; the Lord darken

11. G. K. Beale, *1–2 Thessalonians*, IVP New Testament Commentary Series (Downers Grove, IL: InterVarsity Press, 2003), 189.

12. John Lillie, *Lectures on Paul's Epistles to the Thessalonians*, Tentmaker Classic Commentaries (1860; repr., Stoke-on-Trent, UK: Tentmaker Publications, 2007), 346.

his face to you and withhold all grace; the Lord turn away his countenance and leave you in despair." R.C. Sproul thus comments of hell: "God turns his back, he departs from us, and he leaves us isolated from his presence with no benefits of his presence and nothing to enjoy."[13] To be separated from God is to be excluded from all good, since the Father is the source of every good gift (James 1:17). This is why Jesus described hell with ultimate expressions of woe, as "the outer darkness," where "there will be weeping and gnashing of teeth" (Matt. 8:12).

Not only are those in hell separated "from the presence of the Lord," but they are also separated "from the glory of his might" (2 Thess. 1:9). We must be careful to realize that nowhere does the Bible teach that those in hell have escaped from God. Reckless unbelievers laugh about having a good time in hell precisely because there will be no God (or Christians, for that matter) to disturb their fleshly pleasure. The Bible reveals that instead they will find fleshly torment, and although they are denied the light of God's presence, they do not escape the dreadful awareness of his sovereign wrath. Paul's statement in verse 9 seems to echo the woes of Isaiah chapter 2, where the prophet describes the damned as being unable to hide from "the terror of the Lord, and from the splendor of his majesty" (Isa. 2:21). Sinners in hell are not barred from the holy terror or sovereign rule of God, nor from the might of the Lord, but rather they are excluded "from the glory of his might" (2 Thess. 1:9). The reigning majesty of the sovereign Christ is a terror for them, not a glory; the very things in which the redeemed most rejoice are for the condemned a great and eternal source of lament.

On Behalf of Christ

As we seek to apply the implications of the biblical doctrine of hell, first we must realize how vital it is that we teach this doctrine without compromise. We may imagine that we are improving or updating the Bible by smoothing over matters to which our generation objects. In reality, however, we are denigrating God's Word and corrupting all the doctrines that are inseparably related. For instance, it is impossible for us to downplay eternal punishment and still maintain what Anselm of Canterbury described as "the exceeding

---

13. R.C. Sproul, "Sacrifice and Satisfaction," in Gabriel N. E. Fluhrer, *Atonement* (Phillipsburg, NJ: P&R Publishing, 2010), 76.

gravity of sin."[14] We cannot suggest a second chance to believe after death without undermining the urgent call of missions and evangelism to believe the gospel now. Most seriously of all, by softening the idea of hell's sufferings, we minimize the sacrifice offered by Jesus Christ on the cross, where God's Son voluntarily embraced the eternal experience of separation from the Father as he suffered for us in his spirit.

Instead of toning down the Scriptures when it comes to difficult matters, we need to elevate the capacity of our faith to accept whatever God has revealed. Doing this will require us to bow before God and submit our minds to his Word. Moreover, to accept the Bible's teaching of hell, we will have to face the ways in which we have not fully imbibed the Bible's teaching elsewhere. If we recoil against God's eternal punishment of sin, then we must not have embraced the Bible's emphasis on the heinous offense of sin and the infinite holiness of the God who responds with such terrible justice. Furthermore, we have surely failed to grasp that the supreme purpose of all things is to glorify the sublime perfection of all of God's attributes, including both his glorious love in the gospel and his glorious wrath in the punishments of hell. It is instructive to us to read how heaven rejoices over the glory of God in the judgment of hell. Gazing out from heaven onto hell, the angels cry, "Hallelujah! The smoke from her goes up forever and ever" (Rev. 19:3).

Here on earth, however, where Jesus wept for sin, the truth about hell calls us to a passionate witness to the gospel of salvation from sin. How can we read of the terrors of hell, into which will go all "who do not know God" and "do not obey the gospel" (2 Thess. 1:8), and fail to do everything possible for them to know and believe the grace of God in Christ? How can we fail to pray for greater zeal in evangelism and for God's power to open the unbelieving hearts to which we speak? Sinclair Ferguson comments: "Few things will clarify our vision of what it means to be ministers of the new covenant than to recognize with stark clarity that our great business in life is to pluck men and women and boys and girls from the eternal burnings . . . [so that] those who otherwise would have been eternally condemned before the majestic righteousness of God [will shine] like stars in the heavens and like jewels in the crowns of our own ministry."[15]

14. Anselm, *Cur Deus Homo* (Edinburgh: John Grant, 1909), 50.
15. Sinclair B. Ferguson, *The Biblical Basis of the Doctrine of Eternal Punishment*, audio recording, available at http://www.desiringgod.org/resource-library/conference-messages/universalism-and-the-reality-of-eternal-punishment-the-biblical-basis-of-the-doctrine-of-eternal-punishment.

As the royal princess asserted to the cathedral dean, if the Scriptures teach and the church confesses the reality of hell, then for God's sake we must tell people. And in speaking about hell, we must never fail to declare the way of forgiveness at the cross of Christ, where God sent his own Son to pay with his blood the debt of sin, "that whoever believes in him should not perish but have eternal life" (John 3:16).

Finally, the most urgent implication of the biblical doctrine of hell is the necessity that each of us should know our own salvation through faith in the Savior, Jesus Christ. Are you aware of your sin against the holiness of God? Are your ears open to God's warning of the eternal punishment of sin in hell? Has it not been declared to you that Jesus Christ died to save sinners from hell through faith in his blood? Then hear the words of the same apostle who wrote to the persecuted Thessalonians, comforting them with the truth that God will judge their oppressors, as he appeals to you for salvation:

> In Christ God was reconciling the world to himself, not counting their trespasses against them . . . . Therefore . . . we implore you on behalf of Christ, be reconciled to God. . . . Behold, now is the favorable time; behold, now is the day of salvation. (2 Cor. 5:19–6:2)

29

GLORIFIED IN HIS SAINTS

2 Thessalonians 1:10–12

. . . when he comes on that day to be glorified in his saints, and
to be marveled at among all who have believed. (2 Thess. 1:10)

*I*n 1644, the Puritan minister Richard Baxter was suffering
under such a depressed spirit that he virtually despaired of
any desire to go on living. A number of factors contributed
to his despondency. His ministry in the town of Kidderminster had been
forestalled by the English Civil War, so that he was kept from his spiritual
flock. Having served as a chaplain in the Parlimentary Army, he found
himself shunned by its leader, Oliver Cromwell, because of Baxter's strident
spiritual views. Close friends had died in the war, and his father had been
imprisoned by the Royalist forces. Moreover, Baxter's health had broken
down, leaving him ill and weak.

In this sad condition, Baxter undertook a study that would not only lift
his own spirits but also be used by God to do the same for many others.
Published as *The Saints' Everlasting Rest*, the book meditated on the Bible's
teaching concerning the return of Christ and heaven. Baxter displayed for
his readers all the blessing and glory awaiting them in heaven. He also
urged that by frequently thinking about the everlasting rest, believers are

motivated to lead useful and zealous lives of faith. He wrote: "The frequent believing views of glory are the most precious cordial in all afflictions: first, to sustain our spirits, and make our sufferings far more easy; secondly, to stay us from repining and make us bear with patience and joy; and, thirdly, to strengthen our resolutions, that we forsake not Christ for fear of trouble."[1]

In urging suffering saints to realize the inheritance they possess in glory, Baxter was following the example of the apostle Paul in his ministry to the persecuted believers of Thessalonica. The apostle began his second letter by expressing thanks for their "steadfastness and faith . . . in the afflictions that [they were] enduring" (2 Thess. 1:4). Paul asserted that God would "repay with affliction those who afflict you" (v. 6), punishing them with "eternal destruction" (v. 9). Christ's return would also bring eternal glory to his faithful servants who suffered in his name during this life. Paul concluded with words that would later be employed by Baxter, teaching that Christ "comes on that day to be glorified in his saints, and to be marveled at among all who have believed" (v. 10). By knowing this great deliverance, still future to the beleaguered church of Christ, believers are emboldened to live with a heavenly purpose while still on earth.

MARVELING IN HIS GLORY

Paul's teaching on the return of Christ in 2 Thessalonians 1 culminates in the glorification of Christ by the people whom he has come to save. It is difficult for believers now to imagine how greatly we will praise our mighty Savior on the day of his coming. We can best anticipate this rejoicing by looking to descriptions in the Bible. For instance, Isaiah chapter 11 tells of the Lord's coming, using language that the New Testament applies to the return of Christ: "He shall strike the earth with the rod of his mouth, and with the breath of his lips he shall kill the wicked" (Isa. 11:4). The next chapter relates the praise of the godly: "Shout and sing for joy, O inhabitant of Zion, for great in your midst is the Holy One of Israel" (12:6).

How satisfying it will be for Christ's people when the whole of his redemptive work comes to fruition on that day. Jesus came to the earth not in glory but in humiliation. He "made himself nothing, taking the form of a servant," and ultimately "humbled himself by becoming obedient to the point

1. Richard Baxter, *The Saints' Everlasting Rest* (Vancouver: Regent College Publishing, 2004), 115.

of death, even death on a cross" (Phil. 2:7–8). Even after Jesus was raised from the dead and ascended to the throne of God in heaven, his glory was unobserved by the majority of the human race. Hebrews 2 echoes Psalm 8 in saying, "At present, we do not yet see everything in subjection to him," even though we know that in heaven Jesus is "crowned . . . with glory and honor" (Heb. 2:7–9). But on that great day yet to come, Jesus' resplendent glory will be unveiled to all creation "so that at the name of Jesus every knee should bow . . . and every tongue confess that Jesus Christ is Lord" (Phil. 2:10–11). How greatly Christ will be glorified in the hearts of his adoring people on the day of his unveiling before all!

Paul adds that Christ will "be marveled at among all who have believed" (2 Thess. 1:10). We may consider this in several ways. First, we will marvel to see true manhood glorified. When Jacob's sons went to Egypt seeking food, they trembled in awe before the majesty of the prince of Egypt. But the greater marvel was their realization that this prince was none other than their brother Joseph. We will likewise behold the glory of Christ in his return and marvel that the Lord is our brother and fellow man. Benjamin Morgan Palmer wrote, "When we are raised to sit with Him upon His throne, we shall behold His glorified humanity—behold Him, not as His disciples beheld Him, 'the man of sorrows and acquainted with grief,' but in that glorified human form in which He shall always be present to the sight and to the embrace of the saints above."[2]

While we marvel at the perfection of Jesus' manhood, it will be the glory of his deity that shines upon us. A vision of Christ's divine glory was granted to his disciples at certain key points in Jesus' earthly ministry. When Peter, James, and John saw him on the Mount of Transfiguration in splendor, "they came up and took hold of his feet and worshiped him" (Matt. 28:9). We will give the same honor when Jesus returns to reveal his divine glory to our eyes. Our worship of Jesus in the radiance of his unveiled glory will provide the ultimate satisfaction for our souls, of which our present worship on earth is the closest foretaste.

Moreover, on the day of Christ's coming, his people will marvel at his mediatorial glory in his office as Redeemer and head over the church. The exalted Jesus revealed himself in this way to the apostle John in the book of Revelation, dressed in the garb of the heavenly high priest: "clothed with a

2. Benjamin Morgan Palmer, *Sermons*, 2 vols. (1875; repr., Harrisonburg, VA: Sprinkle, 2002), 1:399.

long robe and with a golden sash around his chest" (Rev. 1:13). This is why the scenes of worship in the book of Revelation show that it is the Lamb upon the throne who is worshiped with great awe and joy. John tells us that at the center of heaven's worship he saw "a Lamb standing, as though it had been slain" (5:6). "Worthy is the Lamb who was slain," the heavenly chorus cried, "to receive power and wealth and wisdom and might and honor and glory and blessing!" (v. 12). So also, "when he comes on that day to be glorified in his saints," Christ's people will marvel at the gospel that they believed on earth and then see embodied in the return of the Messiah in all his glory as our Savior.

Preparing for His Glory

While the Bible's teaching on the return of Christ points to the future, its purpose is found in the present, to inspire and inform practical Christian living. Paul reasons that if we are sure of Christ's coming, then instead of fretting over our present troubles, we will employ ourselves in preparing for the glory that will be revealed.

Paul made clear the relevance of the present work of the church by noting in 2 Thessalonians 1:10 that Christ will be glorified in his saints "because our testimony to you was believed." The connection between faith and witness shows that emphasizing the sovereign glory of Christ in salvation does not minimize the significance of gospel preaching and evangelism today. Christ will be glorified among the Thessalonians because Paul preached the gospel to them and because by God's power they had believed.

In his Great Commission as recorded by Luke, Jesus identified three things needed for his saving work to be fulfilled: "that the Christ should suffer and on the third day rise from the dead, and that repentance and forgiveness of sins should be proclaimed in his name to all nations" (Luke 24:46–47). Two of these great works had already been achieved when our Lord spoke those words: his death and resurrection. One great task remains to be carried forward in this present age: the preaching of the gospel to the world. In his end-times teaching on the Mount of Olives, Jesus emphasized that the gospel must go out to all the world before he returns: "This gospel of the kingdom will be proclaimed throughout the whole world as a testimony to all nations, and then the end will come" (Matt. 24:14). How essential it is,

Paul therefore shows, that Christians should respond to the Bible's teaching about Christ's return by bearing testimony to the gospel before the world.

According to Jesus' parable of the ten minas in Luke 19:11–27, each believer is given the gospel as our stewardship for Christ in this life, with the command, "Engage in business until I come" (Luke 19:13). When he returns, he will ask his servants "what they had gained by doing business" (v. 15). This parable uses the analogy of business, even though we know that salvation comes only by God's sovereign grace. Evangelism is the divinely appointed means of God's saving work in the world. Christians serve Christ by spreading the gospel. Paul rejoiced to know that Christ will be glorified in his return because Paul's testimony led to the Thessalonians' faith. We, too, are to know the joy of sharing the good news of Christ's death and resurrection so that others will glorify Christ in his coming by believing the testimony that we gave.

When we think of Paul's ministry, we think of both his preaching of the gospel and his fervent prayers for the believers. "To this end we always pray for you," the apostle adds in 2 Thessalonians 1:11, pointing out that he asks God to protect and nurture their faith. This combination of witness and prayer makes effective evangelists. Andrew Young writes: "He knows they need the power of God to work out their faith in acts of practical service. And since prayer is the channel God has provided for obtaining that power, the apostle and his fellow missionaries pray constantly that God would supply what their converts need."[3]

Paul tells us not only that he prayed, but also what he prayed for. If most of us were praying for other Christians who were suffering intense persecution for their faith, some of them to the point of death, we would likely spend almost all our time asking God to remove the outward afflictions. Paul indicates a different approach, however, by praying for their spiritual maturity and growth in faith: "that our God may make you worthy of his calling" (2 Thess. 1:11).

This prayer request shows that in addition to following Paul's example of witnessing the gospel and praying, we must also place a priority on our own spiritual growth and maturity, and we should pray for the same in the lives of other believers. In our own lives, we will pursue maturity by devoting ourselves to God's Word and to prayer. We will join a faithful church

---

3. Andrew W. Young, *Let's Study 1 & 2 Thessalonians* (Edinburgh: Banner of Truth, 2001), 138.

and start exercising our gifts as the need arises. As we learn the Bible, we will begin applying its teaching to one area after another, including our use of time and money, our treatment of other people, and our turning from known sins. We will become active in evangelism and missions, and we will seek opportunities to befriend and encourage the faith of other Christians. In all these pursuits, Paul places the priority on living in such a way that is worthy of the calling we received from God in our salvation.

We should note well what Paul is and is not saying in this statement. Paul is not saying that we merit our salvation by being worthy of what God has given us in Christ. As sinners, we could never deserve God's favor, since our nature is corrupted by sin and our record includes countless violations of God's law. It is instructive, then, for us to go back to 2 Thessalonians 1:10 and see that Paul writes of Christ's being glorified "in his saints." Saints are those who are set apart by God through the work of the Holy Spirit. This description applies to every Christian, who is born again by the Spirit and set apart by Christ to live for the glory of God. It is as a "holy one" that I am to live in a manner worthy of what I have received. When Paul urges us to be "worthy of his calling," he is referring to the effectual call of God by which our hearts were changed when we heard the gospel, so that we believed and were saved. Having been called by God's power to a salvation that includes holiness, Christians are now to prepare for the glory that is coming by living a life worthy of that call.

Moreover, note that Paul does not say that we make ourselves worthy, but prays "that our God may make you worthy of his calling" (2 Thess. 1:11). The Christian's growth in grace and godliness is God's work in our lives, although we actively participate. Elsewhere Paul wrote: "Work out your own salvation with fear and trembling, for it is God who works in you, both to will and to work for his good pleasure" (Phil. 2:12–13). Through God's Word, prayer, and the worship of the church, God is working his grace into believers' lives. Our duty is to work out his salvation in every area of our lives, so that when Christ returns he will be glorified by what he has done in us through the Holy Spirit's ministry (see 2 Cor. 3:18).

In 2 Thessalonians 1:12, Paul states that his goal is that "the name of our Lord Jesus may be glorified in you." The "name" of the Lord is not only who he is but also what he has promised to do. Christ has put his name on us, and by his Spirit, through the ministry of the Word and prayer, he desires us to be sanctified so that his reputation will be exalted through our lives. Christ is "glorified in his saints," that is, his "holy ones." Therefore, if we want our lives to glorify his name, we will pursue holiness in this present life, knowing with joy that when Christ returns, our holiness will be perfected through our resurrection into glory.

Knowing that part of Christ's glory is bound up in our holiness forms a powerful motivation for our sanctification. When I grew up, I was proud of my father. We were an army family, and my father was usually one of the highest-ranking officers on the post. Moreover, I was keenly aware of the personal respect that many had for his character. I do not remember ever being told that I had to live up to my father's reputation, but I remember that I desired to do so. I had done nothing to bear his name, but people knew who I was, and this was a strong motivator in leading me to praiseworthy conduct. Christians bear the name of Jesus Christ, who is coming again to reveal his glory to all the earth. It is in part by our holiness that he will be glorified on that day "in his saints." Realizing this should motivate us to practical holiness and godly character for the sake of Christ's praise.

Paul adds a fourth way in which we prepare for the glory that is coming, saying that God will "fulfill every resolve for good and every work of faith by his power" (2 Thess. 1:11). Remember that the apostle was writing to persecuted Christians, yet he directed them to the work that God had given them and that God would empower them to do. This work undoubtedly involved duties in the home and in the church, as well as in the world. Later in the letter, Paul commands people "to do their work quietly and to earn their own living" (3:12). He exhorts them to "not grow weary in doing good" (v. 13). Later in his ministry, Paul would ask the Greek churches to raise money to send to the famine-stricken believers in Jerusalem. In 2 Corinthians 8:1–5, Paul boasted about how the Thessalonians gave generously, despite their afflictions and material poverty: "They gave according to their means, as I can testify, and beyond their means, of their own accord." The collection for the famished Jews was a "resolve for good" and a "work of faith" that God accomplished by his power. The Thessalonians were using their time well, even while they placed their hope in the coming of Christ.

According to Ephesians 2:10, every believer has good works, "which God prepared beforehand, that we should walk in them." We are all called to witness, to pray, and to grow in godliness, to which we add the good works that God has prepared for us as we prepare for Christ's glorious coming. Every Christian should be zealous to learn what works God has appointed and then accomplish them by God's power as crowns to lay before Christ's feet when he returns.

Sharing in His Glory

In his final statement of chapter 1, in which Paul has sought to encourage the steadfast faith of the persecuted believers, he adds not only that Christ's name will "be glorified in you," and also "you in him, according to the grace of our God and the Lord Jesus Christ" (2 Thess. 1:12). Having shared in the suffering of Christ in this life (2 Tim. 3:12), believers share in his glory for all the unending ages to come after he returns. In Romans 8:17, Paul reasoned that if we are "children, then heirs—heirs of God and fellow heirs with Christ." It is not that Christ gains his great inheritance and each believer gets his or her own little inheritance in glory, but rather that together with Christ, as his coheirs, we inherit the whole of the glory of God. Then Paul adds: "provided we suffer with him in order that we may also be glorified with him" (v. 17).

When General Douglas MacArthur signed the documents to accept the surrender of Imperial Japan and end World War II, he insisted that he be joined by two generals who had been captured early in the war and suffered terribly at Japanese hands. Finally sitting before the formal surrender, MacArthur took his pen and wrote his first name only: "Douglas." He then handed the pen to General Wainwright, who added "Mac," and then to General Percival, who completed the name by adding "Arthur." In a similar manner, when Christ returns, those who have suffered for him and with him in this present age will partake of his victory and celebrate his glory together with him.[4]

Paul's statement that Christ is glorified in you "and you in him" echoes the request that Jesus made in his great High Priestly Prayer on the night of his arrest: "Father, I desire that they also, whom you have given me, may be with me where I am, to see my glory that you have given me because you loved me before the foundation of the world" (John 17:24). Jesus did not say merely that he wills for his people to enter into heaven, but that they may be

---

4. *Perfect Illustrations for Every Topic and Occasion* (Wheaton, IL: Tyndale House, 2002), 264.

"with me." He longs for fellowship with his people and for us to enter into the glory that reflects his own love relationship with the Father. It is for this that he is returning to take us to himself and into his glory.

We all know the longing to be with our own people, those whom we love and who love us. Whose face has not been streaked with tears at the parting of dear ones? Who has not also known the joy of a long-awaited reunion with family and dearly beloved friends? In departing, Jesus prayed for the glorious reunion that will happen when he returns. Matthew Henry writes: "Christ speaks here as if he did not count his own happiness complete unless he had his elect to share with him in it."[5] As much as we look forward to our deliverance from affliction in the world, Jesus looks forward to having us to "eat and drink at my table in my kingdom" (Luke 22:30) and, after conquering in his name, "to sit with me on my throne, as I also conquered and sat down with my Father on his throne" (Rev. 3:21).

Jesus will return to be glorified in us, and we in him, and this is only by "the grace of our God and the Lord Jesus Christ" (2 Thess. 1:12). While no sinner can ever earn the glory of Christ, God has ordained it for all who believe the gospel to which Paul gave testimony and that the Bible declares today. Everyone who wishes to be saved must therefore receive the gospel, trusting the death and resurrection of Jesus to deliver us from our sins. If we refuse to believe, rebelling against the gospel that God has revealed concerning his Son, we must "suffer the punishment of eternal destruction" (v. 9) on that day when Christ returns. If we believe, surrendering our lives now in preparation for the glory to be revealed, we can know through faith that the grace of God has ordained that we be glorified together with Christ, his Son. On "that day," the day of Christ's coming and of judgment for the world, believers will marvel at the glory of Christ in order for that glory to enter into us.

CONQUERING FOR HIS GLORY

The next chapter will provide further details about the second coming of Christ, dealing with the problem of a false report stating that Christ had already returned. As we conclude chapter 1's teaching on Christ's appearing,

5. Matthew Henry, *Commentary on the Whole Bible*, 6 vols. (Peabody, MA: Hendrickson, n.d.), 5:942.

we should remember the Thessalonians' context of a suffering and persecuted church. Jesus taught that "because you are not of the world, but I chose you out of the world, therefore the world hates you. . . . If they persecuted me, they will also persecute you" (John 15:19–20). In light of this fact, our concern should not be how to avoid persecution and affliction, but how to respond to it. Paul's teaching in this chapter yields surprising but vitally important answers, which we may sum up in three brief practical applications.

First, Paul reasons that Christians should not lament but rather rejoice in persecution for Jesus' sake. This is not to say that we enjoy trouble and suffering—we do not—but rather that we know the joyful truth of what suffering for Christ brings. Enduring under persecution both proves and improves our faith (1 Peter 1:6–7), yielding a crop of godly character (see Rom. 5:3–5). Moreover, persecution bears testimony to our union with Christ and our eventual victory together with him. Suffering with and for Christ—not because of our sins or some other worldly cause—ensures that when he returns, Christ will be glorified in our faith and we with him (2 Thess. 1:12). As Jesus put it in the Sermon on the Mount: "Blessed are you when others revile you and persecute you and utter all kinds of evil against you falsely on my account. Rejoice and be glad, for your reward is great in heaven" (Matt. 5:11–12).

Second, whatever our circumstances are in this life, our great concern must be to promote the glory of Christ's name, not only by our conduct now but also on that day when he comes "to be glorified in his saints" (2 Thess. 1:10). It may fall to us to suffer gloriously as others have done. In the book of Daniel, Shadrach, Meshach, and Abednego provided an example for us when they would not bow before the golden statue of Nebuchadnezzar. "Our God whom we serve is able to deliver us from the burning fiery furnace," they told the king. But they declared that even if he chose not to do so, "we will not serve your gods or worship the golden image that you have set up" (Dan. 3:17–18). Christ came to save those three stalwart servants, and he will come on the last day to save all his faithful people. With that coming in mind, knowing that soon Christ will be revealed in glory, we must have as our chief goal to live at all times in such a way that his name is glorified in us by his grace and power.

Finally, remembering Paul's statement that Christ would be glorified in his saints "because our testimony to you was believed" (2 Thess. 1:10), we

313

must all put a premium on our calling to spread the gospel to others. The importance of this calling is highlighted in Revelation chapter 12, which presents a symbolic history of the spiritual warfare of this world. The dragon had made war on the church, symbolized by the woman who gave birth to the child Messiah. The dragon was cast down from heaven in defeat, and seeing "that he had been thrown down to the earth, he pursued the woman" (Rev. 12:13). This states that Satan persecutes the church out of frustration for his knowledge of defeat at the hands of Christ. In the midst of that symbolic history, we are told of the saints' salvation and victory: "They have conquered him by the blood of the Lamb and by the word of their testimony, for they loved not their lives even unto death" (v. 11). Christians do not conquer by avoiding troubles or by rising high in the structures of worldly power. They conquer in affliction by the blood of Jesus, which offers forgiveness to every sinner who believes, and redemption from sin in the power of God. They conquer "by the word of their testimony," even at the cost of their lives.

Every believer today has been saved by believing the testimony of another believer, with the result that Jesus Christ will be glorified by that faith on the day of his returning. Therefore, while he yet waits to return, our testimony today can and will expand the company of the saints, increasing the glory of Christ, and by God's grace enfolding people we love into the company of the glorious redeemed, snatching their souls from the fires of hell. Echoing the words of Isaiah long before, Paul reasons:

> How then will they call on him in whom they have not believed? And how are they to believe in him of whom they have never heard? And how are they to hear without someone preaching? . . . As it is written, "How beautiful are the feet of those who preach the good news!" (Rom. 10:14–15, quoting Isa. 52:7)

30

END-TIMES DANGERS

2 Thessalonians 2:1–3

Now concerning the coming of our Lord Jesus Christ and our being gathered together to him, we ask you, brothers, not to be quickly shaken in mind or alarmed. (2 Thess. 2:1–2)

Together with the book of Revelation and Jesus' Olivet Discourse (Matt. 24; Mark 13; Luke 21), Paul's letters to the Thessalonians provide the most detailed New Testament teaching about the events preceding the second coming of Christ. As we begin our study of 2 Thessalonians chapter 2, it may be helpful to recap Paul's teaching so far on this subject.

The apostle first mentioned Christ's return because of believers who had died. He taught his readers "not [to] grieve as others do who have no hope" (1 Thess. 4:13), since all believers will be rejoined with Christ forever when he returns. His second point taught that Christ will return "like a thief in the night"; the second coming will be unexpected by the world but anticipated by his people (5:1–5). Third, Paul began his second letter by encouraging persecuted believers to trust Christ to "repay with affliction those who afflict you, and to grant relief to you" when he comes again in power (2 Thess. 1:6–7). Christ's return, Paul insisted, is the ringing of good news for his people and the knelling of doom for the evil world.

Paul's fourth and final teaching on Christ's return came in response to a false report that the Lord had somehow already come: "Now concerning the coming of our Lord Jesus Christ . . . , we ask you, brothers, not to be quickly shaken in mind or alarmed, either by a spirit or a spoken word, or a letter seeming to be from us, to the effect that the day of the Lord has come" (2 Thess. 2:1–2). Word had spread, perhaps by a misinterpretation of Paul's first letter or a message falsely ascribed to him—Paul indicates that he does not know exactly how this word has spread—saying that Christ had already returned. The apostle therefore wrote to assure his readers that they had not missed out on Christ's coming and the consummation of their salvation.

From this statement, we learn that the Thessalonians suffered not only from outward persecution but also from false teaching from inside. False doctrine disturbs God's people, which is why it must be corrected by true biblical teaching in order to bring believers to peace. Paul's concern on this occasion points out a problem common to end-times teaching, namely, that many are "shaken in mind" and "alarmed." This effect happens when end-times schemes make Christians fear that they might somehow miss out when Jesus returns, having failed in some way to rightly anticipate the end. One way to avoid being wrongly disturbed about Christ's return, Paul emphasizes, is to know the Bible's teaching about the events associated with the second coming.

THE NEARNESS OF HIS COMING

To begin, we should note statements in the New Testament that indicate the nearness (or *imminence*) of Christ's return. In the Gospels, Jesus spoke in a way that some scholars mistakenly believe committed him to return during the lifetime of his original hearers: "Truly, I say to you, there are some standing here who will not taste death until they see the kingdom of God after it has come with power" (Mark 9:1; see also Matt. 16:28; 24:34; Mark 13:30; Luke 9:27). Careful reflection will conclude, however, that Jesus was referring to the events that began his spiritual kingdom rather than to those that will consummate it. The dramatic events of Christ's resurrection, his ascension into heaven, and the outpouring of the Spirit at Pentecost revealed the kingdom of God in its awesome power, just as Jesus had promised.

Other passages call believers to anticipate Christ's return as something to happen soon, especially in the book of Revelation. Jesus said to the church of Philadelphia: "I am coming soon. Hold fast what you have, so that no one may seize your crown" (Rev. 3:11). Later he added: "And behold, I am coming soon. Blessed is the one who keeps the words of the prophecy of this book. . . . Behold, I am coming soon, bringing my recompense with me" (22:7, 12). Similarly, in the next-to-last verse of the Bible, John writes: "He who testifies to these things says, 'Surely I am coming soon.' Amen. Come, Lord Jesus!" (v. 20).

Since we are told by our Lord to expect him soon, we can understand why Christians are anxious to be certain about their salvation when Christ returns. Paul describes Christ's coming as the time of "our being gathered together to him" (2 Thess. 2:1). What a tragedy it would be to live for Christ and even suffer for his gospel, but somehow to miss out on Christ's return and not be gathered into his glory! The primary answer to this concern is the inseparable link between faith in Christ now and our future gathering to him on the day of the Lord. Jesus made it clear that to believe on him in this life is to gain eternal life in the next: "All that the Father gives me will come to me, and whoever comes to me I will never cast out. . . . For this is the will of my Father, that everyone who looks on the Son and believes in him should have eternal life, and I will raise him up on the last day" (John 6:37–40). Therefore, a true and saving faith in Christ now assures the believer of being gathered to Christ for salvation on the day of his return.

ANXIETY OVER CHRIST'S SOON COMING

In light of the Bible's teaching of the nearness of Christ's coming, there are three common errors. First, since we are told to expect Christ's coming soon, people occasionally claim to have calculated the date of Christ's return. The chief problem with this is the clear biblical teaching denying this possibility. Instead of looking to a foreknown date, Christians are to expect Christ at any time. Jesus urged, "Watch therefore, for you know neither the day nor the hour" (Matt. 25:13).

A second error associated with the nearness of Christ's return was warned against in Jesus' Olivet Discourse: believing that Christ has returned secretly and is present somewhere on earth. Jesus warned: "Then if anyone says to you, 'Look, here is the Christ!' or 'There he is!' do not believe it" (Matt. 24:23). False christs may even have power from Satan to "perform great signs and wonders" that deceive the unwary. We can be sure, however, that all such claims are false, for the simple reason that Jesus is now located not on earth but in heaven and will return only at the ending of the age. Therefore, Jesus said, "If they say to you, 'Look, he is in the wilderness,' do not go out. If they say, 'Look, he is in the inner rooms,' do not believe it" (v. 26). Christians can be absolutely sure that every claim to Christ's physical presence on earth is false, however plausible it may seem, since we know that he will not return before the cataclysmic events of the second coming. Jesus concluded that his coming will be so obvious that no one will need to be told about his coming when it occurs: "For as the lightning comes from the east and shines as far as the west, so will be the coming of the Son of Man" (v. 27).

A third error associated with the nearness of Christ's coming is given by Paul in our passage. Through a variety of possible sources, word might come "to the effect that the day of the Lord has come" (2 Thess. 2:1). The biblical designation "day of the Lord" refers in the New Testament to the final judgment that will consummate history at the return of Christ (1 Cor. 1:8; 5:5; 2 Cor. 1:14). The false report in Thessalonica might have suggested that the final sequence of events had already started, which seems to be why some members of that church had stopped working and become idle, a problem that Paul addresses in chapter 3. Alternatively, the false message might have stated that there had been a spiritual second coming of Christ in such a way that the believers thought themselves at risk of missing the resurrection and the new heavens and earth. A modern version of this error was announced by the founder of the Jehovah's Witnesses, Charles T. Russell, when he asserted that Christ came invisibly on October 1, 1914, and argued that believers should not look for a visible return of Christ or for any future hope in his coming.[1] Paul mentions exactly this heresy as having spread to Ephesus through men "who have swerved from the truth, saying that the resurrection has already happened" (2 Tim. 2:17–18). According to Paul, the denial that Christ is still coming not only "upset[s] the faith of some," but leads "people into . . . ungodliness" (vv. 16, 18).

UNDERSTANDING THE TIMES

Paul asserts that we can be certain that Christ's coming has not yet happened by knowing the signs that precede Christ's return. He explains: "Let no

1. G. K. Beale, *1–2 Thessalonians*, IVP New Testament Commentary Series (Downers Grove, IL: InterVarsity Press, 2003), 201–2.

one deceive you in any way. For that day will not come, unless the rebellion comes first, and the man of lawlessness is revealed, the son of destruction" (2 Thess. 2:3).

In considering Paul's teaching on the events preceding Christ's return, we see that he is drawing on Jesus' Olivet Discourse. Jesus gave this teaching shortly before his crucifixion. Seeing his disciples gaping at the splendor of the temple buildings, Jesus predicted their destruction. In reply, the disciples asked, "Tell us, when will these things be, and what will be the sign of your coming and of the close of the age?" (Matt. 24:3). Jesus' answer followed the order of these questions, first predicting the fall of Jerusalem and then telling about his second coming.

In the Olivet Discourse, so named because it was spoken on the Mount of Olives, Jesus foretold signs that will precede his return and the final judgment. Before considering the signs, we should make some general observations. The first is that the signs of the end are not necessarily obvious to everyone. When the Jewish leaders asked for "a sign from heaven" that would enable them to believe, Jesus rebuked them for not believing God's Word. They might be able to read the signs of the weather, Jesus said, "but you cannot interpret the signs of the times" (Matt. 16:1–3). Similarly today, Christian faith is not anchored in extraordinary supernatural signs but in a discerning faith that draws on the Bible in order to understand history. Those who do not rely on God's Word are likely to miss the signs of Christ's return.

Second, it is a mistake to look on the signs as events that will all occur immediately before Christ's return. Some of the signs that Jesus gave were fulfilled in the fall of Jerusalem in A.D. 70. This helps to explain why the Christian church escaped virtually unscathed from that cataclysm. The first Christians believed Jesus' prophetic warning: "When you see Jerusalem surrounded by armies, then know that its desolation has come near" (Luke 21:20). This prophecy plainly referred to events that transpired in the first century. Other signs were given to characterize the entire age between Christ's first and second comings. Jesus said that "you will hear of wars and rumors of wars. See that you are not alarmed, for this must take place, but the end is not yet" (Matt. 24:6). Whenever there are wars, people wrongly assume Christ's soon return. Yet Jesus explicitly said that military upheaval is not a sign of the end but rather of his sovereign control in judging nations throughout this age. According to Cornelis P. Venema, signs such as war

319

"confirm that the present course of history is moving towards the day of the Lord."[2]

Third, when it comes to interpreting Christ's signs, there are three general approaches that people take. One approach is called *preterism*, which comes from the Latin word *praeter*, meaning "past." Under this view, virtually all the prophecies made by Jesus and the apostles were fulfilled in the first-century persecutions of the Roman emperor Nero (A.D. 64) and the fall of Jerusalem (A.D. 70). The strength of preterism is in noting the important ways in which some New Testament eschatology is rooted in first-century history, along with the reality that many New Testament prophecies do have events such as the fall of Jerusalem in mind.

A second approach to eschatology is the *historicist* approach, which notes that the apostles saw the signs of the end as characterizing the entire period between Christ's first and second comings. Paul warned Timothy that "in the last days there will come times of difficulty" (2 Tim. 3:1). Then he described the very troubles facing Timothy's church and common to our churches as well. Moreover, the apostle John explicitly took a historicist view when he wrote: "Children, it is the last hour, and as you have heard that antichrist is coming, so now many antichrists have come" (1 John 2:18). It was under this approach that the Protestant Reformers were virtually unanimous in declaring the pope as the Antichrist, since the Roman Catholic Church seemed to be fulfilling his role of false teaching and government-sponsored persecution.

A third approach is the *futurist* approach to eschatology, which understands virtually all New Testament prophecy to concern only future events that have not yet happened but will immediately precede Christ's return. The strength of this approach is its awareness that much of the New Testament's end-times teaching is associated directly with Christ's coming and the end of the age.

This brief survey makes the point that there are valuable insights to all three positions: preterist, historicist, and futurist. The problem occurs when each of these is made the only approach to eschatology. The error of preterism is in believing that all of the Bible's teaching on Christ's return refers to the fall of Jerusalem and the persecutions of Nero. The error of historicism is to so emphasize general historical trends as to deny their final amplification

2. Cornelis P. Venema, *The Promise of the Future* (Edinburgh: Banner of Truth, 2000), 114.

before the coming of Christ. The error of futurism is to extract eschatology from its first-century soil, as though the apostles had no concern for their own churches, and to divorce the dramatic events of the end from the pattern seen throughout the church age, starting in the first century. The best approach combines all three approaches, realizing that the prophetic signs had a first-century fulfillment, establishing a trend that would typify the whole church age and would have a final concentrated fulfillment in the time immediately before Christ's return. A sensitive reading of the New Testament will see all three emphases—preterist, historicist, and futurist—in the biblical text.

THE SIGNS OF CHRIST'S COMING

With this understanding of how the signs of Christ's coming operate, we may consider Jesus' Olivet Discourse, which Paul summarizes in part in 2 Thessalonians. In his helpful book *The Bible and the Future*, Anthony Hoekema organizes the signs into three groups. The first category is "signs evidencing the grace of God." The second category involves "signs indicating opposition to God," and the third category consists of "signs indicating divine judgment."[3]

The first group—"signs evidencing the grace of God"—centers on the preaching of the gospel throughout the world. Jesus said: "This gospel of the kingdom will be proclaimed throughout the whole world as a testimony to all nations, and then the end will come" (Matt. 24:14). As the preterist approach would emphasize, this prophecy had a near-fulfillment through the apostles, as the gospel spread "in Jerusalem and in all Judea and Samaria, and to the end of the earth" (Acts 1:8). Historicists would add that this sign continues throughout church history in obedience to Jesus' commission, "Go therefore and make disciples of all nations" (Matt. 28:19). Futurists note that there will be a dramatic conclusion to this evangelistic work, including the fulfillment of Paul's dramatic prophecy that "all Israel will be saved" (Rom. 11:26). Just as the early church was birthed out of Jewish believers and as church history has involved the ongoing evangelism of Jews, so also the end of history will be preceded by some mass conversion of Jewish people.

Hoekema's third category involves "signs indicating divine judgment." As Psalm 2 said, "The kings of the earth set themselves, and the rulers take

3. Anthony A. Hoekema, *The Bible and the Future* (Grand Rapids: Eerdmans, 1979), 137.

counsel together, against the LORD and against his Anointed" (Ps. 2:2). In response, as Christ reigns over history from heaven's throne, the nations fall under his judgment, so that every secular kingdom and nation will fail in its utopian schemes and be destroyed through conflict and war. Jesus foretold that "you will hear of wars and rumors of wars. See that you are not alarmed, for this must take place, but the end is not yet. For nation will rise against nation, and kingdom against kingdom, and there will be famines and earthquakes in various places" (Matt. 24:6–7). This pattern of warfare, pestilence, and natural disasters was pronounced in the first century, with its wars and with the eruption of Mount Vesuvius in A.D. 79, destroying the Roman civilization of Pompeii. The same pattern dominates the history of virtually every century, illustrating "that the world still lies under the curse of God (Gen. 3:17)," and reminding us "that the wrath of God continues to be revealed from heaven against all the ungodliness and wickedness of men (Rom. 1:18)."[4] Revelation 16:14–16 foretells a great end-times battle that will culminate this pattern of history, with the kings of the earth arrayed against God's people in the battle of Armageddon, and the Lord's returning to conquer for and with his people (Rev. 17:14; 19:19–20).

It is Hoekema's second category, indicating the world's opposition to God, that is highlighted by Paul: "Let no one deceive you in any way. For that day will not come, unless the rebellion comes first, and the man of lawlessness is revealed, the son of destruction" (2 Thess. 2:3). Jesus spoke of this sign in terms of the Antichrist, who would bring great tribulation on the church, resulting in the falling away of many professing believers: "They will deliver you up to tribulation and put you to death, and you will be hated by all nations for my name's sake. And then many will fall away and betray one another and hate one another" (Matt. 24:9–10). As Paul makes clear, a single Antichrist figure will come in the time before Christ's return—a figure that he describes as "the man of lawlessness," in whose time a great "rebellion" will occur within the church, leaving only the remnant of true believers to be saved in the coming of Christ (2 Thess. 2:3).

HOW TO WAIT FOR CHRIST'S RETURN

Paul begins the material in 2 Thessalonians 2 with a concern that the believers should not be "quickly shaken in mind or alarmed" (2 Thess. 2:2)

4. Venema, *The Promise of the Future*, 180–81.

by false reports of Christ's coming. He points out the signs of Christ's coming that had not yet been fulfilled. In concluding this introduction to Paul's teaching on the delay of Christ's return, we can note additional dangers and draw applications on how rightly to await the return of our Lord.

The first danger when it comes to the signs that precede Christ's coming is the wrong idea that we can be certain when he will return. Jesus warned the Jewish leaders that it is easy to miss the signs of his coming (Matt. 16:3), which shows that the signs might not be obvious in their first appearing. Geerhardus Vos famously stated that signs such as the coming Antichrist are "among the many prophecies, whose best and final exegete will be the eschatological fulfillment."[5] We should observe, by way of analogy, how hard it would have been to make precise sense of the prophecies of Christ's first coming: he would be born in Bethlehem (Mic. 5:2), "out of Egypt I called my son" (Hos. 11:1), and "he shall be called a Nazarene" (Matt. 2:23). Similarly, a precise calculation of the events preceding Christ's second coming is impossible before their fulfillment.

With this in mind, our first attitude in awaiting Christ's return must be *patience*. In assuming that Christ will return during our lifetimes, we may very well be mistaken. In a survey of church history, Kim Riddlebarger notes that practically every generation of Christians has been quite certain that Christ must return during their time. Augustine believed that the Roman Empire fell in the fifth century in order to make way for the Antichrist. Pope Urban II justified the first crusade partly on the grounds that the capture of Jerusalem must initiate the sequence of end-times signs. Martin Luther was certain that the pope was the Antichrist and that the return of Christ was therefore imminent. It was a settled conviction among virtually all the Puritans that Christ was on the brink of returning, with most agreeing on the year 1650 as the most likely date. Jonathan Edwards was persuaded that the Antichrist would arrive in 1866, followed by the church's age of glory with Christ.[6] Just as these great Christians were mistaken in the certainty that Christ would come in their time, the same conviction today is potentially mistaken. And yet, on the other extreme, we should never assume that Christ is not coming simply because certain signs seem yet to be fulfilled.

5. Geerhardus Vos, *The Pauline Eschatology* (Princeton, NJ: Princeton University Press, 1930; repr., Phillipsburg, NJ: P&R Publishing, 1994), 133.
6. Kim Riddlebarger, *The Man of Sin: Uncovering the Truth about the Antichrist* (Grand Rapids: Baker, 2006), 135–65.

Venema observes: "No one should be so confident of his understanding of the Bible's teaching about [the signs] that he concludes that Christ could not return in the near future."[7]

A second danger pertaining to the signs of the end involves our need to be prepared. Thus, in addition to a posture of patience, Christians must maintain *readiness* for Christ's coming. It might or might not be possible for us to immediately recognize the final events before Christ's coming, but we can know how we should always respond to such occurrences. Christians must never betray our Lord despite persecution; we must never follow any false christs who claim to have come; and we must never worship any government or church leader in the place of Jesus our only Lord.

In Matthew 25, Jesus followed up his teaching on the signs of the times with a parable that shows the necessity of always being ready. Ten virgins were watching for the groom's arrival. When his coming took longer than expected, five foolish virgins had their lamps burn out, so they were not ready when he came. The five wise virgins, by contrast, had brought oil for their lamps and were ready (Matt. 25:1–10). The message is that we must always keep our faith vibrant, in communion with Christ through the Holy Spirit, by means of God's Word and prayer. "Watch therefore," Jesus said, "for you know neither the day nor the hour" (v. 13).

Jesus added a second parable, the point of which provides our third application in waiting for Christ's return. First, we must be patient, knowing that Christ may come either soon or in the distant future. Second, we must be ready at all times. Third, because of the danger that we would neglect the present out of concern for the future, we must keep *busy* in the present. While we patiently wait for Christ's return and maintain our readiness for his coming, Christians must labor with zeal in the cause of the gospel and the building of the church.

In Jesus' parable of the talents, three servants were entrusted with money while their master went away: one five talents, another two, and another one. When the master returned, he demanded to see the profit that they had earned (Matt. 25:14–19). The first servant presented five talents earned and the second two more talents. "Well done, good and faithful servant," the master told each of them. "You have been faithful over a little; I will set you over much. Enter into the joy of your master'" (vv. 21, 23). Meanwhile,

---

7. Venema, *The Promise of the Future*, 158.

the third servant had gained nothing for the master and was cast out as one who did not belong to his household (v. 30). If you are looking for things to do while waiting for Christ, just skim through Paul's letters to the Thessalonians! Devote yourself to studying God's Word and spreading Christ's gospel. Look for ways to encourage the faith of fellow Christians and to comfort those who are hurting. Work hard in your vocational calling, and use your money to support the church and help those in need. In short, be faithful to the opportunities that Christ gives you, and you will be plenty busy until he returns.

Can we know when Christ is coming? No, although we learn much from his prophecies about what to expect both now and at the end: signs of salvation through the spread of the gospel; signs of judgment through wars, famines, and disasters; and signs of opposition through persecution and apostasy. Christ's people should expect all of these without dismay. And while we patiently wait for our Savior to come, he calls us to maintain the readiness of a living faith and to occupy the time he has given us in the work of his kingdom. By being faithful to Jesus, we can be certain to hear from him, whenever he returns: "Come, you who are blessed by my Father, inherit the kingdom prepared for you from the foundation of the world" (Matt. 25:34).

31

THE MAN OF LAWLESSNESS

2 Thessalonians 2:3–10

For that day will not come, unless the rebellion comes first,
and the man of lawlessness is revealed, the son of destruction.
(2 Thess. 2:3)

*I*n the end-times novel *Left Behind*, Nicolae Carpathia explains to a journalist his plan for world peace: "We must disarm, we must empower the United Nations, we must move to one currency, and we must become a global village."[1] Propelled by this vision, he soon becomes Supreme Potentate of the newly formed Global Community. Despite presenting himself publicly as a benevolent pacifist, Carpathia is eventually revealed as the Antichrist foretold in the Bible, the enemy of God's people in the last days before Christ's return.

Left Behind's portrayal of the Antichrist is one of history's many attempts to configure current events in light of the Bible's end-times teaching. Christians in the fifth century were convinced that Attila the Hun fit the biblical portrait, just as nineteenth-century Christians saw Napoleon Bonaparte as a likely Antichrist candidate. Attila, Napoleon, and the fictional Nicolae all

---

1. Tim LaHaye and Jerry B. Jenkins, *Left Behind: A Novel of the Earth's Last Days* (Wheaton, IL: Tyndale House, 1995), 279.

have in common an ambition for world dominance and a ruthless employment of violent power. In this respect, they are seen as good candidates for what Paul described as "the man of lawlessness . . . , the son of destruction" (2 Thess. 2:3).

It is easy to ridicule false Antichrist sightings. Yet according to Paul, Christians are to anticipate a powerful figure who will exalt himself in power and oppose Christianity "by the activity of Satan with all power and false signs and wonders" (2 Thess. 2:9). Paul mentioned this figure in order to counter an alarming report from Thessalonica that Christ had already returned. "Let no one deceive you in any way," he replied, "for that day will not come, unless the rebellion comes first, and the man of lawlessness is revealed" (v. 3). The Antichrist's coming is associated with a great apostasy in the church, made possible only by the removal of a divinely imposed restrainer. Despite his great success, the lawless one will be destroyed by the coming of Christ in the glory of his appearing. These are the themes that Paul presents in this fascinating chapter, which we will consider in successive studies.

THE BEASTS OF DANIEL AND REVELATION

In our previous study of the chapter's opening verses, we saw that Paul's eschatology agrees substantially with Jesus' Olivet Discourse. In considering the Antichrist, we should note as well the correspondence between Paul and the prophecies of Daniel and Revelation. Remembering that Scripture is always the best interpreter of Scripture, it may be helpful to consider the general portrait given by those prophecies as a safeguard for our interpretation of Paul's portrait.

During Israel's Babylonian exile, Daniel was shown a vision of beasts that symbolized four great empires in ancient history: a winged lion for Babylon, a bear for Medo-Persia, a four-winged leopard for Greece, and a ten-horned beast for the Roman Empire (Dan. 7:1–8). This succession of beasts led to the appearing of "one like a son of man," who conquered and "was given dominion and glory and a kingdom . . . that shall not be destroyed" (vv. 13–14). In this way, Daniel saw how wicked earthly kingdoms will rise up one after another, only to have their idolatry and violence swept away by Christ's glorious appearing.

327

Reading Daniel, it might have been tempting to believe that Rome was the last of the beasts to come upon the earth. Yet the book of Revelation employs similar imagery, at one point describing "a beast rising out of the sea" (Rev. 13:1) that combines features from all four of the beasts from Daniel's vision. Like the beasts of Daniel, Revelation's beasts are violent rulers that destroy and oppose God's kingdom. As a composite of Daniel's four beasts, Revelation 13:1's beast depicts the phenomenon of violent worldly powers that recurs throughout history and finds ultimate expression in the final days. Paul speaks of "the lawless one" who is empowered "by the activity of Satan" (2 Thess. 2:9). Revelation likewise states that the "beast" receives authority from "the dragon," an obvious image for Satan (Rev. 13:4).

From Revelation we note that the end of history will see the return of a world power like the kingdoms of Nebuchadnezzar and the persecuting Roman emperors. Furthermore, like Daniel's beasts, the beasts of Revelation subject the church to great tribulation: "The beast was given a mouth uttering haughty and blasphemous words, and it was allowed to exercise authority for forty-two months" (Rev. 13:5). Forty-two months, or three and a half years, was the duration of the persecution of the Jews under Antiochus Epiphanes in the third century B.C., as predicted by Daniel. Just as "1776" reminds Americans of the Declaration of Independence and "1066" reminds the English of the Norman Conquest, to the ancient church "42 months" symbolized satanic, idolatrous persecution.[2] Like Antiochus of old, Revelation's beast will blaspheme against God and "make war on the saints" so as "to conquer them" (v. 7). A second beast will pursue the same agenda. Appearing in the guise of Christ as a false prophet, he will speak "like a dragon" with the agenda of Satan. Wielding violent power, he will lead the nations into idolatry, supported by "great signs" that he performs to deceive the nations (vv. 11–17).

The book of Revelation was probably written over forty years after Paul's letters to the Thessalonians, accurately describing what the early Christians would endure under the regimes of Domitian and later Roman emperors. Like the beasts of Revelation, the emperors wielded terrible violence against the church, exhibited satanic evil, and demanded worship for themselves as gods. During Nero's persecution, in which Paul probably died, Christians

---

2. Noted from D. A. Carson, "This Present Evil Age," in Richard D. Phillips and Gabriel N. E. Fluhrer, *These Last Days* (Phillipsburg, NJ: P&R Publishing, 2011), 25–26.

were dipped in pitch to be used as living torches for the emperor's gardens or fed to wild animals in the Colosseum. Through its portraits of the dragon and his beasts, Revelation accurately describes the combination of government persecution and idolatrous demands for worship that would try the faith of Christians in the years after Paul's letter.

Revelation's dragon and his beasts not only depicted what Christians faced in the late first century (as preterism emphasizes) and would continue to face all through history (as historicism shows), but also supported the futurist understanding that these events will come to an ultimate expression when the final Antichrist arises before the return of Christ. Together with his alliance of worldly kings, the Antichrist "will make war on the Lamb, and the Lamb will conquer them, for he is Lord of lords and King of kings, and those with him are called and chosen and faithful" (Rev. 17:14). According to Robert Mounce, the very themes depicted in Revelation chapters 13–20 were first summarized in Paul's prediction of "the lawless one with his deceitful practices and pretentious claims who is to be utterly destroyed at the revelation of Jesus Christ."[3]

THE ANTICHRIST OF 2 THESSALONIANS

Not only does Paul summarize Revelation's later portrait of the Antichrist, with his violent persecution and idolatrous demands, but Paul also makes it particularly clear that the final Antichrist must be taken as an individual human being in service to Satan. Scholars have sometimes understood prophecies such as that of Revelation merely to depict historical tendencies. But Paul indisputably identifies a personal Antichrist who arises at the end of the age, and is, according to Leon Morris, "the last and supreme embodiment of evil, one who will make his appearance only in the last time."[4]

Focusing on this final, ultimate, and individual Antichrist, Paul offers four descriptions. First, he is "the man of lawlessness" (2 Thess. 2:3). In Satan's cause, the Antichrist will rise up against the ruling rights of God as expressed in his law. Daniel 12:9–10 foretold that in the end "the wicked shall act wickedly," and Paul indicates that the Antichrist will be their champion

3. Robert H. Mounce, "Pauline Eschatology and the Apocalypse," *Evangelical Quarterly* 3 (1974): 165.
4. Leon Morris, *The First and Second Epistles to the Thessalonians*, New International Commentary on the New Testament (Grand Rapids: Eerdmans, 1959), 220.

in flouting God's rule. According to William Hendriksen, "the principle of lawlessness, always present, will finally become embodied in 'the man of lawlessness.'"[5]

Second, the Antichrist is "the son of destruction" (2 Thess. 2:3). Jesus used the same description for Judas Iscariot, who alone of his twelve disciples would be lost (John 17:12). This comparison suggests that Paul's Antichrist is doomed to hell. "Son of" could also mean that he is the destroyer who embodies all that his predecessors have stood for—the violent tyrants of history from Pharaoh to Nebuchadnezzar to Antiochus Epiphanes to Nero and to Hitler and Stalin—all of whom by violent means would oppose and overthrow what is right.

Third, the Antichrist is not content with rebellion and destruction, but demands worship: he "opposes and exalts himself against every so-called god or object of worship . . . , proclaiming himself to be God" (2 Thess. 2:4). In place of God, the man of lawlessness demands religious veneration for himself. The word that Paul uses for *opposes* (Greek *antikeimenos*) is also used in 1 Timothy 5:14 to describe Satan as "the adversary" of the church. The man of lawlessness opposes true and saving faith so as to secure worship for himself. This is precisely what the Roman emperors of the early church demanded, as their Christian victims would have recognized in reading the book of Revelation. More recently, imperial worship finds its analogy in the deified secular state, whether in the Communist tyrannies of the East or the socialist democracies of the West. The spirit of antichrist demands that its subjects look to the state and its ruler for provision and deliverance rather than to God. Today's anti-Christian politicians employ science and popular culture to push God and his rule out of society. This same historical impulse will come to a final and ultimate expression in the tribulation imposed by the Antichrist.

The fourth description shows that the Antichrist will seek not only to persecute but also to control the church from within. Paul takes up the language earlier used by Daniel and then by Jesus in his Olivet Discourse, saying that the Antichrist "takes his seat in the temple of God, proclaiming himself to be God" (2 Thess. 2:4). Undoubtedly, Paul is pointing to what Daniel described as "the abomination that makes desolate" (Dan. 11:31), a

---

5. William Hendriksen, *1 and 2 Thessalonians*, New Testament Commentary (Grand Rapids: Baker, 1974), 171.

prophecy first fulfilled by Antiochus Epiphanes. In 169 B.C., this Antichrist precursor entered the Holy of Holies in the temple, erected an altar to Zeus, and sacrificed a pig on it. But this would not be the end of desecration. In 63 B.C., the Roman general Pompey desecrated the temple by intruding into the Holy of Holies, gaining the Jewish name of "the lawless one."[6] Lest we think this was all past tense by the time of Christ, Jesus foretold the same thing happening during the fall of Jerusalem in A.D. 70: "When you see the abomination of desolation spoken of by the prophet Daniel, standing in the holy place (let the reader understand), then let those who are in Judea flee to the mountains" (Matt. 24:15–16). During Paul's lifetime, the emperor Caligula commanded that an image of himself be erected in the temple. The Jews responded with such protest that even evil Caligula relented. Paul sees a similar atrocity happening again before Christ's return, when the man of lawlessness "takes his seat in the temple of God" (2 Thess. 2:4).

The question is raised as to what Paul means in saying that the Antichrist "takes his seat in the temple of God" (2 Thess. 2:4). Dispensationalists take this statement to refer to a rebuilt temple in Jerusalem, which the Antichrist will physically occupy for personal veneration. The chief of many problems with this view is that not once in all his writings does Paul use the word *temple* to describe a rebuilt temple structure. Rather, contrary to the dispensational denial of the connection between Israel and the church, Paul sees Israel's physical temple as finding fulfillment in the spiritual building that is the Christian church (see Eph. 2:20, for instance). Moreover, the idea of God's being worshiped again by his people at a physical temple, complete with animal sacrifices, is utterly repugnant to the New Testament, which sees the temple sacrifices as being fulfilled in the once-for-all atoning death of Jesus Christ (Heb. 10:1–9).

A second view believes that Paul's reference to the Antichrist seated in the temple is metaphorical. The point would be that just as one might go into the temple and physically take the place of God, the Antichrist will similarly demand worship for himself. While this is a possible interpretation, a third view makes better sense of Paul's usual use of the word *temple*. Paul sometimes speaks of the individual Christian as a "temple of the Holy Spirit" (1 Cor. 6:19). But predominantly Paul refers to the temple in terms

6. John R. W. Stott, *The Message of 1 & 2 Thessalonians*, The Bible Speaks Today (Downers Grove, IL: InterVarsity Press, 1994), 163.

of the Christian church as a whole. The church, he says, is "built on the foundation of the apostles and prophets" and "grows into a holy temple in the Lord" (Eph. 2:20–21). G. K. Beale therefore comments that "the church community is the place where end-time prophecies about Israel and its temple will take place."[7]

With this in mind, we note that Paul's fourth statement regarding the Antichrist indicates that he will pursue his idolatrous agenda not only through government power but also from within the formal Christian church. Paul concludes: "Do you not remember that when I was still with you I told you these things?" (2 Thess. 2:5). According to the apostle, it was important for Christians to realize the pattern at work in history and to be aware of how the great tribulation of the end will take place. Empowered by "the activity of Satan" (v. 9), the Antichrist will rebel against God by seizing both worldly power and religious authority, using them to bring tribulation on believers and gain worship for himself on Satan's behalf. We cannot now be certain how the Antichrist will manipulate religious authority, but it is likely to involve the worldly corruption of church offices, and it will certainly involve the spread of false teaching. Christians can thus oppose him now by upholding biblical standards in the ministry, the spiritual focus of the church, and above all the defense of sound biblical doctrine.

THE SATANIC WAR

In studies that follow, we will consider in greater detail the rebellion that takes place in the coming of the "man of lawlessness." Against the backdrop of Daniel and Revelation, Christians are forewarned by Paul to expect both outward persecution and internal satanic infiltration within the church. Looking on Paul's teaching, we not only learn what will happen before the end, but also gain insight into the pattern of satanic warfare that we can expect to face in all times. In short, we can see here Satan's primary *aims* in war against Christ and his church, Satan's primary *methods* of war, and the *means* of Satan's final defeat.

First, it is clear that Satan's aim through the Antichrist is to secure two primary goals: apostasy and idolatry. The devil seeks to destroy, or at least

---

7. G. K. Beale, *1–2 Thessalonians*, IVP New Testament Commentary Series (Downers Grove, IL: InterVarsity Press, 2003), 207.

harm, the Christian church by leading as many as possible astray from the gospel and allegiance to Christ. This is "the rebellion" that Paul says must come before Christ returns (2 Thess. 2:3). Through persecution and false teaching, Satan desires people to abandon Christianity and reject the church, in this way securing the damnation of as many people as possible by binding them in unbelief and afflicting the true church, which he hates but is unable to destroy.

Joined to the aim of apostasy is Satan's goal of securing idolatrous worship for himself. This is the very aim that the evil one revealed when he tried to seduce Jesus through our Lord's temptations in the desert. Showing Jesus "all the kingdoms of the world and their glory," Satan made a diabolical offer: "All these I will give you, if you will fall down and worship me" (Matt. 4:8–9). Jesus refused, in obedience to God's Word: "You shall worship the Lord your God and him only shall you serve" (v. 10). Having failed with Jesus, Satan will seek to usurp God's place through his counterfeit messiah, the Antichrist, whom he will empower to seduce the nations through false signs and wonders.

In addition to discerning Satan's war *aims*, we need to understand his war *methods*. First, the Antichrist employs coercive power as he "opposes and exalts himself" (2 Thess. 2:4). Paul adds a second method of satanically empowered deception: "The coming of the lawless one is by the activity of Satan with all power and false signs and wonders, and with all wicked deception for those who are perishing, because they refused to love the truth and so be saved" (vv. 9–10).

It has always been through deception that the devil has gained his greatest victories, starting with Adam and Eve's fall into sin in the garden of Eden. Paul was concerned, therefore, to counter deception and error. "Let no one deceive you in any way" with false reports that Christ had already come (2 Thess. 2:3). The danger of deception will be far greater in the time of the Antichrist. Leon Morris states: "The Man of Lawlessness will come expressly to deceive men. He will be well equipped to do this. He will have 'all' deception. . . . The Lawless One will be out to lure men to their destruction. To that end he will be armed with every weapon of Satan."[8]

Christians are in this way reminded that when evil forces gain power, Satan's intent is to employ this power to deceive people against the gospel and

8. Morris, *First and Second Thessalonians*, 232.

into idolatry. Examples of this agenda in Western society abound. The role of Christian faith in the growth of Western civilization is being expunged from school history books. Vast government and media powers are arrayed against Christian sexual morality and the biblical idea of marriage. Moreover, Christianity is successfully portrayed as a religion of hatred and bigotry for opposing homosexuality. In light of these trends, Christians should be careful never to replace our gospel clarity with legislative agendas that are likely to go astray. As Paul wrote to the Ephesians, our struggle is never merely "against flesh and blood," but always against "spiritual forces of evil" (Eph. 6:12), whose primary goal is to obscure our gospel witness and deceive the masses into turning away from Christ to the worship of idols.

Finally, Paul shows the *means* of the Antichrist's final and total destruction: "The lawless one will be revealed, whom the Lord Jesus will kill with the breath of his mouth and bring to nothing by the appearance of his coming" (2 Thess. 2:8). In light of Christ's coming to save his afflicted church and cast down our enemies at his glorious appearing, Christians are called to persevere in faith to the end. Thus, after foretelling the first beast and his warfare, the book of Revelation gives us this exhortation: "Here is a call for the endurance and faith of the saints" (Rev. 13:10).

STANDING ON THE TRUTH

Paul's description of the Antichrist, who not only will appear before Christ's return but will be represented in the spiritual warfare of every age, along with the insights that we have gained about Satan's approach to war, points to some applications for us today.

First, Christians are forewarned not to be surprised at opposition to the gospel both from the world and within the church. Believers have a tendency, especially when studying times of past revivals, to expect the church to grow and faith to spread virtually automatically. Certainly there have been times when the Spirit was so abundantly poured out that faith in Christ advanced almost explosively. Yet even in those times, and all the more in times when God has not ordained obvious revival and church growth, the gospel is opposed by Satan in deadly earnest. Geerhardus Vos writes: "The idea of the Antichrist in general and that of the apostasy in particular ought to warn us . . . not to take for granted an uninterrupted progress of the cause of Christ through all ages on toward the end. As the reign of the truth will be gradually extended, so the power of evil will gather force towards the end."[9] Contrary to postmillennial eschatology, which sees Christ returning only after a golden age in which the church has triumphed over the world in Christian faith and culture, Paul's teaching on the Antichrist urges us to anticipate such a concentrated expression of satanic power that only the sudden appearing of Christ can save the church from destruction.

Second, since Satan aims to provoke apostasy from Christ and idolatrous worship for himself, Christians must never swerve from the gospel and an exclusive devotion to God alone through faith in Jesus Christ. The original recipients of the book of Revelation were ruthlessly slaughtered by the beastly emperor Domitian because they refused to acclaim Caesar as Lord. Persecution over the imperial cult almost certainly supplies the background for the "mark . . . of the beast" mentioned in Revelation 13:17. The word *charagma* that John used for the beast's "mark" denoted the official imperial stamp certifying that homage had been paid to an image of Caesar. These blasphemous images of the ruler were set up throughout the empire, and without the mark certifying worship one could neither buy nor sell in the marketplace. Thus, Revelation 13:17 observes that "no one can buy or sell unless he has the mark" of the beast. The original context of the "mark" and Revelation's insistence that it is tied to worship of the beast (v. 15) make it clear that whatever form the mark may take in the last days, Christians must never agree to false worship in any form—whether in ungodly worship practices, false doctrines, or government veneration—but steadfastly uphold our devotion to the Lord Jesus Christ through faith in the gospel he proclaimed and the Spirit recorded in God's Word.

Third, Christians should face every form of spiritual opposition—whether it is outward persecution or inward corruption in the church—with a joy that flows from complete confidence of victory in the soon appearing of Jesus Christ. We should make every effort to absorb what Paul and other biblical writers say, while at the same time modestly admitting that full clarity about the Antichrist is not provided to us in Scripture. But when it comes to the return of Christ, we have detailed knowledge of the sure salvation that he is soon coming to bring: he will raise the dead, gather his people,

9. Geerhardus Vos, *The Pauline Eschatology* (Princeton, NJ: Princeton University Press, 1930; repr., Phillipsburg, NJ: P&R Publishing, 1994), 134–35.

overthrow all evil and darkness, justify those who have believed his gospel, and condemn unbelievers in the final judgment. And in the eternal reign that follows, "we will always be with the Lord" (1 Thess. 4:17).

The issue, therefore, is not what we know about the Antichrist but where we stand with respect to Jesus Christ. Are we worshiping false gods such as money, pleasure, power, or self? However events are moving forward to the Antichrist, Satan always seeks to lure the unwary into worshiping things over which he wields influence, rather than honoring God alone by surrendering our lives in faith through Jesus Christ. Despite all present evil and dark clouds of darkness on the horizon, the way to live in joyful security is to commit yourself in trusting service to Jesus Christ, who will come on the clouds to save all whose hearts are devoted to him.

Therefore, though believers know how deadly the deceits of Satan are, we stand securely on the truth revealed in God's Word, and we rejoice in a sure salvation. Though Satan will marshal violent forces to oppose and oppress us, we lift our hearts in prayer, often with broken hearts, and we rejoice in knowing that Jesus hears us and is coming soon to wipe away all our tears. Faithful to the Word, fervent in prayer, and loyal in service to Jesus above every other name—all by his sovereign grace alone—we rejoice to know that he will come again. And when that day comes, as Paul long ago declared: "The God of peace will soon crush Satan under your feet" (Rom. 16:20).

32

THE GREAT APOSTASY

2 Thessalonians 2:3, 9–12

*The coming of the lawless one is by the activity of Satan with all power
and false signs and wonders, and with all wicked deception for those
who are perishing, because they refused to love the truth
and so be saved. (2 Thess. 2:9–10)*

*I*n the last of his New Testament letters, the apostle Paul shared some of his burdens with his protégé Timothy. Paul was in prison expecting to be martyred for Christ and was looking forward to receiving "the crown of righteousness" in the life to come (2 Tim. 4:8). Having stood alone before the emperor, he praised the Lord for strengthening him in his time of need (v. 17). He asked Timothy to come before winter set in, with a cloak, his books, and above all his Bible parchments (vv. 13, 21). While all these matters reflected difficulties, there seems to have been only one issue that deeply grieved Paul's heart: "Demas, in love with this present world, has deserted me" (v. 10). Here was a sore grief, which struck much deeper than mere trial or persecution: the apostasy of a close associate. In earlier letters, Demas is mentioned by Paul as a fellow believer and a colaborer in spreading the gospel (Col. 4:14; Philem. 24). Now, when the apostle was in need, Demas turned his coat to return his allegiance to the anti-Christian world. In Paul's brief notice of this event, we can read the bitterness and pain that apostasy brings. He would have happily embraced many other trials, if only he could have been spared his friend's desertion of faith in Christ.

THE DOCTRINE OF APOSTASY

However painful his experience might have been, Paul could not have been surprised by the reality of apostasy. Many years before writing 2 Timothy, he had notified the Thessalonians that there would be a great rebellion against the gospel before Christ's return. "Let no one deceive you in any way," Paul wrote. "For that day will not come, unless the rebellion comes first" (2 Thess. 2:3). One of Satan's chief goals, especially through the future "man of lawlessness," is to induce people to abandon Christianity. Paul therefore knew that some people who profess faith in Jesus Christ will later renounce that faith, to their own destruction.

The Greek word translated in 2 Thessalonians 2:3 as "rebellion" is *apostasia*. This word refers to the turning away from a former position or the abandonment of prior loyalties. It can be used of a political rebellion, such as when the historian Josephus used the word for the Jewish revolt against Rome.[1] In the Bible, however, the word is used to describe a turning away from the true faith. Paul used a verb form of the same word in 1 Timothy 4:1, saying that "in later times some will depart from the faith" by embracing false doctrines and idolatry. Hebrews 3:12 urges vigilance, "lest there be in any of you an evil, unbelieving heart, leading you to fall away from the living God." Apostasy reflects an evil heart that embraces unbelief after previously professing faith.

Does apostasy, however, describe a person who once truly believed and was saved, and who then, by losing his or her faith, lost salvation as well? The answer to this question is No. The Bible clearly teaches that those who possess a true and saving faith cannot be lost, for the simple reason that genuine faith results from the grace of God, and God never loses any of those whom he has saved. Jesus said of his true sheep: "I give them eternal life, and they will never perish, and no one will snatch them out of my hand" (John

---

1. Josephus, *Life*, 1:43, cited in Robert J. Cara, *1 & 2 Thessalonians* (Darlington, UK: Evangelical Press, 1995), 200.

10:28). He added: "My Father, who has given them to me, is greater than all, and no one is able to snatch them out of the Father's hand" (v. 29). It is true that salvation requires us to persevere in our faith. Yet the Bible also teaches that all true believers will persevere. Peter wrote that true Christians "by God's power are being guarded through faith" for salvation (1 Peter 1:5). Similarly, Paul told the Philippians that "he who began a good work in you will bring it to completion at the day of Jesus Christ" (Phil. 1:6).

If believers in Christ can never be lost for salvation, then what is an apostate? An apostate is a professing believer and outward member of the church who, having never truly believed, falls back into unbelief and condemnation. John explained: "They went out from us, but they were not of us; for if they had been of us, they would have continued with us. But they went out, that it might become plain that they all are not of us" (1 John 2:19). How, then, do we tell that a professing believer is really an apostate? In most cases, it is difficult if not impossible to tell until he or she actually abandons the faith. It seems, for instance, that the other disciples never suspected Judas Iscariot of his falseness even up to the night on which he betrayed Jesus to his death.

What, then, is the difference between an apostate such as Judas and a true believer who temporarily falls away, as Peter did on the same night when he denied Jesus three times? The difference is often seen only in that the backsliding believer repents and returns to Christ, whereas the apostate does not. In the biblical description of Judas and Peter, there is an obvious qualitative difference between them. When Jesus confronted Judas with his betrayal, the apostate hardened his heart in hostility (John 13:27–30). By contrast, when Jesus looked at Peter after his third denial, the disciple "wept bitterly" over his sin (Luke 22:61–62). By the morning of the resurrection three days later, Peter had returned to his allegiance, and he remained a faithful servant to the end.

If professing believers may fall away, how can a Christian know that his or her faith is genuine and therefore eternally secure? Should believers worry that their faith is actually false and that sometime in the future they might apostatize? John addressed this issue in his first epistle, when he wrote "that you may know that you have eternal life" (1 John 5:13). According to John, there are three tests of a true, saving faith. One is a *doctrinal* test, focused on faith in the person and work of Jesus: "Everyone who believes that Jesus is the Christ has been born of God" (v. 1). Another is a *moral* test: "By this we may know that we are in him: whoever says he abides in him ought to walk in the same way in which he walked" (2:5–6). This does not mean that true Christians never sin or are as perfect as Jesus is. Yet true Christians have taken up the calling to follow Jesus in practical godliness, turning from sin and pursuing holiness. Third is the test of *love*: "everyone who loves the Father loves whoever has been born of him" (5:1). True Christians are drawn to other believers and gain a love for the church that reflects the family love of God. According to the Bible, these three tests—dealing with theology, ethics, and love—provide Christians with a testimony from God's Word as to the assurance of their salvation.

Additionally, in his parable of the soils, Jesus noted differences between true and false professions of faith. He spoke of a seed that grew among weeds, which choked away its life. This compares to a faith that never separates from a love of the world, as well as "the deceitfulness of riches," which "choke the word" (Matt. 13:22). Jesus also mentioned a false faith that is like a seed that fell in shallow soil: "This is the one who hears the word and immediately receives it with joy, yet he has no root in himself, but endures for a while, and when tribulation or persecution arises on account of the word, immediately he falls away" (vv. 20–21). One of the best tests of true, saving faith, then, is our response when we are persecuted for the sake of Christ. Christians who believe the gospel, are changing morally, love their fellow Christians, are willing to turn from the world, and then hold fast to Christ even when persecuted have many good reasons to be confident that they belong to Jesus, who will never let them go.

This understanding of apostasy shows why Paul was so pleased with the news that the Thessalonians were holding fast to the gospel and embracing a lifestyle of godliness and love (2 Thess. 1:3). They were steadfast in faith under persecution, as their worldly goods and even their lives were threatened (v. 4). According to Paul, this confirmed that they were "worthy of the kingdom of God" (v. 5); that is, their lives manifested a true and saving faith in Jesus.

SATAN'S WORK IN APOSTASY

Yet the day will come, Paul warns, when a great apostasy will fall upon the church. Christ will not return "unless the rebellion comes first" (2 Thess. 2:3).

Having understood the doctrine of apostasy, we learn from verses 9–12 that a great apostasy will occur in the end, both by the working of Satan and by God's sovereign judging of unbelief.

In verse 3, Paul had linked the great apostasy to the coming of "the man of lawlessness," often known to Christians as the Antichrist. In 2 Thessalonians 2:9, the apostle makes it clear that the rebellion is the work of this evil person: the great apostasy by which multitudes of professing believers abandon the Christian faith and turn against the church results from "the activity of Satan" in "the coming of the lawless one."

Paul makes three statements relating the coming Antichrist to the great apostasy that he inspires. First, the man of lawlessness comes as a counterfeit of Christ. Paul indicates this by applying to the Antichrist the same word that he has frequently used of Christ's coming. Second Thessalonians 2:9 speaks of the *parousia* "of the lawless one," mirroring verse 1's statement of the *parousia* "of our Lord Jesus Christ" (see also 1 Thess. 4:16). Just as God the Father has ordained the coming of his Son, Jesus, back to earth, Satan has planned the "coming of the lawless one."

To advance this counterfeit of Christ, Satan will empower miracles like the ones Jesus performed to validate his ministry: "The coming of the lawless one is by the activity of Satan with all power and false signs and wonders" (2 Thess. 2:9). The Bible uses all three of these words—*power, signs*, and *wonders*—of Jesus Christ (Acts 2:22). The first term, *power*, denotes the supernatural force behind the Antichrist's deceptions. The second term, *signs*, notes that these miracles seek to prove the false claims of the lawless one. Third, the word *wonders* points out that these actions have no natural explanation and therefore make a strong impression on those who witness them. Whether or not these signs will be actual miracles, it is clear that supernatural power will be extended by Satan to persuade people of the Antichrist's false claims. This is why 1 John 4:1 warns us: "Do not believe every spirit, but test the spirits to see whether they are from God." Long before, Moses had warned Israel that false prophets might be able to work wonders and predict the future (see Deut. 13:1–3). True prophets were identified not by wonders, therefore, but by their faithfulness to the Word of God and their refusal to worship false gods. "For the LORD your God is testing you," Moses said, "to know whether you love the LORD your God with all your heart and with all your soul" (v. 3). Jesus warned that "false christs and false prophets will arise and perform great signs and wonders, so as to lead astray, if possible, even the elect" (Matt. 24:24). Paul identifies the same agenda as characterizing the appearing of the Antichrist. He will offer impressive displays of supernatural power that will induce the unwary to worship him as God.

Second, Paul says that these false signs employ "all wicked deception for those who are perishing" (2 Thess. 2:10). John Stott writes that "the coming of Antichrist will be such a clever parody of the coming of Christ that many will be taken in by the satanic deception."[2] If we wonder how people can be deceived by false miracles, we need only consider the many examples that abound today. For instance, in 1858 a Roman Catholic woman named Bernadette Soubirous claimed that the virgin Mary had appeared in the French village of Lourdes. Today, five million pilgrims journey to Lourdes each year, seeking miraculous healings, so that the town of fifteen thousand residents boasts 270 hotels, second in France only to Paris. In 1996, the curvature of window panes in a Tucson, Arizona, office building was thought to outline Mary's figure. Over the next ten years, hundreds of thousands of people paid homage to the glass panes, many claiming to have received miraculous healings as a result.[3] Meanwhile, charlatan charismatic "faith healers" fill stadiums with people seeking healings and then fill their bank accounts with the offerings they receive from their gullible audiences.

In light of the power of these recent imaginings and frauds, consider how great will be the deception of the Antichrist when he appears with satanic power, performing genuine wonders so as to deceive the unwary, foolish, and needy. D. Michael Martin writes: "Deception is the alluring mask worn by evil. Those deceived are led to destruction,"[4] especially as they follow Satan's leading in rejecting the true God and worship the man of lawlessness.

Paul's warning of Satan's deception points out how perilous it is for anyone to neglect the saving truth revealed in God's Word. Jesus stated that these wondrous deceptions will be so powerful that "if possible, even the elect" would be persuaded (Matt. 24:24). How much success, then, Satan

2. John R. W. Stott, *The Message of 1 & 2 Thessalonians*, The Bible Speaks Today (Downers Grove, IL: InterVarsity Press, 1994), 172.

3. Chris Tisch, "For Mary's Faithful, a Shattering Loss," *St. Petersburg Times* (March 2, 2004), available at http://www.sptimes.com/2004/03/02/Tampabay/For_Mary_s_faithful__.shtml.

4. D. Michael Martin, *1, 2 Thessalonians*, New American Commentary (Nashville: Broadman & Holman, 1995), 245.

will have with those who have rendered themselves vulnerable by rejecting biblical truth.

Paul's third statement regarding the satanic strategy in apostasy states that his victims are deceived "because they refused to love the truth and so be saved" (2 Thess. 2:10). Though Satan is unable to undo the salvation of true believers, his targets "inevitably accept the deception because that is all that is left to them once they have rejected the truth."[5] These dupes are "those who are perishing" (v. 10) and who "find in the end that they have followed [Satan] to their own irreparable loss."[6]

When Paul points out that Satan's targets refused to love the truth, he inevitably includes worldly malice toward Jesus Christ himself, who said, "I am the way, and the truth, and the life" (John 14:6). They hated the gospel because it offended their self-righteous pride and threatened their lifestyle of cherished sins. For those who reject the gospel truth of Jesus Christ, there is no salvation from God but only a path leading away from him, to Satan, and with Satan to eternal condemnation. Many people today who "refuse to love the truth" become unknowing servants of Satan, but in the last days the naked idolatry involved in all unbelief will be especially evident.

GOD'S JUDGMENT IN APOSTASY

One of the perennial mistakes in thinking about Satan is to view him as God's virtual equal, squaring off for deadly combat. Nothing could be further from the truth, however, as Paul shows in 2 Thessalonians 2:11–12. In seducing those who "refused to love the truth," Satan merely accomplishes God's will in judging unbelief. The Bible does not present "a dualistic struggle between good and evil gods," but "the working out of the divine will so that even those who exercise their freedom to do evil will ultimately discover that their actions have paradoxically served the divine economy."[7] Being sovereign over all things, God rules even the will and actions of Satan, who in the end is God's tool for the judgment of those who hated truth and loved sin. J. Philip Arthur rightly describes Satan as "the instrument used by the Almighty to accomplish his wider purposes," since all of Satan's schemes,

---

5. Ibid., 246.
6. Leon Morris, *The First and Second Epistles to the Thessalonians*, New International Commentary on the New Testament (Grand Rapids: Eerdmans, 1959), 232.
7. Martin, *1, 2 Thessalonians*, 248.

"along with everything that ever comes to pass, fall within the scope of the sovereign purposes of God."[8]

When Paul considers God's purposes in the great apostasy, he says that in the coming of the Antichrist, "God sends them a strong delusion, so that they may believe what is false, in order that all may be condemned who did not believe the truth but had pleasure in unrighteousness" (2 Thess. 2:11–12). Here Paul observes that the unbeliever not only refuses to love the saving truth that God sent through the blood of his Son, but also delights in the things that transgress God's law and give offense to God's holy person. In judging this hardened state of rebellion, even before his final judgment when Christ returns, God hands obstinate rebels over to the wickedness they have chosen and the folly they have loved instead of truth in order to secure their condemnation on the last day.

Paul's statement that unbelievers have "pleasure in unrighteousness" exposes the moral cause that lurks behind the supposedly intellectual claims of unbelief. In his autobiography, the infamous atheist Aldous Huxley admitted that his ferocious opposition to Christianity had begun with sensual rather than intellectual motives:

> For myself, as, no doubt, for most of my contemporaries, the philosophy of meaninglessness was essentially an instrument of liberation. The liberation we desired was simultaneously liberation from a certain political and economic system and liberation from a certain system of morality. We objected to the morality because it interfered with our sexual freedom; . . . I had motives for not wanting the world to have a meaning; consequently I assumed that it had none, and was able without any difficulty to find satisfying reasons for this assumption.[9]

So it is, as Paul describes it, that hatred for the truth of Christ and a love for unrighteousness are bound together in unbelief. In judging this rebellion, God sends "a strong delusion, so that [these rebels] may believe what is false, in order that all may be condemned" (2 Thess. 2:11–12). Thinking that he is opposing God's will, the man of lawlessness will instead accomplish God's purposes against his own evil allies.

---

8. J. Philip Arthur, *Patience of Hope: 1 and 2 Thessalonians Simply Explained*, Wellwyn Commentary Series (Ross-shire, UK: Evangelical Press, 1996), 126–27.

9. Aldous Huxley, *Ends and Means*, quoted in Ravi Zacharias, *Can Man Live without God?* (Nashville: Thomas Nelson, 2004), 30.

The idea of God's judging obstinate sinners with a spirit of delusion has strong biblical support. A classic example is the hardened heart of Pharaoh in the time of Moses. The Bible states both that Pharaoh hardened himself against God's demands (Ex. 9:34–35) and that God in turn punished Pharaoh by hardening his heart even further (10:20). When wicked King Ahab had long rebelled against God and persecuted the true prophets, God sent "a lying spirit in the mouth of all his [false] prophets," to lead Ahab into destruction (1 Kings 22:22–23). In Romans 1, Paul noted that when men and women have willfully suppressed truth (Rom. 1:18) and "exchanged the glory of the immortal God" in order to worship idols (v. 23), God "gave them up" to a wholesale delusion of condemning wickedness (v. 24).

To read Paul's catalogue of the kinds of sins into which God gives malicious unbelievers is to survey the moral condition of America and the West today after decades of secular humanism. Generations ago, America began turning away from the Bible and pushing God's truth out of public life. Paul asserts that God gives such rebels over "in the lusts of their hearts to impurity" (Rom. 1:24) and then "to dishonorable passions" in which men "gave up natural relations with women and were consumed with passion for one another" (vv. 26–27), and finally "to a debased mind to do what ought not to be done" (v. 28), so that society begins to completely fall apart (vv. 29–32). One can hardly find a more accurate description of the moral and spiritual decline of America in our times.

In the final days, the judgment of delusion that God gives to those who deliberately turn away will come to unbelievers through the deceits of Satan's "man of lawlessness." Having rejected God's truth, apostates will then believe virtually anything so long as it involves idolatry and sensual sin.

Lovers of Truth

The Bible's prophecies of the end fit the pattern both of what the early Christians faced and of the tendencies that will challenge the church throughout her history. John wrote: "Children, it is the last hour, and as you have heard that antichrist is coming, so now many antichrists have come. Therefore we know that it is the last hour" (1 John 2:18). The coming of the lawless one will put an exclamation point on what takes place throughout the present era, which Hebrews 1:2 calls "these last days." Thus, Paul's teaching about the great apostasy and the man of lawlessness warns all Christians and provides an agenda for our watchfulness in faith.

For instance, Paul's teaching about Satan's deception makes clear the peril of anyone who has heard the message of salvation in Jesus Christ and has yet to believe. The gospel is not merely an invitation to salvation but a sovereign summons from God, calling us to the obedience of faith (see 2 Thess. 1:8). To hear and refuse the gospel of Christ's atoning death for sin on the cross is not merely to go your own way and make your own decisions about truth. Rather, to turn from the gospel is to cast yourself down a path leading to the lake of fire (Rev. 20:15), where God will eternally punish those who hated his truth and loved unrighteousness. Therefore, the gospel call demands immediate acceptance in trusting faith: "Behold, now is the favorable time; behold, now is the day of salvation" (2 Cor. 6:2).

Moreover, when we consider the Bible's teaching on the danger of apostasy, we are reminded that a bare profession of faith in Christ is not enough to provide assurance of salvation. True saving faith is seen in the living fruit it bears: believing the Bible, changing morally, and loving fellow believers. Saving faith requires one to turn his or her back on sinful worldly pleasures and to remain steadfast under persecution. Our approach to evangelism should reflect this biblical definition of saving faith. The Great Commission calls us to more than a shallow acceptance of Jesus; it calls us to bring sinners into obedient discipleship as members of Christ's church: "Go therefore and make disciples of all nations, baptizing them in the name of the Father and of the Son and of the Holy Spirit, teaching them to observe all that I have commanded you" (Matt. 28:19–20). Obeying this commission, rather than following the shallow church-growth fads popular today, will produce converts who bear fruit for Christ and are assured of salvation.

Finally, since Satan's followers in the final days are described as haters of truth and lovers of unrighteousness, then surely Christians should be known as lovers of truth and pursuers of righteousness. This is why Paul praised the Thessalonians in his first letter: they "received the word in much affliction, with the joy of the Holy Spirit," and turned "from idols to serve the living and true God" (1 Thess. 1:6, 9). To this end, the Westminster Larger Catechism instructs Christians in the proper manner of responding to God's Word:

It is required of those that hear the Word preached, that they attend upon it with diligence, preparation, and prayer; examine what they hear by the Scriptures; receive the truth with faith, love, meekness, and readiness of mind, as the Word of God; meditate, and confer of it; hide it in their hearts, and bring forth the fruit of it in their lives. (WLC 160)

By receiving God's Word in this way, believers will escape the deceptions of our enemy that ensnare so many who neglect to love the truth. And they will receive great assurance of salvation, with abounding joy in our Savior, Jesus Christ.

33

THE MYSTERY OF LAWLESSNESS

2 Thessalonians 2:5—8

*For the mystery of lawlessness is already at work. Only he
who now restrains it will do so until he is out of the way*
(2 Thess. 2:7)

s we study the important teaching by the apostle Paul in
2 Thessalonians 2 on the return of Christ, we might easily
overlook an important word in verse 7. Embedded in Paul's
teaching of the dreadful events that will come in the appearing of the Antichrist is a small word that connects directly with us today. The word is *now*:
"Only he who now restrains it will do so until he is out of the way" (2 Thess.
2:7). Such a statement reminds us that biblical eschatology pertains to us
by showing not only what God has planned for future times but also what
God is doing now to shepherd history to his predetermined goal. Along
with whetting our desire for the return of our Lord from heaven, biblical
teaching about the end times is given to make us wise about the days in
which we currently live, moving forward under God's sovereign control to
the glorious appearing of Jesus Christ.

THE RESTRAINER OF THE ANTICHRIST

One challenge in understanding the teaching of this chapter is that Paul
interacts with material that he had taught his readers in person but that

he does not repeat in this letter. One of these matters is the "restrainer" to which Paul refers in 1 Thessalonians 2:6–7 and that has kept Satan from unleashing the "man of lawlessness" to bring tribulation on the church. "Do you not remember that when I was still with you I told you these things?" Paul asks. "And you know what is restraining him now so that he may be revealed in his time" (vv. 5–6). At the time of Paul's writing, this restraint was keeping the Antichrist in check, and since these final events have yet to take place almost two thousand years later, we must presume that the same restraint is still operating.

The natural question to ask concerns who or what this restraint is that is holding back the Antichrist and his great apostasy. One factor in answering is to observe that in 2 Thessalonians 2:6 Paul describes the restrainer in the neuter gender, so that it is translated impersonally: "what is restraining him." In verse 7, however, Paul uses the masculine gender and speaks of a person: "he who now restrains it." Any solution will therefore have to account for both an impersonal and a personal description. Moreover, any answer will need to reflect the fact that Paul does not plainly identify the restrainer, but appeals to his in-person teaching while in Thessalonica (v. 5). The Thessalonians know what the restraint is, but we do not know with the same clarity. With this in mind, the most important thing for us to realize is that some power is at work restraining Satan from fully venting his fury through the coming of the Antichrist. Knowing this, Paul's readers were not to be confused into thinking that Christ had already returned (v. 2).

In seeking to identify the restrainer, G. K. Beale lists seven primary options, three of which are most worthy of note.[1] One approach identifies the restraining power with the Roman Empire and its system of law and order, personified by the emperor. The thought behind this answer is that the power of law is the ideal restrainer of the man of lawlessness. Since Paul teaches in Romans 13:1–5 that government power is established by God for upholding righteousness, and since Paul himself was protected by righteous rulers on some occasions (including during the period when this letter was likely written; Acts 18:12–16), then the restrainer might have been civil authority.

1. G. K. Beale, *1–2 Thessalonians*, IVP New Testament Commentary Series (Downers Grove, IL: InterVarsity Press, 2003), 214–16.

A second option holds that the restrainer is the Holy Spirit. This is the view held by dispensational Christians, whose teaching includes a secret rapture before Christ's return. Part of the rationale for the secret rapture is that with the departure of Christians, the Spirit will no longer be in the world. It is in this way that the restrainer is seen to be removed. The major problem with this approach, as we have seen, is that the idea of a secret rapture is utterly contrary to Paul's description of the second coming in both 1 and 2 Thessalonians.[2] Moreover, while it is true that the Holy Spirit indwells Christians, it is inaccurate to consider his presence bottled up as if Christians were containers in which the omnipresent Spirit could be restricted. Even if Christians were all removed, there is no reason why the Spirit would not continue to exercise his power on earth (see Ps. 139:7–12).

The third main option for the restrainer of the Antichrist is the preaching of the gospel. This idea is attractive in light of Jesus' teaching that before his return "the gospel must first be proclaimed to all nations" (Mark 13:10). In this view, the personified "restrainer" of verse 8 is God himself, who controls the man of lawlessness according to his own redemptive-historical schedule. By God's will, the present age that began during Paul's lifetime and continues today is the time for the spreading of the gospel and the ingathering of believers for salvation. The time will come when God will prepare to bring this age of salvation to a close and his restraining hand will be removed, permitting Satan to operate with unusual power in the career of the man of lawlessness. It was Paul's own preaching of the gospel that was pushing back the forces of darkness in Asia Minor and Greece, and by God's power that same gospel will hold back a complete rebellion until the time appointed from heaven.

One reason why this last option is probably best is its agreement with a similar passage in Revelation 20:1–3, where John wrote:

> I saw an angel coming down from heaven, holding in his hand the key to the bottomless pit and a great chain. And he seized the dragon, that ancient serpent, who is the devil and Satan, and bound him for a thousand years, and threw him into the pit, and shut it and sealed it over him, so that he might not deceive the nations any longer, until the thousand years were ended. After that he must be released for a little while.

2. See my prior discussion of this issue in chapter 18.

Notice that in John's vision there is a restraint that has the effect of curtailing Satan's activities, which will be removed in the last days. Premillennial Christians take the "thousand years" to represent a literal period during which Christ reigns after his second coming, after which there is a brief rebellion before the final day of judgment. One problem with this view is that Matthew 25:31 clearly places the final judgment at the same time as Christ's return from heaven: "When the Son of Man comes in his glory, and all the angels with him, then he will sit on his glorious throne." This teaching does not seem to allow for a thousand years between Christ's return and the final judgment. Moreover, in the visionary literature of the book of Revelation, numbers should be taken symbolically, not literally. It seems best, therefore, especially in light of its correspondence with Paul's teaching, to identify the "thousand years" of Revelation 20 with the church age. This view is known as *amillennialism*, so named because of its teaching that the thousand years of Revelation 20 is symbolic for the church age rather than a literal thousand-year period.

Premillennial scholars object to this teaching, since Revelation 20:3 depicts Satan as being completely under wraps. This, they argue, cannot describe any scenario in this present age. This objection fails to note, however, what effect the binding of Satan is said to have: "that he might not deceive the nations any longer" (Rev. 20:3). This deceiving work exactly fits Paul's description of what Satan and the Antichrist will do once the restraint is removed (2 Thess. 2:9–12). In the meantime, during the age of the Great Commission, which commands Christians to take the gospel throughout the world (Matt. 28:18–20), Satan is kept from effectively hindering that mission by means of deceit. Thus Jesus rejoiced when his seventy-two witnesses returned from preaching the gospel throughout Israel, saying, "I saw Satan fall like lightning from heaven" (Luke 10:18). Jesus understood the binding of Satan to involve the free rein for the gospel to be preached in all the world. Cornelis P. Venema writes: "Satan is bound so that he can neither prevent the spread of the gospel among the nations nor effectively deceive them. This vision confirms the teaching that the period between Christ's first coming and his second coming is one in which the gospel of the kingdom will powerfully and effectively go forth to claim the nations for Jesus Christ."[3] The personified restrainer whom Paul mentions in 2 Thessalonians 2:7—"he who now

3. Cornelis P. Venema, *The Promise of the Future* (Edinburgh: Banner of Truth, 2000), 319.

restrains it"—appears in John's vision in the form of the angel who came from heaven with "the key to the bottomless pit and a great chain" (Rev. 20:1). This angel probably represents God's sovereign will, just as the chain signifies God's binding power. Venema writes of this image: "The angel is properly equipped to execute God's purpose to bind and restrict the activities and wiles of Satan."[4] G. K. Beale concludes: "At the very end of the age, God will remove the angel (or its restraining influence), and 'all hell will break loose.'"[5]

Comparing Revelation 20:1–3 and 2 Thessalonians 2:6–7 argues strongly in favor of viewing the gospel mission of the church as the restraint on Satan's plans, under God's sovereign plan for history. If this is the case, then we can see how urgent is the church's commission to do everything possible to spread the gospel during this present age. There are many kinds of work that the church and Christians are called to do, but *the work* of this age, which is restraining Satan from deceiving the nations, is the work of proclaiming the gospel. Realizing this priority will cause Christians and churches to rethink the priority they are placing on preaching the gospel, witnessing to unbelievers, and supporting missionary causes. Surely, if Satan is now bound by God for the sake of the gospel, then evangelism and missions should be at the forefront of any biblically zealous church's priorities, plans, resource allocations, and also prayers.

LAWLESSNESS AT WORK

In depicting the binding of Satan, Revelation 20:3 uses strong images, such as a pit into which the devil is cast and sealed. The effect is that he is unable to "deceive the nations any longer" until the gospel age is over. It would be mistaken, however, to conclude that this binding keeps the devil from engaging in any form of warfare against God and his people. Revelation 12 takes up similar imagery and language, showing Satan as conquered and cast down from heaven to earth (Rev. 12:7–9). This symbolic depiction of history also shows, however, that a defeated and cast-down Satan is still a terrible and violent dragon. John writes: "When the dragon saw that he had been thrown down to the earth, he pursued the woman who had given birth to the male child" (v. 13). Though kept from successfully opposing the

---

4. Ibid., 316.
5. Beale, *1–2 Thessalonians*, 216.

gospel by deceiving the nations, Satan remains a deadly and active enemy filled with venom against the church. Despite being cast down, Satan makes continual warfare against God's people and in opposition to the gospel. The fact that this warfare cannot succeed in this age, since Satan's binding effectively inhibits his effectiveness, does not mean that there is a shortage of evil that Christians need to confront.

Paul makes this very point about the activity of Satan by saying that "the mystery of lawlessness is already at work" (2 Thess. 2:7). In Paul's usage, a "mystery" is not a puzzle to be solved but rather a truth that is not capable of clear understanding until its revelation in the coming of Christ. This mystery relates to Daniel's prophecy of the "abomination that makes desolate" (Dan. 11:31). The prophet foresaw idolatry within God's temple as the work of the Antichrist. By speaking of the "mystery" of the Antichrist's work, Paul is saying that Daniel would not have foreseen exactly how this would come about. In particular, in saying that "the mystery of lawlessness is already at work," the apostle indicates that what Daniel foresaw about the end of history is also a threat that is presently at work within history. Beale writes: "Paul sees that, though this fiend has not yet come so visibly as he will at the final end of history, he is nevertheless *already at work* in the covenant community through his deceivers, the false teachers." This teaching agrees with John's warning that "as you have heard that antichrist is coming, so now many antichrists have come" (1 John 2:18). Even now, behind the scenes, the same work that will come to mighty expression before the end is opposing the gospel. John Stott writes:

> His anti-social, anti-law, anti-God movement is at present largely underground. We detect its subversive influence around us today—in the atheistic stance of secular humanism, in the totalitarian tendencies of extreme left-wing and right-wing ideologies, in the materialism of our consumer society which puts things in the place of God, in those so-called "theologies" which proclaim the death of God and the end of moral absolutes, and in the social permissiveness which cheapens the sanctity of human life, sex, marriage, and family, all of which God created or instituted.[6]

In fact, the lawless work of Satan has been at work throughout history, starting with his deception of our first parents in order that they would

---

6. John R. W. Stott, *The Message of 1 & 2 Thessalonians*, The Bible Speaks Today (Downers Grove, IL: InterVarsity Press, 1994), 171.

fall into sin (Gen. 3:1–7). Even during times when the church is advancing behind mighty gospel works, the agenda of the enemy is striving to keep pace. This opposition is often noted during revivals, when the Holy Spirit's power is bringing many people to Christ. Satan is also there, distracting with false conversions, infiltrating with false doctrines, and tempting with the false allure of numerical success in ministry. Similarly, in ordinary times of ministry, the devil is always trying to make inroads in order to divide, deceive, or distract people from the gospel fruits of faith and love. In the midst of a wedding service, for instance, the mystery of lawlessness is at work. In gatherings for prayer, in services of worship, and in seminary classrooms, Satan is seeking to lay seeds for his ill-intended fruit. John Bunyan depicted the danger in *Pilgrim's Progress* by placing beside the path to the Porter's Lodge two chained lions, which though roaring could not quite reach Christian as he passed by. Likewise, God is holding Satan back for the sake of the gospel, yet still he roars and, as Peter warned, "prowls around like a roaring lion" (1 Peter 5:8), seeking to devour those who wander off the path of obedience to God's Word.

Knowing that this lawlessness is at work, believers must not merely look to the future day of trouble but also watch for its precursors now and stand guard over the precious things of God. This was Paul's concern, so he urged his readers not to be taken in by false teachers. If we respond to his end-times teaching by exclaiming, "I am so glad not to live in the times of the Antichrist!" we fail to heed the warning of "the mystery of lawlessness . . . already at work" (2 Thess. 2:7). If we do not guard our speech, watch our hearts, and live in careful obedience to Scripture, we may well feel the sting of Satan's bite and suffer great loss to our churches, our families, and our work because of our carelessness and complacency.

In the Splendor of His Coming

While God is currently restraining our enemy for the sake of the gospel, the day will come when he removes his restraint. "Then," Paul says, "the lawless one will be revealed" (2 Thess. 2:8). The apostle uses a verb form of the word *apokalupsis* to speak of this revealing—a word (previously used of Christ's second coming) that indicates the display of something previously present but hidden to sight (1:7). The mystery of lawlessness has been at work all along, but then the man of lawlessness will appear to have his day.

As we saw in our study of 2 Thessalonians 2:1–4, the coming of the Antichrist will lead to tribulation for the church and deception of the world so that a general rebellion against God will drive the church underground. Christians need to know that God has ordained this day of trouble for the world. More importantly, we need to know that the Antichrist's revealing will signal the coming of Christ: "Then the lawless one will be revealed, whom the Lord Jesus will kill with the breath of his mouth and bring to nothing by the appearance of his coming" (v. 8).

The Greek word translated as "kill" is *anaireo*, which literally means to "take up" so as to remove; it was used of those condemned to be executed. Revelation 20:10 reveals that in Christ's return, "the devil who had deceived them was thrown into the lake of fire and sulfur . . . [to] be tormented day and night forever and ever." Leon Morris argues that in verse 8 emphasis is placed on the name "the Lord Jesus" in expressing "the glory of Him who first came in lowliness. Though He had once been despised and rejected, at the supreme moment of history He will be seen in all His glorious majesty."[7]

The majesty of Christ will be heightened by the ease of his victory over Satan and his Antichrist. Jesus "will kill with the breath of his mouth" (2 Thess. 2:8). The main idea here is simply the indomitable power that Christ wields merely by his breath. But in Revelation, Christ is first revealed with "a sharp two-edged sword" coming from his mouth (Rev. 1:16), the apparent meaning of which is the gospel Word with its power to either save or condemn. Revelation 19 then presents Christ as the conqueror on a white horse, adding that from "his mouth comes a sharp sword" (19:15). With these precedents, we should think of Christ as opening his mouth to overthrow Satan by means of his sovereign Word. In Christ's coming, all creation will be reminded that the Savior who died on the cross is the Creator Son, who by merely speaking wields almighty power over every creature, small and great. The same voice that cried "Peace! Be still!" on the Sea of Galilee, so that the winds and waves obeyed (Mark 4:39), will speak with commanding power over evil in this world, and Satan's power will crumble before him.

7. Leon Morris, *The First and Second Epistles to the Thessalonians*, New International Commentary on the New Testament (Grand Rapids: Eerdmans, 1959), 230.

As Paul foresees it, Satan, the Antichrist, and all who had joined in the great apostasy against the church will come to nothing merely "by the appearance of his coming" (2 Thess. 2:8). The "coming" of Christ (Greek *epiphaneia*) will display such radiant splendor that as light floods a dark room and immediately subdues every shadow, so will the coming of Christ in glory conquer the entirety of creation with holiness. The Bible proclaims that Christ's glory is so great that in the courts of heaven even the glorious seraphim cover their faces before him (Isa. 6:2). For believers, the effect of Christ's appearing will be our own transformation into glory: John says that "when he appears," believers will "be like him, because we shall see him as he is" (1 John 3:2). The same appearing of Christ will cause Satan to take up the words once spoken by Isaiah the prophet, when he became aware of his sinfulness before the glory of Christ: "Woe is me! For I am lost" (Isa. 6:5). Satan's destruction will be followed by the judgment of all who worshiped idols and joined in the great rebellion against God. William B. Collyer writes of that coming day:

> But sinners, filled with guilty fears, behold his wrath prevailing;
> For they shall rise, and find their tears and sighs are unavailing:
> The day of grace is past and gone; trembling they stand before the throne,
> All unprepared to meet him.[8]

THE PRESENT DAY OF GRACE

As we conclude our study of Paul's teaching on the awesome events preceding Christ's return, we should take note, first, of the absolute sovereignty of God that this passage displays. Far from drawing the conclusion that Satan's power is something to shake the foundation of a Christian's faith, exactly the opposite should result from Paul's teaching. The apostle can foretell these events because God has foreordained them. Having announced the exact course of the coming of the Antichrist and his great rebellion, God is the One who controls the future and determines its outcome.

In the sure and certain hope of God's victory, Christians should joyfully submit to God's care, doing everything in our power to serve him and give praise to his glorious grace. More important even than knowing *what* is

---

8. William B. Collyer, "Great God, What Do I See and Hear!" (1812).

going to happen is knowing *who* has ordained events by his sovereign will. D. Michael Martin writes: "For the people of God, then, peace and assurance come not from a full knowledge of the times and seasons but from a personal knowledge of the God who rules the times and seasons."[9] Paul has removed the veil enough for us to know about the coming of the lawless one and the great tribulation of God's people. In these prophecies, we see even more clearly the sovereign control of the God who holds our salvation and the certain defeat of all that we might fear in the day of Christ's glorious return.

Second, having been made wise not only about the future man of lawlessness, but also about the present "mystery of lawlessness," Christians are reminded of our great resource in opposing the evil one now. Elsewhere the apostle James tells us, "Submit yourselves therefore to God. Resist the devil, and he will flee from you" (James 4:7). Earlier Paul said that the way to resist the devil is by putting on "the breastplate of faith and love" and "for a helmet the hope of salvation" (1 Thess. 5:8). Now Paul reminds us of the prevailing power of God's Word. We will see Satan destroyed at Christ's coming by "the breath of his mouth" (2 Thess. 2:8). Martin Luther powerfully expressed this hope in his most famous hymn:

And though this world, with devils filled, should threaten to undo us,
We will not fear, for God has willed his truth to triumph through us.
The prince of darkness grim, we tremble not for him;
His rage we can endure, for lo! his doom is sure;
One little word shall fell him.[10]

Do you doubt the sufficiency of that "one little word"—God's Word, the Bible—for ministry today? Then consider its effect in the coming of Christ! Let the sword of our Bibles never become rusty through disuse, but let us practice wielding God's Word for our own salvation and the defense of Christ's church.

Finally, how important it is, in light of what Paul has revealed concerning history, for each of us to be saved through faith in Christ now. I earlier compared Satan's woeful demise when Christ appears to the reaction of the prophet Isaiah when he was confronted with a vision of Christ's majestic

---

9. D. Michael Martin, *1, 2 Thessalonians*, New American Commentary (Nashville: Broadman & Holman, 1995), 242.

10. Martin Luther, "A Mighty Fortress Is Our God" (1529).

holiness. Isaiah responded in the way that all sinners must respond—either now in repentance or in his return with hopeless dismay—when their eyes are opened to see the holiness of Christ: "Woe is me! For I am lost" (Isa. 6:5). How important that you should see your need of forgiveness now, in the day of grace when you can still be saved through faith in Jesus! Whereas Satan will be destroyed by the appearing of Christ's glorious holiness, Isaiah was saved by calling in faith in the grace of God revealed in Christ. He cried, "My eyes have seen the King, the LORD of hosts!" (v. 5).

Two things happened when Isaiah responded to the vision of Christ in faith. The first is that he was cleansed of his sins by the atoning blood of Jesus. Isaiah 6:6 depicts this by saying that "one of the seraphim flew to me, having in his hand a burning coal that he had taken with tongs from the altar." This was a way of saying that the atoning sacrifice was applied to Isaiah's sin: "he touched my mouth and said: 'Behold, this has touched your lips; your guilt is taken away, and your sin atoned for'" (Isa. 6:7). In this present day of grace, before the gospel restraint is removed, you, too, may be forgiven and cleansed by believing in Jesus—by realizing your sin and trusting his death to atone for your guilt.

Second, Isaiah heard God asking who would go forth to serve him with the gospel: "And I heard the voice of the Lord saying, 'Whom shall I send, and who will go for us?' Then I said, 'Here am I! Send me'" (Isa. 6:8). We have seen the holy glory of Christ, experienced the cleansing of our sin by his blood, and now realize what is at stake in the world and what the future holds in the sovereign plan of God. Every Christian should therefore enlist in the service of the Sovereign Lord, each of us answering the call that God sets before us, in whatever way God gives us opportunity to advance his gospel. The cause is glorious, the end is certain, and the present need is great. How is God calling you to serve the cause of his gospel? Seeing in God's Word the same vision that Isaiah saw of a sovereign, holy, victorious Christ enthroned with grace, surely we, too, must answer every call to pray, to give, to witness, and to serve, "Here am I! Send me."

34

To Obtain the Glory

2 *Thessalonians* 2:13–15

To this he called you through our gospel, so that you may obtain
the glory of our Lord Jesus Christ. (2 Thess. 2:14)

*I*n 1957, the Chinese evangelist Watchman Nee published his lectures on Ephesians in a book titled *Sit, Walk, Stand.* While the book contains some flawed theology, the three-fold outline helpfully unfolds Paul's teaching. As Nee saw it, Christian faith begins by being seated in God's grace through faith in Christ, as Paul taught in Ephesians 1–3. Being seated in God's grace, the believer then walks by the power of the Holy Spirit, as detailed in Ephesians 4–5. Finally, in response to the spiritual warfare described in Ephesians 6, the believer stands against the onslaughts of the devil. *Sit, Walk, Stand.* Nee writes: "No Christian can hope to enter the warfare of the ages without learning first to rest in Christ and in what he has done, and then, through the strength of the Holy Spirit within, to follow him in a practical, holy life here on earth. . . . It is with these two lessons well and truly learned that he comes to appreciate the third principle of the Christian life now summed up in the word 'Stand.' "[1]

1. Watchman Nee, *Sit, Walk, Stand* (Fort Washington, PA: Christian Literature Crusade, 1977), 52.

As Paul concludes his end-times teaching, written to protect his readers from the erroneous idea that Christ had already come, we may see a similar pattern at work. In 2 Thessalonians 2:13–15, as in Ephesians, the apostle's doctrine of salvation is thoroughly Trinitarian. Considering first the sovereign will of the Father, he urges us to be seated in the truth of God's election to salvation. Moving to the Spirit's sanctifying work, he urges us to walk in holiness and truth (2 Thess. 2:13–14). Continuing to the glory that believers share through union with Christ, God's Son, Paul urges us to "stand firm" in the gospel truth committed to us through the apostles (v. 15).

SEATED IN THE FATHER'S ELECTION

It is significant that Paul begins a passage that James Denney called "a system of theology in miniature"[2] with the word *But*. Realizing this, we note the connection between Paul's confidence of salvation here and his alarming portrayal of the Antichrist in the preceding verses. The apostle's point is that while there is great evil in this world that poses a deadly threat, there remain the strongest reasons for confidence when it comes to true believers in Jesus Christ. "But we ought always to give thanks to God for you, brothers" (2 Thess. 2:13), Paul writes, going on to note the mighty work of the triune God that secures salvation for his people.

Paul's first ground for confidence against the evil afoot in the world is the sovereign election of the Father: "But we ought always to give thanks to God for you, brothers beloved by the Lord, because God chose you . . . to be saved" (2 Thess. 2:13). Believers are secure in salvation because their destiny was decided by God's choice of them before any decision on their part. Some Christians think of their salvation as beginning when they first heard and believed the gospel. But the Bible teaches that from God's perspective our salvation began in eternity past, when he chose us to be saved through faith in Christ. Romans 8:30 begins a chain of saving links—similar to Paul's teaching in Thessalonians—with reference to God's sovereign predestination: "Those whom he predestined he also called, and those whom he called he also justified, and those whom he justified he also glorified."

2. Quoted in John R. W. Stott, *The Message of 1 & 2 Thessalonians*, The Bible Speaks Today (Downers Grove, IL: InterVarsity Press, 1994), 175.

Opponents of election reply that God merely chose that whoever believes in Jesus will be saved. Or they argue that God did not choose any particular people before their faith, but only foresaw who would believe in Jesus and predestined that by believing they would be saved. The problem with these views is what the Bible actually says! Second Thessalonians 2:13 says not that God chose a principle of salvation but that "God chose you . . . to be saved." Election is of *persons* to salvation. Moreover, God did not choose the elect because he foresaw their faith, but simply because of his sovereign love for them. Paul declares, "In love he predestined us" (Eph. 1:4–5). This is consistent with how Jesus described election in his High Priestly Prayer to his Father, saying that he had received authority "to give eternal life to all whom you have given him" (John 17:2).

Paul goes on to specify when this divine election took place. The English Standard Version translates 2 Thessalonians 2:13 as saying that God chose his people "as the firstfruits to be saved," in which case Paul would be observing that God chose the Thessalonian believers to be the first among a great host of people to be saved through faith in Christ. This would be a true statement, except that it is far more likely that the translation given by most other English versions is correct: "from the beginning."[3] On this view, Paul is making a point virtually identical to that of Ephesians 1:4, which informs us that God "chose us in [Christ] before the foundation of the world." In eternity past, God sovereignly chose certain persons to be saved by means of Christ's redeeming work. Those persons are identified in the present by faith in Jesus, and through this faith they have the certainty of salvation because of God's unbreakable sovereign will.

The doctrine of election is rooted not only in eternity past but also in the unconditional love of God. It is not incidental that Paul identifies his readers as "brothers beloved by the Lord" (2 Thess. 2:13). We noted the same affection in Ephesians 1:4–5, where Paul notes that we were predestined "in love." Love is the foundation of a believer's security, despite the awful threat posed by Satan and his antichrists. God said of old: "I have loved you with

3. The manuscript evidence between *from the beginning* (Greek *ap' arches*) and *firstfruits* (Greek *aparchein*) is mixed. The argument in favor of *firstfruits* notes that the expression *from the beginning* is not found in any other Pauline letter, whereas *firstfruits* is common in Paul. See Gene L. Green, *The Letters to the Thessalonians*, Pillar New Testament Commentary (Grand Rapids: Eerdmans, 2002), 326. In favor of *from the beginning* is the argument that this represents Paul's normal teaching of election and fits best in this context. See G. K. Beale, *1–2 Thessalonians*, IVP New Testament Commentary Series (Downers Grove, IL: InterVarsity Press, 2003), 225.

an everlasting love; therefore I have continued my faithfulness to you" (Jer. 31:3). It is God's loving faithfulness to his elect people that secures us for salvation in the face of evil and spiritual danger.

To employ the metaphor of *sitting*, which Watchman Nee drew from Ephesians 1–3, Paul urges his readers to rest all their hopes of salvation on the eternal decree of God in their election. Believers do not enter into union with Christ by walking with him or standing up for Jesus, though both play a part in the working out of our salvation. Rather, we first trust God's will that is declared to us in sovereign grace. This idea of resting in God's sovereign will is enhanced by the particular word that Paul uses for *chose* in 2 Thessalonians 2:13 (Greek *haireo*). This word highlights not merely God's choosing but his covenantally declaring "that they are his people, his treasured possession."[4] The Thessalonian Christians are secure in salvation as God's preferred and treasured people forever, elected in Christ "from the beginning."

WALKING IN THE SPIRIT'S SANCTIFICATION

The Christian's salvation is rooted in eternity past but lived out in the power that comes from the Holy Spirit. The image of walking in the Spirit's sanctifying power is Paul's second ground for the believer's confidence. Whereas 2 Thessalonians 2:13 begins by saying that believers are saved by God's electing grace, Paul continues to see us as saved "through sanctification by the Spirit and belief in the truth."

The word *sanctification* often refers to the believer's subjective transformation from sin into holiness. Yet the idea of sanctification also has a broader, objective meaning, which Paul has in mind here. God chose his people in eternity past, but in the present he set them apart for service to himself. With this definite act of God in mind, G. K. Beale urges the term *consecration* to capture Paul's idea of setting us apart to God for holy service.[5] This is the apostle's second reason for rejoicing that his readers will not be made captive by Satan: God has set them apart once and for all to be holy to himself.

If we ask how God has consecrated believers, Paul's first answer is "by the Spirit" (2 Thess. 2:13). What God the Father ordained in eternity past

4. Ben Witherington III, *1–2 Thessalonians: A Socio-Rhetorical Commentary* (Grand Rapids: Eerdmans, 2006), 232.
5. Beale, *1–2 Thessalonians*, 228.

is brought to bear in our present lives by the work of the Holy Spirit. It is by the Spirit that believers have been born again to new life, and the Spirit's power then enables Christians to resist the temptations of the evil one. As we have seen, in the last days, the "man of lawlessness" will seduce the world into idolatry and rebellion against God; indeed, the "mystery of lawlessness is already at work" (vv. 3, 7–10). How are God's people secured from this nefarious influence? Paul's answer is the same as the one that John gave in his first epistle, speaking of the Holy Spirit: "He who is in you is greater than he who is in the world" (1 John 4:4).

The second way in which Paul sees Christians as separated to God is "through . . . belief in the truth" (2 Thess. 2:13). Jesus said that the Holy Spirit would come to "glorify me, for he will take what is mine and declare it to you" (John 16:14). Therefore, the Spirit's power in a Christian's life is always joined to the truth of God's Word, which came to us by the inspiration of the Holy Spirit (see 2 Peter 1:20).

Notice the close relationship in 2 Thessalonians 2:13 between God's sovereign election and the Spirit's work of bringing the elect to saving faith. Geoffrey Wilson explains: "When God determines the end, he also ordains the means. Hence this eternal election to salvation was realized in their sanctification by the Spirit and belief in the truth. Such trust in the truth is the evidence of having been set apart for God by his Spirit."[6] This means that the way to know that you are elect is to believe the gospel of Jesus Christ. Andrew Young writes: "If we have heard and believed the gospel and experienced the transforming work of the Holy Spirit in our lives, then we have good grounds to believe that we are God's elect people."[7]

We see here, as well, the contrast between the work of the Antichrist in leading sinners to unbelief and the work of the Holy Spirit, who sanctifies God's people through belief in the truth. J. Philip Arthur writes: "On the one hand, there are those who embrace lies and falsehood (2:11), while on the other, there are those who believe the truth." Believing God's truth ultimately "involves a commitment to Jesus Christ, who is himself the supreme expression and the embodiment of truth."[8]

6. Geoffrey B. Wilson, *New Testament Commentaries*, 2 vols. (Edinburgh: Banner of Truth, 2005), 2:196.
7. Andrew W. Young, *Let's Study 1 & 2 Thessalonians* (Edinburgh: Banner of Truth, 2001), 154.
8. J. Philip Arthur, *Patience of Hope: 1 and 2 Thessalonians Simply Explained*, Wellwyn Commentary Series (Ross-shire, UK: Evangelical Press, 1996), 131.

363

Conventional wisdom in today's society urges that belief in certain truths is not as important as sincerity in whatever you may choose to believe. But according to Paul, the mark of those who are saved by God is their belief in *the* truth. Such saving faith results only from the sovereign ministry of the Holy Spirit in a person's life. G. K. Beale comments: "Faith arises as a gift from God. Not until our stone heart is taken out and a spiritual heart is put in can we exercise saving faith in Christ."[9] Elsewhere Paul explained the divine role in human faith: "For by grace you have been saved through faith. And this is not your own doing; it is the gift of God" (Eph. 2:8). Therefore, to possess this gift of faith in the gospel and to walk in the power of the Holy Spirit is to know that you have been secured by God from the evil in this world in order to be saved through Jesus Christ.

STANDING IN THE SON'S GLORIFICATION

The believer's security from the coming evil is experienced by being seated in God's eternal election and by walking in faith through the sanctifying power of the Holy Spirit. In 2 Thessalonians 2:14, Paul turns finally to the glorification of God the Son, Jesus Christ—a transformation to which Christians are called through the gospel. By standing with Christ in his glorification, believers are made secure against the coming onslaught of the evil one.

Paul connects believers to Christ by our calling through the gospel. This completes the Trinitarian outlook on salvation. According to these verses, the Father *elects* his people, who are then *sanctified* by the Holy Spirit and *called* through the gospel to salvation in Christ. Paul refers here to what theologians define as the *effectual call*, which is the preaching of the gospel as it goes forth with God's power to open the heart to saving faith in Christ. This saving call joins the believer to Christ as he or she trusts and begins following him. Levi the tax collector rose up when Jesus said, "Follow me," leaving his seat of sin and becoming the disciple Matthew (Matt. 9:9). The Savior's call on his life had an immediate effect. Likewise, everyone who is saved is called by God to believe in and stand with Jesus before the world. This effectual call is always "through [the] gospel" (2 Thess. 2:14), the good news of Christ's saving work for sinners.

9. Beale, *1–2 Thessalonians*, 230.

Christians usually think of salvation in terms of deliverance from sin and its penalty, which it certainly is. Paul's emphasis here, however, lies in another direction: "so that you may obtain the glory of our Lord Jesus Christ" (2 Thess. 2:14). We can see the forward-thinking structure of Paul's thought in the parallels between verses 13 and 14. He says in verse 13 that "God chose you . . . to be saved," and that this took place "through sanctification by the Spirit and belief in the truth." In verse 14 he restates God's saving purpose as to "obtain the glory" of Christ "through our gospel." God's will is for Christians to be saved from sin and to glory. If this is how Paul thinks about us, we should likewise ground our identity and destiny in God's saving will for us to "obtain the glory of our Lord Jesus Christ." John Stott writes:

> There is nothing narrow-minded about the apostle Paul! His horizons are bounded by nothing less than the eternities of the past and of the future. In the eternity of the past God chose us to be saved. Then he called us in time, causing us to hear the gospel, believe the truth and be sanctified by the Spirit, with a view to our sharing Christ's glory in the eternity of the future. In a single sentence the apostle's mind sweeps from "the beginning" to "the glory."[10]

We see again why Paul feels constrained to thank God for the salvation of his Thessalonian readers. Yes, the power of evil stalks the land, tempting sinners into unbelief and idolatry. But Christians have been chosen, sanctified, and called into the glory of Christ. Therefore, every time a Christian receives the cup of the Lord's Supper, having believed the gospel and answered the call to stand with Christ before the world, the sacrament attests to the spot reserved for him or her at the wedding feast of the Lamb in the age to come (Rev. 19:9). Jesus declares the security of all who are sovereignly called into true discipleship with him: "I give them eternal life, and they will never perish, and no one will snatch them out of my hand" (John 10:28). Since "the gifts and the calling of God are irrevocable" (Rom. 11:29), true Christians will "obtain the glory of our Lord Jesus Christ" (2 Thess. 2:14). The certainty of salvation constrains Paul "always to give thanks to God for you, brothers beloved by the Lord" (v. 13). We, too, should use the administration of the Lord's Supper as an occasion to express thanks to God for our blessings and to respond in acts of love toward one another.

10. Stott, *The Message of 1 & 2 Thessalonians*, 176–77.

STANDING FIRM, HOLDING FAST

Whenever God's sovereign grace in salvation is emphasized, as it certainly is in 2 Thessalonians 2:13–14, there is a tendency for some readers to draw the conclusion that nothing is therefore required on our part as believers. Paul makes it clear, however, that this is far from the truth. It is God who saves us, to be sure, but the gift of salvation requires a wholehearted commitment to Christ and his saving truth. "So then, brothers," Paul concludes, "stand firm and hold to the traditions that you were taught by us, either by our spoken word or by our letter" (2 Thess. 2:15).

This verse brings us to the third word that Watchman Nee uses to outline Paul's approach to Christianity. First, we are *seated* in God's sovereign work in Christ. Second, we *walk* with him in the power of the Holy Spirit. Finally, we wage the kind of spiritual warfare about which Paul has written in this chapter, as he calls us to *stand* in the victorious conquest achieved by Jesus Christ. Christ has won the victory over Satan through his cross and resurrection, defeating sin and the grave. Nee makes the point that we engage in spiritual warfare not by advancing into enemy-held territory but by standing on the ground secured for us by Christ. "In Christ we *are* conquerors—nay, 'more than conquerors' (Rom. 8:37). In him, therefore, we *stand*. Thus today we do not fight *for* victory; we fight *from* victory. We do not fight in order to win but because in Christ we have already won."[11]

How, then, do Christians stand against enemy attack in the victory won by Jesus? Paul explains by urging us to "hold to the traditions that you were taught by us, either by our spoken word or by our letter" (2 Thess. 2:15). Far from being able to relax as Christians, we must lay hold of the gospel truth in the same way that a man at sea braces himself against the mast in the thrashing winds of a storm. "Stand firm!" Paul cries. "Hold fast!" This is how we withstand the present course of evil working through intimidation, temptation, and false teaching in the world. Paul warned the Ephesians not to be infantile Christians, "tossed to and fro by the waves and carried about by every wind of doctrine, by human cunning, by craftiness in deceitful schemes." Instead, "speaking the truth in love," we must hold fast to Christ and grow up in him (Eph. 4:14–15).

Paul specifically calls us to hold fast to "the traditions" (2 Thess. 2:15). Here

---

11. Nee, *Sit, Walk, Stand*, 55.

we see the Bible's emphasis on a body of doctrinal truth that Christians receive and believe. Similarly, Paul urged Timothy to "follow the pattern of the sound words that you have heard from me" (2 Tim. 1:13). These statements refute the idea that Christians do not need to know theological terminology ("sound words") and doctrinal truth ("the traditions") that are handed down to us. On the contrary, it is valuable for churches to profess creedal statements in our public worship, thereby holding "to the traditions" of biblical Christianity.

It is vital, however, for us to distinguish between apostolic tradition and traditions that are merely fabricated by men. The Roman Catholic Church, for instance, refers to tradition in the form of church teaching that is not derived from the Scriptures. Rome propagates traditions such as purgatory, the mediation of Mary and the saints, and the infallibility of the pope. These traditions, which are contradicted by the teaching of God's Word, are not what Paul referred to in urging us to hold fast to what we have received. Roman Catholicism is not the only church to hold unbiblical traditions, however; all believers should reform their traditions to reflect God's Word faithfully.

Paul specifies that the true Christian "tradition" is the apostolic teaching of the Scriptures: "hold to the traditions that you were taught by us, either by our spoken word or by our letter" (2 Thess. 2:15). Any doctrine that we embrace must therefore be based on and built upward from the written record of the Bible. John Stott comments: "To 'stand firm and hold to the teachings' means . . . to be uncompromisingly loyal to the teaching of Christ and his apostles. This is the road to stability. The only way to resist false teaching is to cling to the true teaching."[12]

SET FREE BY THE TRUTH

Let me conclude by asking: Is holding fast to biblical truth really so decisive for our lives? Can believing what the apostles wrote long ago about Jesus and salvation really make so sweeping a difference in this life and in eternity, protecting us from the evil forces that seek to destroy our souls?

One man who experienced the reality of evil and then the liberating power of Christ's truth was Louis Zamperini. An Olympic athlete before World War II, Zamperini had his bomber plane shot down by the Japanese off the Marshall Islands in 1943. He was rescued by his enemy, who for two

12. Stott, *The Message of 1 & 2 Thessalonians*, 178.

years subjected him to near-starvation and savage brutality as a prisoner of war. Louis was set free from this evil by the Allied victory. Haunted by his experiences, however, he fell captive to another evil in the form of alcoholic self-abuse. In 1949, however, a Christian neighbor invited Zamperini and his wife to attend a Billy Graham crusade. Louis refused to attend, but his wife returned having trusted in Jesus Christ. Through her witness, Louis began attending the rallies, and God's Spirit brought him to salvation through belief in the gospel. He later recalled "an enveloping calm that let me know that I had come to Christ and he had come to me."[13]

What difference did believing the biblical teaching about Jesus and his saving death make in Louis Zamperini's life? The answer is that Zamperini was set free from the power of evil in every way. Zamperini was delivered from the guilt of his sin by the cross of Christ. He was freed from sinful habits, from violent anger, and even from his hatred of the Japanese. In 1950 he returned to Japan to face his former captors, and at a prison for war criminals, Louis preached Christ's message of forgiveness. Some of them believed as a result. Returning to America, and remembering his own troubled youth, Zamperini founded the Victory Boys Camp, which God used to turn around the lives of multitudes of young men.

What difference does it make to us, beset in a world of darkness, idolatry, and empty unbelief, to believe in the gospel? Jesus put it this way: "If you abide in my word, you are truly my disciples, and you will know the truth, and the truth will set you free" (John 8:31–32). Interviewed in 2004, Louis Zamperini echoed those words from his own experience: "Christ told us in the Scripture, 'I am the way, I am the truth, and I am the life. Whoever comes to me I will never drive away.' Christ is the way to God. I believe that eternal life starts now by faith in Jesus Christ."[14]

According to Paul, eternal life is grounded in God's sovereign election "from the beginning" and comes to life in us as we answer the call to believe the gospel and follow Jesus Christ. If we are seated in God's sovereign grace, walk in the Spirit's power, and stand firm with Christ against unbelief, holding fast to the truth, not only will we be freed from the evil powers of sin and death, but we will also "obtain the glory of our Lord Jesus Christ" (2 Thess. 2:14) so that God's saving blessings are forever glorified in us.

13. Quoted in Don Stephens, *War and Grace* (Darlington, UK: Evangelical Press, 2005), 36.
14. Ibid., 42.

35

ENCOURAGED AND ESTABLISHED

2 Thessalonians 2:16—17

*Now may our Lord Jesus Christ himself, and God our Father, who
loved us and gave us eternal comfort and good hope through grace,
comfort your hearts and establish them in every good work and word.*
(2 Thess. 2:16–17)

O n the night of his arrest, Jesus expressed concern for his disciple
Simon Peter, who faced a threat that was too great for him.
Peter had boasted that he would be more faithful than the others, not knowing what was in store for him that very night. Jesus warned:
"Simon, Simon, behold, Satan demanded to have you, that he might sift
you like wheat" (Luke 22:31). Under this diabolical pressure, Simon Peter
failed utterly that night, denying Jesus three times before the rooster crowed
(vv. 34, 54–62).

The apostle Paul's converts in Thessalonica faced a similar threat under
persecution for their faith. So far they had done well, and Paul had boasted
of their steadfastness (2 Thess. 1:4). There would be greater tribulation yet to
come, however, because of the Antichrist's opposition. How would believers
hold firm in faith when beset by supernatural evil attacks?

Paul's answer to the Thessalonians' need was the same as the answer that

Jesus gave to Peter on his dark night of the soul: "I have prayed for you that your faith may not fail" (Luke 22:32). Though Peter stumbled, he did not ultimately fall because Jesus interceded on his behalf. In the benediction of 2 Thessalonians 2:16–17, Paul likewise appeals to Christ's intercession on behalf of his church. The final verses of chapter 2 are a benediction, a "good word," uttered by the apostle in the authority of his office. These verses express not merely a personal prayer desire but an apostolic declaration of Christ's intercession and the resulting blessings that flow from the Father: "Now may our Lord Jesus Christ himself, and God our Father, . . . comfort your hearts and establish them in every good work and word" (2 Thess. 2:16–17). Jesus told Peter, "I have prayed." Similarly, Paul declared to his needy friends, "Christ will pray for you." His benediction therefore consists, first, of a reminder of the God to whom he prays, second, of the saving love that ensures our blessing, and third, of his desire for them to persevere despite trials in a life of practical godliness.

THE DEITY OF CHRIST

Paul begins his benediction by reminding the Thessalonians of the God to whom he prays. In doing this, he incidentally makes a striking assertion of the deity of Jesus Christ: "Now may our Lord Jesus Christ himself, and God our Father," he begins (2 Thess. 2:16).

Liberal scholars have argued that the doctrine of Christ's deity was invented long after the age of the apostles by church power-brokers. This notion was popularized in the best-selling novel *The Da Vinci Code*, which alleged that Jesus' deity was invented by the Roman emperor Constantine three centuries after Christ's life. The fictional character Leigh Teabing explains that until the Council of Nicaea in A.D. 325, "Jesus was viewed by his followers as a mortal prophet . . . a great and powerful man, but a man nonetheless, a mortal." "Not the Son of God?" asks his fictional pupil. "Right," Teabing replies.[1]

Paul's benediction in our passage easily refutes these statements. Note, first, that Paul lists Jesus together with God the Father, praying with equal respect to both persons. Moreover, the apostle lists Jesus' name first, which would be blasphemy if he did not believe in the full deity of Christ. The

1. Dan Brown, *The Da Vinci Code* (New York: Doubleday, 2003), 233–34.

probable reason for this unusual ordering is Paul's emphasis in the preceding verses on the victory of Christ in his return. Additionally, he uses a compound subject—*Christ* and the *Father*—but in 2 Thessalonians 2:17 he employs singular verbs. This suggests that Paul saw the Father and Son working as one God. Moreover, he provides a divine title for Jesus: "our Lord Jesus Christ." In Paul's numerous quotations of the Old Testament, he always translates the covenant name of God, *Yahweh*, with the Greek word *kurios*. It is this sovereign title, *kurios*, Lord, that Paul ascribes to Jesus Christ. When we consider that this letter was written within twenty years of the resurrection of Christ, we may conclude that the deity of Christ was an established fact between the apostle and his converts, an essential tenet of the earliest Christian teaching.

Another reason that Paul named Jesus first might be that Christians pray to the Father through the Son. As the incarnate Christ, Jesus is the Mediator between man and God (1 Tim. 2:5). The Bible teaches, therefore, that the trajectory of prayer is "through [Christ]" and "to the Father" (Eph. 2:18). Matthew Henry writes that we "should pray in [Jesus'] name unto God, not only as his Father but as our Father in and through him."[2]

Paul's benediction raises a question as to your notion of Jesus Christ. Alexander Maclaren comments: "Do you regard Him as the sharer in the divine attributes and in the divine throne? It was a living Christ that Paul was thinking about when he wrote these words, who could hear him praying in Corinth, and could reach a helping hand down to these poor men in Thessalonica."[3] The question now comes to you: Does your faith accept the Bible's teaching of Jesus as the Son of God? Without this belief, you cannot be a Christian. The apostle John wrote: "No one who denies the Son has the Father. Whoever confesses the Son has the Father also" (1 John 2:23).

GIFTS FROM THE FATHER'S LOVE

Having identified the recipients of his prayer, Paul continues by noting the ground of his petition. He prays for God's help in the future on the basis of God's acts of salvation in the past: "who loved us and gave us eternal comfort and good hope through grace" (2 Thess. 2:16).

2. Matthew Henry, *Commentary on the Whole Bible*, 6 vols. (Peabody, MA: Hendrickson, n.d.), 5:645.
3. Alexander Maclaren, *Expositions of Holy Scripture*, 17 vols. (Grand Rapids: Baker, 1974), 15:270.

This brief statement contains some of the greatest claims ever made. First, the apostle says that he prays to God "who loved us." It makes sense that he would do this, since we naturally turn for help to those who have loved us previously. When trouble strikes and we need somewhere to turn, we look to those who have sacrificed for us in the past and have thus proved their loyalty and affection. This is why Paul now directs us to God.

But what acts of God does Paul have in mind when he says that God has "loved us"? It could be that he is thinking about how God chose us "from the beginning" (2 Thess. 2:13 NIV), sovereignly setting his love on us in eternity past and ordaining our salvation. After all, it was "in love" that "he predestined us for adoption as sons" (Eph. 1:4–5). Paul might also be thinking about the incarnation, when God "so loved the world, that he gave his only Son" (John 3:16). While these past acts certainly displayed God's amazing love, it would follow Paul's normal way of thinking if he meant that God "loved us" specifically in Christ's atoning death. Romans 5:8 proclaims, "God shows his love for us in that while we were still sinners, Christ died for us."

Let the impact of Paul's words sink in. God loves you, if you are in Christ. Does that truth shape all the rest of your thinking about life and God? It should, because the Bible over and over declares God's love. George Robinson wrote, "Loved with everlasting love, drawn by grace that love to know . . . I am his and he is mine. / Heav'n above is deeper blue, earth around is sweeter green, . . . since I know, as now I know, I am his and he is mine."[4] God loved the world by sending Jesus from heaven to earth. But God loved you with his special, saving love when Jesus gave himself to pay the debt of your sins on the cross. You may be beset with many troubles, just as Paul's readers faced deadly persecution. But if the omnipotent, eternal God loved you at the cross, he will continue to work that love in and for you. Love always desires to give, and God in love has given Christ to you. This is the ground of the Christian's hope in all circumstances: God "loved us and gave us" (2 Thess. 2:16).

God's love for us is the spring of every comfort and encouragement that flows to those who trust in Christ. Paul goes on to note the "eternal comfort" that God has given his people. The meaning of his word for *comfort* is not so much "sympathy" as it is "encouragement." Because God's comfort to those who trust in Christ is eternal, it will "outlast the afflictions of this age and

---

4. George W. Robinson, "Loved with Everlasting Love" (1890).

the judgment to come." God gives "encouragement that sustains us until we experience fully eternal life."[5] In this life, the trials of the world oppress and threaten us. But God has given us comfort that reaches into the age to come and provides us with the resources of heaven to endure in faith. What a comfort it is to know that our sins are all forgiven, that we are accepted into God's kingdom as beloved children in Christ, and that the precious things for which we labor and suffer now will endure forever to the glory of God. Matthew Henry writes: "The spiritual consolations God gives none shall deprive them of; and God will not take them away: because he loves them with an everlasting love, therefore they shall have everlasting consolation."[6]

Paul adds God's gift of "good hope" (2 Thess. 2:16). Eternal comfort speaks to our present blessing with God, whereas "good hope" speaks to our confidence for the future. Since God has loved us by sending his Son to secure our salvation, Christians are optimistic about what the future holds, even when persecution rages against us. Paul's "good hope" relates specifically to the return of Christ, who comes "to repay with affliction those who afflict you, and to grant relief to you who are afflicted" (1:6–7). If the future holds the overthrow of all evil and the consummation of our entry into eternal glory with Christ, then Christians have every reason to live in hope for the future.

Paul's readers then, as now, had reasons to need the eternal comfort and good hope for which the apostle prays. Alexander Maclaren writes:

> They were a young Church, just delivered from paganism. Like lambs in the midst of wolves, they stood amongst bitter enemies, their teacher had left them alone, and their raw convictions needed to be consolidated and matured in the face of much opposition. No wonder then that over and over again, in both letters, we have references to the persecutions and tribulations which they endured, and to the consolations which would much more abound.[7]

We, too, need eternal comfort and a good hope. Knowing God's love for us, we are encouraged to trust God to save us. As we mature in faith, we esteem more and more the comforts that God gives compared with the comforts of this world. Maclaren writes:

---

5. Michael William Holmes, *1 & 2 Thessalonians*, NIV Application Commentary (Grand Rapids: Zondervan, 2011), 255.

6. Henry, *Commentary*, 5:645.

7. Maclaren, *Expositions of Holy Scripture*, 15:267.

There are consolations enough in the world, only none of them are permanent; and there are hopes enough that amuse and draw men, but one of them only is "good." The gift of Christ, thinks Paul, is the gift of a comfort which will never fail amidst all the vicissitudes and accumulated and repeated and prolonged sorrows to which flesh is heir, and is likewise the gift of a hope which, in its basis and in its objects, is equally noble and good.[8]

It is worth noting that this comfort and hope in Christ come to us through God's Word. Paul told the Romans that "whatever was written in former days was written for our instruction, that through endurance and through the encouragement of the Scriptures we might have hope" (Rom. 15:4). What Paul calls "eternal comfort" in Thessalonians, he names "the encouragement of the Scriptures" in Romans, the hope-giving Word of God. Since it is God's Word that will lift up our hearts and grant us a good hope in Christ, Christians should be devoted to the study of the Bible and should treasure each of God's promises for salvation that are found in its pages.

One of the reasons that the Bible is so encouraging is that, contrary to the expectation of many people, its message is one of grace. The Bible does not present you with a list of things that you need to fulfill in order to get yourself together sufficiently to be accepted by God. Instead, the Bible tells you that you are such a sinner that there is nothing you can ever do to earn your way into God's favor. The good news is the message that Paul has given about God's love for us, and the comfort and hope that come "through grace" (2 Thess. 2:16). The Bible tells us that whereas we could do nothing to earn salvation, having broken God's law and being corrupted by sin, God has loved us by his grace, as a free gift offered from infinite mercy. God sent his Son to bear the condemnation that our sins deserved, and Jesus bestowed righteousness on us so that we may stand justified before God.

We should pause again and realize the implications of what Paul is saying. God loved believers through the saving work of his Son. We have a comfort that will endure forever because in Christ our sins have been forgiven, we are adopted into God's family, and God has secured for us eternal life and glory. Realizing this, how could we ever shrink back from enduring worldly scorn on Jesus' behalf? We have been saved by God's grace so that our eternal blessings will bring glory to his gracious character. Since all our blessings are

8. Ibid., 15:272.

"to the praise of his glorious grace" (Eph. 1:6), Christians may rely utterly on God's unchanging grace for those who belong to Jesus Christ through faith.

Established for Good Works

Paul has set before us God's love and his gifts of eternal comfort and a good hope. So far, all of this is still the preface to his actual prayer request. These blessings in Christ are the ground on which Paul stands as he turns to God to meet the needs of his afflicted readers. God's love and saving gifts, eternally confirmed to all who believe in Christ, are the soil in which bold confidence in prayer may flourish and the rock on which Paul may stand to pronounce that God is certain to meet his people's needs. If God has confirmed his love for me and has given me eternal comfort and a good hope for the future, then I may appeal to heaven in my attempts to lead a godly life and be certain not only of being heard but also of being helped. To this end, Paul prays that God will "comfort your hearts and establish them in every good work and word" (2 Thess. 2:17).

When we remember that this benediction appears at the end of Paul's teaching about the coming Antichrist and the great tribulation that will lead to worldwide apostasy and idolatry, it is almost staggering to see what the apostle prays for God to do. We might expect him to pray for the latest military technology to enable us to fight back against Satan. Or we might expect him to pray against the local powers bringing affliction to his friends in Thessalonica. Contrary to our expectation, however, Paul focuses not on the great events in his reader's outward circumstances, but rather on God's work in the hearts of the persecuted believers so that their lives may honor him.

First, Paul prays that God would "comfort your hearts." This is the same word for *comfort* that he used in 2 Thessalonians 2:16, with the emphasis on "encouragement." Earlier, Paul reminded us that God had given us reasons for eternal encouragement; now he prays that God would work these gospel truths into our hearts so that we receive the inward benefit of them. The Father and Son do their work, we know, through the ministry of the Holy Spirit. Paul made the same request for the Spirit's work with more detail in Ephesians 3:16–17, asking God to "grant you to be strengthened with power through his Spirit in your inner being, so that Christ may dwell in your hearts through faith."

In addition to inward strengthening through the encouragement of the gospel, Paul prays that the believers would be "established" (2 Thess. 2:17). This word (Greek *sterizo*) means to "support" in the way that buttresses are set up to strengthen a wall. In Ephesians 3:17, Paul went on to pray that believers would be "rooted and grounded in love," much in the way that a tree is grounded firmly in good soil or a building is well established on a sure foundation. This soil or foundation, Paul urges, is God's love for us that was proved in Jesus Christ. The importance of this subject to Paul is seen in his use of the same two words—*establish* and *encourage*—when he explained the mission for which he had sent Timothy back to Thessalonica: "We sent Timothy, our brother and God's coworker in the gospel of Christ, to establish and exhort you in your faith" (1 Thess. 3:2).

Paul's prayers, recorded across the span of his ministry and throughout his epistles, clarify the priority for our lives as Christians. We are to be established in our knowledge of God's love for us—a love declared in the past but now applied inwardly to our hearts by the Holy Spirit—and encouraged so that we have spiritual motivation to live for Christ. So much of our daily focus is given to seeking positive outward circumstances, whereas Paul argues instead that God wants to be glorified by making us flourish spiritually even in barren settings. God showed his power by feeding Israel with manna in the wilderness and making water spring from a rock. God glorifies his grace by causing roses to bloom in the desert. We keep expending our efforts to gain positive settings, not realizing that God sometimes keeps us in trials so as there to glorify himself in us. Therefore, Paul prays for God to give "eternal comfort and good hope through grace," in order to "comfort [our] hearts and establish them in every good work and word."

Does this describe you? Are you certain of God's love for you—which he proved in the offering of Christ—so that you have comfort and hope amid your trials, with a desire to live for Christ's glory? Is your life a testimony to the power of God to bless and encourage despite fleshly weakness and earthly difficulty? If not, the most likely reason is that you are not fully appropriating the comfort and hope that God has for you, as promised in the Bible alone. G. K. Beale writes: "The Christian's confidence about present and future salvation is inextricably linked to one's awareness of God's Word."[9]

9. G. K. Beale, *1–2 Thessalonians*, IVP New Testament Commentary Series (Downers Grove, IL: InterVarsity Press, 2003), 233.

Beale tells of a six-year-old boy whose parents asked whether he wanted to profess his faith in Christ. He answered that he was not sure that he believed. Later, his parents asked him again whether he wanted to profess faith in Jesus. The boy spoke of doubts, since it was hard to believe that someone could die and rise from the dead. When the boy advanced to second grade, however, his church presented Bibles to all the children of that age, and the boy began reading it every day. After a few weeks, his parents asked him once more whether he wanted to believe and be admitted to the sacrament of the Lord's Supper. This time, the boy answered, "Yes, I want to have the Lord's Supper with you." What had occurred to encourage the boy in God's love and establish him in saving faith? Paul gave the answer in Romans 10:17: "So faith comes from hearing, and hearing through the word of Christ." The boy had been reading his Bible, and suddenly his doubts vanished and his reluctance to profess faith in Jesus was gone. Beale concludes:

> There is something about the Bible that can instill confidence in God in a way that nothing else can. This is as true for adults as it is for children. As we read the Scriptures, God speaks to our hearts through his Spirit, and we come into closer relation to him. And as we grow closer to him, our hearts are assured that he is true. To avoid being filled with doubts about God's electing love, God's people must spend time in his Word and prayer, both of which enable them to know him well and do what pleases him.[10]

The result of this encouragement and establishment is immensely practical. Paul concludes his benediction by praying for us to be established "in every good work and word" (2 Thess. 2:16–17). The apostle is referring to a lifestyle of practical godliness, with works and words that follow the teaching and example of Christ. Isn't it remarkable that in the midst of the great affairs of history and the mighty clash of heaven and hell about which Paul has been writing, he concludes by saying that what really matters is the way that we live before God, doing all kinds of good works and saying all kinds of godly words?

In concluding his end-times teaching with an appeal for practical godliness, Paul matches Jesus' emphasis in teaching on the same subject. Jesus concluded his Olivet Discourse on the second coming by telling of the praise

10. Ibid., 233–34.

he will give to his sheep when they are gathered to him in the final judgment: "For I was hungry and you gave me food, I was thirsty and you gave me drink, I was a stranger and you welcomed me, I was naked and you clothed me, I was sick and you visited me, I was in prison and you came to me" (Matt. 25:35–36). Jesus then indicated that the glorified believers will be surprised that he noticed such seemingly unimportant works. But the Lord responded by saying how much our daily godliness and love mattered to him: "Truly, I say to you, as you did it to one of the least of these my brothers, you did it to me" (v. 40). By Jesus' own reckoning, in light of the awesome events planned by God for history, the thing that matters most is the daily love of God shown in the works and words of the people who claim his name. The supportive visit, the welcoming meal, the fervent prayer, and the timely word of truth are esteemed so highly by our returning Lord that he takes them as offered to himself.

OUR LIVES A BENEDICTION

Paul has offered a benediction—a good word—reminding us of God's love and praying for God to apply his gospel grace to our lives. His purpose is that we would become a living benediction to the glory of God through "every good work and word" (2 Thess. 2:17). When Jesus returns, he will then have another good word—another benediction—to say to those of us who trusted in him and lived out his love: "Come, you who are blessed by my Father, inherit the kingdom prepared for you from the foundation of the world" (Matt. 25:34). The apostle's benediction *for us* is designed to become a benediction *in us* so that Christ may speak a benediction *to us* on the day of his coming.

Is your life a benediction for the blessing of others and the glory of Christ? It can be, if you will follow the advice sung by children and heard by St. Augustine on the day of his conversion. The children sang in Latin: "*Tolle lege, tolle lege.*" It means: "Take and read, take and read."[11] Establish your life in the love of God revealed in the Bible, and you will find the encouragement and power you need to live as a benediction to the blessing of others and to the praise of God's glorious grace.

11. Augustine, *Confessions: Books I–VIII*, trans. Henry Chadwick (Oxford: Oxford University Press, 1982), 13.12, at 152–53.

36

PRAYING WITH CONFIDENCE

2 Thessalonians 3:1–5

Finally, brothers, pray for us, that the word of the Lord
may speed ahead and be honored, as happened among you.
(2 Thess. 3:1)

he book of Acts contains the record of Paul's ministry, describing enough opposition and suffering to discourage anyone from following in his steps. In Cyprus, a magician sought to turn the Roman proconsul against the apostle (Acts 13:8). In Pisidian Antioch, civic leaders stirred up persecution that drove him from the city (v. 50). In Iconium, Paul narrowly escaped a stoning (14:5–6); at Lystra, he was stoned and left for dead (v. 19); and in Philippi, Paul and Silas were beaten with rods and thrown into prison (16:22–24). All these events took place before Paul's ministry in Thessalonica, where his preaching caused a riot in which several believers were arrested and beaten, and the apostle himself had to flee (17:5–9).

In light of these ceaseless trials, the last thing we would expect from Paul is confidence about his ministry. Yet he writes to the Thessalonians that "we have confidence in the Lord about you" (2 Thess. 3:4). Indeed, throughout his letters Paul exudes confidence in the success of his ministry enterprise (see 2 Cor. 3:4; Gal. 5:10; Eph. 3:12). If we wonder at the source of this optimism, we find it in the apostle's appeals for prayer. "Finally, brothers," Paul begins the final section of his letters to the Thessalonians, "pray for us" (2 Thess. 3:1). Here is the secret not only of Paul's success in ministry but especially of his confidence in the face of ministry trials: his confidence that God answers prayers.

THE NECESSITY OF PRAYER FOR MINISTRY

Paul begins his final section not by writing just about prayer in general but specifically seeking prayer for the ministry of the gospel. As the apostle sees it, prayer is necessary for gospel ministry, so that "the word of the Lord may speed ahead and be honored" (2 Thess. 3:1).

If anyone could seem to get by without prayer, that person would be the apostle Paul. Naturally endowed with a towering intellect and a strong will, Paul communicated with the risen Jesus Christ and served as a vehicle of divine revelation. He had the ability to perform miracles in order to prove his message. Nonetheless, throughout his letters Paul solicits the prayers of fellow Christians. In Romans 15:30 he writes: "I appeal to you, brothers, . . . to strive together with me in your prayers to God on my behalf." John Calvin comments: "Though the Lord powerfully aided him, and though he surpassed all others in earnestness of prayer, [Paul] nevertheless does not despise the prayers of believers, by which the Lord would have us aided. It becomes us, after his example, to desire this aid, and to stir up our brethren to pray for us."[1]

For his own part, Paul was devoted to praying for others. It seems that he made it his practice to pray for someone whenever he heard or thought about the person. "I thank God," he wrote to Timothy, "as I remember you constantly in my prayers night and day" (2 Tim. 1:3). In the same spirit, Paul encouraged the Thessalonians to "pray without ceasing" (1 Thess. 5:17). We find this same commitment to prayer in practically every Christian who has been greatly used by the Lord. The story is told of Roman Catholic opponents who once sent an agent to spy out Martin Luther's weaknesses. The spy came back lamenting, "Who can overcome a man who prays like this?" John Calvin often rose at 4:00 am for prayer. John

1. John Calvin, *Commentaries*, 22 vols. (1854; repr., Grand Rapids: Baker, 2009), 21:347.

Knox cried out to God, "Give me Scotland, or I die!" Jonathan Edwards spent whole days in prayer for his preaching. We see a similar emphasis on prayer in biblical heroes such as Moses, David, and Daniel, and especially in the life of our Lord Jesus Christ. Can you imagine the divine help that would come if Christians today took up this same mantle and prayed "without ceasing"?

Despite his grave personal difficulties, Paul did not ask his readers to pray for his well-being but "that the word of the Lord may speed ahead and be honored, as happened among you" (2 Thess. 3:1). The word translated as "speed ahead" means to "run so as to win a race" (Greek *treche*) and speaks of Paul's desire for the gospel to spread and conquer unbelief. He desired as well for God's Word to be "honored," or "glorified" (Greek *doxazo*). This happened in Pisidian Antioch, where the Gentiles believed and "began rejoicing and glorifying the word of the Lord" (Acts 13:48). Whenever the gospel is received with the joy and power of salvation, God's Word is glorified.

Desiring for his gospel ministry to make rapid progress and glorify God, Paul appealed to his friends for prayer. He realized that the success of God's Word does not rely on natural factors such as oratorical ability and a dynamic personality. Rather, since the gospel aims to bring spiritually dead unbelievers to saving faith, it relies on God's power to convey spiritual life to those who hear and believe. Since the gospel requires the Holy Spirit's working to open the hearts of those who would otherwise never believe, Paul knew that prayer is needed for the gospel to speed ahead and glorify God.

Remember that Paul wrote this letter during a frustrating time of ministry in the city of Corinth. He clearly longed for his earlier experience in Thessalonica, when large numbers of people were speedily converted by his preaching of Jesus Christ. "Among you," Paul recalls, God's Word raced forward and was glorified. Now facing opposition in Corinth, Paul appeals to his friends' prayers as a sort of spiritual artillery to blast open a way for the message of salvation.

I wonder whether we realize today how important prayer is to the preaching of the gospel in the church. Ours is a generation that is captivated by celebrity preachers and the display of God's gifts in the ministry of successful pastors. Yet there is no minister of God's Word, however gifted, who like the apostle Paul does not need to rely utterly on the prayers of believers to empower his message. Every minister who longs to follow Paul in being used by God for the salvation of many will echo his heartfelt plea: "Brothers, pray for us, that the word of the Lord may speed ahead and be honored" (2 Thess. 3:1). E. M. Bounds wrote: "Without prayer, the gospel can neither be preached effectively, promulgated faithfully, experienced in the heart, nor be practiced in the life. And for the very simple reason that by leaving prayer out of the catalogue of religious duties, we leave God out, and His work cannot progress without Him."[2] Since only the power of God through the Holy Spirit can make gospel preaching effective, Andrew Young comments: "Prayer and preaching must be intertwined if the word of the Lord is to spread rapidly and be honoured among men."[3]

Another reason why Paul urgently desired prayer was to counter opposition to his ministry: "that we may be delivered from wicked and evil men. For not all have faith" (2 Thess. 3:2). In Corinth, Paul was "opposed and reviled" by Jews who opposed the gospel (Acts 18:5–6, 12–13). He may well have these specific people in mind when he speaks of "wicked and evil men." The word translated as "wicked" is better rendered as "unreasonable" or "wrongheaded" (Greek *atopos*). To be "unreasonable" and "evil" go together in hatred of the gospel. Geoffrey Wilson explains: "When those without faith exhibit their enmity towards the truth, this antagonism is completely in accord with their nature and their destiny."[4]

If you have heard but rejected the gospel, consider the Bible's description of your unbelief as "unreasonable" and "evil." Do you not realize that it makes no sense to reject Jesus Christ, and that spurning him condemns you for wickedness? What could be more unreasonable than to reject the message of God's saving grace to grant eternal life to sinners? What could be more wrongheaded than to prefer the fleeting pleasures of this passing world over the joy of fellowship with God and eternal life in the kingdom of Christ? Do you not realize, if your mind is closed to the gospel, that beneath your objections is a moral rebellion against the God who made you and who offers you forgiveness through the blood of his Son? How much better it would be to open your heart to the message of a Savior in Jesus Christ, who offers you salvation through faith in him.

2. E. M. Bounds, *A Treasury of Prayer* (Minneapolis: Bethany Fellowship, 1961), 159.
3. Andrew W. Young, *Let's Study 1 & 2 Thessalonians* (Edinburgh: Banner of Truth, 2001), 158.
4. Geoffrey B. Wilson, *New Testament Commentaries*, 2 vols. (Edinburgh: Banner of Truth, 2005), 2:199.

And yet, Paul says, "not all have faith." The apostle mentions this to point out that faith is God's sovereign gift and that opposition to the gospel is inevitable. We should never be dismayed when people rise up in anger at the message of God's grace or when worldly powers misrepresent the gospel as something narrow or bigoted. Without the regenerating work of the Holy Spirit, no one has faith and everyone hates the light that Jesus shines. Jesus explained: "This is the judgment: the light has come into the world, and people loved the darkness rather than the light because their works were evil" (John 3:19). The reality of this opposition urges us not to despair but to prayer. Charles Spurgeon said: "If we cannot prevail with men for God, we will, at least, endeavor to prevail with God for men."[5]

OUR CONFIDENCE IN PRAYER FOR MINISTRY

Even as Paul appeals for prayer in light of the slow advance of his preaching in Corinth and the serious opposition against it, he simultaneously expresses his confidence in this very ministry. "We have confidence in the Lord," he writes (2 Thess. 3:4), just as we should have confidence in our own prayers for gospel ministry.

If we ask why Paul was so confident in prayer for the gospel, the first answer is found in 2 Thessalonians 3:3, where he declares that "the Lord is faithful." The apostle states this to form a decisive contrast. Our problem is that "not all have faith." "But the Lord is faithful," and this is what really matters. Like Paul, we should pray for gospel success in preaching, in witnessing, and in raising our children, not because we trust our own labors or because we see spiritual promise in those whom we seek to reach, but solely because we trust God to be faithful to bless and empower his gospel for the salvation of those whom he will call. Leon Morris comments: "Paul turns away from the difficulties of man to the God on whom all men must depend. . . . He knows that the really significant factor is the character of his Lord, not the might of the enemy."[6]

God's faithfulness to the ministry of his Word is one of the Bible's great themes. Moses declared: "The LORD your God is God, the faithful God who keeps covenant and steadfast love with those who love him and keep

5. Quoted in Helmut Thielicke, *Encounter with Spurgeon* (Philadelphia: Fortress, 1963), 119.
6. Leon Morris, *The First and Second Epistles to the Thessalonians*, New International Commentary on the New Testament (Grand Rapids: Eerdmans, 1959), 246.

his commandments" (Deut. 7:9). Isaiah promised that sinful Israel would be redeemed "because of the LORD, who is faithful, the Holy One of Israel, who has chosen you" (Isa. 49:7). In surveying the biblical witness, Richard Mayhue notes five categories in which the Bible specifically describes God as faithful. The Lord is faithful: to complete the salvation of those who believe (1 Cor. 1:9); to enable believers to resist temptation (10:13); to fulfill all his promises (2 Cor. 1:18; Heb. 10:23); to vindicate believers who suffer (1 Peter 4:19); and to cleanse those who confess their sins and believe: "If we confess our sins, he is faithful and just to forgive us our sins and to cleanse us from all unrighteousness" (1 John 1:9).[7] So magnificent is the attribute of God's faithfulness that amid the wreckage of fallen Jerusalem, the weeping prophet Jeremiah still prayed with hope: "The steadfast love of the LORD never ceases; his mercies never come to an end; they are new every morning; great is your faithfulness" (Lam. 3:22–23).

Whereas the best intentions of men often fail, God remains faithful because of his other attributes. God is holy, and therefore his faithfulness is not tempted by sin. God is almighty, so no power can thwart his faithfulness in doing his will. Moreover, God is immutable, or never-changing, and therefore always remains faithful to himself and to his people. With this truth in mind, Thomas Chisholm wrote:

> Great is thy faithfulness, O God my Father;
> There is no shadow of turning with thee;
> Thou changest not, thy compassions, they fail not;
> As Thou hast been thou forever wilt be.[8]

Paul expresses confidence not only in God's faithfulness to his present ministry of the gospel but especially in God's saving work among the Thessalonians: "We have confidence in the Lord about you" (2 Thess. 3:4). The key phrase is "in the Lord." Paul knows that his readers possess union with Christ through saving faith; he is confident about them because they are "in the Lord."

This is a second source of our confidence: the decisive difference it makes to be in Christ and to have Christ in us, experiencing saving faith and the

---

7. Richard Mayhue, *1 & 2 Thessalonians: Triumphs and Trials of a Consecrated Church* (Ross-shire, UK: Christian Focus, 1999), 200.
8. Thomas O. Chisholm, "Great Is Thy Faithfulness" (1923).

reality of the new birth. However unpromising Christians may seem, we know that great things are in store. We might come to Christ with great problems, character defects, and crushing failures in life. We do not seem to be the kind of "movers and shakers" who will make a great difference in this world. Yet Paul wrote that "if anyone is in Christ, he is a new creation. The old has passed away; behold, the new has come" (2 Cor. 5:17). For this reason, whenever someone is "in the Lord," we anticipate supernatural power for change and spiritual growth. Former blasphemers are given lips to preach good news of salvation. Former thieves are motivated to work hard for the well-being of others. Castoffs from lives of sexual sin and relationship failure are purified and joined to fellow Christians in bonds of love.

Knowing the difference it makes for someone to be "in the Lord," we should have our prayers exude confidence and high expectations. We pray for God to glorify himself by using weak and sinful people like us to play a significant role in the gospel work of our generation. We pray for God to break patterns of sin and strengthen weary hands for ministry. We pray for opportunities to share the gospel and for hardened hearts to become soft. We pray confidently for all these things because the mighty God of grace whom we serve is faithful to keep his covenant commitment to those who are in Christ.

Notice how our confidence in prayer is linked to a priority on the gospel. God has not promised to bless civic campaigns, political movements, or social good works, but he has promised his power for the advancement of the gospel. This is why the work of the church centers on the gospel message that brings sinners to forgiveness and ushers rebels into saving union with Christ. The gospel alone is "the power of God for salvation to everyone who believes" (Rom. 1:16). Through the gospel and union with Christ in faith, Paul is confident that God will do "far more abundantly than all that we ask or think, according to the power at work within us," to his own glory "in the church and in Christ Jesus throughout all generations" (Eph. 3:20–21).

We should note that God's faithfulness does not mean that he will answer prayers exactly as we wish. Paul often experienced prayer answers that puzzled and even frustrated him. A notable example is his seeking to take the gospel to the province of Asia, recorded in Acts 16. Despite his prayers, God hindered Paul's plans for Asia and directed him instead to Greece, through a vision of a man of Macedonia pleading for the gospel. God sovereignly redirected Paul and in this way brought salvation to Thessalonica (Acts 16:6–10).

A famous example of God's sovereign manner of answering prayer is seen in Monica, the mother of the great theologian Augustine. Monica pleaded with God to save her son, and especially begged God not to permit him to travel to Rome, where he was sure to become more enmeshed in the ways of sin. How crushed she was, having spent a night in prayer for her son, to learn that he had boarded a ship for that very city. Yet it was in Italy that Augustine came under the influence of the great preacher Ambrose of Milan. In time he was converted and began his remarkable ministry of teaching and writing. God had answered Monica's prayer in his own way and timing. Augustine later wrote to God: "In your deep counsel you heard the central point of her longing, though not granting her what she then asked, namely that you would make me what she continually prayed for."[9]

God's faithfulness does not relieve us from needing to persevere in prayer. Instead, confidence in God will keep us praying until God has sped forth the gospel and overcome spiritual opposition. I know a man who was converted to Christ and brought his reluctant wife to a gospel-preaching church. He prayed for her salvation, but she was offended at the clear Bible teaching she heard. Soon she began writing outraged notes to the preacher, who patiently answered her objections and met with her husband weekly to pray for her salvation. The woman's spiritual opposition continued for over a year, yet her husband and the pastor persevered in ministry and in prayer. Finally, without advance warning, the pastor opened another note from the woman. Its brief message made his eyes grow moist with tears. "Dear Pastor," she had written, "God has removed the veil from my eyes and I believe in Jesus Christ. Thank you for patiently ministering and praying for my soul."

God's Answers to Prayers for Ministry

In this exhortation to prayer, Paul notes the kinds of things that God does in answer to our prayers for blessing in ministry. Second Thessalonians 3:3–5 thus presents a brief description of what God does in saving us through faith in Christ.

---

9. Augustine, *Confessions: Books I–VIII*, trans. Henry Chadwick (Oxford: Oxford University Press, 1982), 5.8, at 82.

First, Paul rejoices that God is faithful to "establish you and guard you against the evil one" (2 Thess. 3:3). This is the apostle's way of describing a true conversion to faith in Christ. Faith does not involve a bare profession of faith, but our being rooted in Jesus Christ. In the terms of Jesus' parable of the soils, true salvation is not like the seed that falls amid the thorns of worldly cares and desires, which choke faith to death, or like the seed that falls in shallow soil, where the heat of tribulation causes it to wither (Matt. 13:20–22). Instead, saving faith is like the seed that falls in good soil, so that it "bears fruit and yields" (v. 23).

God not only establishes believers in faith but also protects them from Satan's attacks. True believers withstand mockery, social rejection, and even the kind of severe persecution that Paul's readers were facing, because God is faithful to guard their salvation in response to prayer. Leon Morris writes: "The faithfulness of the Lord means that His people will not be left to the mercy of any and every temptation that may assail them, but they will be settled in the faith."[10]

Second, God enables believers to obey his Word. Paul writes: "We have confidence in the Lord about you, that you are doing and will do the things that we command" (2 Thess. 3:4). Contrary to the easy-believism practiced so widely today, biblical evangelism includes obedience to the Bible. Jesus' Great Commission tells us to "make disciples . . . , teaching them to observe all that I have commanded you" (Matt. 28:19–20). We must therefore pray for the obedience of those who profess faith in Christ, trusting God's faithfulness and the Holy Spirit's power to train them to a life of practical godliness.

Third, in 2 Thessalonians 3:5, Paul speaks of God's bringing believers to spiritual maturity: "May the Lord direct your hearts to the love of God and to the steadfastness of Christ." Scholars debate whether the apostle refers to God's love for us or our love for God, and then to Christ's steadfastness as our Savior or our steadfastness in trusting him. In reality, both sides always go together. Growing in our knowledge of God's love, we mature in our love for God. Relying on Christ's faithfulness as our Savior, we persevere through steadfast faith in him. Paul particularly notes that in maturing us, God directs our hearts to spiritual maturity. This is something that we should pray for: "O God, direct my heart!" We can be confident that God will answer. In the words of Hebrews 13:21, he will equip us "with everything

10. Morris, *First and Second Thessalonians*, 247.

387

good that [we] may do his will, working in us that which is pleasing in his sight, through Jesus Christ, to whom be glory forever and ever."

Learning to Pray with Confidence

We should conclude our study by asking whether we have the same confidence in prayer that Paul shows in these verses. Most of us will probably say that we do not. So how can we learn to pray with greater confidence in the Lord?

First, we will gain confidence in prayer by increasing in our knowledge of what God is like. Knowing God comes only through study of the Bible. For instance, the Bible assures us that through faith in Christ we become God's dearly beloved children. As a faithful Father, God is certain to receive our prayers with love and concern. In one of his parables on prayer, Jesus said, "What father among you, if his son asks for a fish, will instead of a fish give him a serpent; or if he asks for an egg, will give him a scorpion? If you then, who are evil, know how to give good gifts to your children, how much more will the heavenly Father give the Holy Spirit to those who ask him!" (Luke 11:11–13). Notice that, according to Jesus, our prayers are answered not because of any worthiness on our part but because of God's love as a faithful Father. The way to have your prayers answered, then, is to become God's child through faith in Jesus. As God's children, Christians pray with confidence. Jesus promised: "Ask, and it will be given to you; seek, and you will find; knock, and it will be opened to you" (v. 9).

Second, we grow confident in prayer through positive experiences in which we clearly see how graciously God has intervened. One reason to start praying about our needs, and especially for ministry situations, is that we will learn how powerful prayer is in the hands of our gracious God. As soon as possible, start praying for the needs of a missionary friend, and watch to see how your prayers make a difference. Start praying for God to give you an opportunity to share the gospel with someone you know, that he will give you the words to say and open your friend's heart in faith. As you experience God's faithfulness and see the eternal difference it makes when you pray, you will grow in confidence in prayer and thus in usefulness to Christ.

Third, we gain confidence as we pray for the things that our Lord desires in our lives. Jesus said, "Whatever you ask of the Father in my name, he will give it to you" (John 16:23). "In Jesus' name" means "in accordance with Jesus' will." We do not know whether God wants us to have a certain job or improved health. But we do know that God wants us to repent of sins, grow in godly character, and offer ourselves for the spread of the gospel. When we pray for these and other gospel priorities of Christ, we can be certain of a positive answer. Praying with confidence thus starts with seeking from God the things that God is seeking in and through us. As we grow spiritually and become more committed to Christ's work of salvation in our lives and in the lives of others, our confidence in prayer soars through God's power.

Sometimes our prayer is wrong, so God answers, "No." Sometimes our timing is wrong, so God answers, "Slow." Sometimes we're not ready, so God answers, "Grow." But when we seek what God desires, when the timing is right and we are ready for what God desires, he answers, "Go!"[11] As we gain confidence with God, we learn to persevere in prayer. Then when God is ready to answer, we will be ready to do anything for him in the confidence of faith.

---

11. Bill Hybels, *Too Busy Not to Pray* (Downers Grove, IL: InterVarsity Press, 1988), 74.

37

WILLING TO WORK

2 Thessalonians 3:6–15

*For even when we were with you, we would give you this
command: If anyone is not willing to work, let him not eat.*
(2 Thess. 3:10)

n the 1840s, William Miller began preaching the imminent
coming of Jesus Christ and the end of the world, which he predicted would take place between March 21, 1843, and March 21,
1844. By using newsletters and posters, Miller spread his message to as
many as a hundred thousand adherents. Expecting Jesus to appear at any
moment, these "Millerites" sold their belongings and took to the mountains,
waiting for the end. When Jesus did not return on schedule, Miller changed
the date and then explained his mistake by remodeling his theology as the
Seventh-day Adventist movement.

Miller was mistaken not only about the timing of Christ's return but also
about the response to the soon appearing of Jesus. In 2 Thessalonians 2, Paul
responded to a false report that Jesus had already come or that the day of
the Lord was upon them. In 2 Thessalonians 3, he deals with an erroneous
response to that false report. Like the later Millerites, these Thessalonians
had stopped working and carrying on their lives because they expected

Jesus at any moment. Paul complains, "We hear that some among you walk in idleness, not busy at work, but busybodies" (2 Thess. 3:11). This is the problem that the apostle confronts in the final section of his second letter to this church. Instead, the way to respond to the thought of Christ's return is to go on working in the callings that God has given us. Paul summarizes: "As for you, brothers, do not grow weary in doing good" (v. 13), even if today might be the last day that we have to live on this present earth.

A CHRISTIAN LIFESTYLE

Before looking at the details of Paul's teaching on work, we should make two important general observations from this passage. The first observation is that, according to Paul, there is a Christian tradition in which we are to live. He mentions this biblical lifestyle in 2 Thessalonians 3:6, where he speaks of a person "who is walking in idleness and not in accord with the tradition that you received from us." Paul previously spoke of the Christian tradition in 2:15, referring to the doctrinal teaching of the apostles. Now he uses the same term (Greek *paradoseis*) to refer to the manner of living that follows from the doctrinal teaching.

Paul emphasizes the Christian lifestyle in Ephesians 4:1, urging believers "to walk in a manner worthy of the calling to which you have been called." The apostle sees Christianity as involving a "walk" or "manner" of living that is consistent with Scripture and the high calling of discipleship to Jesus. The way a person walks tells you much about him or her. A proud man will walk with his chin held high. A busy person will move briskly. A woman trying to get attention will sway. Paul urges his Christian readers to consider the manner of their walk, that it would be "worthy of the calling" in Christ. As Paul sees it, Christianity is not something that takes up just a corner of our lives but instead involves the whole manner by which we live. It is a lifestyle that says Yes to some things and No to other things, because of the truths that we believe and that govern our walk.

The book of Hebrews stresses that this biblical tradition or lifestyle does not substantially change from one generation to the next. The reason is that "Jesus Christ is the same yesterday and today and forever" (Heb. 13:8). This means that the Bible's teaching of salvation and morality is not irrelevant to modern or postmodern man. In the face of the world's complaint that ours is an outmoded creed, we reply: "Jesus Christ is the same." This means that Christians are now to live in a manner that would be recognizable to those who came before us in the faith. Our forerunners have passed down to us a body of doctrinal truth and a pattern of life received from Jesus. Paul therefore commands Christians to walk "in accord with the tradition that you received" (2 Thess. 3:6).

We should be careful to note that when Paul speaks of a Christian lifestyle, he does not mean a uniform approach in which all believers get up at the same time, wear the same clothes, eat the same foods, or do the same things. Christianity not only embraces but celebrates individuality within the spiritual bond of faith in Christ. Yet there remain commitments of discipleship to Jesus that all believers must share. These include Bible study and prayer, worship and service in a faithful church, moral living in keeping with God's law, and, as Paul emphasizes in this chapter, hard and honest work to provide for our needs.

AN EXAMPLE OF CHURCH DISCIPLINE

Nonetheless, for all the commitments that Christians are bound to keep, there remains a need for correction and church discipline. In this matter, just as in Paul's description of a true Christian lifestyle, his writing is perfectly suited to our contemporary needs. In this case, church discipline is directed to the sin of sloth: "Now we command you, brothers, in the name of our Lord Jesus Christ, that you keep away from any brother who is walking in idleness and not in accord with the tradition that you received from us" (2 Thess. 3:6).

It is necessary for church discipline to exercise spiritual authority rightly. Paul speaks here directly on the authority of Christ: "We command you . . . in the name of our Lord Jesus Christ." It is because Christ is the Lord of all believers that those granted authority by Christ are to be obeyed. Paul held his authority as an apostle. Today it is the elders of the church who wield Christ's authority in church discipline, so that when they insist on biblical standards of faith and conduct, they are acting in Christ's name. The key passage on this topic is Matthew 18:15–20, in which Jesus requires believers to "listen . . . to the church" (Matt. 18:17). According to Jesus, church discipline actually starts at the individual level. When someone sins against you, you should go to him or her privately and "tell him his fault, between you and him alone" (v. 15). If he will not repent, then you should go back with "one or two others," who can be witnesses to the exchange (v. 16). If the sinning believer still will not repent, Jesus directed, "tell it to the church. And if he refuses to listen even to the church, let him be to you as a Gentile and a tax collector" (v. 17). Congregationalists understand this authority to be wielded by the entirety of the church members, meeting together in public. Presbyterians take note that the Bible ordains elders to "shepherd the flock" by "exercising oversight" of the church (1 Peter 5:2; see also 1 Tim. 3:1–2; Titus 1:7). Since Paul says that the elders "care for God's church" (1 Tim. 3:5) and Hebrews 13:17 requires Christians to "obey your leaders and submit to them," Christ's authority for church discipline in the church seems to rest in the care of the elders.

The primary purpose of church discipline is to restore a member who has fallen into serious sin. Paul identifies the purpose of his action to be "that he may be ashamed," so as to repent and thus rejoin the church fellowship (2 Thess. 3:14). To this end, he directs sanctions to be taken against the idlers who are refusing to obey. In this case, the unrepentant sinners are to be shunned by their Christian friends: "keep away from any brother who is walking in idleness and not in accord with the tradition" (v. 6); "take note of that person, and have nothing to do with him" (v. 14). D. Michael Martin writes: "By ostracizing such persons the church as a body was able to express its disapproval in a manner that the offender could not dismiss lightly. Ultimately the goal of the church was to see the errant one repent, return to a Christ-like lifestyle, and return to the fellowship of believers."[1]

We should notice as well the procedural deliberation in Paul's approach to discipline. He had noted the problem of freeloading in his first letter, responding both with a general exhortation "to mind your own affairs, and to work with your hands" (1 Thess. 4:11) and with a command to "admonish the idle" (5:14). Apparently this was done, but the idle were still idling! Having refused a rebuke from Paul, and presumably from their elders, the idlers were to be shunned by the church. The apostle says to "keep away" from these unrepentant sinners, using a term (*stellesthai*) bearing the nautical meaning of taking in sails on a ship. Likewise, the church was to pull back from the idler, being careful not to be caught up in the idler's sin and

1. D. Michael Martin, *1, 2 Thessalonians*, New American Commentary (Nashville: Broadman & Holman, 1995), 273.

to bring shame on the brother for the sake of his repentance. In terms of how church discipline is sometimes practiced today, this step is similar to public admonition, and it presumably included suspension from the sacrament of the Lord's Supper. Paul uses stronger language in 2 Thessalonians 3:14, saying that the church must "have nothing to do with him." Most commentators urge that this likely did not involve excommunication, a full expulsion from the communion of believers, since Paul still refers to the person as "a brother" (v. 15).[2] In 1 Corinthians 5:1–2, however, he commands the excommunication of a particularly heinous sexual offender. Within that context, the apostle commands the church "not to associate with sexually immoral people" (1 Cor. 5:9). Since that language is so similar to what Paul writes in 2 Thessalonians 3:15, it may be that he ultimately envisions the removal of unrepentant idlers from the church so that they are no longer considered believers—in a word, *excommunication*. The process of discipline must ultimately be brought before the congregation so that, whether excommunication was in view or not, the strong public rebuke could be delivered before all. Andrew Young writes: "Church members are not to welcome such a person into the intimacies of home and church fellowship as they might have done in the past. When words fail, they are to exert pressure upon them by withdrawing personal intimacy."[3]

There are two main errors when it comes to the contemporary practice of church discipline. The first is for churches simply to neglect or even refuse to discipline gross and scandalous sinners. J. Philip Arthur writes that "there are those fellowships that will never act no matter how flagrant the offence."[4] Such churches neglect an important duty that is necessary both to maintain the honor of Christ's church in the world and to reclaim hardened sinners. The other error is to exercise a harsh church discipline, in which the church employs a heavy hand against its members and exerts "an intrusive measure of control over matters which are, properly speaking, the concern of no one but the individuals concerned."[5] Paul warns against malice or undue harshness, writing: "Do not regard him as an enemy, but warn him as a brother" (2 Thess. 3:15). However unrepentant the person may

---

2. For this view, see ibid., 286.

3. Andrew W. Young, *Let's Study 1 & 2 Thessalonians* (Edinburgh: Banner of Truth, 2001), 168.

4. J. Philip Arthur, *Patience of Hope: 1 and 2 Thessalonians Simply Explained*, Wellwyn Commentary Series (Ross-shire, UK: Evangelical Press, 1996), 145.

5. Ibid.

be, the rebuke is given in a brotherly fashion and with tender concern. One way to guard against undue harshness is to work in a slow and measured way, giving plenty of opportunity for the Holy Spirit to work in answer to the elders' prayers. At its best, proper church discipline will combine "a steady refusal to have any truck with the evil thing, and a genuine concern for the well-being of the wrong-doer."[6]

THE CHRISTIAN COMMAND TO WORK

The main pastoral problem in Thessalonica was the unwillingness of some church members to work. Paul writes: "For we hear that some among you walk in idleness" (2 Thess. 3:11). The word translated as "idleness" (Greek *ataktos*) more generally means to "be unruly." Originally it was a military term that described a soldier who got out of line. Here it applies to professing Christians who are not living up to their obligations. Specifically, they were not working hard so as to provide for their own needs, but instead were relying on gifts from the church and from other Christians.

There are a number of possible reasons for this laziness. We know that in the Greek culture of the Thessalonians' time, manual labor was looked down on as unworthy of a cultured man. The most likely reason, however, is linked to the other matter that Paul wrote about in this letter, namely, the return of Christ. Like the attitude of the Millerites of the nineteenth century, and that of many others before and afterward, the belief that Christ was about to appear had led these people to stop performing their duties in life. Because of their sloth, other Christians were being wrongly burdened and the gospel was suffering disgrace in the society.

Moreover, as is usually true of the idle, the men who refused to work were stirring up trouble elsewhere. Paul derides them as "not busy at work, but busybodies" (2 Thess. 3:11). So not only were these people burdening the resources of the church, but they were also disrupting their fellow Christians. Paul's basic meaning is that they were meddling in the affairs of others and gossiping about them. William Barclay comments: "There may be greater sins than gossip but there is none which does more damage in the Church."[7]

6. Leon Morris, *The First and Second Epistles to the Thessalonians*, New International Commentary on the New Testament (Grand Rapids: Eerdmans, 1959), 259.
7. William Barclay, *The Letters to the Philippians, Colossians, and Thessalonians* (Louisville: Westminster, 1975), 218.

We can also imagine such persons badgering other Christians with fantastic eschatological theories based on their own "discoveries" in the Bible. "They may well have considered themselves the more spiritual members of the church," writes Young, "and seen it their duty to reproach others for their lack of zeal."[8] What is certain is that their free time as idlers was related to the trouble that they were stirring up. The hardworking generally do not have time left to cause much trouble for others, but the idler has plenty of time on his hands to burden and badger other people.

Paul responded to this problem with a command, an example, and a precept. His command was simple: "Now such persons we command and encourage in the Lord Jesus Christ to do their work quietly and to earn their own living" (2 Thess. 3:12). First, Christians are to apply themselves to their work. Christians have various callings in the workplace and in the home. Men and women have professions or trades, mothers have a calling to their children and to the home, and students have a calling to their studies. The duty of Christians is to labor in these callings. Paul adds that we should do this "quietly." His meaning seems to be that we should work without disrupting others—the very opposite of what the busybodies were doing in their idleness. The aim of our work is to provide for the earthly needs of ourselves and our families. In this way, hardworking Christians will fulfill their obligations in life, will avoid depleting the church's resources, and will gain the respect of watching unbelievers in the surrounding society.

THE CHRISTIAN ATTITUDE TOWARD WORK

Paul's command reflects the general Christian attitude toward work that often conflicts with a low view of work in secular society. John MacArthur notes the theology of work seen on bumper stickers. One says, "I owe, I owe, so off to work I go," indicating that work has no other value in a debt-ridden society than paying for a pleasure-seeking lifestyle. Another reads: "Work fascinates me—I can sit and watch it for hours." This makes inactivity an occupation! Yet another states, "I'd rather be fishing"—or "playing golf," or "camping," or anything else other than working.[9] Many people today approach work by doing only enough to avoid being fired. In contrast, the

8. Young, *Let's Study 1 & 2 Thessalonians*, 166.
9. John MacArthur, *1 & 2 Thessalonians* (Chicago: Moody, 2002), 300.

Bible teaches that man's basic calling before God is to work: "The Lord God took the man and put him in the garden of Eden to work it and keep it" (Gen. 2:15). Work is not a punishment but a gift from our Creator by means of which we may bear his image in doing his will. John Lillie thus describes labor as "Heaven's first law." He writes:

> Assuredly there is a dignity in labour, whether of the study, or the field, or the workshop, when, enlightened by the truth, cheered by the grace, and trusting in the strength and promises of God, we go at it as the task assigned us by Him, and the faithful performance of which not only our daily bread and present comfort but our future happiness also, and the welfare of society, and the honour of the gospel, and the glory of our Lord and Savior are all alike concerned.[10]

Work was not caused by the fall, though Adam's fall into sin caused work to become painful and frustrating (Gen. 3:19). But when all is redeemed in the eternal age of Christ's glory, Christians will revel in the privilege of working with and for the Lord. According to Jesus' parable of the talents, his reward for faithful service in this life is the privilege of greater work in the age to come: "Well done, good and faithful servant. You have been faithful over a little; I will set you over much. Enter into the joy of your master" (Matt. 25:21, 23). With this in mind, Christians should do all our work—earning money, raising and educating children, studying for future usefulness—as given to us by Christ. As Paul wrote in Colossians 3:17, "Whatever you do, in word or deed, do everything in the name of the Lord Jesus, giving thanks to God the Father through him."

Paul reinforced his command with an appeal to his own example in Thessalonica: "For you yourselves know how you ought to imitate us, because we were not idle when we were with you, nor did we eat anyone's bread without paying for it, but with toil and labor we worked night and day, that we might not be a burden to any of you. It was not because we do not have that right, but to give you in ourselves an example to imitate" (2 Thess. 3:7–9). As an apostle of Christ, Paul had the right to ask for material support. He chose not to do so, however, in order both to avoid the accusation of wanting only

10. John Lillie, *Lectures on Paul's Epistles to the Thessalonians*, Tentmaker Classic Commentaries (1860; repr., Stoke-on-Trent, UK: Tentmaker Publications, 2007), 435–36.

the Thessalonians' money and also to set an example of industry. Paul did not intend his example to set the policy for ministers of the gospel: he makes it clear in his letters that churches should provide for the material needs of their pastors so that God's servants may devote themselves fully to the ministry of the gospel among the people (see 1 Tim. 5:17–18). Paul wrote in 1 Corinthians 9:9, 14: "You shall not muzzle an ox when it treads out the grain. . . . In the same way, the Lord commanded that those who proclaim the gospel should get their living by the gospel."

What Paul's example does require is that ministers work hard, providing an example of a disciplined, diligent lifestyle that is given over to glorifying God through faithfulness in our daily work. There is, in fact, more to do in the gospel ministry of a church than any minister or pastoral staff can possibly do: ministers should therefore be expending themselves in doing all that they can for the salvation of the lost and the upbuilding of the saints. In this way, the spiritual leaders of the church should encourage faithfulness in all worldly duties, just as parents set the standard for their children.

Paul concludes with a precept: "For even when we were with you, we would give you this command: If anyone is not willing to work, let him not eat" (2 Thess. 3:10). Notice that this command pertains to those who are unwilling to work, not to those who are unable to work, whether because of disability or a lack of employment. There will be times when the church is happy to gather resources to provide for the needs of a family whose wage-earner has suffered a disease, injury, or other hardship. In such cases, the recipients of the help should do all that they can to provide for their own needs, to provide material help to the church, or at least to engage diligently in the all-important work of intercessory prayer. But when someone simply is not willing to do the work needed to provide for himself, as Paul commands, "let him not eat." The idea is, first, that sloth has forfeited a claim on the resources of other Christians. Furthermore, hunger will provide a motivation to work that is otherwise absent.

In cases in which unwillingness to discipline one's life and work hard is the problem, Christians are not to step in to alleviate needs but instead are commanded to "have nothing to do with him, that he may be ashamed" (2 Thess. 3:14). This is invaluable counsel, especially to parents of adult children who will not grow up or have given themselves over to wanton lifestyles. Like the father in Jesus' parable of the prodigal son, such parents are advised to allow their children to learn through painful consequences, while loving prayers are offered up and open hearts anticipate a more joyful reunion by God's grace.

Notice that while Paul's teaching might not explicitly endorse every aspect of modern capitalism, he certainly condemns the kind of socialism in which income is redistributed from those who earned it to those who did not. To be sure, there are many inequities in capitalist societies that should be addressed, and many causes for people with means to show mercy to the poor. But the Bible insists that property and wealth belong to those who earn it. Paul anticipates in this passage the many evils that will arise from an idle class that has grown used to "entitlements" that are purported to come from the government but in fact come from hardworking people whose property was confiscated by the government in order to give to others. Just as the idlers of Thessalonica became "busybodies," the welfare class in America has necessarily become a seedbed for immorality, family dissolution, crime, and despair. Christian mercy will do many good deeds for the poor and will be happy to sacrifice in legitimate ways that lift up the needy. But the socialist idea that people possess a right to the fruits of other people's work is alien to the Bible and condemned by Paul's teaching to the Thessalonians.

Three Reasons to Work Hard

Let me conclude this study with a biblical perspective on reasons that Christians should work hard, as well as motives that should shape our attitude to the work that we do.

The first reason Paul gives for working hard is to provide for ourselves so as not to be a burden to others. Then we can also rejoice in gaining the resources that we can use to provide for others in genuine need. Paul saw this desire to work hard in providing for ourselves and others as a mark of Christ's redemption: "Let the thief no longer steal, but rather let him labor, doing honest work with his own hands, so that he may have something to share with anyone in need" (Eph. 4:28). Christians should therefore work hard in order to make money. We should also be wise in investing and saving our money, so that it may be used in providing for those placed under our care and for those who truly cannot help themselves. Young men, especially, should diligently secure the education and training that will enable them

399

to take responsible roles as heads of households. Young women should also make sure that they have the ability to support themselves financially as needed, not burdening their families. If they are married, they should be competent to help their husbands in time of need. All Christians should be especially motivated to support the work of the gospel. Instead of delighting in spending money on ourselves, we should rejoice in helping others and in supporting the work of the gospel for the salvation of souls.

A second reason to work hard is that we may do good in the world through our talents, training, and labors. This aspiration should shape the kind of work that we seek to do. Most people today evaluate work strictly in terms of the money they make. But Christians will desire to expend their labor in worthy causes, as part of sound organizations. Whether your work is admired by the world or considered menial, Christians should rejoice in every opportunity to serve others. The nurse should take satisfaction in ministering to the sick, the teacher should rejoice in enlightening young minds, the police officer should apply himself to the safety of the people, and the manager should delight in the opportunity to mold the character of employees and to provide them with honest work. Paul wrote in Galatians 6:10: "So then, as we have opportunity, let us do good to everyone, and especially to those who are of the household of faith."

Finally, Christians should realize that the primary purpose of all that we do, including our work, is to serve and glorify God. This was Paul's ultimate reason for writing, "As for you, brothers, do not grow weary in doing good" (2 Thess. 3:13). Christians should not allow resentment over the idle, or over government redistribution of wealth, to harden our hearts when there are real needs that call for mercy. Moreover, our work ethic provides a compelling testimony that will often provide openings for a gospel witness.

The story is told by a famous theologian of a Christian office worker who caught the eye of an executive in London. He would often pass by and notice how this one woman was so much more diligent than the other typists, working faster, taking fewer breaks, and getting much more done. He finally asked someone in the office about the woman, and was told, "Oh, that's Mildred. She is a Christian." After a few more weeks, the executive approached Mildred herself to discuss her work performance. She answered, "I'm a Christian and I serve Christ. I work heartily for him, and not merely for my human boss." That conversation led to a witness to the gospel of

Christ and the salvation of the executive. Some years later, that convert was speaking at a Christian businessmen's gathering, and through his story of Mildred another man was converted—a man who went on to be a noted theologian.[11]

Mildred's example exposes the folly of the Millerites and their forerunners in Thessalonica. It turns out that in Jesus' own teaching about his second coming, he emphasizes the value and significance of the work that we have done on his behalf. When he returns, Jesus will point to our work of mercy, provision, and service, saying: "Truly, I say to you, as you did it to one of the least of these my brothers, you did it to me" (Matt. 25:40). Then we will have the privilege of marveling not only at how Jesus was blessed by the diligent, faithful work we have done in his name, but also at how Jesus has blessed others, many of them with eternal life that came about at least in part through the work that we did for him.

11. G. K. Beale, *1–2 Thessalonians*, IVP New Testament Commentary Series (Downers Grove, IL: InterVarsity Press, 2003), 253–54.

38

WITH HIS OWN HAND

2 *Thessalonians* 3:16–18

Now may the Lord of peace himself give you peace at all times in every way. The Lord be with you all. (2 Thess. 3:16)

fter the end of the Civil War, a Union cavalry troop was riding along the road from Richmond, Virginia, to Washington, D.C. Suddenly a soldier in tattered gray stumbled out of a bush. "Can you help me?" he called out. "I am starving to death. Can you give me some food?" The Union captain questioned why he was starving. "Why don't you just go into Richmond and get what you need?" he asked. The soldier answered that if he went to Richmond, he would be arrested. "Three weeks ago I became so discouraged because of our losses that I deserted and I have been hiding in the woods ever since." He had broken the law of his country, and if found he would be shot. "Haven't you heard the news?" the captain asked. "Why, the war is over. Peace has been made. General Lee surrendered to General Grant at Appomattox two weeks ago." "What!" cried the soldier. "Peace has been made for two weeks, and I have been starving in the woods because I didn't know it?"[1]

There is an analogy between that soldier, who feared the just punishment

1. Harry Ironside, *Addresses on the Gospel of John* (Neptune, NJ: Loizeaux Bros., 1942), 637–38.

of death for his crime of desertion, and the sinner, who fears God's justice. Like the deserter, hiding in the woods and starving, the unbelieving sinner hides from God, suffering a spiritual death as one cut off from the resources of life. The Christian faith, however, declares news similar to that of the cavalry captain. Peace has been declared through the saving conquest of God's Son, Jesus Christ. It is for this reason that Paul concluded his letters to the Thessalonians with a benediction of peace: "Now may the Lord of peace himself give you peace at all times in every way" (2 Thess. 3:16).

THE SIGN OF GENUINENESS

It was essential that Paul's letter, as a message declaring the peace of Christ, be validated as an official apostolic writing. As was common in the ancient world, Paul seems to have dictated his letter to a secretary and then taken up the pen himself for the final verses. "I, Paul," he says, "write this greeting with my own hand." He explains further that this was his normal procedure: "This is the sign of genuineness in every letter of mine; it is the way I write" (2 Thess. 3:17; see also 1 Cor. 16:21; Gal. 6:11; Col. 4:18).

This is an interesting statement, since scholars are agreed that Paul's Thessalonian letters were among his earliest known writings. It seems that Paul had other letters that have not been preserved by the Holy Spirit. Moreover, the problem of false letters made it imperative for Paul's letters to be authenticated. Second Thessalonians 2:2 mentioned "a letter seeming to be from us" that falsely stated that the Lord had returned. By writing the final verses in his own handwriting, Paul provided the church leaders with a basis for comparison with 1 Thessalonians and perhaps with earlier samples of his writing.

Paul's statement of authentication raises a question: how do we know that these letters are genuine apostolic writings, and therefore messages from the risen Jesus Christ, when we do not have the original copies and cannot examine the handwriting for ourselves? There are many good answers to this question. First, we have the testimony of the early church, which includes this letter in its official collection of apostolic writings. We call this *canonization*, the process by which the church formally recognized apostolic writings as divine Scripture. It is important to realize that the church never decided that certain books should be regarded as God's Word, but rather recognized and received the letters whose apostolic origin was attested by the original recipients. The earliest record of the New Testament canon is found in the Muratorian Canon, dating from A.D. 170, which lists all thirteen of Paul's known letters as acknowledged Scripture, including 1 and 2 Thessalonians.

In addition, the earliest known writings of Christian leaders—including second-century figures such as Ignatius, Justin Martyr, and Irenaeus—cite Paul's letters as sacred Scripture. Finally, and most importantly, we receive these writings as Scripture today by the inward testimony of the Holy Spirit "bearing witness by and with the Word in our hearts" (WCF 1.5). Just as Paul authenticated his letter to the original readers in his own hand, Jesus Christ has sent forth the hand of the Holy Spirit to certify to our hearts the divine origin of these letters.

Peace That Is from God

We should be impressed not merely that Paul wrote with his own hand, but also with the context of these final verses. Here, the apostle identifies peace as the ultimate answer to his readers' needs. We may summarize his final message as setting forth the peace that is from God, that meets our every need, and that is granted by the grace of Jesus Christ.

Paul generally concluded his letters with a benediction, and these prayers often referred to "the God of peace" (see Rom. 15:33; 16:20; 2 Cor. 13:11; Phil. 4:9; 1 Thess. 5:23). In this way, Paul indicates that peace is a quality of God's inner being. John MacArthur writes:

> God is at all times at perfect peace, without any discord within Himself. He is never under stress, worried, anxious, fearful, unsure, or threatened. He is always perfectly calm, tranquil, and content. There are no surprises for His omniscience, no changes for His immutability, no threats to His sovereignty, no doubts to cloud His wisdom, no sin to stain His holiness. Even His wrath is clear, controlled, calm, and confident.[2]

Unlike the worldly idea of peace, God's peace does not merely consist of the absence of strife but involves harmony, wholeness, and prosperity. Leon Morris comments, "Paul . . . is not saying here that he trusts that the . . .

---

2. John MacArthur, *1 & 2 Thessalonians* (Chicago: Moody, 2002), 313.

believers will not find themselves caught up in a war. He is speaking about the deep and abiding peace that comes when people are right with God."[3] A minister friend of mine likes to quote the Puritan William Perkins's definition of *peace* when he tells people what he does for a living. He describes himself as a teacher of "the science of living blessedly forever."[4]

Paul's conclusion makes it clear that true peace comes only from God: "Now may the Lord of peace himself give you peace" (2 Thess. 3:16). Our great need for peace is not met, therefore, by something that we can do but rather by receiving the peace that originates with God and that he alone can give. This is what God's peace provides: a blessed life forever.

Even the most basic summary of human history will prove how great is our need for peace. History is largely the record of warfare and conquest, showing that, as James Montgomery Boice wrote, "wars are the chief legacy of every culture."[5] Among the earliest of all historical records is a Sumerian bas-relief from Babylon (about 3000 B.C.) depicting soldiers in close battle lines wearing helmets and carrying shields. The glory of ancient Greece was shattered by the twenty-seven-year-long Peloponnesian War. Rome declared "peace" by slaughtering its neighbors, a fact enshrined when Emperor Augustus built his Altar of Peace on the Field of Mars, the god of war. The bloodiest of all centuries was the most recent one, in which hundreds of millions of people died in two world wars and a succession of violent revolutions. Politicians respond with peace initiatives and peace treaties, yet the one result they never achieve is peace itself. James Montgomery Boice comments that "the ink is scarcely dry on these treaties when guns begin to sound for the next fierce encounter."[6]

The reason why wars do not cease is that people themselves do not possess peace. Men and women are not content with what they have and who they are, so they seek to increase and enhance themselves at the expense of others. Isaiah eloquently described sinful humanity's inner turmoil: " 'the wicked are like the tossing sea; for it cannot be quiet, and its waters toss up mire and dirt. There is no peace,' says my God, 'for the wicked' " (Isa. 57:20–21). James 4:1–2 asks: "What causes quarrels and what causes fights among you?

3. Leon Morris, *Expository Reflections on the Letter to the Ephesians* (Grand Rapids: Baker, 1994), 13.

4. Quoted in J. I. Packer, *A Quest for Godliness: The Puritan Vision of the Christian Life* (Wheaton, IL: Crossway, 2010), 64.

5. James Montgomery Boice, *Romans*, 4 vols. (Grand Rapids: Baker, 1995), 4:1902.

6. Ibid., 4:1903.

Is it not this, that your passions are at war within you? You desire and do not have, so you murder. You covet and cannot obtain, so you fight and quarrel."

The root of mankind's lack of peace is the warfare that exists between man and God. Sinners have rebelled against God by violating his law and refusing his lordship. Paul summarized the problem in Romans 1:21: "For although they knew God, they did not honor him as God or give thanks to him." To honor God is to recognize his right to rule your life by his Word and accept your duty to worship, obey, and glorify him in all things. The worst news is that because of our war against God in refusing these things, God is also at war with us. Romans 1:18 says that "the wrath of God is revealed from heaven against all ungodliness and unrighteousness of men." Even worse, we ourselves are unable to end our warfare with God, since our very nature has been corrupted by sin. According to Romans 8:7, the natural mind "is hostile to God, for it does not submit to God's law; indeed, it cannot." Having rebelled against God, we are now "dead in trespasses and sins" and "by nature children of wrath" (Eph. 2:3).

When we diagnose the problem of sinful mankind in a biblical way, we see that man can be saved only through a peace that comes from God. Our sinfully corrupt natures will never be able to attain to the contentment, serenity, and stability that peace requires, nor will God permit us to forge our own peace while we remain at war with him. Therefore, our salvation requires "the Lord of peace" to give us the peace that he possesses and that he alone can provide.

PEACE THAT MEETS OUR NEED

The good news of the Christian gospel is that God gives us the peace that meets our every need. We see this in Paul's prayer for God to "give you peace at all times in every way" (2 Thess. 3:16). His point is that God provides peace to his people in every circumstance of life.

If we survey Paul's two letters to this church, we can see a number of circumstances in which God provides us with peace. For instance, in his first letter he noted his readers' need to advance in sanctification: "how you ought to walk and to please God . . . . For this is the will of God, your sanctification" (1 Thess. 4:1, 3). The challenge of sanctification consists in the unruly passions and unholy desires of remaining sin within our hearts. God combats our sin and works for peace within us as the Holy Spirit ministers to us through God's Word and in prayer. The Bible often connects the disciplines of prayer and Bible study to a life of peace: Psalm 19 assures us that God's Word "is perfect, reviving the soul," that its testimony "is sure, making wise the simple," and that its precepts "are right, rejoicing the heart" (Ps. 19:7–8). God's peace comes into our minds and hearts as we commit to a lifestyle of study and meditation on God's Word, which Hebrews 4:12 tells us "is living and active, sharper than any two-edged sword, piercing to the division of soul and of spirit." Likewise, 1 Corinthians 10:13 promises that when we pray, "God is faithful, and he will not let you be tempted beyond your ability." Philippians 4:7 adds that through prayer "the peace of God, which surpasses all understanding, will guard your hearts and your minds in Christ Jesus." The question, therefore, is whether we are making use of the protection of prayer and the Word designed by God to subdue our sin and convey his peace to our hearts.

Paul proceeded to address the anxiety that was disturbing the peace of the church, namely, anxiety over those who had died. The apostle did not want them to "grieve as others do who have no hope" (1 Thess. 4:13). And so in answer to the anguish of death, he pointed to the coming of Christ. Believers learn that when Jesus returns, "God will bring with him those who have fallen asleep" (v. 14). This means that Christians who die are with the Lord in glory as their souls wait to rejoin their bodies for the glorious resurrection: "For the Lord himself will descend from heaven with a cry of command, with the voice of an archangel, and with the sound of the trumpet of God. And the dead in Christ will rise first" (v. 16). Katharina von Schlegel wrote of the peace that this knowledge brings:

Be still, my soul: the hour is hast'ning on when we shall be forever
    with the Lord,
when disappointment, grief, and fear are gone, sorrow forgot,
    love's purest joys restored.
Be still, my soul: when change and tears are past,
all safe and blessed we shall meet at last.[7]

Paul went on to warn against those who have a false hope for "peace and security," because they rest their anxieties on worldly resources such

7. Katharina von Schlegel, "Be Still, My Soul" (1752).

407

as money and power. Those who seek peace in the world will experience "sudden destruction" when Christ returns, "as labor pains come upon a pregnant woman, and they will not escape" (1 Thess. 5:3). Christ's return will "inflict[ ] vengeance" on God's enemies and "grant relief" to suffering believers (2 Thess. 1:7–8). Paul tells us that there will be a great rebellion when the "man of lawlessness" is set loose against the church (2:3). In fact, even now, "the mystery of lawlessness is already at work" (v. 7), so that our peace is often disturbed by persecution, false teaching, and apostasy. Again, the knowledge of Christ's return to destroy Satan and his servants "with the breath of his mouth" (v. 8) is designed to give us peace even in the midst of trials and persecution.

Finally, against the problem of idlers in the church who were stirring up trouble, Paul commends the peace that results from the church's refusal to tolerate gross sin. In the name of Jesus, leaders in the church were empowered to discipline the unruly and even, if needed, to remove them from their fellowship (2 Thess. 3:6, 14). Then they would possess the clean and peaceful conscience of knowing that they had sincerely worked for the well-being of unrepentant sinners.

In speaking of the peace that God gives "at all times in every way," Paul adds the prayer, "The Lord be with you all" (2 Thess. 3:16). In all circumstances, peace results from the presence of Christ, which Jesus promised through the ministry of the Holy Spirit: "I will ask the Father, and he will give you another Helper, to be with you forever, even the Spirit of truth . . . . You know him, for he dwells with you and will be in you" (John 14:16–17). Jesus saw the Spirit working in us primarily by means of his Word: "When the Spirit of truth comes, he will guide you into all the truth . . . . He will glorify me, for he will take what is mine and declare it to you" (16:13–14). Moreover, Paul asserts in Romans 8:16–17 that the Spirit bears an inward testimony to believers of the privileges of our adoption in Christ: "The Spirit himself bears witness with our spirit that we are children of God, and if children, then heirs—heirs of God and fellow heirs with Christ." With Christ's Spirit testifying to us by the Scriptures and bearing witness in our hearts to God's fatherly love, believers experience the peace of God that results from union with Christ in faith.

Even as we experience inward peace now, through our faith, we look forward to the final peace that will come at the return of Jesus. J. Philip Arthur writes of a memorable experience shortly after his teenage conversion to faith in Christ. One January night, he attended a Christian meeting, after which a noisy throng of young believers spilled out of the church into the street. He writes: "The sky was as black as ink and the stars were spangled across it in riotous profusion. We soon fell silent at the grandeur of it. A friend came up to me, and overwhelmed by the brilliance of the night sky said, 'Wouldn't it be great if the Lord were to come back now?'"[8] This is how Christians often feel when the reality of God's holiness is impressed on our spirits. "We want Jesus to be *here!*" our hearts cry. It gives us peace to know that someday soon Jesus is going to part the sky and return to us in the full splendor of his glory. Even as we long for his unveiled presence on that coming day, his presence now by his Spirit and through his Word conveys a wondrous peace that enables us to continue in faith and love. "Behold, I am with you always, to the end of the age," Jesus told the disciples before he departed to ascend into heaven (Matt. 28:20). "The Lord be with you all," Paul prayed (2 Thess. 3:16), knowing that Christ's presence brings the peace of God for the blessing of his people.

Peace That Is Granted by Grace

Having prayed for the peace that only God can give, the peace that meets all our needs, Paul concludes in the final verse by declaring that peace is granted by the grace of God in Jesus Christ: "The grace of our Lord Jesus Christ be with you all" (2 Thess. 3:18). Grace is God's loving favor to those who deserve his hostility and wrath. Therefore, when Paul concludes with a prayer for God's grace, he notes that the divine peace that we can never earn or win by any efforts of our own, since we are condemned by our sin and unable to earn God's favor, God grants as a free gift through his grace in Jesus Christ. As Paul sees it, a Christian is someone who is at peace with God through saving grace in Christ.

The final verse makes it clear that when Paul spoke of God in 2 Thessalonians 3:16 as "the Lord of peace," he specifically had in mind the Lord Jesus Christ. This agrees with Isaiah's prophecy, which foresaw the coming of Jesus as the "Prince of Peace" (Isa. 9:6). According to Paul in Ephesians

8. J. Philip Arthur, *Patience of Hope: 1 and 2 Thessalonians Simply Explained*, Wellwyn Commentary Series (Ross-shire, UK: Evangelical Press, 1996), 149.

2:14–16, it was on the cross especially that the grace of Christ made peace with God for sinners: "For he himself is our peace, who has . . . broken down in his flesh the dividing wall of hostility . . . [to] reconcile [sinners] to God in one body through the cross." Holy justice separated us from divine blessing, but Christ satisfied that justice by paying the debt of our sins with the coin of his own blood. However many or great our sins may be, we may have peace with God by confessing our sins and looking to the cross of Christ in faith, asking Jesus to forgive our sins and reconcile us to God. In Christ, Paul said, "we have redemption through his blood, the forgiveness of our trespasses, according to the riches of his grace" (Eph. 1:7).

Having been forgiven of our sins by the grace of Christ, we are accepted as God's children and enter into his spiritual provision, experiencing peace through our access to God in prayer (Phil. 4:7). We receive the peace and security of knowing that history will end with Christ's return to bring his people together with him into glory. With these and many other blessings in mind, Jesus promised his disciples on the night before he died: "Peace I leave with you; my peace I give to you. Not as the world gives do I give to you. Let not your hearts be troubled, neither let them be afraid" (John 14:27).

When Paul concludes his letter with an appeal for the grace of Christ to be with us, he intends for that grace to unite Christians together in the bond of peace. This lifestyle of spiritual unity and peace does not come easy to us, given our many differences and sins, which is why the grace of Christ is needed.

One Christian who showed how peace is possible was the great Dutch theologian Cornelius Van Til. For decades, Van Til had pursued a disagreement with another great Dutch theologian, Herman Dooyeweerd, over a technical matter of theology. Both scholars had written numerous articles opposing each other, and even as frail old men they continued to dispute their differing views. During their final exchange, when both of them were near to death, Van Til explained his position one last time, along with the reasons that he thought he was right and Dooyeweerd was wrong. He concluded that last meeting, however, with words that enabled the two opponents to experience a bond of Christian peace: "Soon we shall meet at Jesus' feet."[9] If that is how two differing theologians can experience peace in Christ, how

9. Quoted in Joseph Ryan, *That You May Believe: New Life in the Son* (Wheaton, IL: Crossway, 2003), 318.

much more should husbands and wives, parents and children, and Christians living together in the church embrace the peace that comes from knowing a shared destiny together in Christ. We sin against one another and fail to meet one another's expectations. But soon we will meet at Jesus' feet, having received peace from God. The grace of Christ enables us to live now in peace with one another in his name.

His Hand and Ours

In concluding his letter, Paul wrote out the final verses in his own hand. The words for which he took up the pen express the heart of his gospel: God's peace through the grace of Jesus Christ. This reminds us that while Paul's own hand completed this letter, it was Christ, by his own hand, who secured that peace by his gift of grace. Jesus extended his hands upon the cross, gaining the peace of forgiveness with God through sin-atoning death.

Our hands, as well, have a role to play. First, we receive saving grace by opening our hands in humble faith, believing God's Word and receiving Jesus Christ as the giver of peace with God. Then, like Paul, we should surely reach out our hands to others who do not yet know God's peace in the grace of Christ for all who believe in his gospel.

How many today are like the starving soldier who never knew that the war was over and peace was at hand, and therefore remained fearfully aloof from the provision that he needed? How many unbelieving people, burdened by the guilt of their sin, remain distant from God out of fear of his wrath, not knowing that forgiveness has been gained through the blood of Jesus Christ? With his own hands, Jesus gained peace for you so that you may live blessedly forever in the glory of God. Will you open your hands in faith to receive this precious gift? And will you reach out your hands to others, offering the priceless good news about the peace of God that is freely given from heaven by the grace of Jesus Christ?

Select Bibliography of Commentaries Cited and Consulted

Arthur, J. Philip. *Patience of Hope: 1 and 2 Thessalonians Simply Explained.* Wellwyn Commentary Series. Ross-shire, UK: Evangelical Press, 1996.

Barclay, William. *The Letters to the Philippians, Colossians, and Thessalonians.* Louisville: Westminster, 1975.

Beale, G. K. *1–2 Thessalonians.* IVP New Testament Commentary Series. Downers Grove, IL: InterVarsity Press, 2003.

Bruce, F. F. *1 & 2 Thessalonians.* Word Biblical Commentary 45. Waco, TX: Word, 1982.

Calvin, John. *Commentaries.* 22 vols. 1854; repr., Grand Rapids: Baker, 2009.

Cara, Robert J. *1 & 2 Thessalonians.* Darlington, UK: Evangelical Press, 1995.

Gorday, Peter, ed. *Colossians, 1–2 Thessalonians, 1–2 Timothy, Titus, Philemon.* Ancient Christian Commentary on Scripture, New Testament 9. Downers Grove, IL: InterVarsity Press, 2000.

Grant, James H., Jr. *1 & 2 Thessalonians: The Hope of Salvation.* Wheaton, IL: Crossway, 2011.

Green, Gene L. *The Letters to the Thessalonians.* Pillar New Testament Commentary. Grand Rapids: Eerdmans, 2002.

Hendriksen, William. *1 and 2 Thessalonians.* New Testament Commentary. Grand Rapids: Baker, 1974.

Holmes, Michael William. *1 & 2 Thessalonians.* NIV Application Commentary. Grand Rapids: Zondervan, 2011.

Lightfoot, J. B. *Notes on the Epistles of St. Paul.* Peabody, MA: Hendrickson, 1993.

Lillie, John. *Lectures on Paul's Epistles to the Thessalonians.* Tentmaker Classic Commentaries. 1860; repr., Stoke-on-Trent, UK: Tentmaker Publications, 2007.

MacArthur, John. *1 & 2 Thessalonians.* Chicago: Moody, 2002.

Maclaren, Alexander. *Expositions of Holy Scripture.* 17 vols. Grand Rapids: Baker, 1974.

Martin, D. Michael. *1, 2 Thessalonians.* New American Commentary. Nashville: Broadman & Holman, 1995.

Mayhue, Richard. *1 & 2 Thessalonians: Triumphs and Trials of a Consecrated Church.* Ross-shire, UK: Christian Focus, 1999.

Morris, Leon. *The First and Second Epistles to the Thessalonians.* New International Commentary on the New Testament. Grand Rapids: Eerdmans, 1959.

Shenton, Tim. *Opening Up 1 Thessalonians.* Leominster, UK: Day One, 2006.

Stott, John R. W. *The Message of 1 & 2 Thessalonians.* The Bible Speaks Today. Downers Grove, IL: InterVarsity Press, 1994.

Thomas, Robert L. "1, 2 Thessalonians." In *The Expositor's Bible Commentary,* edited by Frank E. Gaebelein, 11. Grand Rapids: Zondervan, 1978.

Venema, Cornelis P. *The Promise of the Future.* Edinburgh: Banner of Truth, 2000.

Wanamaker, Charles A. *Epistles to the Thessalonians.* New International Greek Text Commentary. Grand Rapids: Eerdmans, 1990.

Wilson, Geoffrey B. *New Testament Commentaries.* 2 vols. Edinburgh: Banner of Truth, 2005.

Witherington, Ben, III. *1–2 Thessalonians: A Socio-Rhetorical Commentary.* Grand Rapids: Eerdmans, 2006.

Young, Andrew W. *Let's Study 1 & 2 Thessalonians.* Edinburgh: Banner of Truth, 2001.

INDEX OF SCRIPTURE

25:24–28—53
25:30—325
25:31—351
25:31–32—154, 176
25:32—174
25:34—154, 174, 325, 378
25:35—248
25:35–36—378
25:40—378, 401
25:41—174, 299
25:46—298
26:40—208
26:41—208
26:53—289
28:9—306
28:18–19—191
28:18–20—351
28:19—23, 247
28:19–20—33, 231, 346, 387
28:20—151, 409

Mark
4:15—91
4:39—355
9:1—316
9:48—299
12:30—261
13—315
13:8—350
13:10—350
13:26—153
13:26–27—290
13:30—316
13:32—196

Luke
1:46–47—261
2:10—251
2:14—8
4—91
8:11—30
9:23—49

9:23–24—39
9:24—83
9:27—316
9:34—188
10:1—4
10:7—59
10:18—351
11:9—110, 388
11:11–13—388
12:43—191
17:4—243
19:11–27—308
19:13—308
19:15—308
21—xiii, 315
21:20—319
22:3—91
22:30—312
22:31—369
22:31–32—151
22:32—370
22:34—369
22:54–62—369
22:61–62—339
24:39–43—172
24:46–47—307

John
1:4—206
1:8—300
1:12—108
3:16—303, 372
3:19—383
3:36—201
4:34—245
5:21—177
5:24—158, 165, 201, 245
5:28–29—174, 176
6:37—180
6:37–40—317
6:39—180
6:40—180

8:12—206
8:21—245
8:24—297
8:31–32—368
8:56—251
10:12—187
10:27–28—73
10:28—338–39, 365
10:29—339
11:11—162
11:25—169
11:35—163
12:46—206
13:1—89
13:15—249
13:27–30—339
13:34—137, 146, 278
13:35—138
14:3—51, 152, 290
14:6—343
14:16–17—408
14:27—9, 410
15:16—262
15:19–20—284, 313
16:7—152
16:13—4
16:13–14—408
16:14—363
16:23—389
16:33—40, 214, 245
17:2—361
17:3—248, 300
17:12—330
17:17—81, 100, 206, 266
17:24—311
20:19—172
20:21—42

Acts
1:8—4, 5, 321
1:9—151
1:11—187

417

421

Index of Subjects and Names